Public Opinion

Public Opinion
Democratic Ideals, Democratic Practice

Rosalee A. Clawson
Purdue University

Zoe M. Oxley
Union College

CQ PRESS

A Division of Congressional Quarterly Inc., Washington, D.C.

CQ Press
2300 N Street, NW, Suite 800
Washington, DC 20037

Phone: 202-729-1900; toll-free, 1-866-4CQ-PRESS (1-866-427-7737)

Web: www.cqpress.com

Cover design: Vincent Hughes
Cover image: Media Bakery
Composition: Auburn Associates, Inc., Baltimore, Md.

∞ The paper used in this publication exceeds the requirements of the American National Standard for Information Sciences—Permanence of Paper for Printed Library Materials, ANSI Z39.48-1992.

Printed and bound in the United States of America

12   11   10   09   08   1   2   3   4   5

Library of Congress Cataloging-in-Publication Data

Clawson, Rosalee A.
  Public opinion : democratic ideals, democratic practice / by Rosalee
A. Clawson, Zoe M. Oxley.
     p. cm.
  Includes bibliographical references and index.
  ISBN 978-0-87289-304-7 (alk. paper)
  1. Democracy. 2. Public opinion. 3. Political socialization.
  4. Mass media and public opinion. 5. Political participation. I. Oxley,
Zoe M. II. Title.
  JC423.C598 2008
  321.8—dc22

                                                                2008003220

To my parents, Dale and Janice Clawson, who taught me that people matter.

To my mother, Rachel Oxley, whose encouragement and optimism never wavered, and to my entire family for supporting my endeavors.

Brief Contents

Contents

Tables, Figures, and Features

Tables

Figures

Boxes

Public Opinion in Comparative Perspective

Preface

At the 1999 Southern Political Science Association meeting in Savannah, Georgia, James Headley, then the national sales manager at CQ Press, approached Rosie Clawson and asked if she would be interested in writing a public opinion text with Zoe Oxley. A few weeks later, he e-mailed Zoe to see if she wanted to coauthor this text with Rosie. Rosie and Zoe jumped at the opportunity to work together on this project and were especially excited to work with the wonderful people at CQ Press. Since neither had tenure at the time, it took a while to move the project beyond the planning stages. Now, more than eight years, two tenures, and two babies later, we finally have completed our book!

While we never anticipated that writing this text would take so many years, our goals for the book remained the same throughout the process. We want students to grasp how fascinating and important it is to study politics generally and public opinion more specifically. What better way to attain that goal, we think, than to discuss public opinion in the context of democratic thought. After all, it is the particular salience of public opinion within a democracy that makes its study so vital and interesting. To that end, we situate the field's empirical research within a normative framework, specifically theories of democracy, and focus on especially important and revealing studies rather than tediously summarizing every available piece of research. We organize the text into six sections, each of which poses a normative question that is significant for democratic theory, such as: What should be the relationship between citizens and their government? What should be the role of citizens in a democracy? Are citizens' opinions pliable? Do citizens organize their political thinking? Do they demonstrate an understanding of and commitment to the democratic "basics"? That is, are they knowledgeable? Interested? Attentive? Do they support civil rights and civil liberties? The chapters in each section present evidence to help students answer the question at hand, giving them both the content and context of public opinion. This organization encourages students to understand and interpret the empirical evidence in light of normative democratic theories, thus enhancing their critical analysis skills.

We want students to appreciate the thrill of conducting research and producing knowledge and to learn that conclusions about public opinion emerge from original scholarship on the topic. Yet we also want them to understand that no one piece of research is perfect and that the ability to evaluate the strengths and weaknesses of a piece of research is a vital skill. So we devote attention to explaining specific studies in some depth throughout the text. Rather than presenting only the conclusions that are drawn from a study, this approach lets students see how those conclusions were reached, exposes them in a fairly organic way to the range of research methods used in the study of public opinion, and illustrates how the choice of method influences the conclusions that researchers draw. We thus use an "embedded" research method approach throughout the book rather than consign methods to one stand-alone chapter. Additionally, we provide an appendix that encapsulates the basic information students need on key public opinion methods.

This text includes other important pedagogical features. We focus heavily on American public opinion, but chapters 2 through 11 contain feature boxes called "Public Opinion in Comparative Perspective" that highlight public opinion issues in a variety of countries and serve to deepen students' understandings of American public opinion. A wealth of data is presented in more than eighty tables and figures throughout the book to help students grasp important research findings. Core concepts are bolded in each chapter and included in a list of key concepts at the end of each chapter. The key concepts are also defined in a glossary at the end of the book. Each chapter contains a list of suggested sources for further reading. Brief explanatory annotations are provided with each suggested source to guide students as they delve deeper into a topic.

ACKNOWLEDGMENTS

Completing this book required the assistance of many people. A long-standing debt of gratitude is owed to our graduate school advisers, Paul Allen Beck, Thomas Nelson, and Katherine Tate. They opened our eyes and minds to the study of public opinion and trained us to be political scientists. From the day Tom arrived at Ohio State, he involved us in every stage of his research and taught us how to produce rigorous scholarship. Tom also demonstrated the importance of engaging writing, a skill we have both worked hard to hone. As for Paul, we most appreciate his generosity of time. No matter how busy he is (and as department chair and now university dean, he is busier than most), he always responds to any query we have, whether for feedback on our scholarship or professional advice. We also greatly appreciate and admire Katherine Tate. Of the many valuable lessons we learned from Katherine, one was to stay attuned to and ground our scholarship in the real world of politics. We kept that advice in mind as we wrote this text.

We were also extremely fortunate to have wonderful undergraduate mentors. While attending Bowdoin College, Zoe's honors thesis adviser was Janet Martin.

Janet was the first person to suggest to Zoe that she consider graduate school in political science (and told her how to apply for PhD funding!). Since then, Janet has been very supportive of Zoe's career and continues to provide useful guidance. Bruce Stinebrickner was Rosie's favorite political science professor at DePauw University. Their shared interests in politics and women's basketball have turned them into close friends over the years. Rosie thanks Bruce for all his advice, enthusiasm, and good cheer.

We are so grateful to the many people who provided valuable and specific feedback on this text. Our prospectus and chapter outlines were improved by suggestions from Jeremy Zilber, Keith Shimko, Suzanne Parker, Richard Fox, and George Bizer. For reading completed chapters, or portions thereof, we thank Cary Funk, Ewa Golebiowska, Jennifer Jerit, and John Zumbrunnen. Janice Clawson read many of our chapters, and we are very appreciative of the time she devoted to this. Some of our students also read individual or multiple chapters, including Evan Reid, students in Rosie's Human Basis of Politics course, and students in Zoe's Political Psychology course. For reading many chapters thoughtfully and carefully, we especially thank Ben Bauer and Mike Grady. The quality of the material in this text is due in no small part to those who read early versions of our chapters.

We would also like to thank the professors CQ Press commissioned to review the manuscript at various stages, including Scott Basinger, Stony Brook University; John Bruce, University of Mississippi; Ted Jelen, University of Nevada–Las Vegas; Mary Fran T. Malone, University of New Hampshire; Tom Nelson, Ohio State University; Shayla Nunnally, University of Connecticut; Robert Y. Shapiro, Columbia University; and Matt Wilson, Southern Methodist University. Their guidance was invaluable as we drafted and revised the manuscript.

We received support in other important ways as well. Larry Baum and John Clark gave us loads of good advice along the way. We thank them for their words of wisdom. For helping us with *Chicago*-style documentation, we thank Mary Cahill (who gave us her copy of the *Chicago Manual of Style*) and Carol Cichy (who converted early chapters that were formatted using APSA style). The Dean of Arts and Sciences at Union College funded essential travel so that we could be together to work on the book during the early days. Richard Fox allowed Zoe to arrange her teaching schedule to free up time to write, which was most welcome. Lisa Howell and Evan Reid hunted down articles and wrote helpful summaries. Helen Willis spent part of her middle-school summer vacation searching for material to be included in the text. Zoe thanks Helen for her careful work and predicts for her a bright future in politics or political science. Andrea Olive and Bill Shaffer offered Rosie words of encouragement at key times. Michelle Conwell assisted Rosie with pop culture references and various computer issues; her sassiness and irreverence were also invaluable. We must also mention our many Ohio State friends, who supported and encouraged us throughout the book-writing process. We greatly appreciate them.

Early on, we were told that CQ Press is a wonderful press to publish a first book. We were happy to hear that then, and even happier that our experience confirmed this. Everyone we worked with at CQ was supportive, professional, and friendly. James Headley not only encouraged us to consider writing the text but also helped us understand the book publishing process. When we told him that we would have to wait a couple years before starting the project, he demonstrated enough faith in our ability to write this text to wait until the time was right for us. College director Brenda Carter also displayed early interest in our project. We are especially grateful for their patience. Substantial patience was also displayed by chief acquisitions editor Charisse Kiino. As various professional and personal engagements slowed down our early work on the book, Charisse did not falter in her enthusiasm for this text and optimism that we would finish it. Furthermore, during points when our writing progress was stuck, Charisse's advice helped motivate us and pushed the project along. Development editor Elise Frasier skillfully and efficiently shepherded the text through the final development stages, always with good cheer. For responding to our many, many questions clearly, we also thank Elise. She made straightforward what could have been a confusing and anxiety-inducing process. Elaine Dunn's diligent copyediting improved our prose, and the speed of her editing allowed the book to proceed on schedule despite our lateness in getting material written. Steve Pazdan, managing editor, and Talia Greenberg, project editor, were also very efficient, including responding to e-mails on weeknights and weekends.

While it does not quite take a village to raise our children, with working spouses, we have needed help from many to care for our sons. Knowing that they were in the hands of loving and responsible caregivers enabled us to write without worry. For this, Zoe thanks Joyce von Elburg, Anna Ott, Becky Broadwin, Rachel Bennett, Amanda Roosevelt, Kelly Lannan, Caitlin Milbury, Katie Monroe, and her parents-in-law, Millie and Wilbur Miller. Rosie thanks Kara Wuethrich, Helen Bartlett, the wonderful daycare staff at the YWCA, and especially her mom, Janice Clawson.

Finally, we owe special thanks to our families. We were both raised by parents who placed priority on education and who encouraged us to pursue whatever channels most interested us. Their faith that we would succeed in our chosen career paths provided us with the confidence to try to do just that. Sadly, Zoe's mother passed away before this book was completed. She was very pleased to learn that we were writing a text, and we know that she would be proud to see the completed version. When Rosie's husband was deployed (over and over again), support came from family near and far. Rosie thanks Dale and Janice Clawson; Tammy, Mike, and Jared Harter; Jill, Scott, Liv, and Sadie Castleman; and her Cleveland cousins.

Our sons Alonzo and Owen bring us tremendous joy. And as they both enter toddlerhood, we expect to have many opportunities to practice our skills at persuasion! To our husbands, Dale and Des, we can only begin to articulate our gratitude. Writing this book required many, many hours of work beyond the normal workweek—time that we would have much rather spent with them. Yet they wholeheartedly supported us. This included giving us the time to write, of course, but also listening to endless conversations about public opinion, reading over some material, and providing help on figures and other technical matters. Mostly, though, we thank them for their love and for making our lives much happier than they were before they entered them.

PART I

What Should the Role of Citizens Be in a Democratic Society?

CHAPTER 1

Public Opinion in a Democracy

IN A DEMOCRATIC society, public opinion matters. Let's consider a few examples.

When the U.S. Congress did not pass an immigration reform bill in the summer of 2007, President George W. Bush stated: "Legal immigration is one of the top concerns of the American people and Congress's failure to act on it is a disappointment."[1] In response, the White House announced that it would work to prevent illegal immigration through better enforcement of existing laws. Republican Senator Mitch McConnell applauded this move, saying that "countless well-informed Americans [had spoken] up about the need to enforce our borders and our laws."[2] While running for the 2008 Democratic presidential nomination, Senator Hillary Clinton said: "What's important is what's happening in the lives of the American people and the kind of change I'm interested in is how we help more Americans get to the American dream and that means universal health care."[3] Senator Clinton also asked the public to select her campaign song. The winner? "You and I" by Celine Dion. Thus, from the mundane to the most vexing issues of our times, what the public thinks about political and social issues is important.

In a democracy, such as the United States, we expect the public to have a role in governmental decision making. Yet, the precise role that citizens should play in a democracy has been argued over for centuries. Whether the public actually can and really does live up to democratic expectations is also a debatable topic. In the pages that follow, we explore the normative issues related to how the public *ought* to function in a democracy. Throughout this text, we review empirical studies of public opinion that describe how the public *does* function in America. We then link these studies back to the normative theories of how citizens should behave in a democracy. Focusing on public opinion from these two angles will, we hope, provide you with a broad understanding of this important topic.

THEORIES OF DEMOCRACY

A simple definition of democracy is "rule by the people." What exactly, though, does rule by the people mean? Answering this, and related questions about democracy, is neither easy nor straightforward. In fact, many people across many centuries have devoted their lives to examining democracy and delineating the proper characteristics of a democracy. **Democratic theory** is "the branch of scholarship that specializes in elucidating, developing, and defining the meaning of democracy."[4] Among other topics, democratic theorists deliberate over how the people should rule in a democracy (by voting directly on all laws or by electing representatives for this task) as well as who should qualify as a democratic citizen (all adults, only those who are educated, etc.). Democratic theorists also focus on citizens' ruling capabilities and the role of the public in a democracy, as indicated by the following overview of major democratic theories.

Classical Democratic Theory

The earliest Western democratic societies emerged in the city-states of ancient Greece. In Athens' direct democracy, for example, governing decisions were made by the citizens, defined as all nonslave men of Athenian descent. All citizens were eligible to participate in the Assembly, which met at least forty times per year. Assembly members debated all public issues, often at great length, before making any final decisions. The Assembly tried to reach a consensus on all matters, and unanimous decisions were preferred, under the belief that the common interest would only be realized when everyone agreed.[5] When unanimity was not possible, votes were held to resolve differences of opinion. The implementation of the Assembly's decisions was conducted by smaller groups of men, who had been selected by lot or directly elected by the Assembly. These officials served for short periods of time and were not allowed to serve multiple terms in a row. These procedures ensured that many different men would serve in this executive capacity and that all citizens would have an equal chance of fulfilling these roles.[6]

One of the few surviving descriptions of Athenian citizens and their democratic participation is contained in Pericles' oration at a funeral for fallen soldiers:

> It is true that our government is called a democracy, because its administration is in the hands, not of the few, but of the many; yet while as regards the law all men are on an equality for the settlement of their private disputes, as regards the value set on them it is as each man is in any way distinguished that he is preferred to public honors, not because he belongs to a particular class, but because of personal merits; nor, again, on the ground of poverty is a man barred from a public career by obscurity of rank if he but has it in him to do the state a service.... And you will find united in the same persons an interest at once in private and in public affairs, and in others of us who give attention chiefly to business, you will find no lack of insight into political matters. For we alone regard the man who takes no part in public affairs, not as one who minds his own business, but as good for nothing; and we Athenians decide public questions for ourselves or at least endeavor to arrive at a sound understanding of them, in the belief that it is not debate

that is a hindrance to action, but rather not to be instructed by debates before the time comes for actions. For in truth we have this point also of superiority over other men, to be most daring in action and yet at the same time most given to reflection upon the ventures we mean to undertake; with other men, on the contrary, boldness means ignorance and reflection brings hesitation.[7]

As Pericles portrays, Athenian democracy was characterized by the active participation of public-spirited men. In fact, he labeled "good for nothing" those men not partaking in public affairs. This passage also alludes to other key characteristics of democratic citizenship that appear in **classical models of democracy,** such as high levels of attention to and interest in political matters, and the capability of deciding matters in favor of the general interest rather than only to advance one's own selfish interests.

Writing centuries later, Jean-Jacques Rousseau proposed a theory of democracy that has much in common with the classical model. Rousseau strongly advocated **popular sovereignty,** arguing in *The Social Contract* that "sovereignty [is] nothing other than the exercise of the general will" and "since the laws are nothing other than authentic acts of the general will, the sovereign can act only when the people is assembled."[8] Rousseau also distinguished the "general will" from the "will of all": "the general will studies only the common interest while the will of all studies private interest, and is indeed no more than the sum of individual desires."[9] In other words, the general will is not determined by simply adding up every person's individual opinions but rather reflects what is in the best interest of the entire society. Procedurally, Rousseau favored a **direct democracy** in which all citizens (restricted to property-owning free men) were to meet, discuss, and decide on the content of the laws. As in the Athenian Assembly, Rousseau envisaged vigorous legislative debate with a preference for unanimous decisions. Active political participation by the citizenry served multiple purposes for Rousseau. It was the only method by which the general will could be reached and enshrined in law. Active participation was also beneficial for the individual participants; in other words, political participation had "intrinsic value ... for the development of citizens as human beings."[10]

Rousseau's theory did depart from classical democratic theory in two important ways. First, Rousseau preferred that the citizens not be as involved in implementing the laws as they were in crafting legislation. He placed less faith in the public's ability to execute laws and proposed that a body of administrators be selected for this duty.[11] The administrators would be selected by the citizens and would be expected to follow the general will but would be distinct from the citizen assembly. Second, Rousseau's vision of democracy relied on relative economic equality among citizens, as enshrined by all free men having only a limited right to property. This does not mean that Rousseau favored strict equality of property but rather that he opposed unlimited accumulation of wealth. Short of this, some inequality was acceptable. Further, and more problematic for Rousseau, a citizen would not be able to make decisions for the benefit of all if he were motivated by fear of losing his economic independence. The right to enough property to make each citizen economically free from other citizens would prevent the formation of groups motivated by economic self-interest. Rousseau feared that the existence of such groups would undermine the creation of laws benefiting the common good.[12]

Later democratic theorists and practitioners have criticized classical democratic theory as unworkable for most societies. First, the city of Athens and Rousseau restricted citizenship rights to a degree that has become unacceptable for many democracies. In both cases, only free men were citizens; women and slaves were not given political rights. Further, the existence of a slave economy in Athens and the reliance on women for unpaid domestic labor created much leisure time for the free men to participate in government.[13] The amount of time necessary to participate in the Assembly's debates (forty times per year!) is simply not feasible for most contemporary working adults. Second, most democratic polities are larger than were the Greek city-states or the eighteenth-century towns of Rousseau's Europe. In fact, both the Greeks and Rousseau assumed that "[only] in a small state, where people could meet together in the relative intimacy of a single assembly and where a similarity of culture and interests united them, could individuals discuss and find the public good."[14] One of the primary reasons more modern democratic theories, including those that follow, departed from the classical variants was to accommodate popular rule in large, diverse, and populous nation-states. And, because democratic theory has evolved away from classical democracy in an attempt to speak to actual conditions in present-day societies, we will devote less attention to classical democracy than to other theories in this book.

Theories of Democratic Elitism and Pluralism

In contrast to classical democracy, theories of democratic elitism and pluralism do not allocate to citizens direct involvement in governmental decision making. Rather, the citizenry exerts indirect control. **Democratic elitists** view frequent competitive elections as the primary mechanism by which citizen preferences are expressed. Voters select their preferred candidates, and the elected officials deliberate over and vote on the nation's laws. These officials (or political elites) are accountable to the public in that they must periodically run for reelection. Thus, the elites have an incentive to represent the wishes of the public, and the will of the public will be reflected, to some degree, in governmental decisions. Yet, the daily decisions are made by the elites, who, by their knowledge and expertise, are better able to make these decisions. Joseph Schumpeter outlined his theory of democratic elitism as follows:

Suppose we reverse the roles of these two elements [the selection of representatives and the decision-making power of the voters] and make the deciding of issues by the electorate secondary to the election of the men who are to do the deciding. To put it differently, we now take the view that the role of the people is to produce a government.... And we define: the democratic method is that institutional arrangement for arriving at political decisions in which individuals acquire the power to decide by means of a competitive struggle for the people's vote.[15]

Pluralists also view competitive elections as one important mechanism by which citizens hold elected leaders accountable. Unlike democratic elitists, however, pluralists emphasize the essential role performed by groups, as intermediaries between the public and the elites, in representative democracies. **Interest groups** are especially important for transmitting the wishes of the citizenry to government officials in between elections. Such groups, which represent a wide variety of issues and concerns, attempt to influence elected officials and other governmental decision makers. Bargaining ensues, and the public policies that result are compromises among various groups.[16] Because interest group leaders have the desire and knowledge to lobby government officials, members of the public do not need to be actively involved to have their views represented in lawmaking. For example, citizens who care about human rights do not need to write letters to their elected officials but can instead have their concerns vocalized by an interest group such as Amnesty International or Human Rights Watch. Leader responsiveness to public concerns should result, argue pluralists.

Why have democratic elitists and pluralists proposed a more minor role for citizens in democratic politics? Simply put, "the individual voter was not all that the theory of democracy requires of him."[17] In practice, much evidence suggests that not all citizens are interested in or knowledgeable about politics, that levels of citizen apathy run high, and that many do not participate in politics. This evidence, collected by social scientists beginning in the 1940s, contributed to the development of democratic elitism and pluralism.[18] Indeed, it was the disconnect between dominant democratic theories and the reality of life in existing democracies that focused theorists' attention on actual democratic practices.[19] As described by a prominent political theorist, one way "to construct a theory of democracy ... is to consider as a single class of phenomena all those nation states and social organizations that are commonly called democratic ... and by examining the members of this class to discover ... the distinguishing characteristics they have in common."[20] Note that deriving a democratic theory based on observations from contemporary democracies would result in a very different theory than that which emerged from ancient Athens.

Contemporary democratic elitism and pluralism can trace their intellectual roots to earlier theorists of **representative democracy,** such as the English philosophers Jeremy Bentham and James Mill and the United States' James Madison.[21] These earlier theorists, especially Madison, advocated that most people are not capable of democratic citizenship in the classical sense. In *Federalist* No. 10, written in 1787, Madison argues that humans are self-interested and will pursue what benefits themselves rather than the nation as a whole. In societies where the liberty of individuals to form their own opinions and pursue their own goals is ensured, groups of similarly interested people will form. By Madison's definition, such groups, or **factions,** consist of citizens "who are united and actuated by some common impulse of passion, or of interest, adverse to the rights of other citizens, or to the permanent and aggregate interests of the community."[22] To overcome the negative effects of such factions, the causes of which are "sown in the nature of man," Madison proposes a republic whereby a few citizens are elected by the rest of the public to serve in the national government.[23] In his own words,

> The effect of [a representative democracy] is ... to refine and enlarge the public views by passing them through the medium of a chosen body of citizens, whose wisdom may best discern the true interest of their country and whose patriotism and love of justice will be least likely to sacrifice it to temporary or partial considerations. Under such a regulation it may well happen that the public voice, pronounced by the representatives of the people, will be more consonant to the public good than if pronounced by the people themselves, convened for the purpose.[24]

Similar beliefs in the decision-making superiority of elite officials are reflected in the writings of democratic elitists and pluralists. In an especially uncharitable view of the public, Joseph Schumpeter stated as fact "that the electoral mass is incapable of action other than a stampede."[25] More broadly, he argues that the public is capable of voting, but little else, and that the elites should be allowed to make decisions in between elections without public interference. Some theorists also emphasize that elites are more supportive of democratic norms and values, especially the civil rights and liberties of marginalized and/or unpopular groups, than are members of the public. In general, they suggest, this is beneficial to a democracy where decision making is in the hands of the elite.[26] The elites are not immune from public pressures to restrict individual liberties but will typically sort out such issues among themselves, with a preference toward maintaining such liberties.

Critiques of democratic elitism and pluralism have come from many quarters. Participatory democrats, as we describe below, interpret the empirical evidence related to citizen participation vastly differently than do democratic elitists and pluralists. Others have contradicted the pluralist assumption that interest groups will represent all points of view and/or that governmental officials are responsive to these groups. Government officials can choose to ignore a group's demands, especially when they believe the group lacks widespread public support. As just one

BOX 1-1 Use of Male Nouns and Pronouns

"... factions, the causes of which are 'sown in the nature of man ...'"
James Madison, 1787

"... make the deciding of issues by the electorate secondary to the election of the men who are to do the deciding."
Joseph Schumpeter, 1976 (originally published in 1943)

"The individual voter was not all that the theory of democracy requires of him."
Bernard Berelson, Paul Lazarsfeld, and William McPhee, 1954

When you read the above quotations in this text, did they sound unusual to you? Did you stop and wonder whether the original writers really meant their statements to refer only to men? Or are women implicitly included as well? Would these statements have sounded as odd, or more odd, if a female noun or pronoun had been used? What if Madison had stated that the causes of factions are "sown in the nature of woman"? Would you have paused and wondered about that statement? Today, writers often substitute "him or her" for "him" or even alternate usage of "him" and "her" or "man" and "woman" when their statements apply equally to men or women. This was not always the case, however, and certainly was not the norm in the 1700s or even as recently as the 1950s.

One way to determine whether the authors did mean to refer only to men when they wrote the above sentences would be to read more writings by these authors to try to determine their opinions regarding the political roles and rights of women. It is useful to bear in mind, though, that women's increasing involvement in politics has been accompanied by changes in language usage (not coincidentally). Early theorists might not have made their views toward women's role in politics known, because this role was minimal, by law and by custom. Furthermore, when women did engage in political activities, they were not viewed as political actors and could more easily be overlooked. Thus, in some instances, it can be difficult to sort out whether these writers really meant to refer to men only or whether by "man" they really meant "human." We encourage you not to just assume that using "man" implies women as well, but rather to consider the time period in which the author was writing and the nature of his or her conclusions regarding women and men in politics. In other words, do stop and think

(continued)

when you encounter "him" or "man" rather than merely breezing over these words.

Our approach in this book is to alternate using male and female nouns and pronouns when our statements are meant to apply to both women and men. So, unless otherwise specified, when we say "her" or "woman" we could have also said "him" or "man."

example, Amnesty International's pleas in 2003 to the United States military to stop the abuse of Iraqi prisoners in Abu Ghraib prison went largely unheeded until the news media became aware that photographs of the abuse existed, photographs that were eventually released to the American public in 2004.[27]

Further, some groups possess more resources than others and thus have more influence over policymaking: "The flaw in the pluralist heaven is that the heavenly chorus sings with a strong upper-class accent."[28] This fact did not go unnoticed by pluralists. Some accepted the inequality of political resources but argued that the inequalities did not accumulate within certain types of people but rather were dispersed throughout society. In other words, "Individuals best off in their access to one kind of resource are often badly off with respect to many other resources.... Virtually no one, and certainly no group of more than a few individuals, is entirely lacking in some influence resources."[29] Pluralists, however, did not fully develop the implications of group inequalities, an oversight that has been somewhat rectified by more recent neo-pluralist theorists.[30] Assumptions of noncumulative inequalities have also been challenged. Business groups, these critics contend, occupy a privileged position in U.S. politics due to their accumulation of advantages.[31]

Finally, Jack Walker's assessment of democratic elitism takes quite a different form. He charges the democratic elitists with changing "the principal orienting values of democracy."[32] Earlier democratic theorists had stressed the importance of citizen participation and the personal benefits that accrue to individuals from this participation. In contrast, under democratic elitism, "emphasis has shifted to the needs and functions of the system as a whole; there is no longer a direct concern with human development. ... [Elitists] have substituted stability and efficiency as the prime goals of democracy."[33] Participatory democracy, the final democratic theory we examine, represents a shift back toward the developmental functions of democracy that Walker supports.

Participatory Democracy

As its name suggests, **participatory democracy** emphasizes the importance of political participation by the public. While participatory democrats recognize the need for representative democracy in nations as large as the United States, they also see the possibility and benefits of more political involvement by the public than is currently practiced.[34] Because participation is linked to social class and wealth today, participatory democrats advocate greater political involvement of all citizens as a means to redress inequality. "This is not to say that a more participatory system would of itself remove all the inequities of our society," writes one theorist. "It is only to say that low participation and social inequity are so bound up with each other that a more equitable and humane society requires a more participatory political system."[35]

This theory of democracy originated during the protest movements of the 1960s and also represented dissatisfaction with the democratic elitist and pluralist models that were dominant at that time.[36] Participatory democrats agreed with these other theorists that levels of disinterest and apathy ran quite high among the American public, but they disagreed over the source of these attitudes. Rather than being politically disinterested by nature or preferring to spend one's time on other pursuits, such as family, work, and leisure time, participatory democrats argue that the political system, with its relatively few opportunities for meaningful citizen influence, breeds apathy. To political scientist Benjamin Barber, people

> are apathetic because they are powerless, not powerless because they are apathetic. There is no evidence to suggest that once empowered, a people will refuse to participate. The historical evidence of New England towns, community school boards, neighborhood associations, and other local bodies is that participation fosters more participation.[37]

Citizen apathy is thus a problem to be examined and solved rather than an accepted fact of political life in modern democracies.[38]

Participation in democratic decision making provides many personal benefits to those who engage in this activity, according to participatory democrats. On this point, they agree with democratic theorists of earlier eras, especially the nineteenth century's John Stuart Mill.[39] Citizens become more politically and socially educated and can develop their intellect and characters through political participation. By communicating with and learning from other members of the public, individuals can look beyond their own self-interest and come to know what is best for the community or nation as a whole. In short, participation, in and of itself, can produce better democratic citizens.[40] Peter Bachrach, in articulating his vision of democracy as fostering individual self-development, states, "the majority of individuals stand to gain in self-esteem and growth toward a fuller affirmation of their personalities by participating more actively in meaningful community decisions."[41]

According to some participatory democrats, a fully participatory society necessitates more citizen involvement in decision making in governmental as well as nongovernmental institutions, such as the workplace or school. Why should people be excluded from decision making by private organizations when these decisions strongly affect their own lives and livelihoods, asks Bachrach.[42] Further, engaging in decision making at work and in other nongovernmental venues could increase governmental participation. Engagement in workplace decision making fosters civic skills, provides valuable experience, and, if effective, could create more confidence in one's ability to influence governmental decisions.[43] The flipside of this argument is that the lack of involvement in decision making in one's daily life will likely translate into disengagement from political participation, as the following clearly demonstrates:

> After spending the day following orders without question at the factory, a worker cannot be expected to return home in the evening to act like the civics textbook's inquiring, skeptical, self-actualizing citizen. Students who are taught primarily to obey authority in school are not likely to grow into effective democratic citizens.[44]

Skeptics of participatory democracy argue that the public does not respond to participatory opportunities as the theorists contend they will. When barriers to political participation are eliminated or reduced, citizens have not necessarily become more politically active. For example, the National Voter Registration Act of 1993, more commonly known as the motor-voter bill, made voter registration easier and, supporters alleged, would increase voter turnout once enacted. Levels of turnout, however, have not substantially increased in the wake of this registration reform.[45] More broadly, some scholars conclude that participatory democrats' assumptions about the public are unrealistic.[46] Rather than desiring to become more involved in politics, many citizens actually dislike politics and wish to avoid the type of conflict that typically emerges during decision making. In other words, while citizens might in fact learn from one another, as participatory democrats suggest, others argue that the more likely response is to bypass any opportunity for deliberation, especially if the chance of disagreement is high.

Democratic Theory and Public Opinion

As you can see, these theories of democracy are quite broad, addressing many features of democratic governance. In our overview here, we have highlighted the aspects of the theories that are most relevant for the study of public opinion. We have also organized this textbook around what we consider to be key democratic theory debates about the public. Specifically, the chapters that follow pertain to one of four questions that are central to evaluating democratic citizens and democratic nations:

- Are citizens pliable?
- Do citizens organize their political thinking?

- Do citizens endorse and demonstrate democratic basics?
- What is the relationship between citizens and their government?

The first two questions pertain to public competence, and we selected them because, as you just learned, democratic theorists disagree over assumptions regarding the political capabilities of the public. The third question brings our attention toward public support for some fundamental features of democracies (civil liberties, political rights, etc.). Democratic theorists focus on this topic not only because it is relevant for evaluating the public but also because democratic societies require some level of support for certain values and norms. Finally, the fourth question highlights the relationship between the public and leaders as well as what role the public should play in governmental decision making. These are topics that are important for democracy but toward which democratic theorists provide different views.

WHAT IS PUBLIC OPINION?

Public opinion is, on the one hand, a term that is familiar to most people and, on the other hand, rather difficult to define. Popular conceptions of public opinion might include phrases such as "the voice of the people." For most of us, public opinion is probably best represented by the results from opinion polls, such as those reported on the evening news or in the newspaper. Among public opinion observers and scholars, many different definitions have been proposed. While researchers do not agree on one single definition of public opinion, some commonalities exist across specific definitions. First, most emphasize that public opinion refers to opinions on governmental and policy matters rather than on private matters (such as one's favorite flavor of ice cream or favorite movie). This characteristic is implied by a description of public opinion as "those opinions held by private persons which governments find it prudent to heed."[47] Of course, what constitutes a private matter might be in dispute. For centuries the problems of domestic violence and rape within marriage were considered to be private affairs best left to a married or intimate couple to resolve. Societal views on this topic have changed, however, so that now people assume governments have to be involved in addressing these serious problems.

Second, in recent decades a consensus definition of public opinion has emerged. As one example, public opinion has been defined as "simply the sum or aggregation of private opinions on any particular issue or set of issues."[48] In this view, public opinion refers to the preferences of individuals, tallied such that each person's opinion counts equally. Following the consensus, this is the definition that we use in this book.

However, despite the consensus, some have raised important objections to defining public opinion as a "one person, one vote" aggregation. One of the earliest critiques came from sociologist Herbert Blumer. Society, according to Blumer, is organized hierarchically and "is not a mere aggregation of disparate individuals."[49] Certain individuals have more influence over the formation and expression of people's opinions, and treating each person's opinion as equal ignores this simple fact. For example, leaders of labor unions not only attempt to influence the opinions of their members but also present their members' views to government policymakers. Simply tallying up individuals' opinions on a specific issue also overlooks the dynamic opinion formation processes among groups and among people. In Blumer's words, public opinion "is a function of a structured society, differentiated into a network of different kinds of groups and individuals having differential weight and influence and occupying different strategic positions."[50] Blumer further attacked the "one person, one vote" accounting of opinions by arguing that not all opinions were treated equally by government policymakers, in part because not all opinions of the public actually reach these policymakers. Opinions that do not come to the attention of decision makers will not influence their decisions.

Blumer directed his criticisms toward the **public opinion polling** industry, arguing that polls were incapable of capturing public opinion as he understood the concept. By reporting the opinions from a random selection of individuals, polls epitomize the "one person, one vote" aggregation of people's preferences. Not only were polls an unnatural forum for expressing one's opinions, argued Blumer, but they also were unable to capture the opinion formation process that he identified. Opinion polls do not report, for example, whether a poll respondent "belongs to a powerful group taking a vigorous stand on the issue or whether he is a detached recluse with no membership in a functional group; whether he is bringing his opinion to bear in some fashion at strategic points in the operation of society or whether it is isolated and socially impotent."[51] Blumer wrote at a time when public opinion polling was in its infancy. Despite his concerns, which were also shared by others, opinion polls have grown in use and influence, becoming the dominant method by which public opinion is assessed. Further, as this one method has dominated, there has been a narrowing in our understanding of public opinion—a narrowing around the consensus definition described above.[52]

Robert Weissberg is not much bothered by the manner in which the concept of public opinion is defined.[53] Rather, he is worried when the public's social welfare policy opinions *as measured by polls* too strongly influence the decisions of elected officials. Compared to the complex choices officials confront, poll respondents are often faced with simple options, such as whether social welfare spending should be increased, be decreased, or remain at current levels. When responding to such a poll question, an individual might consider what the trade-offs to increased spending would be, such as whether taxes would increase or other areas of government spending would decrease, or she might not consider these trade-offs. Knowing that a majority of the public support increased spending not only does not provide specific enough policy advice to policymakers but might also result in representatives rushing to follow the wishes of the public without considering the budgetary implications of doing so. "Governance via public opinion polling," concludes Weissberg, "does not fortify democracy."[54]

Others have also emphasized the poor quality of public opinion as assessed by polls, arguing that survey respondents often provide snap, top-of-the-head judgments. Contrast this with **public judgment,** a state that exists when "people have engaged an issue, considered it from all sides, understood the choices it leads to, and accepted the full consequences of the choices they make."[55] Encouraging and cultivating thoughtful public judgment, according to this view, is necessary if we want the public—and not only those people with specialized knowledge and expertise—to govern in a democracy.

We mention these criticisms not because we find them superior to the consensus definition of public opinion. We are, however, sympathetic to the latter concerns because we find the "public opinion as aggregation of individual views" definition too limiting. In addition to the concerns outlined above, we are troubled that this consensus approach draws our attention only to one feature of public opinion: the content of people's political opinions. While it is important to know how the public feels about an issue, focusing only on the content of people's opinions overlooks many equally important features of public opinion. Understanding public opinion requires us to explore other topics, such as the sources of those opinions, the processes by which opinions are formed and altered, the organization of an individual's opinions, and the impact of public opinion on public policy. In the chapters that follow, we describe studies that illustrate a variety of definitions of public opinion. Along the way, therefore, we touch on the many facets of public opinion. But, as will become evident, most scholars of public opinion do rely on the consensus definition of public opinion, whether implicitly or explicitly.

DEFINING KEY CONCEPTS

Each of the chapters in this text addresses a specific aspect of public opinion in America. In these chapters, you will repeatedly encounter a few of the same concepts and terms. We define those concepts here, so that you will understand the later chapters more thoroughly.

Attitude and Opinion

Two terms that we use frequently in this book are attitude and opinion. These words are undoubtedly familiar to you, and you will likely agree that they are similar to each other. They both have sparked considerable attention to their meanings, however, and numerous definitions have been proposed for each, especially for attitude. The term **attitude** is one of the most important concepts in psychology and has been for many years. Over seventy years ago, a prominent social psychologist presented a "representative selection" of sixteen definitions of attitude and then proposed his own comprehensive definition.[56] In the many decades since, still more scholars have discussed and debated the meaning of attitude. Of the many possible definitions, we prefer this one: "Attitude is a psychological tendency that is expressed by evaluating a particular entity with some degree of favor or disfavor."[57] A similar approach defines an attitude as "a general and enduring positive or negative feeling about some person, object or issue."[58]

These two definitions highlight some key features of an attitude. First, people hold attitudes toward targets ("entity" or "person, object, or issue"). In the realm of political attitudes, possible types of objects for which we have attitudes are policy issues, political candidates or politicians, groups (such as feminists or the National Rifle Association [NRA]), and institutions of government. Second, attitudes represent an evaluation of an object, generally articulated as favorable or unfavorable, as liking or disliking, or as positive or negative. So, in terms of specific political attitudes, your friend might favor school prayer, like President George W. Bush, dislike feminists, support the NRA, and disapprove of Congress. It is also possible to have a neutral (neither favorable nor unfavorable) attitude toward a target. Neutral attitudes might result from not being informed enough about an object to evaluate it positively or negatively. Alternatively, you might assess certain features of an object positively and other features negatively. If these cancel each other out and prevent you from an overall positive or negative evaluation of the object, you might conclude that your attitude is neutral.

So, now, what is an **opinion**? Similar to an attitude, an opinion refers to a specific object and expresses a preference, such as support or opposition, toward that object. As with attitudes, opinions vary in that not everyone holds the same opinion toward an object. While acknowledging these similarities, many scholars distinguish between these two concepts by stating that an opinion is an expression of a latent attitude. That is, whereas an attitude is not observable, an opinion is a verbal or written expression of that attitude. Distinctions such as these are more common in the field of psychology than in political science. In political science you are not only likely to see the terms used synonymously but are also more likely to encounter the concept opinion than attitude. We view these two terms as much more similar than dissimilar and thus use them interchangeably in this book. This no doubt reflects our training as political scientists, but it also reflects common usage of the terms. In fact, in most thesauruses, opinion and attitude are presented as synonyms of each other.

When thinking about a specific attitude or opinion, it is obviously important to consider its *direction* (support versus oppose, favorable versus unfavorable, etc.). For the study of public opinion, we also need to bear in mind two other characteristics of attitudes and opinions: extremity and importance. The **extremity** of an opinion refers to whether support (or opposition) for the opinion object is slight or strong. You might, for example, slightly favor U.S. intervention in foreign military conflicts but strongly favor laws that prohibit testing cosmetics on animals. **Attitude importance,** in contrast, focuses on how meaningful a specific attitude is to you or how passionately you care about the attitude. While we may have attitudes toward a wide range of political and social objects, not all of these attitudes will be of equal importance, at least for most of us. The more important an attitude is, the less likely it is to change over time, and the more likely it directs certain behaviors, such as thinking about the attitude object or influencing our vote preferences for political candidates.[59] While it is often the case that more extreme attitudes are also more important, this does not necessarily have to occur.[60] Take the two examples presented above. Although you might have a more extreme opinion toward animal testing than U.S. military intervention, the latter opinion might be more important to you, especially when it comes to evaluating national politics, such as the performance of political leaders.

Opinion Ingredients: Beliefs, Values, and Emotions

Specific political opinions do not stand alone in people's minds but are instead often related to, even guided by, other mental constructs, most especially beliefs, values, and emotions. These three often have evaluative content—content that can help to determine one's specific opinion toward a related entity. **Beliefs** are thoughts or information a person has regarding an attitude object, often regarding what the person thinks to be true about the object. One might, for example, believe that the possibility of a very severe punishment, such as the death penalty, will not deter most people from committing a serious crime. Someone possessing this belief would be more likely to oppose capital punishment than would someone who believed in the deterrent power of death penalty laws. Beliefs about the characteristics of members of social groups, such as blacks or Christian fundamentalists, have a specific name: **stereotypes.** Stereotypes can be positive or negative, and people can hold both positive and negative stereotypes toward the same group. Examples of positive and negative stereotypes include blacks as athletic or lazy and Christian fundamentalists as charitable or intolerant. Believing certain stereotypes is often related to support for public policies that affect the group in question. White Americans who believe most blacks are lazy, for instance, are unlikely to support social welfare policies, especially when compared with people who do not believe this stereotype.[61]

Values are specific types of beliefs. According to a prominent values researcher, "a value is an enduring belief that a specific mode of conduct [instrumental value] or end-state of existence [terminal value] is personally or socially preferable to an opposite or converse mode of conduct or end-state of existence."[62] Examples of instrumental values include independence, responsibility, and self-control, whereas examples of terminal values include a peaceful world, family security, and freedom. Unlike other types of beliefs, values refer to ideals. Notice that this definition of

BOX 1-2 "When Ideology Is a Value," by Michael Kinsley

It's been less than a month since the gods decreed that because of the election results American political life henceforth must be all about something called "values." And I gave it my best. Honest. But values won. I'm sick of talking about values, sick of pretending I have them or care more about them than I really do. Sick of bending and twisting the political causes I do care about to make them qualify as "values." News stories about values-mongers caught with their values down used to make my day. Now the tale of Bill O'Reilly and phone sex induces barely a flicker of schadenfreude.

Why does an ideological position become sacrosanct when it gets labeled as a "value"? There are serious arguments and sincere passions on both sides of the gay-marriage debate. For some reason, the views of those who feel that marriage requires a man and a woman are considered to be a "value," while the views of those who believe that gay relationships deserve the same legal standing as straight ones barely qualify as an opinion.

Those labels don't confer any logical advantage. But they confer two big advantages in the propaganda war. First, a value just seems inherently more compelling than a mere opinion. That's a big head start. Second, the holder of a value is held to be more sensitive to slights than the holder of an opinion. An opinion can't just slug away at a value. It must be solicitous and understanding. A value may tackle an opinion, meanwhile, with no such constraint.

No doubt there are strategists all over Washington busily reconfiguring their issues to look like values. Highway construction funds? Needed to help people get to Grandma's house for Christmas. You got something against family values, buddy? Or Christmas? Especially humiliating are efforts by liberals to reposition the issues they care about as conservative and therefore, we hope, transform them into values. Welfare? It (like nearly everything else) is about families, of course. And affirmative action is about work and opportunity. Liberals' motivation—a simple instinct that a prosperous society ought to mitigate the unfairness of life to some reasonable extent—isn't considered a value. So let's keep that one among ourselves . . .

Source: Washington Post, November 28, 2004, sec. B, final edition.

Note: Michael Kinsley is editorial and opinion editor of the *Los Angeles Times.*

values differs quite substantially from the usage of the term in political discourse immediately following the 2004 presidential election. In Box 1-2, an excerpt from an editorial written in late November of that year demonstrates the latter usage.

Values are also assumed to be quite stable over time for individuals, as highlighted by this definition: "By values we mean general and enduring standards."[63] Whereas value change can and does occur, stability is more common. Some have even argued that values are central to people's political belief systems, certainly more central than are attitudes.[64] Further, much public opinion research demonstrates that values are quite important in influencing people's specific political attitudes. For instance, opposition to social welfare spending is more likely among those who value responsibility, a sense of accomplishment, and economic individualism and less likely among those who value equality.[65] Finally, certain values are more salient in American political culture than others in that they guide political opinions more strongly. These include individualism, equality, and limited government.[66] Not all Americans value these three, to be sure, but whether one values or does not value each is related to opinions on many specific political matters.

Whereas beliefs are considered to be the cognitive components of attitudes, **emotions** comprise the affective component.[67] Emotions are feelings that a person has toward the attitude object. Emotions are especially common when it comes to evaluating political individuals or groups. You might feel warmly toward a politician and thus evaluate her (and even her job performance) highly. In contrast, fearing a politician would likely lead to poor assessments of her but also might transfer into not supporting issues that she supports. Negative affect that is felt toward a specific group is commonly referred to as **prejudice** and can influence attitudes toward politicians from the group as well as policies designed to benefit the group. Emotional reactions can also influence opinions toward political issues or public policies. Anxiety that a foreign leader could detonate a nuclear weapon somewhere on U.S. soil could lead one to support a strong national defense and a preemptive foreign policy. Finally, people can feel positively toward an attitude object but also hold negative beliefs about the object. For example, someone could admire black culture while at the same time hold negative stereotypes about blacks.

Party Identification

Throughout this book, we present examples of many different political opinions. One opinion that we refer to often, because it is a core opinion for many Americans and crucial to understanding the nature of public opinion in the United States, is party identification. **Party identification** refers to a person's allegiance with a political party (typically the Democratic or Republican Party) or identification as independent of a party. It is a self-classification rather than a description of one's behavior, as the following excerpt from *The American Voter,* a classic study about voting first published in 1960, highlights:

Only in the exceptional case does the sense of individual attachment to party reflect a formal membership or an active connection with a party apparatus. Nor does it simply denote a voting record, although the influence of party allegiance on electoral behavior is strong. Generally this tie is a psychological identification, which can persist without legal recognition or evidence of formal membership and even without a consistent record of party support. Most Americans have this sense of attachment with one party or the other. And for the individual who does, the strength and direction of party identification are facts of central importance in accounting for attitude and behavior.[68]

In other words, a person could consider himself to be a Republican without ever formally registering as such or without always voting for Republican candidates. Party identification is instead an attitude one has about his attachment to a political party. Typically, then, to determine someone's party identification, you would not ask whom she voted for most recently but rather ask her whether she identifies with a particular party, emphasizing the self-identification component of this attitude. To illustrate, two examples of questions used by national survey organizations to assess the party identification of the American public follow:

> Generally speaking, do you usually think of yourself as a Republican, a Democrat, an Independent, or what? [If Republican or Democrat:] Would you call yourself a strong (Republican, Democrat) or a not very strong (Republican, Democrat)? [If Independent, Other or No Preference:] Do you think of yourself as closer to the Republican or Democratic Party?[69]

> No matter how you voted today, do you usually think of yourself as a Democrat, Republican, Independent, [or] Something else?[70]

We highlight party identification here because it is important in American political culture for a number of reasons. First, for an individual, party identification is quite stable over time, certainly more stable than other political attitudes.[71] When movement does occur, it is most likely due to people switching from identification with one of the two major parties to considering themselves to be independent or vice versa. That is, switching from identifying with one of the parties to the other does not occur very often. Second, party identification is a global attitude that is related to many specific political attitudes (such as policy opinions, evaluations of political leaders, etc.). Third, one's party identification can influence the interpretation of newly encountered information. When learning of damaging information about a Democratic president, for example, a Democrat is likely to interpret this information quite differently than a Republican. Relatedly, one's party identification can help one to make sense of political issues and topics, especially those that are unfamiliar. We will elaborate on these and other aspects of party identification throughout the rest of this book.

With which of the two major political parties are Americans most likely to identify? In Figure 1-1, we present the breakdown of Americans' party identification (as Democratic, Independent, or Republican) since 1952. Focusing first on the solid lines, a few trends are evident. American adults are much less likely to identify with the Democratic Party now than they were in the 1950s and 1960s (when around one-half of the population considered themselves Democrats). This does not necessarily mean, however, that Americans are now identifying as Republicans in much larger numbers. Republican self-identification is higher now than it was in the 1950s, but not much higher (even though Republican identifiers were less common in the intervening decades).

The most significant change in party identification the past fifty years is the switch from **partisans** to **partisan independence.** In fact, beginning in 1988, in presidential election years Independents have been more common than either Democrats or Republicans in all but one (1996). There was a substantial increase in Independents during the 1960s, as you can see from Figure 1-1. Whereas only about 23 percent of the population considered themselves to be Independent in 1960, more than 31 percent did so by 1970. These figures, however, include people who lean toward supporting one of the major parties. That is, when initially asked whether they consider themselves to be Democratic, Republican, or Independent, they claim to be Independents. Yet, when then asked if they are closer to one of the parties, most of these Independents do indicate closeness to one

Figure 1-1   Party Identification, 1952–2004

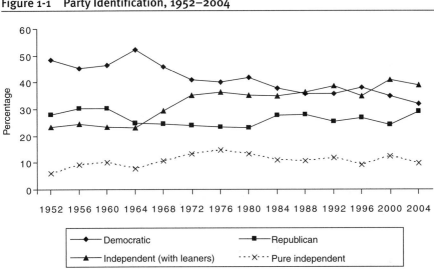

Source: Analysis of American National Election Studies Cumulative Data File, 1948–2004.

party. Removing these **leaners** from the analysis (as we did for the dotted line at the bottom of the figure) presents a very different picture. While there are more pure Independents now than there were in the 1950s, the increase has not been very large (6 percent in 1952 to 9.7 percent in 2004). Most of the increase in Independents, thus, seems to have been among the leaners, people whose initial identity is as Independent but who ultimately think and act like partisans. Finally, recently leaners are more likely to feel close to the Democratic than Republican Party. Thus, when placing the leaners in their partisan camp rather than grouping them with the pure Independents, the gap between Democrats and Republicans is larger than what is graphed in Figure 1-1. There, we show that 32.1 percent of the public was Democratic in 2004 and 29 percent was Republican. When leaners are included as partisans, the respective figures are 49.6 percent and 40.7 percent.

EMPIRICAL ASSESSMENTS OF PUBLIC OPINION

As should have been clear from the summaries of democratic theory we presented earlier, the main goal of these theories is to present **normative** conclusions. That is, most theorists outline how a democratic government and society ought to be structured, including what ought to be the role of the citizenry. Democratic theories are not entirely normative, however. According to one view, the best models of democracy

> have been both explanatory and justificatory or advocatory. They are, in different proportions, statements about what a political system or a political society is, how it does work or could work, and statements of why it is a good thing, or why it would be a good thing to have it or to have more of it.[72]

To rephrase, theories of democracy contain normative and empirical components. The empirical features are statements about how a society actually is, based on observations of democratic societies. These observations of reality can be important components of democratic theories and can complement or contribute to a theory's normative conclusions, as we discussed above with the theories of democratic elitism and pluralism. In contrast to the normative focus of democratic theories, **empirical analyses** of public opinion place primacy on accurately describing and/or explaining real-life phenomena. Any broader conclusions, whether normative or otherwise, are of secondary importance for fields of empirical study.

Most public opinion scholars, and nearly all that we feature in this book, are empiricists. Examining public opinion empirically requires, of course, that this phenomenon be measured in some way. Measuring public opinion is not an easy or obvious task, however. What if, for example, you wanted to know whether the public supports the death penalty. How would you determine public opinion on this issue? You could stop people on the street, ask them if they support capital punishment, and tally up the responses. You could read letters to the editor in the newspaper to gauge public sentiment on the death penalty. You could look to elected officials' statements about the public to determine how citizens feel about this issue or assume that most people do support the death penalty because the majority of states in America have death penalty laws. These are just a few possibilities, and although each has its advantages (and disadvantages), none can be ruled out as clearly inappropriate. In fact, all are examples of approaches that have been used, at one time or another, to measure public opinion. The Appendix of this text discusses a variety of public opinion research methods, methods that we will illuminate throughout the chapters of this book.

THEMES OF THE BOOK

By reading this book, you will learn a lot about public opinion in the United States. One way that we try to fulfill this goal is by linking normative democratic theories with findings from empirical studies of public opinion. Rather than only considering what researchers have concluded about public opinion, throughout this book we discuss the democratic theory implications of a study or a body of research. We hope this approach will encourage you to evaluate the public opinion research through the lenses of the democratic theories outlined above, and also to evaluate the democratic theories in light of the empirical studies. This, we hope, will deepen your assessments of these democratic theories and provide you with a broad understanding of public opinion.

There are many, many empirical studies on public opinion. Summarizing all of these would be a daunting task for us, and would produce a book that would be tedious for you to read. Thus, we have not attempted to discuss every relevant study on each topic. Instead, in each chapter, we focus on prototypical and especially influential studies that bring the fundamental questions into sharp focus. Our discussions of these prototypical studies are detailed and are meant to illustrate the strengths and weaknesses of each study. To evaluate well the conclusions from a study, you need to know what is good about the research and what its limits are. Using this approach will, we hope, encourage you to consider how public opinion is studied as well as better understand how a choice of methodology can influence the conclusions that researchers draw. We also anticipate that this feature of our text—what we call "embedded methods"—will teach you about specific research methods better than if the topics were presented in a separate chapter devoted only to methodology. If at any point you want to have more information about a method you are reading about, however, you can always turn to the Appendix for details about the specific method.

Finally, we have organized the chapters of the book into sections. Each section poses a question that is important for democratic theory, and the chapters in the section present evidence and arguments to help you answer that question. We will not answer these questions, however. In fact, these questions do not have "correct" answers. Instead, we present evidence and tools to help you think through the material critically and challenge you to make your own judgment regarding the capacity of citizens to function effectively in a democracy.

Chapters in the next section address the following question: Are Citizens Pliable? Topics included in the three chapters of this section include the sources of people's opinions, how the mass media shape public opinion, and the stability of attitudes. The following section asks, Do Citizens Organize Their Political Thinking? Chapters 5 and 6 consider this question by examining whether people's opinions are shaped by factors such as political ideology, personality, self-interest calculations, values, historical events, or reference groups (based on party identification or racial identification, for example). The three chapters in the next section address the question: Do Citizens Endorse and Demonstrate Democratic Basics? The democratic basics we focus on are knowledge and attention to politics, support for civil liberties, and support for civil rights. The question guiding chapters 10 and 11 is, What Is the Relationship between Citizens and Their Government? The first of these chapters takes up the topics of citizen trust in government and support for the institutions of government, whereas the second chapter examines the relationship between public opinion and public policy. In the final section, we take a broad assessment of the role of public opinion in America, asking, What Do We Make of Public Opinion in a Democracy? The concluding chapter of the text reviews normative debates over the role of citizens in a democracy and summarizes the empirical evidence that speaks to these debates.

KEY CONCEPTS

attitude / 15	opinion / 16
attitude importance / 17	participatory democracy / 10
beliefs / 17	partisan independence / 21
citizen apathy / 11	partisans / 21
classical models of democracy / 5	party identification / 19
democratic elitists / 6	pluralists / 7
democratic theory / 4	popular sovereignty / 5
direct democracy / 5	prejudice / 19
emotions / 19	public judgment / 15
empirical analyses / 22	public opinion / 13
extremity / 16	public opinion polling / 14
factions / 8	representative democracy / 7
interest groups / 7	stereotypes / 17
leaners / 22	values / 17
normative / 22	

SUGGESTED SOURCES FOR FURTHER READING

Each chapter in this book ends with a list of readings and Web sites. If you wish to investigate any of a chapter's topics further, perusing these lists of suggested sources will be a good step to begin your exploration.

Bachrach, Peter. *The Theory of Democratic Elitism: A Critique.* Washington, D.C.: University Press of America, 1980.

Pateman, Carole. *Participation and Democratic Theory.* Cambridge: Cambridge University Press, 1970.

Walker, Jack L. "A Critique of the Elitist Theory of Democracy." *American Political Science Review* 60 (1966): 285–295.

These three authors are proponents of participatory democracy. In these works, they present reasons for supporting this theory and explain why democratic elitism is problematic.

Bryan, Frank M. *Real Democracy: The New England Town Meeting and How It Works.* Chicago: University of Chicago Press, 2004.

Bryan presents an in-depth and illuminating analysis of the New England town meeting. Unlike representative democracies, these meetings involve all eligible citizens coming together to debate and vote on town matters. For this reason, Bryan labels the town meeting "real democracy."

Dahl, Robert A. *Who Governs? Democracy and Power in an American City.* New Haven: Yale University Press, 1961.

Schumpeter, Joseph A. *Capitalism, Socialism and Democracy,* 5th ed. London: Allen and Unwin, 1976.

The theories of democratic elitism and pluralism are discussed in these works.

Held, David. *Models of Democracy,* 2nd ed. Stanford: Stanford University Press, 1996.

Macpherson, C. B. *The Life and Times of Liberal Democracy.* Oxford: Oxford University Press, 1977.

Macpherson and Held have organized the numerous variants of democratic theory into a manageable number of models (four for Macpherson and nine for Held), some of which we presented in this chapter. For a description of similarities and differences among theories of democracy or an introduction to specific theorists, these books are recommended.

Marcus, George E., and Russell L. Hanson, eds. *Reconsidering the Democratic Public.* University Park: Pennsylvania State University Press, 1993.

This volume brings together democratic theory and empirical studies of citizens in "an attempt to better understand American democratic practices and the requirements of democratic theory" (p. xiii). The chapters demonstrate the richness of combining these two branches of scholarship.

American Association for Public Opinion Research: www.aapor.org

AAPOR is the professional organization for public opinion researchers. This Web site contains information about the organization, statements regarding the misuse of polls and poll results, links to Web sites that contain polling data, and a helpful list titled "Fifty books that significantly shaped public opinion research, 1946–1995."

PART II

Are Citizens Pliable?

DO UNITED STATES' citizens hold stable political attitudes? Or are many people pliable, with their attitudes frequently changing? These questions highlight a core difference among the democratic theories we profile in this book: beliefs regarding the political capabilities of the public. Which view suggests a more capable public? Is it best for people to hold opinions that stay the same over years or for people to be open to new perspectives? Put another way, do citizens need to be open to new ideas, fresh leaders, and policy innovations? Is it possible to guarantee that but not have citizens susceptible to a politician's every whim?

These are important questions for any student of the democratic public to consider. Before reaching any firm answers, however, it is important to know where people's opinions originate, when and under what conditions they are likely to change, for whom opinions are likely to be stable versus changeable, and what role external communication sources play in influencing opinions. These topics are addressed in this section with specific chapters on the topics of political socialization, the mass media, and attitude stability and change.

CHAPTER 2

Political Socialization

THINK ABOUT YOUR political opinions. Where did they originate? In other words, where did you get your political attitudes? Once you developed specific political opinions, have they changed very often? If you are like most people, your opinions have been influenced by a variety of sources, including your family, the schools you have attended, and the media, to name a few. Some of your political opinions were even formed when you were a child, and perhaps some of these have not changed much since then. Thus, an examination of the stability versus pliability of citizens' opinions should properly begin by considering how and when political opinions are first formed.

The manner by which we all learn about politics and develop political opinions is called **political socialization.** "Political socialization is the process by which people acquire relatively enduring orientations toward politics in general and toward their own particular political systems."[1] This process begins at a very early age, and, for most people, socialization occurs throughout the entire lifetime.

The study of socialization began "with a single-minded focus on childhood and the family."[2] A key assumption of this research was that political opinions and outlooks gained during childhood and adolescence would persist into adulthood. At some level, this supposition justified the extensive study of childhood political opinions. Why else would examining the attitudes of those without any power in the political system be useful, unless such study taught us something about the opinions of future political actors? The notion that preadult attitudes remained relatively stable was especially thought to be the case with one specific attitude: party identification. It was assumed that individuals' partisanship was quite well formed by the time that they left adolescence and remained very stable throughout adulthood.

There are many sources of people's political opinions. Important **socialization agents** include schools, peers, and the news media. Primary among these, though, is the family. In fact, among researchers, the family was thought to play the most influential socializing role. One of the very first books on the topic of political socialization contained the following: "Foremost among agencies of socialization into politics is the family."[3] Combining this assumption with the belief that party identification is socialized at a young age, a picture emerges. Children of, for example, Republican parents were assumed to identify as Republicans by the time they reach adulthood and remain Republicans throughout their lives.

These expectations about the source and stability of partisanship have been the focus of much socialization research over the past few decades. As we will show in this chapter, understandings of the persistence of preadult opinions as well as the role of the family in transmitting opinions have been revised since the earliest examinations of these topics. In terms of the specific organization of the chapter, we discuss the key characteristics of socialization at three stages of life: childhood, adolescence, and adulthood. For each, we describe which political attitudes are developed in that stage and what the key socialization agents of these attitudes are. For adolescence and adulthood, we also focus on whether previously socialized attitudes persist over time.

Another way to think of political socialization is as the transmission of key political values and norms from one generation to the next. This view of socialization focuses on how societies "inculcate appropriate norms and practices in citizens, residents or members."[4] David Easton and Jack Dennis were proponents of this approach, linking socialization to the maintenance of a democratic political system.[5] In particular, Easton and Dennis described the main goal of early socialization as fostering confidence and trust in as well as positive affect toward the political system. They further argued that widespread holding of these attitudes is important for the persistence of a nation's government. Failure to transmit these norms to new generations of children could threaten a nation's stability.

Consistent with Easton and Dennis's view, successful socialization would result in citizens who support the nation's system of government and who respect political authority. Such outcomes would please democratic elitists. First, socializing citizens in such a way could lead them to defer to political leaders and the leaders' expertise. This would preserve the dominance of elite decision making with lesser involvement from the citizens, as democratic elitists prefer. Second, this type of socialization emphasizes system support over individual development, a goal that democratic elitists support, but one that other democratic theorists, most especially participatory democrats, find worrisome.

In contrast, pluralists hope that socialization develops strong political identities and a clear sense of how one's interests are best represented in the political system. With a clear sense of their own similarities to the political parties—"[t]he major vehicle through which the public works its will in pluralist theory"—citizens can more easily pursue their interests and hold elected officials accountable for representing them.[6] Thus, pluralists would favor a socialization process that results in strong partisan identification. To what degree does socialization accomplish the goals of these democratic theorists? We return to this question at the end of the chapter.

CHILDHOOD SOCIALIZATION

Political socialization begins quite early in life. Children begin to learn about the political world and develop political orientations during the elementary school years. From the fourth grade, "children move from near—but not complete— ignorance of adult politics to awareness of most of the conspicuous features of the adult political world" by the eighth grade.[7] One of the earliest political attitudes formed is a highly positive evaluation of the nation. Children believe that the United States is better than other nations and at an early age develop a strong emotional attachment to the nation.[8]

Benevolent Leader Images

Another notable political orientation of elementary school children is their ideal- ization of leaders, especially the president. Fred Greenstein asked fourth through eighth graders in New Haven, Connecticut, to rate specific political executives.[9] Substantial majorities of children who knew these leaders rated them as "very good," whereas barely any children (less than 1 percent) rated the leaders as "bad." For example, 71 percent of the children evaluated the president's job performance as very good, with a further 21 percent feeling that the president was doing a "fairly good" job. These evaluations were higher than adult assessments of the president. During the time of Greenstein's study, 58 percent of the adult public approved of Dwight Eisenhower's performance. Similar positive assessments by children emerged in another study.[10] Children from a Chicago suburb in grades two through eight were asked to compare the president to "most men" on a number of charac- teristics. Large majorities of children felt that the president is more honest, is more knowledgeable, and works harder. When asked to evaluate the president as a per- son, nearly all (over 90 percent for most grades) students said the president is "the best person in the world" or a "good person."

The words children use to describe political leaders and their duties are quite interesting and further demonstrate the positive attitudes they hold. Greenstein asked the children in his study, "What kinds of things do you think the Mayor [President, etc.] does?"[11] Some of their responses appear in Table 2-1. These chil- dren generally describe the leaders doing "good" deeds and providing for people's basic needs. Further, this **benevolent leader imagery** exists for most children in the absence of factual information about the leaders. As the examples in the table demonstrate, some children do not describe the leaders' duties accurately, such as assuming that the mayor pays workers or makes swings. Yet, this does not prevent them from possessing positive attitudes about the leaders.

Research conducted by Roberta Sigel also demonstrates that children possess positive evaluations of the president.[12] However, she found that children's assess- ments are based on more cognitive details than Greenstein's conclusion suggests. In particular, Sigel assessed children's attitudes toward President Kennedy after

Table 2-1 Children's Descriptions of Political Leaders

Leader	Description
The president ...	"gives us freedom" (8th grader)
	"[does] good work" (6th grader)
	"has the right to stop bad things before they start" (5th grader)
	"is doing a very good job of making people be safe" (4th grader)
	"deals with foreign countries and takes care of the U.S." (8th grader)
The mayor ...	"makes parks and swings" (5th grader)
	"sees that schools have what they need and stores and other places too" (5th grader)
	"pays working people like banks" (5th grader)
	"helps everyone to have nice homes and jobs" (4th grader)
	"sends men to build parks for us and make our city be a good one" (4th grader)
The board of aldermen ...	"gives us needs so we could live well" (4th grader)

Source: Fred I. Greenstein, "The Benevolent Leader: Children's Images of Political Authority," *American Political Science Review* 54 (1960): 939.

his assassination. When asked what they remembered most about Kennedy, 55 percent of these children focused on personal qualities and emotional responses, as we might expect given Greenstein's research. Nearly one-third of these children, however, provided specific political examples, such as "he tried to get us Medicare but failed" and "he was a leader and defender of my Negro race." [13] Further, in response to a later question asking the children what they remembered Kennedy doing as president, a majority in all grades highlighted political actions, often with much detail. His attention to civil rights (e.g., "worked on programs for civil rights, less segregation" and "tried to let the Negro live an intelligent life") and peace (e.g., "was always trying to stop new wars" and "saved the world [from a war] when there was the Cuban Crisis") were most commonly mentioned. [14] Note that while these examples do contain more cognitive content than Greenstein's students provided in their responses, they also present an image of Kennedy as benevolent and as doing good for the nation and the world.

Age, Class, and Race Differences

Although positive images of political leaders are fairly common among children, there are important exceptions to this trend. Older children were substantially less likely to view leaders in an idealized fashion.[15] Further, children's assessments of a president's personal qualities (honesty, etc.) became more negative over time, but their evaluations of the president's governing-related characteristics (working hard, knowledge, etc.) remained positive. The president is thus "increasingly seen as a person whose abilities are appropriate to the demands of the office."[16] In other words, children are better able with age to distinguish between the role of president and the person who is the president, with the latter becoming somewhat more negative.

Significant class and racial differences also exist in children's evaluations of political leaders. Observing that most socialization research had not examined the attitudes of children from rural areas in the United States, Dean Jaros, Herbert Hirsch, and Frederic Fleron surveyed children in Appalachia (specifically eastern Kentucky).[17] They selected this region because its higher-than-average levels of poverty and relative isolation distinguish Appalachia from most middle- and upper-class regions of the United States. Using the same questions as in the study of suburban Chicago children,[18] Jaros, Hirsch, and Fleron assessed the Appalachian children's images of the president. Their results are strikingly different from Hess and Easton's, with Appalachian children demonstrating much less positive attitudes toward leaders and the political system. Whereas 77 percent of the fifth to eighth graders in the Chicago area, for example, believed that the president works harder than "most men," only 35 percent of the Kentucky children held this view. Also, 26 percent of the children in Appalachia believed that the president is "not a good person" compared with only 8 percent of the Chicago area children. Rather than Greenstein's benevolent leader, Jaros et al. conclude that **malevolent leader imagery** is more common in eastern Kentucky. Their results are important not only for what they demonstrate about political socialization in Appalachia, a region that is not often studied, but also because they caution us against concluding that positive images of political authority are universally held among American children.

Compared with white children, idealized images of the president are less common among black children. In a 1969–1970 study of children's attitudes, 32 percent of black children possessed positive or idealized assessments compared with 55 percent of white children.[19] These racial differences generally exist at all grade levels but are especially notable as children become older. Studies have shown, for example, that whereas attitudes toward the president and police officers were similar for black and white second graders, by eighth grade black children held significantly more negative images than their white peers.[20]

Racial differences also exist when we consider political attitudes other than images of political leaders. White school children tend to have considerably higher levels of political trust and efficacy compared with black school children. **Trust** assesses the degree to which individuals agree that political leaders are honest and act in the public's interest. **Efficacy** refers to the belief that one can influence the decisions of government officials and the belief that these officials are responsive to public wishes. When levels of trust and efficacy by children's race were compared, black children had consistently lower levels of efficacy than did their white peers. Racial differences in trust, however, only emerged in research conducted after the summer of 1967, at which point levels of trust were lower among blacks. Before then, white and black children had similar levels of trust. That year marked a time when the black community became less trusting of the government, in part because urban riots were occurring in the United States and the policy gains achieved during the civil rights movement had seemingly ended.[21]

Ethnic and racial differences in political attitudes continue to exist today. In 2003 and 2004, Kim Fridkin and her colleagues surveyed white, African American, Latino, and Native American eighth graders in and around Phoenix, Arizona.[22] Compared with the minority students, white students displayed more trust in government and higher levels of political efficacy. Native Americans had the lowest levels of both trust and efficacy, with levels of African Americans and Latinos falling in between those of Native American and white students.

What Are the Sources of Children's Political Orientations?

Children come to have political attitudes from a number of different sources. In terms of their idealized images of leaders, children transfer their generally positive feelings toward authority figures they personally know (such as parents) to political leaders.[23] That is, while children might not know exactly what the president does, they understand that the president is a person of authority and deserves respect. Additionally, parents serve as agents of socialization by sharing information and assessments of leaders to children. Although these adults may hold negative attitudes toward specific leaders, they likely temper or sugarcoat their feelings when discussing politics with their children, thus explaining why children's attitudes toward leaders are generally more positive compared with adults' attitudes.[24] The role of parents in communicating their political attitudes to their children also accounts for class and racial differences in children's attitudes. Jaros, Hirsch, and Fleron attribute the Appalachian children's less favorable assessments of leaders and the political system to their parents' views. Among Appalachian adults, "there is a great deal of overt, anti-government sentiment.... Rejection of and hostility toward political authority, especially federal authority, has long characterized the region."[25] Attempts to explain racial and ethnic differences in trust and efficacy also posit a key role for parents. According to one approach, labeled a **political-reality explanation,** minorities have less power than whites in the political system and less reason to believe that political leaders will respond to their wishes. Black, Latino, and Native American children are aware of this reality, perhaps through communication from their parents, thus accounting for their different attitudes compared with white children.[26]

Another important agent of childhood socialization is the school. Elementary school rituals, such as reciting the pledge of allegiance and singing patriotic songs, foster patriotism and loyalty to the nation among children. In school, children also learn to follow rules and obey authority figures, behaviors that they pursue in nonschool settings as well. Political socialization in schools tends to be indirect, highlighting "behavior that relates the child emotionally to his country and impress[ing] upon him the necessity for obedience and conformity."[27] Elementary school curricula and teachers generally do not directly inculcate children to hold specific political attitudes, such as support for a specific public policy.[28] By high school, civics curricula have been shown to influence students' levels of political knowledge and trust in government, but curricular effects on political attitudes of elementary school children are uncommon.[29]

Features of the political context, such as current events, also influence children's attitudes. To try to sort out how much changes in children's attitudes as they grew older were due to cognitive maturation as opposed to actual political events, one study assessed the opinions of Detroit-area children in grades four, six, and eight in 1966 and again in 1968.[30] Two different types of political attitudes were examined: **diffuse support,** or general attachment to the political system, and **specific support,** or opinions toward specific policies and politicians. Consistent with others, these researchers found that children's positive affect toward government declined somewhat, but not greatly, as they grew older, a change they attributed to cognitive development: "greater maturity increases individual capacity for objectivity, which in turn decreases the tendency to idealize government."[31] The decline in specific support among these children was even greater, however. Compared with 1966, in 1968 children were less likely to believe the president is responsive to the people or that the government is helpful to their families. Why? Children became more critical in part because of the events that transpired over these two years, specifically riots in Detroit, the assassination of Martin Luther King Jr., and the escalating war in Vietnam.[32]

The Watergate scandal also had immediate and lingering effects on children's images of the president. In 1972, a burglary occurred in the Democratic National Committee headquarters in the Watergate complex in Washington, D.C. Amid allegations that he tried to cover up his involvement in this burglary, President Richard Nixon resigned from office two years later. To examine the effects of this scandal while events were still unfolding, Fred Greenstein compared the attitudes of children in 1969–1970 with those held in June 1973.[33] Whereas 55 percent of the children interviewed in 1969–1970 possessed positive images of the president, only 45 percent did in 1973. The percentage providing negative assessments increased from 1 percent to 5 percent, with the remainder of the children holding neutral views. Thus, although children viewed the president somewhat less positively, assessments of the president did not become significantly more negative during the early 1970s, at a time when allegations of presidential wrongdoing were widespread (although many of these allegations were not confirmed until after 1973). In a very specific domain, however, children's attitudes toward the president did change. Compared with four years earlier, in 1973 children were much more likely to believe that the president is above the law (respectively, 31 percent versus 58 percent expressed this view).

The Watergate era ushered in a sustained period of increasing negative views of government and politicians among the American public. Recent research suggests that children have not been immune to this increase in negativity.[34] In 2000, Nashville school children were asked the same questions that Greenstein had asked his New Haven children in 1958.[35] The results from 2000 were mostly similar to the earlier results, with children continuing to hold idealized and benevolent images of the *presidency.* One significant difference did emerge: compared to earlier decades, children of today are much more likely to evaluate the *president* negatively. Recall that 71 percent of Greenstein's children felt that the president was doing a "very good" job while another 21 percent evaluated the president's performance as "fairly good." The respective results from the 2000 study were 14 percent and 28 percent. Furthermore, 28 percent of the children in 2000 assessed the president as "bad" whereas only 1 percent of the 1958 children held this attitude.

THE FAMILY AS A SOURCE OF POLITICAL ATTITUDES

As we move into adolescence, we begin to acquire opinions toward policy issues and perhaps even a partisan identification to add to the more general orientations toward government and political leaders that we gained during childhood. Parents are thought to be a key source of these political attitudes, perhaps even the most important source, as the following quotation illustrates: "Whether the child is conscious or unaware of the impact, whether the process is role-modelling or overt transmission, whether the values are political and directly usable or 'nonpolitical' but transferable, and whether what is passed on lies in the cognitive or affective realm, it has been argued that the family is of paramount importance."[36]

In 1965, Kent Jennings and Richard Niemi conducted a study to examine directly the similarity between adolescents' political attitudes and those of their parents.[37] Their research—one of the most influential political socialization studies conducted in the United States—improved on prior socialization studies in important ways.

Parental Socialization

Empirically, one could assess the influence of parents' attitudes on their child(ren) by using a number of different approaches. One method involves surveying the children, asking them their political attitudes, and also asking them to report their parents' attitudes. (Similarly, one could survey parents, querying them about their and their children's attitudes.) This approach is limited, however, because of the possibility that the children either do not know their parents' attitudes or assume that their parents' attitudes are the same as theirs. If the latter occurs, this projection could lead to the parents' and children's attitudes appearing more similar than they really are. To avoid these problems, Jennings and Niemi surveyed children and their parents separately, with members of each group completing their own questionnaires. In total, 1,669 high school seniors took part in their study. For approximately one-third of these students, their father was randomly selected to complete a questionnaire. The mother was randomly selected for another third, and both parents were selected to be surveyed for the final third. Nearly 2,000 parents participated.

Another advantage of Jennings and Niemi's study is that their research participants were selected to represent the entire nation. Rather than studying parents and children from one city or one geographic area, these researchers used a national sample. High schools across the nation were randomly selected, with steps taken to ensure that this sample accurately represented the entire population of high schools in the United States. Thus, the ninety-seven selected high schools included those from cities, suburbs, and rural areas; those with varying numbers of students; those from every geographic region of the nation; and both public and private schools. Within each selected school, fifteen to twenty-one seniors (depending on the size of the school) were randomly selected to participate in the study. This approach to selecting study participants, known as a **national probability sample,** allowed Jennings and Niemi to make inferences from their participants to the entire nation of high school seniors and their parents. With other methods, researchers must be more cautious in their conclusions. Selecting participants from one's local area, for example, does not allow a researcher to draw conclusions about the entire nation. Further, if participants volunteer to participate instead of being randomly selected, we cannot be certain that these self-selected participants' attitudes mirror those of the greater population. In fact, these people very likely may have more intense attitudes or be more politically aware, factors which increase the likelihood that one will voluntarily participate in a political survey.

To assess how thoroughly parents transmit their political attitudes to their offspring, Jennings and Niemi compared a variety of political attitudes between parents and their children. One of their most significant conclusions is that children are more likely to share their parents' party identification than other political attitudes (see Table 2-2). The figures in the table are tau-bs, which measure how closely associated two items are. The possible range of tau-b is 0 to 1.0. For the purposes of Jennings and Niemi's study, the higher the value of tau-b, the more that students share the same attitudes as their parents. Smaller values, then, indicate that students and parents have very dissimilar attitudes. In contrast, if tau-b equals 1.0, students and parents would be in complete agreement.

With a tau-b of .47, the relationship between parental and offspring party identification is stronger than the other political attitudes studied by Jennings and Niemi. Analyzing this relationship in another way, the researchers found that 59 percent of high school seniors have the same general partisanship as their parents (e.g., if the child is a strong Democrat, the parent is either a strong, weak, or

Table 2-2 Similarity of Political Attitudes between Parents and Offspring

Political attitude	Correlation between parents and offspring (tau-b)
Party identification	.47
Political issues/civil liberties	
School integration	.34
School prayer	.29
Communist should be allowed to hold office	.13
Speeches against churches and religion should be allowed	.05
Evaluations of groups	
Catholics	.28
Southerners	.22
Labor unions	.22
Negroes	.20
Whites	.19
Jews	.18
Protestants	.13
Big business	.08
Political cynicism	.12

Source: Data from M. Kent Jennings and Richard G. Niemi, "The Transmission of Political Values from Parent to Child," *American Political Science Review* 62 (1968): 173, 175, 176, 178.

independent-leaning Democrat), and that in only 7 percent of the parent-child pairs is one person a Democrat and the other a Republican, or vice versa. This result led Jennings and Niemi to conclude that the "transmission of party preferences from one generation to the next is carried out rather successfully in the American context."[38] One significant difference in partisanship did emerge from their analysis: the children were more likely to be politically independent than their parents (35.7 percent versus 23.9 percent identified as independent, respectively). Unbeknownst to them at the time, Jennings and Niemi's data capture a snapshot of a decades' long trend of Americans becoming more weakly attached to the political parties.

Political attitudes other than partisanship appear to be passed from parent to child less often, as demonstrated in Table 2-2. Among political issue opinions, parents and students were more likely to hold the same attitudes regarding school integration and school prayer compared with civil liberties items, such as allowing individuals with unpopular views to hold office or give public speeches. Parent-child agreement on evaluations of political groups, such as "Catholics" or "Negroes," falls in between their similarity on attitudes toward policy issues and civil liberties. Finally, there is little agreement between parents and offspring in their degree of cynicism toward politicians and the political system. Overall, seniors are much less likely to be cynical than their parents, a result that coincides with the childhood socialization research presented earlier. Jennings and Niemi attributed this finding to the fact that schools serve as powerful socializing agents, inculcating positive views of the nation (through rituals and curricula) while avoiding much critical analysis of the U.S. government.

With the exception of party identification, Jennings and Niemi concluded that children's attitudes differ quite significantly from their parents'. In fact, this is the second key conclusion of their study: the transmission of political attitudes and values from parents to children is not as "pervasive" as some observers of political socialization had assumed.[39] They posited a few explanations for the low level of parent-child agreement. First, other agents of socialization, most notably the school and mass media, influence the political attitudes of adolescents. Second, it is possible that children's attitudes will change as they age, eventually becoming more similar to their parents'. This explanation, known as a life cycle effect, is elaborated later in the chapter.

Genetic Inheritance of Political Attitudes

From our parents, we inherit, among other things, our hair color, eye color, and height. Could some of our political attitudes also result from **genetic inheritance**? Yes, according to recent research conducted by John Alford, Carolyn Funk, and John Hibbing.[40] Not surprisingly, it is not at all easy to sort out what portion of one's political attitudes might be genetically inherited, influenced by family during early socialization, or influenced by other agents of socialization. After all, we cannot ask a newborn baby whether she is a Republican or a Democrat at the moment of her birth, before her postnatal political socialization begins. Borrowing research approaches from scientists who specialize in genetics, Alford, Funk, and Hibbing necessarily took a very different approach in examining the genetic transmission of political attitudes.

Specifically, Alford et al. compared the similarity in political opinions of monozygotic twins (typically known as identical twins) versus the similarity of dizygotic twins (fraternal twins). The genetic material of identical twins is the same because the conception of these twins involved fertilization of one egg by one sperm. In contrast, fraternal twins are conceived when two eggs are fertilized by two separate sperm at the same time. Thus, these twins' genetic makeup is only 50 percent identical (which is the same for any pair of siblings). This fact regarding known differences in genetic makeup between identical and fraternal twins is an important foundation of Alford et al.'s research. They also assume, as do all who conduct research on twins, that the influence of environmental factors (parental socialization, outside influences on attitudes, etc.) is roughly the same for each type of twin. This does not mean that every twin's attitudes are influenced precisely the same amount and in the same way. Rather, they assume that the impact of environment on attitudes is the same, on average, for identical twins as it is for fraternal twins.

With this foundation in place, Alford, Funk, and Hibbing examined how similar the political opinions of twins are separately for identical versus fraternal twin pairs. Unlike Jennings and Niemi's approach, Alford et al. do not need to compare parents' attitudes with their children's; comparing twins' attitudes across types of twins with known differences in genetic inheritance is sufficient. Alford and colleagues parceled out the proportion of variation in attitudes that is due to genetic heritability versus the twins' **shared environment** (primarily parental and family socialization, but also shared school environments and exposure to the same media) versus their **unshared environment** (any unique experiences, socialization that occurred after adolescence, etc.). The statistical techniques they used are too complex to describe here, but a key premise of their analysis is important to understand. If a political attitude is genetically transmitted, then identical twins will be more likely to share the attitude with each other than fraternal twins will share with each other, since identical twins share more genetic material. For attitudes that originate with environmental factors rather than genes, the likelihood that a pair of twins will have the same attitude will not differ across identical and fraternal twins.

So, what did Alford, Funk, and Hibbing conclude? They found that a portion of political attitudes is genetically inherited, although the role of genetic inheritance differs across types of attitudes (see Figure 2-1). Of the three attitudes that they examined, the largest effect of genetic transmission occurs for political ideology. Close to half of the variation in whether these twins are liberal or conservative is due to genetic inheritance, compared with about one-third for their unshared environment and about one-quarter for the shared environment. In contrast, the unshared environment contributes a much larger share toward **political opinionation** (or whether individuals have opinions on political matters), with genetic factors accounting for just over one-third, and a negligible role for the shared environment. The attitude that is least likely to be genetically inherited is party identification. The twins' shared environment (which is assumed to be largely parental socialization) is a much stronger influence on party affiliation than are genetics (.41 versus .14, respectively).

How can we explain the differences in genetic transmission across types of attitudes? Alford et al. argued that attitudes that are closely related to personality traits are more likely to be genetically inherited, largely because personality has a genetic component. Comparing two of the attitudes in their research, Alford et al. posited that political ideology is more closely related to personality than is party identification. In particular, one core personality trait is the degree to which one is open to other people and other beliefs. This tendency toward openness, argued Alford and colleagues, in part distinguishes conservatives from liberals, with liberals being more open. Rather than being related to personality, party affiliation is instead identification with a group: Democrats or Republicans. Group identifications tend to

Figure 2-1   Genetic versus Environmental Factors Influencing Political Opinions

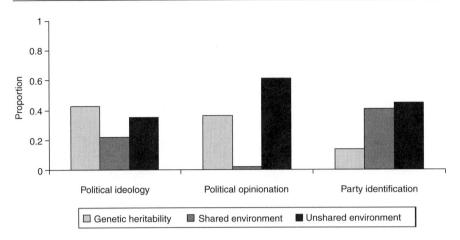

Source: Data from John R. Alford, Carolyn L. Funk, and John R. Hibbing, "Are Political Orientations Genetically Transmitted?" *American Political Science Review* 99 (2005): 160.

Note: Bars represent the proportion of estimated variability in political opinions due to each of the three types of factors.

be the result of socialization rather than genetics. One is not born a Protestant or a Catholic because of genes, for example, but rather has this religious identification because of parental socialization. Alford et al.'s research suggests the same is true with partisan identification.

Despite the fact that Alford et al. do not place primary attention on postnatal political socialization, one of their findings clearly coincides with one of Jennings and Niemi's key conclusions: parental socialization is an important source of individuals' partisanship. These two studies also conclude that nonfamily sources (Alford et al.'s unshared environment) are important agents of socialization, sometimes more important than family is. Reconciling these two studies on another point is not so obvious, however. Recall that Jennings and Niemi found levels of parent-offspring agreement to be lower for political attitudes other than party identification. Yet, Alford and colleagues argued that genetic transmission will be more likely for political attitudes other than party identification. If this were the case, wouldn't we expect to find parent-child agreement to be higher for nonpartisanship attitudes than Jennings and Niemi found? Directly comparing the two studies on this point is difficult because Jennings and Niemi did not sort out how much of parent-child agreement is due to genetic inheritance versus family socialization. If they did, perhaps we would see genetic transmission playing a larger role for issue attitudes versus party identification. The fact that these two studies

Public Opinion in Comparative Perspective
BOX 2-1 POLITICAL SOCIALIZATION IN NIGERIA AND IRAN

In many nations around the world, the primary agents and processes of political socialization are the same as those in the United States. This is especially the case in firmly established democracies. Among nondemocratic nations or those that recently transitioned to democracy, however, the socialization process can look quite different.

Take Nigeria, for example. Since breaking away from British colonial rule in 1960, Nigerians have witnessed multiple military coups and thus a long period of military rule. Civilian, democratically elected leaders have ruled Nigeria since 1999. Not surprisingly, such political instability does affect the public's view of politics. While cynicism toward government does exist among Nigerians, there are also strains of faith in democratic procedures, particularly among citizens with more formal education.[1]

The Nigerian government might have played a role in socializing such support for democratic procedures. In the years before a new Nigerian constitution was adopted in 1999, the nation's military leaders developed programs to prepare the public for a transition to democracy. Specifically, the goals of the government's efforts were to "shape a mass political culture that would be congenial to democracy."[2] Whether such effects were realized is debated in Nigeria, yet these programs demonstrate attempts at government socialization that we typically do not find in the United States or in European democracies.

In most authoritarian or totalitarian nations, schools play a key role in transmitting values and beliefs. Such is the case in the Islamic Republic of Iran, where the schools attempt to create "good Islamic citizens out of young Iranians."[3] Iran has a mixed political system. The nation is a theocracy, with Islamic law dominant over other laws and the Supreme Leader appointed by religious clerics. At the same time, the citizens do elect officials into key positions, such as the president and members of parliament.

The Iranian government attempts to socialize schoolchildren in a variety of ways. Students are required to study Islam, are taught that the nation's rulers before the 1979 Islamic Revolution were immoral, and learn poems criticizing Western nations (most notably the United States). The images in textbooks reinforce national laws, such as by always portraying women wearing veils.

The schools in Iran do not control all political socialization, however. Inside the home, families discuss contemporary politics and historical events,

(continued)

often in ways that counter the government's presentation. Some parents and grandparents, for instance, hold memories of Iran's prerevolutionary leaders and politics that diverge from what the textbooks portray, memories which are passed on to younger generations of Iranians.[4] Thus, the government's messages are being contradicted by other agents of socialization. This diversity of political messages so far has not resulted in Iranian citizens challenging the theocracy's authority. What will happen in the future, though, is very much an open question. As two scholars of Iranian politics conclude, "Whether the regime will be able to accommodate and represent pluralistic discourse or impose the single voice of unity is very much the question facing Iran's authorities. Their decision and capacity in this regard will determine whether Iran will move toward more democratic politics or authoritarianism."[5]

1. Robert J. Mundt, Oladimeji Aborisade, and A. Carl LeVan, "Politics in Nigeria," in *Comparative Politics Today: A World View,* 9th ed., ed. Gabriel A. Almond, G. Bingham Powell Jr., Russell J. Dalton, and Kaare Strøm (New York: Pearson Longman, 2008).
2. Ibid., 681.
3. H. E. Chehabi and Arang Keshavarzian, "Politics in Iran," in *Comparative Politics Today: A World View,* 9th ed., ed. Gabriel A. Almond, G. Bingham Powell Jr., Russell J. Dalton, and Kaare Strøm (New York: Pearson Longman, 2008), 583.
4. Chehabi and Keshavarzian, "Politics in Iran."
5. Ibid., 588.

address different types of attitudes (with the exception of partisanship) also makes it difficult to compare their conclusions more fully. More research on these topics is clearly necessary to sort out these as well as other concerns. However, until and if future research suggests otherwise, Alford et al. make a strong case to include genetics as one source of political attitudes even though many might at first consider this possibility "far-fetched, odd, even perverse."[41]

POLITICAL EVENTS AND ADOLESCENT SOCIALIZATION

So far, we have primarily discussed the role that individuals and institutions play in shaping the political attitudes of children and adolescents. The development of political opinions is also influenced by the political context. Both broader political trends and specific political events can influence the development of political attitudes during the impressionable years, typically late adolescence and early adulthood.

Generational Effects

When changes in the political context influence the political socialization of an entire age cohort, a **generational effect** on political attitudes occurs. In other words, the opinions of an entire generation of people can be influenced by the nature of the times during their formative years. Such was the case with the formation of party affiliation among those who came of age during the post–World War II period, according to Paul Abramson.[42] Abramson was interested in explaining why Americans' identification with political parties had noticeably weakened beginning in the 1960s. Whereas 35–38 percent of the electorate strongly identified with one of the parties between 1952 and 1964, only 24–27 percent had such strong attachments from 1966 until 1974. Similarly, the proportion of Americans claiming political independence rose from approximately 8 percent in the first period to 13 percent in the second.

Abramson attributed these changes to generational replacement. Voters with strong partisan affiliations were being replaced by those with weaker attachments, largely because the latter were socialized at a time when the political parties were weakening on the national stage. Beginning in the 1950s, national politicians began to build personal campaign organizations rather than tie themselves clearly to the national parties. Television coverage of campaigns tended to focus on candidates rather than parties, and the candidates could bypass the parties and their grassroots campaign organizations by using television to disseminate their messages directly to the voters. These changes in the broader context influenced the partisanship of individuals whose formative socialization occurred during this time period. Table 2-3 presents a comparison of two age cohorts as an illustration.

The first cohort includes voters whose late adolescence occurred in the 1920s and 1930s, decades of relatively strong national parties. In 1952, members of this cohort were 37–44 years old and possessed fairly strong partisan attitudes. Nearly one-third identified strongly with one of the parties, whereas only 4 percent affiliated with neither party. Contrast these partisan attitudes to those of the second cohort, who emerged out of adolescence in the 1950s. When this group was 35–42 years old (1974), only 19 percent were strong partisans whereas 15 percent were politically independent, demonstrating significantly weaker partisan attitudes than when the first cohort was approximately the same ages. Focusing again on the first cohort, the percentage of strong partisans in this cohort was the same in 1974 as in 1952, indicating no weakening over time. Yet, the proportion of independents in this cohort did increase (from 4 percent to 11 percent), suggesting that these voters were not entirely immune from effects of the post–World War II political context. Overall, though, their attachment to the political parties was stronger than was the attachment of the younger cohort.

Influence of Political Events

Not only are adolescents' opinions influenced by the political times, but they are also shaped by discrete political events. David Sears and Nicholas Valentino have examined the role of a highly salient political event on adolescent socialization: presidential campaigns. Specifically, they examined whether adolescents make

Table 2-3   Generational Effects on Party Identification

Measure	Cohort 1	Cohort 2
Years of birth	1908–1915	1932–1939
Years when turned 18	1926–1933	1950–1957
Ages in 1952	37–44	13–20
Partisan attitudes in 1952		
% who were strong partisans	32%	NA
% who were independent	4	NA
Ages in 1974	59–66	35–42
Partisan attitudes in 1974		
% who were strong partisans	32%	19%
% who were independent	11	15

Source: Data from Paul R. Abramson, "Generational Change and the Decline of Party Identification in America: 1952–1974," *American Political Science Review* 70 (1976): 470.

socialization gains (such as increases in knowledge or the development of more concrete political attitudes) during presidential election years.[43] To do so, Sears and Valentino examined interviews of Wisconsin adolescents (ages 10–17) conducted in early 1980, in October of 1980, and then again one year later (the autumn of 1981). These adolescents demonstrated significant gains in knowledge, affect, and attitude crystallization between the first two waves of the study, but only for attitude objects centrally related to the campaigns, such as political parties. Gains were much smaller in the year after the election and essentially nonexistent for other types of attitudes, such as racial tolerance, ideology, and political trust.

In terms of **attitude crystallization,** the adolescents began the study with what Sears and Valentino termed as relatively "immature" partisan attitudes.[44] While they did express opinions toward the candidates and the parties, the adolescents' attitudes were not often based on accurate knowledge. Further, their evaluations of candidates were not consistent along partisan lines (e.g., displaying positive evaluations for *both* Democratic and Republican candidates) nor strongly related to their own party affiliation. Months later, near the end of the presidential campaign, these adolescents demonstrated much more crystallized partisan opinions, with higher levels of consistency across candidate evaluations, a stronger relationship between their assessments of candidates and their own party affiliation, and over-time stability in their party identification.

Expanding on these results, Valentino and Sears explored what conditions facilitated such socialization gains during presidential campaigns.[45] The more that these preadults engaged in **interpersonal communication** about the presidential campaign (with family and peers and in school), the larger were their gains. Exposure to **media communication** about the campaign in newspapers and on television was not related to differences in attitude crystallization or increased knowledge. In other words, those adolescents who followed the campaign news more did not have larger socialization gains. Valentino and Sears argued that *active communication* rather than *passive reception* of news produced the gains. They also highlighted the complexities of parental involvement in this socialization. Parents can encourage more interpersonal communication about campaigns by "stimulating a climate of interest in and attentiveness to the campaign, and the motivation for discussing it."[46] Yet, it is communication with a wide range of individuals, not only parents, that encourages socialization gains. And, it appears that the communication between parents and their children is a dialogue, a sharing of opinions, rather than only parents transmitting their partisan attitudes to their children.

Taken together, these two studies contribute to our knowledge of adolescent socialization in a number of important ways. First, Sears and Valentino focus our attention on the importance of the political context and political events. Socialization does not happen in a vacuum. Second, they demonstrate that socialization occurs episodically rather than incrementally. In their own words, "political socialization may typically occur in bursts, during a period when political events make particular attitude objects salient, rather than through the gradual and incremental accretion of experience."[47] Third, they integrate the socializing effects of political campaigns with the agents of socialization that other scholars have shown to be important (particularly family and others through interpersonal communication), thus presenting a more nuanced picture of adolescent socialization.

ADULT SOCIALIZATION

What are the attitudes of adults? How are they formed, and do they change? These questions are similar to those asked by scholars of childhood and adolescent socialization. Studies of adult socialization, however, tend to focus on a related but more focused question: Do attitudes acquired before adulthood remain stable during one's lifetime? Broader questions about the content and sources of adult attitudes form the basis of much other research on public opinion, and thus will be the focus of many of the later chapters in this book. For example, chapter 3 outlines the effect of communication, most notably the media, on the public's attitudes, and in chapter 4 we examine to what degree the attitudes of American adults are stable over time versus variable. In this section, we focus more narrowly on the stability of preadult attitudes throughout the life cycle.

Do Political Attitudes Persist into Adulthood?

There are a number of methods for assessing whether preadult attitudes persist throughout adulthood or whether they change. One of the most effective ways is to survey the same group of people when they are adolescents and then again when they are adults. This method, called a **panel or longitudinal study,** is the approach taken by Kent Jennings and Richard Niemi. In 1973, Jennings and Niemi reinterviewed the high school seniors they had first interviewed in 1965. They then interviewed this group twice more, in 1982 and in 1997. Although they were not able to reinterview all of the 1,669 seniors who had participated in the original study, they did reinterview nearly 1,000 of the participants in all four waves of the study. This study design allows a comparison of the attitudes of these individuals at various points in their life—as high school seniors, at 25–26 years old, at 34–35 years old, and again at 49–50 years old—to directly assess whether their late adolescent political attitudes persisted into and throughout adulthood. Further, where possible in 1973 and 1982, Jennings and Niemi also reinterviewed the parents of these respondents. In 1997 children of the former high school seniors were interviewed, resulting in three generations of participants spread over the four waves. This panel study has resulted in a rich array of information and has produced a number of interesting insights into adult socialization.

One of the first analyses examined the over-time stability of party identification and issue opinions (such as school integration, school prayer, and support for civil liberties) for both the offspring and the parents.[48] Among the younger generation, party affiliation and issue attitudes varied more between 1965 and 1973 than between 1973 and 1982, indicating that the political opinions of the offspring shifted a fair bit during their early 20s. For example, only 22 percent of those who were strong Democrats in 1965 remained so in 1973, with the rest identifying as weak Democrats or independents leaning Democratic (62 percent) or, less often, as independents or Republicans (see Figure 2.2). When their partisanship in 1973 was compared with that in 1982, however, individual partisanship appeared to stabilize when participants were between the mid-20s and the mid-30s. Of the strong Democrats in 1973, 48 percent remained the same in 1982, with 42 percent identifying as weak or leaning Democrats. Jennings and Gregory Markus concluded that "the period between the mid-twenties and mid-thirties witnesses a surge in the crystallization of a variety of sociopolitical attitudes.... Consequently, the kinds of attitudes and values each cohort brings into that crucial stage are likely to define its outlooks for some time thereafter."[49]

This pattern supports an **impressionable years model** of attitude stability, whereby political attitudes change around some during late adolescence and early adulthood, then remain more stable throughout the rest of the life span. Other analyses of the Jennings-Niemi panel data provide further evidence consistent with this model. Results from the fourth wave of the panel are especially useful because they allow us to examine whether the stability in attitudes that exists from the 20s to the 30s persists as one enters middle age. A comparison of the offspring's political attitudes in 1997 to what it had been in 1982 demonstrates such persistence: these individual's party affiliations and issue opinions remained quite stable as they aged from their mid-30s to 50.[50] Additional support for partisan stability after one leaves early adulthood comes from an analysis of the partisan-

Figure 2-2   Over-Time Variation in Party Affiliation of Strong Democrats for Two Time Periods

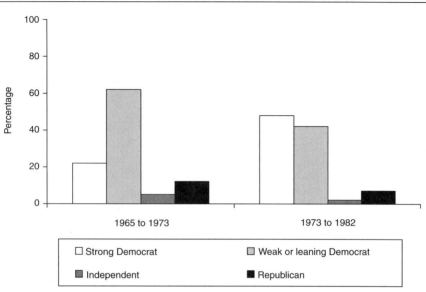

Source: Data from M. Kent Jennings and Gregory B. Markus, "Partisan Orientations over the Long Haul: Results from the Three-Wave Political Socialization Panel Study," *American Political Science Review* 78 (1984): 1004.

Note: Bars represent the percentage of strong Democrats from the first year (1965 or 1973) claiming the specific party identification in the second year (1973 or 1982, respectively).

ship of the parents of the 1965 high school seniors. These parents' party affiliations were very stable between 1965 and 1973 (when they aged from, on average, their mid-40s to mid-50s), and again between 1973 and 1982 (mid-50s to early 60s). For example, fully 53 percent of the parents who were strong Democrats in 1965 also identified as strong Democrats in 1973, with 42 percent still identifying as Democrats, only more weakly. Only 5 percent of the former strong Democrats identified as independent or Republican in 1973.[51] Recall that the offspring's partisanship shifted much more than this during the 1965–1973 time frame.

The transmission of political attitudes from parent to child can be examined two different ways with the Jennings-Niemi panel data. First, with the addition of a third generation in the panel's fourth wave, parent-child transmission can be examined for two different time periods. More specifically, the correspondence between the attitudes of the 1965 high school seniors and their parents (in 1965) can be compared with the correspondence between these former seniors and their children (in 1997). Across a variety of political issues, including partisanship, the likelihood that a child will hold the same attitudes as his parents was roughly the same, whether the child was an adolescent in 1965 or 1997.[52] This result suggests that Jennings and Niemi's initial results were not time bound, that they were not a product of the political times of the 1960s.[53]

Second, it is possible to assess whether the attitudes held by parents when their children were adolescents transmit to the children then and also persist as the children age into adulthood. We already know from Jennings and Niemi's original study that the rate of parent-child transmission is higher for party identification than for other political opinions.[54] As the offspring aged into their 20s (in 1973), the correspondence between their party identification and what their parents' partisanship had been in 1965 declined. In 1982, though, this correspondence was nearly the same as it had been in 1973, and then declined only slightly in 1997.[55] Once the children had initially moved away from their parents' partisanship in their early 20s, then there was little additional movement as this generation aged.

In a particularly illustrative example of this phenomenon, Niemi and Jennings compared parents' party affiliation and offspring affiliation separately for those offspring who held consistently conservative versus consistently liberal opinions toward specific political issues (such as school integration, support for American involvement in Vietnam, and the proper role of government in providing jobs).[56] One might expect that individuals with strong and consistent conservative opinions would identify as Republicans. Yet, for offspring with such conservative opinions who were raised in a home of strong Democrats, the typical party identification at age 18 was weak Democrat. Eight years later, these individuals identified more as political independents, albeit leaning somewhat toward the Democratic Party. Nine years after this, these offspring (now about 35 years old) were quite clearly independent in their political affiliation. So, while the partisanship of these individuals moved away from the Democratic Party and became more in line with their ideological leanings, the pull of their preadult socialization (their parents' partisanship) prevented them from identifying as Republicans, even though they held conservative issue opinions.

Life Cycle and Period Effects

To assess changes in political attitudes throughout adulthood, socialization researchers have focused some attention on two explanations: life cycle and period effects. The **life cycle** explanation presumes that people's political attitudes are strongly influenced by their age (by their place in the life cycle) and do not only result from early socialization. Life cycle effects have been proposed to account for why partisanship varies more for those just leaving adolescence than for those who are in their 30s or are older.[57] According to this understanding, those in their early 20s lack the experience to have consistent party affiliations. In other words, "the political outlooks of young adults typically rest upon a fairly limited experiential base and are therefore particularly susceptible to change in response to attitudinally relevant events," such as national economic growth or decline, or personal changes such as marriage.[58] As young adults grow older, they experience fewer genuinely new politically relevant events, and their partisanship becomes more firmly grounded in their past experiences and thus is more resistant to change.

Period effects occur when salient features of the political period influence the political attitudes of many, regardless of age. Period effects differ from the generational effects discussed earlier in this chapter. Generational effects result when aspects of the political context shape the political attitudes only of those who are in their impressionable years. When this occurs, different generations of people will have noticeably different attitudes that can be traced to changes in the political context.

As an example, think about the 9/11 attacks. One effect of the attacks was to increase patriotism among the public. If patriotism levels remain high for all Americans over the next decades, a period effect will have occurred. If, in contrast, higher patriotism persists only for those who were entering or in early adulthood on September 11, 2001, we will conclude that a generational effect occurred. Also, recall Abramson's research in which he concluded that lessening attachment to political parties was due to a new generation of citizens being socialized in an era when the national political parties were weakening.[59] These are generational effects. In the same study, Abramson also found evidence of period effects. Across many age cohorts, the percentage of those identifying as independents was higher in the 1960s and early 1970s than it had been in the 1950s. This suggests that younger and older adults alike were somewhat influenced by the decline of parties on the national political stage, a clear period effect.

CONCLUSION

The acquisition of political attitudes begins fairly early in life, and often with positive feelings toward the nation and idealized views of political leaders. Would democratic elitists thus be satisfied with the socialization of children in the United States today? While it is true that levels of system support tend to be high among children, as these theorists would hope, support is not uniformly high across all children. For some children, such as those who are older, black, Latino, Native American, or from impoverished backgrounds, childhood attitudes are less benevolent. More worrisome for elite democrats, as American political culture has changed over the past decades with adult citizens evaluating their leaders less favorably, children are also more likely to hold cynical attitudes toward those holding political power. Elite democrats assume that citizens are neither interested in nor knowledgeable about politics and rely on the expertise of elected officials to make governing decisions. As Americans have come to hold these officials in lower esteem, attitudes that are socialized young, there is less deference to political authority than elite democrats prefer. Even when children held more uniformly positive attitudes toward leaders, however, there is good evidence that these attitudes did not persist into adulthood, further undermining elite democrats' hope for socialization to produce system-supporting adults. Much of the earliest childhood socialization research was conducted in the 1950s. Although this generation of children trusted government and possessed idealized images of leaders then, they "wound up rioting in the streets of Chicago or smoking dope in Vietnam or working as carpenters under assumed names in Toronto" to avoid the Vietnam War draft.[60]

Adolescence brings with it the development of partisan leanings and opinions toward a variety of issue opinions. While the role of parents in transmitting these attitudes to their children is less than previously assumed, the family does continue to play an important socializing role, particularly when it comes to party identification. Other agents of socialization—schools, peers, current political events— shape political attitudes more than once thought. In spite of that, over years of socialization research, the family continues to emerge as an important shaper of children's attitudes, whether through genetic transmission or postnatal socialization. The imprint of our parents' political attitudes is often still visible into adulthood, after a period of attitude instability that many of us experience in our early 20s.

Pluralists would be pleased by the fact that the transmission of party identification continues to be more complete than the transmission of other political attitudes. Pluralists, after all, hope for socialization to develop strong political identities before adulthood, chief among these being party identification. Yet the development of preadult partisanship is not as complete as pluralists would prefer, partly because the party affiliation of young adults is not entirely stable. This suggests that adolescents' party identification is not very crystallized, certainly not as crystallized as pluralists would want for citizens about to reach voting age. Also concerning for pluralists is the movement away from strong party affiliations that Americans have experienced over the past few decades. As generations of adolescents have been socialized during a time of weaker national political parties, the effect has been to produce more independent voters who, in the pluralists' eyes, are less able to have their interests represented through the party system.

How would participatory democrats assess the state of political socialization? They would have a more difficult task, given that much political science research on this topic has generally not focused on the features of socialization that these theorists feel are most important. Having said this, there is one conclusion from the research that certainly troubles participatory democrats: the fact that some children (black, Latino, Native American, poor, etc.) develop less trusting attitudes toward government at an early age. The more trust in government citizens have, the more likely they will participate in politics throughout life. Participatory democrats worry that these children who trust government less will grow up to be adults who do not participate in politics, thus undermining the goal of political equality across citizens that participatory democrats value so strongly.

More centrally, for participatory democrats, teaching children to be active participants in democracy is crucial. Most socialization research has not gauged participatory skills and activities of children or adolescents, certainly not to the degree that participatory democrats would like. Rather than emphasize which agents of socialization influenced preadult attitudes most strongly, for example, researchers could focus on "how agents might successfully inspire the development of democratic citizenship values in children and adolescents."[61] This situation is changing somewhat, however, as political scientists begin to examine the many civic engagement and service learning programs that are scattered throughout the nation.[62] Such programs attempt to introduce young people (and young adults) to politics through hands-on experience and also to develop civic skills that are relevant for political participation. Assessing the quality of these programs would provide valuable information for participatory democrats.

Finally, our understanding of political socialization would benefit with forays into a number of other topics also. Political socialization research could return to studies of children. Such studies fell out of favor in the 1970s, in part because early promises of socialization researchers were not met. Studying children was viewed to be important on the assumption that childhood attitudes persist into adulthood and influence adult behavior. When this assumption was brought into question, due to empirical results that contradicted it as well as the experience of the trusting children of the 1950s turning into 1960s protestors, researchers turned their attention away from children and toward the formation of attitudes in adults. However, some political opinions clearly develop before adulthood, and there is much we do not know about which opinions these are, which are susceptible to change later in life, and why any changes occur. Further, while much attention has been placed on understanding the development of party identification, we know much less about the sources of other political attitudes. This includes core values, such as equality and individualism.[63] A return of public opinion scholars to studying preadult socialization could begin to fill these gaps in our knowledge.

KEY CONCEPTS

attitude crystallization / 45	life cycle / 49
benevolent leader imagery / 31	malevolent leader imagery / 33
diffuse support / 35	media communication / 45
efficacy / 33	national probability sample / 37
generational effect / 43	panel or longitudinal study / 46
genetic inheritance / 39	period effects / 50
impressionable years model / 47	political opinionation / 40
interpersonal communication / 45	political-reality explanation / 34

SUGGESTED SOURCES FOR FURTHER READING

Alwin, Duane F., Ronald L. Cohen, and Theodore M. Newcomb. *Political Attitudes over the Life Span: The Bennington Women after Fifty Years.* Madison: University of Wisconsin Press, 1991.

A fascinating study of the social and political attitudes of women who attended Bennington College (Vermont) in the 1930s and 1940s. This book assesses these women's attitudes in 1984, approximately 50 years after their college graduation, examining the over-time stability of their attitudes as well as the influence of the social environment on these women's political opinions.

Easton, David, and Jack Dennis. *Children in the Political System: Origins of Political Legitimacy.* New York: McGraw-Hill, 1969.

The authors adopt a systems-analytical approach to political socialization. They examine the views of children to determine the degree to which political attitudes that support a political system (such as trust in the government) are socialized at a young age.

Gimpel, James G., J. Celeste Lay, and Jason E. Schuknecht. *Cultivating Democracy: Civic Environments and Political Socialization in America.* Washington, D.C.: Brookings Institution Press, 2003.

A study of adolescent political socialization with a focus on the effects of the local context (e.g., racial composition and partisan heterogeneity of one's neighborhood) on socialization.

Jennings, M. Kent, and Richard G. Niemi. *Generations and Politics: A Panel Study of Young Adults and Their Parents.* Princeton: Princeton University Press, 1981.

A thorough summary of the conclusions drawn from the 1965 and 1973 waves of the authors' survey of high school students and their parents.

Niemi, Richard G., and Jane Junn. *Civic Education: What Makes Students Learn.* New Haven: Yale University Press, 1998.

An examination of the influence of civics curricula on levels of political knowledge and political attitudes of twelfth graders. In contrast to much previous research on this topic, the authors conclude that characteristics of civics curricula do increase knowledge and influence attitudes.

Campus Compact: www.compact.org/
City Year: www.cityyear.org/
Kids Voting USA: http://kidsvotingusa.org/

These are three, out of many possible, examples of organizations that focus on civic engagement. These organizations have designed programs that, among other goals, aim to increase the political skills and political activity of adolescents and young adults.

CHAPTER 3

Mass Media

AT 10:00 A.M. on June 23, 2003, the U.S. Supreme Court handed down two decisions regarding the use of affirmative action in higher education. One case involved the University of Michigan's undergraduate admissions policy, and the other involved the university's law school admissions policy.[1] These cases originated when several disgruntled white applicants filed suit against the University of Michigan on the grounds that the university's admissions policies unlawfully provided racial preferences for black, Hispanic, and Native American applicants. In the undergraduate case, *Gratz et al. v. Bollinger et al.,* the plaintiffs argued that the use of a point system that automatically allocated points to each underrepresented minority applicant was unconstitutional because it discriminated against whites on the basis of race. In the law school case, *Grutter v. Bollinger et al.,* the plaintiffs made a similar argument, although here minority status was considered a "plus factor" during the admissions process, and underrepresented students were not assigned a specific number of points. In defense of their admissions policies, the University of Michigan argued that taking race into account was necessary to build a diverse student body. And why is a diverse student body so important? Because, the university argued, *all* students gain educational benefits from learning in a diverse environment. Thus, a diverse student body is a fundamental component of an elite university.

In a 5–4 ruling with Justice Sandra Day O'Connor writing for the majority, the Court ruled in *Grutter* that achieving a diverse student body is a compelling state interest and therefore race can be considered in the law school's admissions process. In contrast, the Court knocked down the undergraduate admissions policy because it was not narrowly tailored to achieve the goal of a diverse student body. In other words, as Chief Justice William H. Rehnquist argued for the 6–3 majority in *Gratz,* race was *the* factor in admissions, not simply *a* factor, making the undergraduate policy unconstitutional. Together, these rulings uphold the University of Michigan's basic argument that the educational benefits stemming from a diverse set of students justify the use of race in admissions procedures; however, the university cannot go overboard and put too much weight on race.

To be sure, these were historic decisions because it was the first time the Supreme Court had addressed affirmative action in higher education since the famous *Regents of the University of California v. Bakke* case in 1978.[2] As evidence of the importance of the Michigan cases, a record number of amicus curiae (i.e., friend of the court) briefs were filed by interested parties, such as the NAACP Legal Defense and Educational Fund, the Cato Institute, Fortune 500 corporations, and retired military officers. The overwhelming majority of these briefs were in support of the Michigan admissions policies, but there were also a few briefs in opposition. As another sign of the importance of the rulings, oral arguments for the cases were made available to the public immediately after the cases were heard on the morning of April 1, 2002. Up to that point, the only other time tapes had been made available so quickly was in the *Bush v. Gore* case, the case that essentially decided the 2000 presidential election.[3]

Although a few political junkies (perhaps some of you reading this book) rushed to their computers or turned on C-Span to listen to (not see, because cameras are not allowed in the Supreme Court) the oral arguments, most citizens relied on journalists to distill the information for them. Likewise, on the day the Court announced its rulings, only a few citizens were permitted in the courtroom to hear the decision read from the bench. And while there were certainly demonstrators waiting anxiously outside the Supreme Court building, most citizens were too darn busy working, raising their kids, or watching Regis and Kelly to drop everything and hang out at the Supreme Court waiting for these rulings to be handed down.

Citizens cannot do everything and be everywhere at once. Thus, they rely on the media to keep them up to date on important political events, such as the Supreme Court's rulings in the *Gratz* and *Grutter* cases. Participatory democratic theorists would argue that providing citizens with information is a fundamental role of the news media in a democratic society. A well-functioning, vibrant democracy requires news organizations that inform and educate citizens. The news media should serve as a critical intermediary transmitting vital information from elites to citizens and vice versa.

Did the media live up to that democratic standard when covering the Michigan affirmative action cases? Well, certainly not in its immediate coverage of the *Grutter* and *Gratz* decisions. By 10:15 a.m. on the morning of June 23, 2003, before the Supreme Court had even finished announcing *one* of its decisions, both ABC and CNN interrupted regularly scheduled programming to run "breaking news" segments (see Box 3-1). Not surprisingly, the quality of the reporting in these segments left much to be desired. Citizens looking for a clear and coherent summary of these complex Supreme Court rulings were not going to get it from watching these reports.

This begs the question then, why would two reputable news organizations rush to put such low-quality fare on the air? One explanation for this lies with an

BOX 3-1 ABC Breaking News Coverage of the University of Michigan Affirmative Action Decisions, June 23, 2003

This is an excerpt from ABC's Breaking News coverage of the Supreme Court's rulings in the University of Michigan affirmative action cases. As you will see, the reporting is incoherent at times, yet self-congratulatory. The segment ends with Peter Jennings saying they will have the cases "sorted out" by the evening newscast.

PETER JENNINGS: Now, Jackie Judd, I believe has a decision in the second case. This is a case brought against the University of Michigan itself, not specifically the law school. Jackie?

JACKIE JUDD: (Off Camera) Right, Peter. This is the case that had to do with the undergraduate admissions program in which there was a 150-point system, 20 points being automatically added to a minority candidate's admission application. The court, another complicated decision, has reversed it in part. They have remanded it, meaning they've sent it back to the lower court for further adjudication. This also was a 5–4 ruling, but this time O'Connor again finds herself in the majority. Chief Justice Rehnquist read the majority opinion from the bench. They said about this program that it was not narrowly tailored. That's an important expression.

JACKIE JUDD: In the first, in the law school decision they said the use of race was not prohibited by equal protection clause. It was narrowly tailored. The undergraduate program they found was not. Pardon me. So, a split decision. But again, the bottom line is that affirmative action, in some form, as the law school configured it, stands. The way the undergraduate program configured it, most of it reversed.

PETER JENNINGS: (Off Camera) So, so, just let me understand absolutely, completely. In the undergraduate case, they've said to the lower court, which ruled in favor or against this? Do you recall?

JACKIE JUDD: (Off Camera) They—they had ruled in favor of the university and against the students. What we don't know yet, Peter, because, again, literally the decisions are still being read from the bench, is what part of this is being sent back. But clearly, from the lines I've been read by our producer inside the courtroom, the underpinning of the program, the 20 point assignment to minority students has been reversed. It's been knocked down, declared unconstitutional.

PETER JENNINGS: (Off Camera) Okay. Many thanks. Jackie Judd at the Supreme Court. Thank goodness she is there.

(continued)

[Peter Jennings then interviews legal correspondent Cynthia McFadden.]
PETER JENNINGS: Just to remind folks at home, 'cause our legal corre-
spondents do this with such dexterity, the rest of us do not always. There
were two cases involved today. One was a case brought against the University of Michigan at the undergraduate level by a young man and a young
woman who said they were denied admission because they didn't get
enough points. And there were points given for candidates on the basis of
their race, 20 points you got for being black. And therefore, that automatically in some cases, they believe, put them ahead. And that is why, with the
encouragement of something called the Center for Individual Rights, they
brought this case on the fact that they had been unfairly denied.

In the case of the law school, the case was brought because the young
woman believed she had been denied a place because the school had used
unfair standards, namely race, as a consideration to admit what she regarded as less qualified candidates. The court agrees with the law school.
And we believe does not agree with the university at the undergraduate
level. We will have to get that sorted out by *World News Tonight*. And you
can always go to abcnews.com to read it in full. I'm Peter Jennings. Thank
you for joining us.

extremely important characteristic of the mass media in the United States: major
media outlets are businesses. And as such, they are in fierce competition with one
another to make profits, which may or may not coincide with excellence in journalism. In this case, being first to report the Supreme Court rulings trumped any
sense of civic obligation CNN and ABC might have to provide quality information to viewers. It is interesting to note that elite democratic theorists would not
be troubled by this coverage because they support a market-based media system.
From the elite democratic perspective, media outlets might not provide high-
quality information in a free market, but they do provide the kind of news that
people want to consume.

News norms also influenced coverage of the Michigan cases. Mainstream
news organizations place a high value on objective reporting, which they define
as providing both sides of a story. For example, journalists from mainstream news
organizations were careful to balance their reporting by presenting the views of both
the white students and the University of Michigan. But keep in mind that not all
news organizations are alike. Some are not as constrained by the norm of objectivity and have other considerations that influence their news coverage.[4]

For example, the black media have different goals than the mainstream media:
the black media report the news from a "black" angle rather than maintain what

they would argue is a façade of neutrality and objectivity. Black newspapers have a long history of acting as a corrective to the mainstream media by challenging the often stereotypical and inaccurate coverage of African Americans.[5] In terms of covering the Michigan affirmative action cases, the black press's primary concern was not objectivity; instead, it was concerned with providing the context for understanding the cases. Journalists from black newspapers emphasized the history of racial discrimination at the University of Michigan and discussed the ways in which the admissions process was biased in favor of white students.[6] Obviously, advocacy newspapers and mainstream newspapers are going to produce different news products.

Did the media coverage of the Michigan affirmative action cases influence public opinion? Since most citizens relied on the media to get news about the Supreme Court cases, it certainly makes sense that the coverage would affect their support for affirmative action. Think about the various ways in which affirmative action policy might be framed by the media.[7] Affirmative action could be described as a program that gives preferential treatment to black students while unfairly discriminating against white students. Let's call this the reverse discrimination frame. Alternatively, the media could present the same affirmative action program as one that benefits all students by ensuring a diverse educational environment. Consider this the diversity frame. See Table 3-1 for examples of each frame. Which media frame do you think would lead to greater support for affirmative action? Most likely the diversity frame because it appeals to the interests of citizens regardless of their race.

This discussion of media coverage of the University of Michigan affirmative action cases illustrates many of the points we will be touching on in this chapter. We begin with a discussion of what we should expect from the news media in a democratic society. We have already mentioned that participatory theorists argue the media should provide citizens with high-quality information, but there are additional roles the media should play to successfully serve as "the fourth branch of government." Next, we examine general characteristics of the mass media that shape news coverage. We have just scratched the surface by highlighting the corporate, and therefore highly competitive, nature of major media outlets in the United States. There are other characteristics we will analyze as well.

Specific features of the news media also influence how stories are covered. Objectivity clearly shaped how (at least some) journalists reported on the Michigan affirmative action cases, but it is just one of several important news norms we discuss below. We also grapple with the effects of media coverage on citizens. Framing affirmative action as a policy that benefits all students through ensuring a diverse learning environment is fundamentally different from framing it as a policy that gives minority students undeserved advantages that result in discrimination against white students. Therefore, we investigate framing and other media effects on citizens' opinions. Along the way, we will remind you that all media are

Table 3-1   Media Framing of the University of Michigan Affirmative Action Cases

Media frame	Example
Reverse discrimination frame	Bob Franken, *CNN Lou Dobbs Tonight,* June 24, 2003, lead story: "The other case involved a challenge to the University of Michigan's more structured undergraduate admissions program with added points assigned to minorities. Chief Justice Rehnquist wrote the 6–3 decision saying 'it violates the Equal Protection Clause that this one went too far in considering race.'"
	Maribel Hastings, *La Opinión,* June 24, 2003, 1: "Los integrantes republicanos de la Comisión Nacional de Derechos Civiles criticaron los fallos. 'Las preferencias raciales son la antítesis de la igualdad de protección bajo la ley. El mejor método de obtener diversidad en la educación superior es mejorar la educación desde el jardín de infantes hasta el duodécimo grado y no seleccionar a los estudiantes por el color de su piel,' dijo el comisionado Peter Kirsanow." ["The Republican members of the U.S. Commission on Civil Rights criticized the ruling. 'Racial preferences are antithetical to equal protection under the law. The best way to obtain diversity in higher education is to improve K through 12 education and not select students based on the color of their skin,' said Commissioner Peter Kirsanow."]
Diversity frame	Jackie Judd, *ABC World News Tonight,* June 23, 2003, lead story: "Good evening, Peter. It was a generation ago that the court ruled in the famous *Bakke* case, establishing that race can be used as a factor in college admissions. Today, the court reaffirmed that position, saying that the creation of a diverse student body is good for American society."
	Chicago Defender, June 24, 2003, 7: "The policy had gained worldwide respect at Michigan, Northwestern University, the University of Chicago and other fine colleges and universities because diversity enriches the educational experience of all students."
	Alfonso Bermudez, *Impacto,* July 1, 2003, 3: "'Siempre he creído que en Estados Unidos, la belleza se encuentra en la diversidad. De esa belleza se nutre nuestra fuerza, nuestra creatividad y nuestra versatilidad. La Corte Suprema hoy apoyo esta posición al confirmar que el gobierno tiene el interés publico de promover la diversidad en las instituciones educativas,' anoto la congresista Pelosi." ["I have always believed that in the United States, beauty is found in diversity. That beauty nurtures our strength, our creativity, and our versatility. Today, the Supreme Court reinforced this position by acknowledging that the government has a public interest in promoting diversity in educational institutions,' noted Congresswoman Pelosi."]

Source: Quotes from Rosalee A. Clawson, Katsuo Nishikawa, and Eric N. Waltenburg, "Coverage of the Supreme Court's Rulings in the Michigan Affirmative Action Cases: Comparing the Mainstream, Black, and Latino Media" (paper presented at the meeting of the Latin American Studies Association, Las Vegas, Nevada, October 2004), 4.

not alike and illustrate how studying a variety of news media provides added insight. We close by reviewing the evidence and considering whether the media play their appropriate role in our democratic society.

WHAT SHOULD CITIZENS EXPECT FROM THE MASS MEDIA IN A DEMOCRACY?

Before reading this section, stop and ask yourself: What do you expect from the mass media in a democracy? How do you think the media should behave? Notice we are not asking how the media act in reality. We will get to that in a moment. For now, we are interested in your ideal vision of how the media should operate in a democratic society.

Probably the first thing that came to mind is that the media should be free from government control.[8] Freedom of the press, of course, is a fundamental tenet in a democracy. The government should not control the media by censoring stories or by forcing the publication of stories. Speaker of the House Nancy Pelosi, for example, should not be able to stop the *Washington Post* from publishing a particular story, nor should she be able to require the newspaper to cover certain events. What about freedom from other external forces? In a democracy, a free press should also be free from economic forces, such as market pressures and advertising dollars. Powerful economic forces should not be able to stop the media from covering important issues of the day and thus limit debate.

A press free from governmental and economic control will have great benefits for citizens because such a press should have several key characteristics. First, the media should act as an **intermediary** between citizens and elites, providing both with the information essential for a well-functioning democracy. Specifically, media organizations should provide citizens with the information and analysis necessary to make informed decisions. Further, the media should cover how citizens think about issues so that elites will be able to make educated decisions on behalf of their constituents. Second, a free press should provide a **forum for diverse views.** Elite and citizen opinion from across the spectrum should be presented in the media. A free press will not stifle critical or alternative voices. Debates should be wide ranging and contain a variety of perspectives. Finally, the media should play the role of a **"watchdog."**[9] Since citizens are unable to attend every city council meeting or participate in every public hearing held by a federal agency, they rely on the media to scrutinize the actions of public officials. The media should provide citizens with the information necessary to hold government accountable. Thus, the media should act like the "fourth estate" (or the fourth branch of government) and provide a check on the judicial, legislative, and congressional branches of government.[10]

This vision of the media is most consistent with the one held by participatory democratic theorists. Participatory theorists, as you will recall, want citizens to be actively engaged in the political process. By providing accurate information, the media will create knowledgeable citizens ready to participate in the give-and-take of politics. Moreover, by presenting diverse viewpoints, the media will ensure that both privileged and marginalized voices will be heard. This will facilitate participation on the part of *all* citizens (thus redressing the inequality in society, a core concern of participatory theorists). Participatory democratic theorists believe that political participation makes people better citizens, and they see the potential for the media to assist in that process.

Elite democrats, on the other hand, would be happy with a press relatively free from governmental control. We say "relatively free" because these theorists might argue that there are circumstances under which governmental elites should have influence over what the media publishes. For example, during the "war on terror," elites might prefer censorship of stories discussing warrantless wiretapping of U.S. citizens by the government. They would argue that since elites are the decision makers it is unnecessary for citizens to know these details, especially because publication of this information could undermine national security. Furthermore, elite democrats would be much less concerned with the effect of economic forces on the media. From their perspective, media outlets should be responsive to market pressures and advertising dollars so that citizens receive the kind of programming they want. As long as the media provide enough basic information to citizens so they can vote, these theorists are not concerned with the quality or diversity of news presented in the media.

WHAT GENERAL CHARACTERISTICS OF THE MASS MEDIA SHAPE NEWS COVERAGE?

Let's turn now to a discussion of the mass media in reality. Here we focus on general characteristics of the media that influence news content. In the United States, the mass media can best be characterized by the three Cs: corporate, concentrated, and conglomerate.[11]

The First C: Corporate

Most media are owned by large **corporations,** the first C. The primary goal of these corporations is to make money for their owners and shareholders, not to serve the interests of citizens in a democratic society. Since they are profit-driven companies, pleasing advertisers, not citizens, is their main objective. And this concerns critics who argue that advertisers prefer programming that puts people in the mood to buy, buy, buy, not vote, vote, vote. Moreover, in the world of advertising, certain people are more valuable than others. Broadcast networks, for example, are most interested in attracting viewers to their news programs who are between the ages of 18 and 49, particularly women who presumably hold the purse strings in many households.[12]

Although many of you will not recall (but your parents and grandparents will), citizens used to turn to one of three broadcast networks for their evening news: ABC, CBS, or NBC. That was it—the big three *were* television news. That seems strange today with literally hundreds of available channels, several of which are dedicated to news coverage. During this time period, these evening news broadcasts were shielded from profit expectations. This changed in the mid-1980s as new owners took over ABC, CBS, and NBC with an eye toward turning these evening news broadcasts into money-making enterprises.[13] Around the same time, technological changes occurred that led to an explosion of cable channels, resulting in a much more competitive environment. Not only were broadcast networks forced to compete with cable news outlets (such as CNN, which debuted in 1980), but they also had to contend with entertainment television (such as MTV, which debuted in 1981). Thus, just as the three broadcast networks were asked to bring home the bacon, the competition became even stiffer.

A widely respected media scholar, Thomas Patterson, argues that news organizations have "softened" their coverage as a result of this increased competition.[14] In their rush to attract larger audiences, the media have turned away from **hard news** coverage of "breaking events involving top leaders, major issues, or significant disruptions in the routines of daily life, such as an earthquake or airline disaster."[15] To examine this supposition, Patterson content analyzed a random sample of 5,331 news stories from two magazines, two broadcast television networks, three national newspapers, and twenty-six local papers. The news stories were published or televised between 1980 and 1999. He found that **soft news,** defined as those stories without a connection to public policy, have increased from roughly 35 percent of all stories during the early 1980s to almost 50 percent of all stories by 1999.[16] News stories with soft news elements, such as sensationalism, human interest, or crime and disaster, have increased substantially during this time period as well.[17] Patterson argued that this increase in crime news coverage may explain why even though crime rates were decreasing in the 1990s, people thought they were rising.[18]

Ironically, Patterson argued that this increase in soft news coverage, which is intended to draw in news audiences, may actually be driving people away. Sixty-three percent of citizens say they prefer hard news (and another 13 percent prefer both hard and soft news equally), according to a national survey conducted by Patterson.[19] For these citizens, the emphasis on soft news is a turnoff. This may explain why news audiences have shrunk considerably over the years. With the exceptions of online newspaper readership (which has increased) and cable TV news viewership (which has stayed basically the same), news audiences have declined significantly since 1993 (see Figure 3-1). The preference for hard news may also explain why the *CBS Evening News* has had its worst ratings in history since Katie Couric took over as anchor. When Couric took over the broadcast, there was a shift toward lighter news fare to take advantage of her "morning-news skills."[20] This approach was met with quite a bit of criticism, and the program returned to a more traditional format fairly quickly.

Figure 3-1   The Declining News Audience

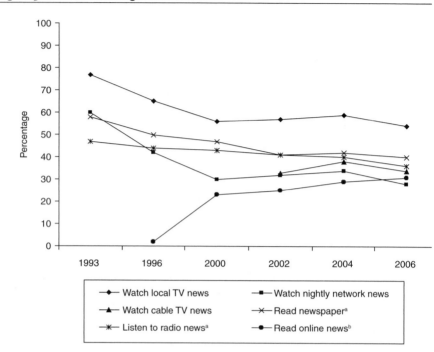

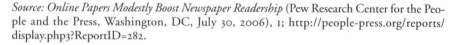

Source: Online Papers Modestly Boost Newspaper Readership (Pew Research Center for the People and the Press, Washington, DC, July 30, 2006), 1; http://people-press.org/reports/display.php3?ReportID=282.

Note: Data on watching cable TV news were only collected from 2002.
[a]1993 data are actually from 1994.
[b]1996 data are actually from 1995.

Citizens who prefer soft news will not be loyal audience members either, according to Patterson. For those who favor soft news—presumably due to its entertainment value—there are other much more entertaining programs available that will draw their attention in the long run. A sensational news story on Paris Hilton, for example, may occasionally draw in people with soft news preferences. During the week of June 4, 2007, 20 percent of those under age 30 indicated the news story they were following most closely was the imprisonment (and release and reimprisonment) of Paris Hilton.[21] But ultimately if that is the type of story people are interested in, there are much better places to turn for soft news than the traditional news media.

Might economic forces also influence the treatment of political topics on entertainment television? Here is one example of how an advertiser influenced whether citizens saw an episode of a television show with political overtones. During the summer of 2001, CBS pulled a rerun of its show *Family Law* because its major advertiser, Procter and Gamble, did not want its ads associated with an episode that dealt with a hot button issue: handgun ownership.[22] To be clear, Procter and Gamble was not upset by the particular political stance the show took on guns; instead, the company was worried that watching a show on such a controversial topic would upset or depress people, thus making them less interested in buying Charmin toilet paper and Crest toothpaste. The association of negative thoughts and feelings with its products is an advertiser's worst nightmare. As a result of Procter and Gamble's influence, citizens did not spend a summer evening grappling with a tough political issue.[23]

Now, we do not mean to imply there was anything illegal about Procter and Gamble pressuring CBS to pull this episode of *Family Law*. Procter and Gamble has a right to advertise its products where it sees fit. Another matter, however, is whether or not it is good for society for an advertiser to influence programming in this way. What do you think? Your response probably depends on how you view the role of the mass media in a democratic nation. On the one hand, you might believe media corporations have a special responsibility to foster debate in a democracy (particularly broadcast television since the public owns the airwaves) and therefore should serve the public interest by airing shows on controversial political topics. On the other hand, you might think that media corporations' only responsibility is to their bottom line, and media executives should do everything possible to keep their advertisers happy, thus serving the financial interests of their stockholders.

The Second C: Concentrated

The second C is **concentrated**: a few large companies own the majority of media in the United States. In 1983, there were fifty dominant media corporations; by 2004, there were five: Time Warner, The Walt Disney Company, News Corporation, Viacom, and Bertelsmann.[24] According to Ben H. Bagdikian, this handful of multinational corporations owns "most of the newspapers, magazines, book publishers, motion picture studios, and radio and television stations in the United States."[25] What this means in practice is that one company can own a television station and eight radio stations in the same community, as CBS (which separated from Viacom in 2005) does in Los Angeles.[26] Thus, what looks like a multiplicity of choices may actually be no choice at all. In recent years, major media corporations have rushed to scoop up lucrative Internet companies. Many of you have profiles on MySpace, but do you know which major media corporation owns the popular social networking Web site? News Corporation bought MySpace during the summer of 2005. News Corporation also owns the Fox Broadcasting Company (think Homer Simpson), the Fox News Channel (think Bill O'Reilly), and *The Weekly Standard* (think Bill Kristol), to name just a few of its other media holdings.

During the summer of 2007, News Corporation made one of its boldest moves yet by acquiring Dow Jones, including the influential *Wall Street Journal.*[27]

Does media concentration have an effect on news coverage? Media critics argue this high degree of media consolidation stifles debate in a democracy. Diverse news content is impossible if just a few companies control the vast majority of the media, according to this perspective.[28] Unfortunately, there is little systematic research on this topic. One study by Martin Gilens and Craig Hertzman, however, makes a substantial contribution to our understanding of the effects of media concentration on news content.[29]

Gilens and Hertzman conducted an innovative study of the influence of media concentration on news coverage of the 1996 Telecommunications Act. The Telecommunications Act had significantly different implications for those media corporations that owned television stations than for those that did not. Specifically, the Telecom Act loosened caps on television station ownership. Thus, media corporations that owned television stations benefited from the legislation, whereas other media corporations did not benefit and were perhaps even put at a disadvantage by the bill. As a result, Gilens and Hertzman hypothesized, newspapers owned by media companies with television interests would cover the Telecom Act more favorably than newspapers that did not have investments in television stations.

To test this hypothesis, Gilens and Hertzman identified three types of newspapers: newspapers in a company with no television stations; newspapers in a company with five or fewer television stations; and newspapers in a company with nine or more television stations. Then they collected 397 articles published in those newspapers between December 1, 1995, and February 28, 1996, that discussed the Telecommunications Act. Of those 397 articles, 113 specifically mentioned the aspect of the bill dealing with loosening the caps on television ownership. Next, Gilens and Hertzman conducted a **content analysis** of the characteristics of the coverage dedicated to the ownership cap issue.

Gilens and Hertzman found the three types of newspapers dedicated roughly the same amount of coverage to the ownership cap issue, as shown in Table 3-2. In terms of the tone of coverage, however, the three types of newspapers differed considerably. The newspapers with television holdings were more likely to focus on the positive impact of the Telecom bill and significantly less likely to mention the negative impact compared with the newspapers with no television ownership. For example, in newspapers without ties to television, 58 percent of the articles mentioned negative consequences of lifting the ownership caps, such as the bill would decrease the diversity of viewpoints and dampen democratic debate in the media. In contrast, only 15 percent of the articles from those newspapers with substantial television interests mentioned any negative consequences.

There was also a difference among the three types of newspapers in whether their coverage included a misleading claim about the Telecommunications Act. Twenty-six percent of the newspapers with major television holdings indicated

Table 3-2   News Coverage among Newspapers with Different Levels of
Television Ownership

Measure	Newspapers with no television ownership	Newspapers with five or fewer television stations	Newspapers with nine or more television stations
Amount of coverage:			
Percentage of all Telecom Act stories that mentioned ownership caps	31%	27%	27%
Positive impact:			
Percentage of ownership cap stories that mentioned positive consequences of Telecom Act	16	34	33
Negative impact:			
Percentage of ownership cap stories that mentioned negative consequences of Telecom Act	58	44	15
Deceptive claim:			
Percentage of ownership cap stories that said companies owning television stations could not own more than one station per market	4	15	26

Source: Data from Martin Gilens and Craig Hertzman, "Corporate Ownership and News Bias: Newspaper Coverage of the 1996 Telecommunications Act," *Journal of Politics* 62 (2000): 378.

that the Telecom legislation would prohibit a media company from owning more than one television station in each market. According to Gilens and Hertzman, this was a deceptive claim because the Federal Communications Commission regularly gave waivers to companies so they could own more than one television station per market, and the Telecom Act specifically increased the number of media markets in which these waivers could be given. Thus, this claim was highly deceptive, if not downright false. Only 4 percent of the newspapers with no television interests reported this misleading claim.

This pattern of news coverage exposed by Gilens and Hertzman raises serious questions about the negative effects of media concentration on news content.[30] Gilens and Hertzman conclude their study on a pessimistic note, "Only the news media can provide the public with the information it needs to participate meaningfully in democratic government; a press that systematically slants the news to further its own business objectives threatens to undermine the very foundations of democracy."[31]

The Third C: Conglomerate

The third C is **conglomerate.** Not only do these large corporations own lots of different types of media, they own lots of nonmedia companies as well. The same company—GE—that reports on the war in Iraq also produces weapons for fighting the war in Iraq: GE owns NBC and produces engines for Black Hawk helicopters and the Abrams Tank.[32] Another example of cross-ownership is Bertelsmann. The global conglomerate includes Random House, which bills itself as "the world's largest general-interest book publisher."[33] It also has corporate divisions that specialize in database management and financial services, and it owns television and radio stations across Europe.[34]

Many observers are concerned with this level of conglomeration. The "willingness to criticize and scrutinize those with political and economic power"[35] is expected from a free press, yet do media conglomerates hold their own accountable? Media critics might argue, for example, that NBC news will not cover expensive weapons systems or investigate fraud and abuse in military procurement because their reporting might reflect poorly on their GE sister companies that regularly do business with the U.S. military. There is also the concern that news organizations will spend time cross-promoting their products rather than covering hard news.[36] *The Early Show* on CBS, for example, dedicates extensive coverage to their network's hit TV show, *Survivor.* This might not raise eyebrows if the morning show was billed as entertainment programming, but it is not. *The Early Show* is part of the CBS news division.[37]

The Walt Disney Company: A Case Study of the Three Cs

To illustrate the three Cs, let's turn to a detailed examination of one huge multinational media conglomerate: The Walt Disney Company.[38] Disney owns the ABC broadcast network, which airs *World News with Charles Gibson,* and ten television stations in major cities across the country. In Chicago, for example, Disney owns a television station and four radio stations; it owns the same in Los Angeles and New York. Disney also holds a variety of cable television stations, including ESPN and SOAPnet, and has partial ownership in E!, Lifetime, and A&E. The Walt Disney Corporation is a publishing powerhouse with its Hyperion book imprint and magazines ranging from *Automotive Industries* to *Family Fun* to *Institutional Investor.* Disney also has four music labels: Buena Vista Music Group, Walt

Disney Records, Hollywood Records, and Lyric Street Records. Disney owns Buena Vista Theatrical Productions, which produces shows such as The Lion King, Tarzan, and the Beauty and the Beast, and owns six film studios, including Touchstone Pictures, Pixar, and Miramax Films. Disney owns the Baby Einstein Company, which produces "developmental media for infants,"[39] and runs the Disney Cruise Line. And, of course, Disney is best known for its resorts and parks in the United States and around the world.

Should we be concerned about this global media conglomerate? Well, it depends whom you ask. On the one hand, it is a little disconcerting when the corporation that produces the Baby Einstein videos also profits from the Kill Bill film franchise. Indeed, observers from both ends of the ideological continuum worry about the effects of large, highly concentrated media conglomerates. Liberals, for example, might be concerned about whether ABC news outlets will report on the environmental damage caused by Disney cruise ships, whereas conservatives might be concerned with the impact of violence in Disney films on our culture. On the other hand, those who favor free markets do not worry about these issues. They believe that free markets provide citizens with the products they prefer. If that happens to be a violence-laden movie, so be it; if that means a news organization does not cover certain political topics, so be it.

Exceptions to the Three Cs

Although corporate, concentrated, and conglomerate characterize most of the media in the United States, there are notable and important exceptions. National Public Radio (NPR) and the Public Broadcasting System (PBS) are **nonprofit media corporations** whose goal is to provide high-quality, noncommercial news and entertainment programming to American citizens. Both corporations are membership organizations and receive significant financial support from their member stations (public radio stations in the case of NPR and public television stations in the case of PBS). NPR and PBS are also underwritten by corporations and private foundations. These underwriters do not air advertisements in the traditional sense but do have their names mentioned during programming. A small portion, less than 2 percent, of NPR's annual budget comes from federal funds, and less than 20 percent of PBS's funding comes from federal money.[40]

Citizens who receive their news from public radio and public television tend to have high levels of knowledge about politics. According to a 2007 poll conducted by the Pew Research Center, 53 percent of regular viewers of PBS's *NewsHour with Jim Lehrer* were among the top one-third most knowledgeable citizens in the United States. Similarly, 51 percent of regular NPR listeners were in this highly knowledgeable group.[41]

In an important study of misperceptions regarding the war in Iraq, Steven Kull, Clay Ramsay, and Evan Lewis found that public media consumers were the least likely to be confused about facts pertaining to the war.[42] These scholars collected survey data from a random sample of 1,362 respondents between June and September 2003. They were interested in whether citizens had misperceptions about the war and whether citizens receiving news from particular sources were more likely to hold those misperceptions.

Kull, Ramsay, and Lewis crafted three questions to measure misperceptions:

Is it your impression that the US has or has not found clear evidence in Iraq that Saddam Hussein was working closely with the al Qaeda terrorist organization?

Since the war with Iraq ended, is it your impression that the US has or has not found Iraqi weapons of mass destruction? (Note that the end of the war wording here refers to the end of major combat operations, as declared by Bush in May 2003.)

Thinking about how all the people in the world feel about the US having gone to war with Iraq, do you think: The majority of people favor the US having gone to war; The majority of people oppose the US having gone to war; or Views are evenly balanced.[43]

Because the United States has not found a clear link between Saddam Hussein and al-Qaeda or weapons of mass destruction in Iraq (despite occasional Bush administration statements that might imply otherwise), answering "has" to the first two questions were coded as misperceptions. Saying world opinion favored the war in response to the third question was also coded as a misperception since public opinion polls showed that most people around the world opposed the war. Kull et al. found that 60 percent of Americans held one or more of these misperceptions about the war.

Next, Kull et al. examined whether citizens' levels of misperceptions varied with their news source. Indeed, they found stark differences in beliefs about the war based on where citizens tended to get their news (see Figure 3-2). Viewers of Fox News were particularly likely to believe one or more of the misperceptions. More than a majority of CBS, ABC, CNN, and NBC viewers held one or more of these misperceptions; slightly less than a majority of print media users were confused about the facts. The striking finding is that three-fourths of the NPR and PBS audience did not hold any misperceptions.

What makes the high level of misperceptions among the public particularly troublesome is that the more misperceptions citizens held, the more they supported the war in Iraq. For example, only 23 percent of citizens who had no misperceptions supported the war, whereas 86 percent of those with three misperceptions supported it. Kull et al. did not demonstrate that the news sources *caused* the misperceptions or that the misperceptions *caused* support for the war. Never-

Figure 3-2   Misperceptions by News Source

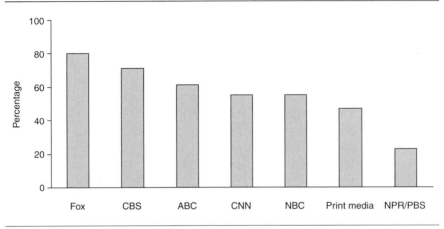

Source: Data from Steven Kull, Clay Ramsay, and Evan Lewis, "Misperceptions, the Media, and the Iraq War," *Political Science Quarterly* 118 (2003–2004): 582.

Note: Bars represent the percentage of people holding at least one misperception about the Iraq War by primary news source.

theless, the associations between news sources and misperceptions and between misperceptions and support for the war raise serious questions about the sources, extent, and effect of misinformation in a democratic society.

For our purposes here, we are most interested in the relative accuracy of the NPR and PBS audience. These findings suggest that public radio and television stations play a crucial role in providing citizens with information necessary to make informed judgments about the most important issues of our day. To be sure, public radio and television are not without their critics;[44] nevertheless, in a media environment dominated by conglomerates, noncommercial outlets are an essential source of reliable and accurate hard news.

Another noteworthy exception to the dominance of media conglomerates is the **minority press.** Let's take the black press as an example. Black newspapers tend to be independent or part of relatively small family-owned chains.[45] The black press is affected by economic forces, but it is also driven by a mission of advocacy. Its goal is to present the news from a "black" angle, and it tries to counter the often incomplete and erroneous coverage of minority communities that appears in the mainstream media.[46] As a result, the black press provides a diversity of voices that are not heard in the mainstream media.[47] Black citizens find this particularly important, especially during periods of racial strife. For example, the *Los Angeles Sentinel*'s circulation increased after the highly publicized videotaped police beating of Rodney King in Los Angeles in 1991, the subsequent acquittal of the police officers involved in 1992, and the uprisings that ensued.[48] Minority presses in other communities serve a similar function.[49] Overall then, by providing a forum for diverse points of view, minority newspapers act as an important, albeit small, counterbalance to the nation's major media outlets.

Finally, what about the **Internet** as an exception to the dominance of media conglomerates? Denis McQuail, a noted media scholar, argues that the Internet "can unlock secrets and make much arcane information readily available to ordinary people very rapidly, with an empowering effect."[50] The Internet provides unprecedented opportunities for citizens to discuss, and even make, the news. Blogs, for example, turn readers into writers.[51] Furthermore, since few resources are required to set up a Web site, independent media organizations can afford to establish a home on the Internet that would be impossible without the technology.

The Internet is not a panacea, however. Citizens are more likely to search the Internet for entertainment news than for political news. For example, in 2000, more searches were conducted for news on Britney Spears than on Social Security. Also in 2000, there were substantially more Web pages that mentioned the X Files or South Park than President Bill Clinton or the Supreme Court.[52] Bloggers are not constrained by journalistic norms of accuracy and objectivity (which we discuss below), and many have no qualms about reporting gossip as fact.[53] It is also the case that media conglomerates have planted their flags in cyberspace. The same companies that control much of the traditional news media also garner significant traffic on their Internet sites. These companies' "brands" are so powerful that citizens turn to them for information; it just happens to be on the Internet rather than on television or in print. Nevertheless, the Internet provides countless opportunities for average citizens, if they so desire, to seek out information from bloggers, independent media organizations, and government, academic, and non-profit Web sites.

WHAT SPECIFIC CHARACTERISTICS OF THE NEWS MEDIA SHAPE THE REPORTING OF POLITICAL EVENTS?

In this section, we discuss **news norms** that influence the reporting of political events. Here we are focusing on norms that shape how journalists—not columnists or pundits—decide what's news. We also provide a critique of those norms. Finally, we examine whether these norms constrain the activities of all media organizations.

News Norms

One of the most important norms that shapes news coverage is **objectivity.** In practice, journalists define objectivity as providing both sides of an issue. To uphold this norm, journalists strive for balance in their reporting. In the U.S. political context, this often means that a Republican viewpoint is balanced with a Democratic one.[54]

A close cousin of objectivity is **neutrality.** According to this norm, journalists do not inject their personal opinions into news coverage. Instead, they report on political events by presenting others' viewpoints in their stories, especially the viewpoints of **official sources.** Official sources include primarily government officials but also other people who are powerful in society.[55] W. Lance Bennett argues that news organizations index "the range of voices and viewpoints in both news and editorials according to the range of views expressed in mainstream government debate about a given topic."[56]

By relying heavily on official sources, journalists are able to do their jobs easily and efficiently. It also allows them to achieve the norm of **accuracy.** Journalists work hard to ensure the information they report is correct. They perceive official sources to be reliable, legitimate, and in the know; thus, journalists regularly turn to these sources in their news coverage. In the words of prominent media scholar Timothy E. Cook, "officials are big fish."[57]

These norms—objectivity, neutrality, and accuracy—are a function of the news media trying to reach as broad an audience as possible. Media corporations want to advertise to large audiences, not just Republicans or Democrats. Thus, they provide news that will not tick off one side or the other (or at least tick off both sides equally). This was not always the case. As Cook notes, "From the infancy of the newspaper in North America in early eighteenth century Boston all the way through the Civil War, politics infused and informed the production of news, in direct, conscious, and unsubtle ways. Support tended to consist of individual sponsorship. Newspapers most often were launched with the help of politically powerful sponsors—officials, factions, or, by the first years of the republic, parties."[58] Technological changes during the mid-1800s, however, allowed publishers to print greater quantities of newspapers in a much shorter time frame. This technological advance allowed for high circulation, which encouraged businesses to own and advertise in newspapers. It became necessary for journalists to report the news in such a way that newspapers appealed to a wide audience; thus, journalists adopted the norms of objectivity, neutrality, and accuracy.[59]

Assigning journalists to **newsbeats** is another journalistic norm.[60] Journalists are assigned to cover specific institutions or topic areas, and these are called beats. For example, major news organizations assign journalists to the White House beat and the Pentagon beat. This allows journalists to gain expertise on certain topics and develop relationships with key players, obviously important because of the heavy reliance on official sources. Assignment to a beat enables journalists to create familiar, reliable routines in a job where events are constantly changing.[61]

Journalists are also influenced by norms of **newsworthiness.** Conflict garners significant media attention. For example, media coverage of Congress focuses heavily on partisan conflict within the institution and strife between the Congress and the president.[62] The emphasis on conflict is also obvious in news coverage of political campaigns. The media tend to focus on the "horse race" aspect of campaigns: who's ahead in the polls and who's behind, who has momentum and who doesn't, and who's leading in fundraising and who's faltering.[63]

Thomas Patterson argues that journalists think of politics as a strategic game.[64] Thus, when covering political candidates, they use a **game schema** to organize their reporting. They use the language of competition to cover the ins and outs of the campaign rather than report on the candidates' policy pronouncements. Patterson writes, "The strategic game is embedded in virtually every aspect of election news, dominating and driving it. The game sets the context, even when issues are the subject of analysis. The game, once the backdrop in news of the campaign, is now so pervasive that it is almost inseparable from the rest of election content."[65] Other scholars argue the emphasis on strategy extends beyond news coverage of political campaigns to news coverage of governance.[66] In other words, once politicians gain office, the news media still assess their every move in terms of competition and gamesmanship rather than substance. An analysis of the debate over health care reform during the Clinton administration shows that two-thirds of newspaper and broadcast news coverage focused on strategy rather than the issue at hand.[67]

Critiques of News Norms

This discussion of news norms may have raised some red flags in your mind. On the one hand, these news norms enable journalists to appeal to a wide audience and do their work in an efficient manner. The norms also ensure that powerful political elites will be able to get their messages out to the public, thus pleasing elite democratic theorists. On the other hand, some of these news norms make it difficult, if not impossible, for the news media to live up to the ideal standards proposed by participatory democratic theorists.

To begin, the norm of objectivity requires journalists to present two sides of an issue. But, what if there are more than two sides? Take abortion, for example. The debate is often characterized in the media as pro-life versus pro-choice, with Republican elites supporting life and Democratic elites supporting choice. Among the public, however, 50 percent of Americans do not fall neatly into either camp. Instead, they believe that abortion should be available under certain circumstances, such as rape, incest, life of the mother, or when some other clear need has been established.[68]

As you can also see from this abortion example, it is problematic to rely so heavily on official sources. Since journalists focus on elite opinion, the abortion debate looks as if it is two-sided. If journalists paid more attention to the opinions of average Americans, however, they would see that the issue is actually much more complex. "Ordinary people do not hold easily and quickly reported press conferences";[69] thus, it is unlikely that journalists will be grappling with the complexities of the issue anytime soon.

We have discussed the limitations of objective reporting when there are more than two sides to an issue, but what about when elites are in agreement and thus there is only one side of an issue? In those circumstances, one of two things happens. First, the norm of newsworthiness emphasizes stories in which there is conflict. If there is no disagreement among elites, there is no conflict. If there is no conflict, there is no story. As a result, many important issues go unreported by the media.

Second, if the issue does get covered, it appears as if there is no debate on the topic. In reality, plenty of debate may be occurring among those who are not powerful enough to be counted as official sources, but that debate rarely hits the front page of newspapers or leads off news broadcasts. In matters of foreign policy and national security especially, it is not uncommon for elites to stake out uniform positions.[70] Thus, on some of the most important issues of our day—war, terrorism, sacrificing civil liberties in the name of national security, nuclear proliferation, and international trade—elites often present a united front, which leads the press to act more as a tool of government than a watchdog. Indeed, both the *New York Times* and the *Washington Post* have expressed regret for not publishing stories that challenged the Bush administration's justifications for going to war in Iraq.[71]

The assignment of journalists to newsbeats results in journalists developing close relationships with government officials on those beats. This leads to the concern that journalists become too cozy with those officials. From this perspective, journalists act more like lapdogs than watchdogs. Some scholars characterize the relationship between journalists and politicians as symbiotic. That is, journalists need politicians to report accurate news, and politicians need journalists to get their messages out to the public. Other scholars go further and say that the relationship is better understood as mutual exploitation: journalists exploit politicians to do their jobs, and politicians exploit journalists to do theirs.[72]

Newsbeats can also lead to **pack journalism.** Major news organizations assign journalists to the same beats. While covering those beats, journalists develop relationships with the same sources. As a result, journalists often end up covering the same set of stories from the same perspectives. Further, newsworthy events may be happening that do not get reported because there is no journalist assigned to that newsbeat.[73] For example, news organizations regularly assign journalists to cover the Pentagon. Those journalists become familiar with weapons systems, military buildups, and troop deployments; they attend press conferences; and they cultivate key sources. Not surprisingly, stories emanating from the Pentagon are regularly featured in news coverage. Reporters are not assigned to cover the Department of Veterans Affairs as a beat, however. As a result, significant stories may be overlooked. An important story about the shoddy treatment of wounded soldiers at Walter Reed Army Medical Center was missed for months, if not years.[74] And of course some stories may never be reported.

The norm of newsworthiness leads journalists to focus on conflict and to emphasize the strategic aspects of political campaigns and governance. Citizens view politics in a very different way, however, according to Thomas Patterson. Instead of a game schema, citizens use a **governing schema.** They want journalists to cover the issues so they can judge whether political candidates will address their problems. This makes for a sharp disconnect between what information journalists deem newsworthy and what information citizens hope to receive.

Do News Norms Influence All Media Organizations?

Do these news norms constrain the activities of all media organizations? No, they do not. Robert M. Entman distinguishes between **traditional journalism, advocacy journalism, tabloid journalism,** and **entertainment.**[75] He argues that traditional journalists (such as those who work for the *New York Times, CBS Evening News,* and *Time* magazine) have a strong commitment to news norms. Advocacy journalism, in contrast, is committed to only some of these norms. Minority newspapers, for example, value objectivity and accuracy, but they are also committed to advocating on behalf of their communities. This often leads to an emphasis on different facts and sources than those covered by the mainstream media.[76] Advocacy journalism also includes magazines with an ideological bent, such as *The Nation* on the left and *The Weekly Standard* on the right. These magazines strive for accuracy, but again, it is accuracy from a particular perspective.

Tabloid journalism is much less committed, if at all, to news norms. Tabloid journalism includes local television news and cable programs such as the *O'Reilly Factor* on Fox News that appeals to a conservative audience and *Countdown* with Keith Olbermann on MSNBC that speaks to a liberal audience. Over the last two decades, the explosion of cable channels has allowed for profitable niche programming. And since these programs do not need to appeal to a wide audience, the norms of objectivity, neutrality, and accuracy have gone by the wayside. In fact, the draw of these cable news programs tends to be the bombastic commentary of their hosts.

Shows such as *The Daily Show with Jon Stewart, Oprah,* and *24* fall into the category of entertainment. These shows clearly have political content, but their primary purpose is to entertain, not inform. Obviously, they are not bound by news norms. Nevertheless, Entman argues these programs are important because they can "provide deep and accessible insights into the impacts of policies, the prevarications and real goals of public officials, and the distribution of wealth and power."[77]

ARE CITIZENS AFFECTED BY THE MASS MEDIA?

In this chapter, we have discussed what citizens should expect from the media in a democracy, and we have addressed the empirical reality of the media in the United States. By now, you should have a good feel for the general and specific characteristics of the media that shape news coverage. The question remains, however, whether citizens are affected by the mass media. That is the topic we turn to in this section.

Public Opinion in Comparative Perspective
BOX 3-2 MEDIA IN ARAB COUNTRIES

"A review of media programmes and research indicates that light entertainment is the most common offering, and is predominantly superficial, repetitive in content, and promotes values that encourage consumerism and a depreciation of work."

"The main focus is still on official news and on senior political officials. Certain news values predominate, notably those favouring celebrities, idiosyncratic behaviour, humour and conflict."

"The news is often presented as a succession of isolated events, without in-depth explanatory coverage or any effort to place events in the general, social, economic and cultural context."

It would be quite reasonable to think these blurbs refer to the news media in the United States. Actually, these comments refer to the media in Arab countries.[1] Criticism of Arab media content sounds remarkably similar to complaints voiced about the U.S. media. This is interesting because important differences exist between the U.S. and Arab media. Unlike the United States where most media are owned by large corporations, the media in Arab countries tend to be state-owned. In other words, the government controls most media outlets. Censorship is common, and newspapers and television channels can be shut down by the government.[2] While political officials in the United States try to spin stories to their advantage and sometimes try to keep stories from being broadcast or published, it would be unthinkable for President George W. Bush to close down a media outlet. Even during Rush Limbaugh's very successful attempts to stir up grassroots anger over the president's support of the immigration bill during the summer of 2007, the Bush administration never considered pulling the plug on Limbaugh's radio show. Another difference is the way journalists are treated. In Arab countries, journalists are often harassed, abducted, detained, jailed, or even murdered. In war-torn Iraq, 32 journalists were killed in 2006 alone.[3] People in Arab countries also have less access to the media. In Arab countries, there are only 53 daily newspapers in circulation per 1,000 people. Contrast that with 285 in circulation per 1,000 people in developed countries.[4] Similarly, Arabs are much less likely to have Internet access: 89 people per 1,000 are Internet users in the Middle East and North Africa compared with 630 per 1,000 in the United States. And several countries trump

(continued)

the United States in terms of Internet access, including Australia (698 per 1,000), South Korea (684 per 1,000), and Sweden (764 per 1,000).[5] Overall, these data suggest that the information necessary for citizens to have informed opinions is not as readily available in Arab countries as it is in other parts of the world.

Dramatic transformations are under way in the Arab world, however. Technological changes continue to make news more available to the average Arab citizen. Private satellite channels and Internet access are increasingly available. Independent newspapers have also emerged, often by relying on the Internet to circumvent state censorship.[6]

1. *Arab Human Development Report 2003: Building a Knowledge Society* (United Nations Development Programme, Arab Fund for Economic and Social Development, New York, 2003), http://hdr.undp.org/docs/reports/regional/ABS_Arab/Arab_States_2003_en.pdf.
2. Ibid., 58–62.
3. Joel Campagna, "As Democracy Falters, Arab Press Still Pushes for Freedom," *Attacks on the Press in 2006: Middle East and North Africa* (Committee to Protect Journalists, 2007), http://www.cpj.org/attacks06/mideast06/mideast_analysis_06.html.
4. *Arab Human Development Report 2003*, 59.
5. *World Development Indicators 2006* (The World Bank, 2007), http://siteresources.worldbank.org/DATASTATISTICS/Resources/table5_11.pdf.
6. *Arab Human Development Report 2003*, 65–66.

The Hypodermic Model

Imagine you are going to the doctor to receive your annual flu shot. The doctor uses a hypodermic needle to inject you with the vaccine. You leave her office with the medicine coursing through your veins ready to fight off any flu bug that might come your way. Receiving a shot in a doctor's office is an (often unpleasant) experience to which we can all relate.

Now, let's translate this phenomenon to the political arena. Take yourself back in time to the Great Depression. Imagine you and your family sitting in your living room listening attentively to one of President Franklin D. Roosevelt's "fireside chats" on the radio. Or imagine you are in Munich, Germany, during roughly the same time period. Picture yourself reading newspapers over which Adolf Hitler has exerted complete control. Are you being injected with messages from the mass media in the same way a doctor injects you with medicine? Are the media messages so powerful and you so weak that resistance is futile?

Bring yourself to the present and take a look around. Why are so many of your friends (and maybe even you) wearing Nike or Sean John T-shirts with the name brands prominently displayed? Is it possible that the advertising campaigns of these companies have "injected" your friends with their messages, thus getting them to buy overpriced clothing and provide free advertising for the company all at the same time?

These examples illustrate what has been called the **hypodermic model** of media effects.[78] The early to mid-1900s saw a huge growth in advertising, numerous technological changes that allowed average citizens access to the media, two world wars, the rise of dictators across Europe, and a powerful president at home. All of these factors led some observers to fear that the media could control citizens. Underlying this fear were two assumptions: (a) that the media are extremely powerful, and (b) that citizens are not sophisticated enough to ward off media messages. The hypodermic model is certainly a compelling metaphor, but is there evidence to support its view of media effects on citizens? It turns out that systematic support for such wide-ranging, persuasive effects of the media never panned out. Instead, scholars came to the conclusion that the media have relatively minimal effects on citizens' political attitudes.

Minimal Effects Model

Whereas the hypodermic model viewed citizens as blank slates waiting to be written on by the mass media, the **minimal effects model** of media influence has a more nuanced understanding of citizens. From the minimal effects perspective, citizens' slates are already marked up with a whole host of prior attitudes and predispositions when they encounter media messages. Citizens rely on these existing attitudes to help them sift through, evaluate, and often filter out media content. Thus, citizens are not passively injected with messages from the media; instead, they are active receivers or rejecters of these messages depending on their predispositions. As a result, the media have minimal effects on citizens' political attitudes.

Evidence of the media's minimal effects was provided by Paul Lazarsfeld, Bernard Berelson, and Hazel Gaudet in their classic study of Erie County, Ohio, during the 1940 presidential campaign between Franklin Roosevelt and Wendell Wilkie.[79] Lazarsfeld et al. trained local interviewers to conduct several in-home interviews with a representative sample of Erie County residents between May and November 1940. To be precise, this panel survey included 600 people who were each interviewed six times over the course of the campaign. Thus, the design of the study allowed the researchers to track residents over time to determine why people voted the way they did in November. In particular, Lazarsfeld and colleagues were interested in the influence of campaign messages on citizens' vote choices. By studying one community in depth, the scholars were able to assess the campaign messages that were circulating in the local media environment and examine what effect, if any, those messages had on voters. In this way, Lazarsfeld et al.'s research provides evidence that allows us to assess the power of the media to influence citizens' political attitudes.

Lazarsfeld et al.'s research findings are striking. First, they discovered that a remarkable 50 percent of citizens already knew in May for whom they were going to vote in November. Obviously, the campaigns' media messages were not changing people's choices because they had already made up their minds before the campaign even got started. Nevertheless, Lazarsfeld et al. argued that political communication still played an important role because it reinforced people's existing decisions. Hence, this was labeled the **reinforcement effect.**

Lazarsfeld et al. also identified an **activation effect** among those people who were initially undecided about which candidate to support. The researchers demonstrated that campaign messages aroused interest in citizens, which led them to pay more attention to the election; however, the fascinating thing was that citizens did not pay attention to all aspects of the campaigns. Instead, citizens honed in on particular magazine articles and newspaper stories that corresponded with their political predispositions. In other words, citizens with Republican-leaning characteristics were more likely to seek out Republican-leaning campaign news, whereas Democratic-inclined citizens sought out pro-Democratic media content. This selective attention to the media activated citizens' prior attitudes, which served to remind citizens of why they held those attitudes in the first place.[80] Thus, citizens' latent predispositions were stimulated and strengthened by the news stories. Rarely were those predispositions challenged, and when they were, citizens were anchored by their predispositions and therefore resistant to change. By November, citizens' preexisting attitudes became crystallized, encouraging them to vote for the presidential candidate who was consistent with their values and predispositions all along.

Finally, Lazarsfeld and colleagues found little evidence of a **conversion effect.** In other words, very few citizens actually changed from one candidate to another during the course of the campaign. We might expect that citizens who had few existing attitudes would be susceptible to campaign messages and thus to conversion; however, those same citizens who did not have strong predispositions also did not expose themselves to campaign news. In other words, those most likely to be persuaded were the least likely to come across persuasive messages. Conversion, then, was a rare phenomenon.

Lazarsfeld et al. also argued that the media's influence was limited because many citizens relied on conversations with politically engaged friends and family, rather than the mass media, to obtain information about the presidential campaign. The researchers described the process as a **"two-step flow of communication."**[81] First, highly interested citizens would gather campaign information from newspapers and the radio. These people were called "opinion leaders."[82] Second, the opinion leaders would talk about the election with their friends and family, passing on information about candidates and issues to those who were much less caught up in the campaign. Therefore, Lazarsfeld et al. did not dismiss the influence of the media entirely because clearly the opinion leaders were gathering information from news organizations, but they did emphasize that personal contacts were more influential for most everyday, average citizens.

Subtle Effects Model

When scholars did not find evidence that the media had widespread persuasion effects, many lost interest in studying the influence (or lack thereof) of the media. Research in this area was dormant for quite a while. Maxwell McCombs and Donald L. Shaw reversed that trend, however, with their research on the agenda-setting role of the media in the 1968 presidential election.[83] McCombs and Shaw acknowledged that the media cannot change people's minds on the issues of the day, but they argued that *"the mass media set the agenda for each political campaign, influencing the salience of attitudes towards the political issues."* [84] Their study marks the beginning of the **subtle effects model** era of media research.

Agenda Setting and Priming. McCombs and Shaw's argument was based on a comparison between what a random sample of Chapel Hill, North Carolina, voters said were the key issues in the 1968 presidential election and actual campaign coverage in the news media relied on by voters in that community. McCombs and Shaw found a strong relationship between the issues emphasized by the media and those issues deemed important by the voters. For example, the mass media devoted a significant amount of coverage to foreign policy and law and order issues, and Chapel Hill voters indicated those topics were major campaign issues. Thus, the media set the agenda by establishing which campaign issues are considered important in the minds of voters. The media "may not be successful much of the time in telling people what to think, but it is stunningly successful in telling its readers what to think *about.*" [85]

McCombs and Shaw's research breathed new life into the study of media effects and spurred a new generation of scholars to further investigate the **agenda-setting phenomenon.**[86] In 1982, Shanto Iyengar, Mark Peters, and Donald Kinder, for example, tackled a significant question left unanswered by McCombs and Shaw's research. Since McCombs and Shaw's conclusions were based on comparing aggregated cross-sectional survey data to media content, they were not able to demonstrate that media coverage *caused* voters to consider certain issues more important than others. To explain further, McCombs and Shaw had surveyed Chapel Hill voters at one point in time (therefore collecting what scientists call cross-sectional data) and then lumped them all together (meaning they aggregated the voters) to compare what voters as a group indicated were their campaign priorities with what issues were covered by the media. Thus, their research was not able to establish that the news coverage *caused* individual voters to consider particular issues important. Why not? Because perhaps it was the case that the media simply reflected the priorities of the voters. The media might have anticipated the interests of voters and therefore covered those issues they thought would draw the largest audience. Figure 3-3 illustrates this conundrum. Thus, the question remains:

Figure 3-3 Sorting Out Causal Relationships

Cross-sectional data do not allow us to sort out the causal relationship between two variables. Let's say we see an association between the amount of media coverage of global warming and the importance citizens assign to that issue. Does the association occur because the media coverage causes people to think global warming is important? Or, does the association occur because people think global warming is important, which causes the media to devote more attention to the issue? This is known as the reverse causality problem. To solve this problem (and thus establish the direction of the causal arrow), scholars often use experimental research designs.

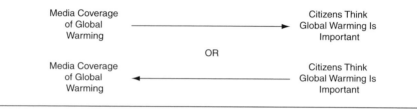

do the media cause voters to think certain issues are important, or do voters think certain issues are important and the media cover those issues as a result?

To untangle this causal relationship, Iyengar, Peters, and Kinder conducted an agenda-setting experiment using citizens of New Haven, Connecticut, as subjects.[87] By paying subjects $20 to participate in their experiment, they were able to recruit a group of participants who mirrored the characteristics of New Haven citizens. Six days in a row during November 1980, subjects reported to an office at Yale University, which had been transformed into a casual setting for television viewing. The researchers "encouraged participants to watch the news just as they did at home."[88] In this way, they tried to make the context as natural as possible to ensure their results could be generalized beyond the experimental setting. Therefore, by recruiting a mix of people to participate in their study and creating a comfortable setting for watching the news, Iyengar et al. took steps to ensure their experiment was high in **external validity.**

When subjects arrived on the first day, they were asked to complete a questionnaire on political topics. Embedded in this survey were questions that asked subjects to rate the importance of several national problems. Over the next four days, subjects watched videotapes of the prior evening's network newscast, or so they thought. On the last day, subjects completed another questionnaire that repeated the problem importance questions.

Now, there are three crucial details here. First, the newscasts were not truly from the night before. Instead, the experimenters created newscasts based partially on what had been shown the night before, but with specific types of stories either added or deleted. Second, the experimenters created two different versions of the newscast. In one version, stories describing problems with U.S. defense capabilities were inserted in the middle of the broadcast, while no such stories were included in the other version. Thus, the researchers had complete control over the characteristics of the experimental treatment (i.e., the newscasts). And third, subjects were randomly assigned to view either the newscasts that emphasized weaknesses in U.S. military preparedness or the newscasts that did not mention the issue. In other words, it was chance alone that determined whether subjects saw the defense-related news stories or whether they saw newscasts without those stories. As a result of this random assignment, the subjects in the two conditions were essentially the same. Overall then, this process of **random assignment** of subjects to conditions and **experimenter control** over the treatment ensures that the only difference between the two groups is that one viewed newscasts with the defense stories and the other did not. Thus, if the subjects in the two conditions express different opinions on the final questionnaire, we know that it is due to the experimental treatment because all other factors have been held constant.

And indeed, this was just the case. Subjects who viewed the newscasts emphasizing the problems with U.S. military preparedness changed their opinions and rated defense issues as much more important in the postexperiment questionnaire than in the initial questionnaire. Before viewing the newscasts, the subjects ranked defense as the sixth most important out of eight problems. After watching the newscasts, defense jumped to the second most important problem. Furthermore, their attitudes on the importance of other issues did not change, and subjects in the control condition did not change their ranking on the importance of defense as a national problem.

In addition to studying agenda setting, Iyengar and colleagues examined media **priming effects** in these two experiments.[89] The researchers hypothesized that the issues emphasized by the media would become the same issues citizens used to evaluate political leaders. For example, if the media covered defense topics, then a president's performance on that issue would become a salient factor shaping opinion toward the president in general. This is exactly what they found. After viewing stories on the inadequacies in the defense system, subjects views' of President Jimmy Carter on *that issue* were a stronger predictor of their overall evaluation of Carter than in the condition in which subjects did not see stories on defense. In other words, the defense stories *primed* citizens to evaluate the president along those lines.

Framing. In addition to agenda setting and priming, scholars have also identified media **framing effects.** Framing is defined as "the process by which a communication source, such as a news organization, defines and constructs a political issue or public controversy."[90] Media frames identify which aspects of a problem are relevant and important, and they imply which characteristics of a problem are not significant. They also influence what aspects of a story are remembered.[91] A framing effect occurs when media frames influence public opinion on the issue being framed. To illustrate frames and framing effects, we turn to another important research project conducted by Shanto Iyengar.[92]

Iyengar examined television news framing of poverty between 1981 and 1986. He identified 191 poverty-related stories on CBS, NBC, and ABC news during this period. The stories were framed in either episodic or thematic terms. **Episodic frames** focused on individual poor people, whereas **thematic frames** emphasized poverty as a societal problem. For example, an episodic story on poverty might focus on a young, single mother who is trying to make ends meet after losing her job. In contrast, a thematic story might discuss the nation's poverty rate. Obviously the topic of both stories is poverty, but one leads your attention to the characteristics of the poor person, whereas the other leads you to focus on poverty as a problem faced by the country as a whole. Iyengar found that the episodic frame dominated news coverage during the early to mid-1980s: two-thirds of the stories on poverty were framed in terms of particular victims of poverty.

Do these media frames influence public opinion? Iyengar answered this question by conducting an experiment to test whether the different frames influenced how people assign responsibility for poverty. Iyengar recruited subjects from the Suffolk County, New York, area and paid them $10 to watch a twenty-one minute videotape containing seven news stories. Subjects were randomly assigned to view either a thematic or episodic story on poverty, which was embedded as the fourth story in the broadcast. After viewing the video, subjects completed a questionnaire asking about responsibility for the problem of poverty. Specifically, to measure **causal responsibility,** individuals were asked, "In your opinion, what are the most important causes of poverty?"[93] And to measure **treatment responsibility,** individuals were asked, "If you were asked to prescribe ways to reduce poverty, what would you suggest?"[94] Iyengar then coded up to four responses for each question. The responses fell into one of two categories: citizens assigned responsibility either to individual poor people or to more general societal factors.

Did the frames influence how citizens attributed responsibility for poverty? Indeed they did. Subjects exposed to the episodic frame were significantly more likely to hold individuals responsible for causing and treating their own poverty and less likely to point to societal factors. The reverse occurred when subjects were exposed to the thematic frame; when the coverage emphasized the general phenomena of poverty, citizens were more likely to point to societal causes and solutions and less likely to hold individuals responsible for their poverty. Ironically, media coverage that highlights individual people and their plight leads citizens to point the finger of blame at the poor themselves. Overall then, the dominance of the episodic frame in media coverage of poverty has clear implications for how citizens think about the issue.

Another important aspect of Iyengar's study is the influence of race on public opinion. In the episodic framing condition, Iyengar also varied whether the poor person depicted in the news story was black or white. When the poor person was black, subjects were significantly more likely to indicate that poor people should solve their own problems and less likely to point to societal solutions for poverty. Thus, citizens' responses to poverty are at least partially driven by whether the poor person is black or white.

Thomas Nelson, Rosalee Clawson, and Zoe Oxley also examined media framing effects, but they took the research a step further by specifying the psychological mechanism that leads to such effects.[95] These scholars studied media coverage of a Ku Klux Klan (KKK) rally held in Chillicothe, Ohio. They identified two frames used by local television news stations to cover the event: **free speech** and **public order.** A newscast using the free speech frame emphasized the right of the KKK to speak and included images of KKK leaders speaking before a microphone. Several Klan supporters were interviewed and said they wanted to hear the Klan's message. One man said, "I came down here to hear what they have to say and I think I should be able to listen if I want to."[96] In contrast, a newscast with the public order frame focused on the possibility that violence would erupt at the rally between protestors and the Klan. The news story included images of police officers standing between the Klan members and the protesters. A bystander who was interviewed said, "Here you have a potential for some real sparks in the crowd."[97]

To examine what impact these frames had on tolerance for the KKK, Nelson et al. conducted an experiment using actual news coverage of the rally. They recruited college students enrolled in introductory political science courses to participate in the experiment. These subjects were randomly assigned to view either the free speech frame or the public order frame and then were asked to complete a survey that included a variety of questions, including two measuring tolerance for the Klan. The first question asked, "Do you support or oppose allowing members of the Ku Klux Klan to hold public rallies in our city?" The second asked, "Do you support or oppose allowing members of the Ku Klux Klan to make a speech in our city?"[98] Subjects responded on 7-point scales ranging from *strongly oppose* (1) to *strongly support* (7). Those exposed to the free speech frame were significantly more likely to support the KKK's right to rally and speak than those in the public order condition (see Figure 3-4). The free speech frame increased political tolerance for the Klan by more than one-half of a point on a 7-point scale. This is both a statistically and substantively significant increase in support for the Klan's right to participate in the public arena.

Nelson et al. also collected data in their experiment to understand the psychological mechanism leading to these framing effects. Previous scholars had hypothesized an **accessibility model** to explain why priming and framing effects occur. This perspective emphasizes that citizens are limited information processors operating in a complex political world. Since there is no way people can deal with all the information in their environment, they make judgments based on the most readily available considerations. The political context, such as news frames, makes certain concepts more accessible than others. In turn, these accessible concepts influence how citizens evaluate the issue that is being framed. For example, the free speech frame makes concepts like freedom and liberty accessible. Thus, when citizens are asked whether the Klan should be allowed to rally after exposure to the

Figure 3-4 Political Tolerance by Framing Condition

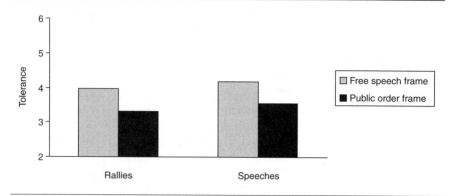

Source: Data from Thomas E. Nelson, Rosalee A. Clawson, and Zoe M. Oxley, "Media Framing of a Civil Liberties Conflict and Its Effect on Tolerance," *American Political Science Review* 91 (1997): 572.

Note: Higher numbers on 7-point scales indicate greater tolerance.

free speech frame, freedom and liberty are uppermost in their minds. These accessible concepts encourage citizens to support the Klan's rights. At least that is the mechanism according to the proponents of the accessibility model.

Nelson, Clawson, and Oxley, however, suggested an **importance model** instead. They argued that not all equally accessibly concepts will have an equal effect on political evaluations. In other words, just because freedom and liberty are accessible does not mean they will automatically influence citizen judgment. Nelson et al. proposed a more thoughtful model of information processing, which says that citizens will judge some accessible concepts more important than others. And those important or relevant concepts will be the ones that influence opinion.

To test these competing hypotheses, Nelson et al. randomly assigned subjects to either an accessibility or importance condition. In the accessibility condition, subjects were asked to respond to series of letter strings flashed on their computer screens. Subjects had to indicate whether each letter string was a word or a nonword. The task included words made accessible by the free speech frame (i.e., freedom, liberty, independence, and rights) and by the public order frame (i.e., violence, disorder, danger, and disturbance). How quickly subjects responded to the words indicates the accessibility of the words. This reaction time task is a standard method that psychologists use to measure accessibility.[99] Nelson et al. found that regardless of the framing condition, the public order and free speech concepts were equally accessible. Thus, differences in accessibility could not explain why subjects were more tolerant in the free speech framing condition than in the public order framing condition. This pattern of reaction time results allows them to rule out the accessibility hypothesis.

Nelson and colleagues provided evidence, however, that the importance model explains how framing effects occur. In the importance condition, subjects were asked to evaluate the importance of certain values related to free speech and public order. For example, subjects were asked to indicate "how IMPORTANT each of these ideas is to you when you think about the question of whether or not the Ku Klux Klan should be allowed to make speeches and hold demonstrations in public": "Freedom of speech for all citizens is a fundamental American right" and "There is always a risk of violence and danger at Ku Klux Klan rallies." [100] The researchers found that public order values were deemed significantly more important after exposure to the public order frame, and free speech values were viewed as slightly more important in the free speech framing condition. As a result, these important values were weighted more heavily when determining support for the KKK's right to participate. In sum, frames influence which values citizens view as most important to the matter at hand, which leads to changes in public opinion regarding the issue.[101]

This research offers a more redeeming view of citizens. Rather than being buffeted around willy-nilly by whichever considerations are made most salient by a media frame as suggested by the accessibility model, citizens engage in a more thoughtful process of weighing the importance of certain values as they form their opinions.[102]

Much of the work on framing effects has been done using experimental methods. Experiments, of course, are wonderful tools for testing causal hypotheses, but they are often more limited when it comes to generalizability because many experiments are conducted on college students. Paul Kellstedt's research on the impact of media framing on racial attitudes provides evidence that framing effects occur beyond the experimental laboratory, thus bolstering the case for the generalizability of these effects.[103]

Kellstedt argued that many citizens hold conflicting core values that influence their thinking on issues of race. On the one hand, citizens value **egalitarianism**; they believe everyone is of equal worth and should be treated the same before the law. On the other hand, citizens value **individualism**; they believe that people should get ahead through their own efforts and should pull themselves up by their own bootstraps. When it comes to racial policy preferences, egalitarians are more likely to support government activities designed to ensure blacks have the same opportunities as whites to succeed, whereas individualists are more likely to oppose such activities. Since many citizens hold both values to be dear, how do they figure out whether to support or oppose government programs intended to assist blacks? Kellstedt argued that citizens rely on egalitarian and individualist cues from the media to help determine their racial policy preferences.

To test this hypothesis, Kellstedt began by examining news coverage of race. Specifically, he content analyzed egalitarian and individualism frames in *Newsweek* stories on race between 1950 and 1994. He found that egalitarianism was a common frame during the 1960s but became less so after the mid-1970s. In contrast, individualism cues were fairly rare until the late 1970s, at which point they were used with greater regularity. The number of individualism cues peaked in the early 1990s.

Next, Kellstedt pulled together aggregate public opinion data on racial issues from this same time period by relying on surveys from a variety of polling organizations. He showed that public opinion on issues of race fluctuated a great deal during this roughly forty-year period. Citizens were significantly more liberal on racial issues in the mid-1990s than they were in the early 1950s, but there was by no means a constant march in the liberal direction. Instead, one might think of the pattern as a dance step: for every two steps forward, you take one step—and sometimes more—back.

Lastly, Kellstedt compared the longitudinal data on media framing with these longitudinal public opinion data. He found that changes in media framing of values explain variations in racial policy preferences across time. When the egalitarian frame became more prominent in the media, citizens' racial attitudes became significantly more liberal. In contrast, the individualism frame led to slightly more conservative racial policy opinions. Thus, Kellstedt's "real world" research confirms what many experimental researchers have found in the laboratory: media frames influence public opinion.

In sum, agenda setting, priming, and framing constitute what are known as subtle media effects. Researchers in this tradition have not found the widespread persuasion effects suggested by the hypodermic model, nor is their evidence consistent with the minimal effects model. Instead, researchers have shown how the media can influence public opinion by (a) affecting what the public thinks about, (b) affecting which issues shape evaluations of leaders, and (c) affecting which considerations are viewed as most important when assessing a political issue.

Limits on Subtle Effects

Are there limits on subtle media effects? Can the media set the agenda to such an extent we would consider it controlling the agenda? Can the media prime issues so much they overwhelmingly determine how candidates and politicians will be judged? Can the media frame political issues and therefore manipulate public opinion? These are important questions that emerge out of the research on subtle effects.

James Druckman moves us toward answering these questions by examining whether there are limits on framing effects.[104] Specifically, he asks, *who* can successfully frame an issue? He argues that citizens look to trusted, credible elites for guidance when determining their issue positions. Therefore, credible communication sources should be able to effectively frame public opinion, while less credible sources should not be able to do so. Druckman set up an experiment to test this hypothesis using a college student sample. He first identified two ways in which assistance to poor people is framed: government expenditures or humanitarianism. The **government expenditures frame** focuses on how providing money to the poor increases government spending, whereas the **humanitarian frame** emphasizes the needs of poor people. Subjects were randomly assigned to read one of those two frames and were then asked to provide their opinion on a 7-point scale regarding whether Congress should increase or decrease assistance to the poor. If the framing effect works, we would expect subjects in the humanitarian condition to be more supportive of spending on poor people than subjects in the government expenditures condition.

There is one more crucial detail, however. Druckman also varied whether the frames were presented by a credible or noncredible source. To identify a credible source and a noncredible source, Druckman conducted a pretest in which he asked participants—also college students—to rate seven people according to how trustworthy and knowledgeable they were about the issue at hand. The seven people were Colin Powell, Ross Perot, Bill Maher, Bob Dole, Geraldo Rivera, Dennis Miller, and Jerry Springer. The participants selected Colin Powell as the most trustworthy and knowledgeable and Jerry Springer as the least.

Based on that pretest, Druckman created (what looked to be) statements from either Colin Powell's Web site or Jerry Springer's Web site (see Table 3-3). Thus,

Table 3-3 Framing Assistance to the Poor: Government Expenditures and Humanitarian Frames

Government expenditures frame	Humanitarian frame
On his Web page, [talk show host Jerry Springer OR former chairman of the Joint Chiefs of Staff Colin Powell] has a section called "Talk Back" where he solicits opinions on various issues and current events. Recently, he posed the following: "In the next few weeks, the U.S. Congress will likely accept one of two proposals that will alter the amount of federal assistance to the poor. One proposal is to increase assistance while the other is to decrease assistance. An increase in assistance to the poor would lead to an increase in government spending. A decrease in assistance would allow the government to cut excessive expenditures. Do you think Congress should increase or decrease assistance to the poor?"	On his Web page, [talk show host Jerry Springer OR former chairman of the Joint Chiefs of Staff Colin Powell] has a section called "Talk Back" where he solicits opinions on various issues and current events. Recently, he posed the following: "In the next few weeks, the U.S. Congress will likely accept one of two proposals that will alter the amount of federal assistance to the poor. One proposal is to increase assistance while the other is to decrease assistance. An increase in assistance to the poor would ensure help for many people who need it. A decrease in assistance would prevent people from receiving basic support. Do you think Congress should increase or decrease assistance to the poor?"

Source: James N. Druckman, "On the Limits of Framing Effects: Who Can Frame?" *Journal of Politics* 63 (2001): 1062.

the assistance to the poor frames were attributed to either Colin Powell in the high-credibility condition or Jerry Springer in the low-credibility condition. If framing effects depend on the credibility of the source as hypothesized by Druckman, then we would expect subjects in the humanitarian condition to be more supportive of assistance to the poor than subjects in the government expenditures condition *only* when the statement is attributed to Colin Powell. And that is exactly what Druckman found. His results are presented in Figure 3-5. Subjects who read the humanitarian message from Colin Powell were significantly more supportive of spending on the poor than subjects who read a Colin Powell government expenditures message. In contrast, subjects exposed to a Jerry Springer message were only slightly more likely to support assistance for the poor in the humanitarian condition than in the government expenditures condition. The difference was not statistically significant. Therefore, returning to Druckman's original question: Who can successfully frame an issue? Credible sources can frame an issue.

As with Nelson, Clawson, and Oxley's research on framing effects, Druckman's study provides a more redeeming view of citizens. His study shows that citizens are not simply victims of manipulation on the part of elites; instead, citizens react to cues that make sense—whether the elite is a credible source. We might be worried, for example, if citizens' opinions on crime policy were influenced by a Jerry Springer show on "how my mother stole my jailhouse boyfriend," but it seems much more reasonable for citizens to look to people such as Colin Powell for guidance on critical issues of the day.

Figure 3-5   Support for Assistance to the Poor by Framing Condition by Source Expertise

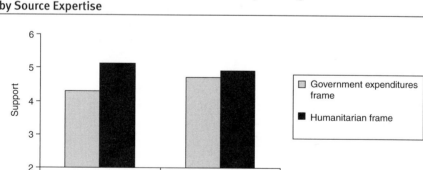

Source: Data from James N. Druckman, "On the Limits of Framing Effects: Who Can Frame?" *Journal of Politics* 63 (2001): 1051.

Note: Higher numbers on 7-point scales indicate greater support for assistance to the poor.

CONCLUSION

Do the mass media live up to democratic ideals? Overall, participatory democratic theorists would say no. In a perfect world, the media should be free from government and economic control, and they should inform and educate the public, provide a forum for diverse views, and hold government officials accountable. The reality is much different. The media in the United States are best characterized by the three Cs: corporate, concentrated, and conglomerate. Further, the norms of objectivity, neutrality, accuracy, beats, and newsworthiness often result in news that is biased toward the perspectives of powerful officeholders. Participatory democratic theorists would argue, however, that all is not lost. Nonprofit media, the minority press, and the Internet offer alternatives to the dominance of conglomerates, and not all journalists are constrained by the news norms that favor elites.

Elite democratic theorists have a much different view about whether the media live up to democratic ideals. Compared with participatory democratic theorists, they have much lower expectations for citizens in a democracy, and as a result, they also have much lower expectations for the media. Because the media are relatively free from government control and provide citizens with enough information to go to the polls and cast a ballot, elite democrats are pleased. The influence of economic forces and the emphasis on official sources simply do not raise the same concerns for elite democrats.

Are citizens influenced by the mass media? The answer to that question has changed over time. Scholars originally proposed a hypodermic model of media effects, which said that the media were extremely powerful and would persuade unsophisticated citizens with their messages. This model went by the wayside, however, when little evidence was found to support it. Next, the minimal effects model emerged. This model argued that citizens would filter media messages through their preexisting attitudes. Instead of converting citizens to a new point of view, media messages were more likely to reinforce and activate current predispositions.

Most recently, scholars have found substantial evidence to support a subtle effects model of media influence. This tradition argues that the media influence citizens through agenda setting, priming, and framing: the media influence what citizens think about, what issues citizens bring to bear when evaluating candidates and officeholders, and what considerations shape their thinking on political issues.

Overall, both participatory and elite democratic theorists can find things to like about the subtle effects model. On the one hand, elite democrats would find it natural for citizens to take cues from the media. Citizens are not expected to follow politics day in and day out; thus, it makes sense that the media would provide guidance for what issues are important and how politicians and issues should be evaluated. On the other hand, participatory democratic theorists would be pleased that citizens take in media messages in a thoughtful way and do not simply fall prey to elite manipulation.

KEY CONCEPTS

accessibility model / 85
accuracy / 73
activation effect / 80
advocacy journalism / 76
agenda-setting phenomenon / 81
causal responsibility / 84
concentrated / 65
conglomerate / 68
content analysis / 66
conversion effect / 80
corporations / 62
egalitarianism / 87
entertainment / 76
episodic frames / 84
experimenter control / 83
external validity / 82
forum for diverse views / 61
framing effects / 83
free speech frame / 85
game schema / 74
governing schema / 76
government expenditures frame / 89
hard news / 63
humanitarian frame / 89
hypodermic model / 79
importance model / 86

individualism / 87
intermediary / 61
Internet / 72
minimal effects model / 79
minority press / 71
neutrality / 73
news norms / 72
newsbeats / 73
newsworthiness / 73
nonprofit media corporations / 69
objectivity / 72
official sources / 73
pack journalism / 75
priming effects / 83
public order frame / 85
random assignment / 83
reinforcement effect / 80
soft news / 63
subtle effects model / 81
tabloid journalism / 76
thematic frames / 84
traditional journalism / 76
treatment responsibility / 84
two-step flow of communication / 80
watchdog / 61

SUGGESTED SOURCES FOR FURTHER READING

Gans, Herbert J. *Deciding What's News,* 25th anniversary ed. Evanston, Ill.: Northwestern University Press, 2004.

This classic book uses content analysis and participant observation to understand how news organizations and journalists decide what is news.

Iyengar, Shanto. *Is Anyone Responsible? How Television Frames Political Issues.* Chicago: University of Chicago Press, 1991.

Iyengar, Shanto, and Donald R. Kinder. *News That Matters.* Chicago: University of Chicago Press, 1987.

In a series of experiments, these authors provide evidence of agenda setting, priming, and framing effects.

Kaid, Lynda Lee, ed. *Handbook of Political Communication Research.* Mahwah, N.J.: Erlbaum, 2004.

This compelling collection of essays provides an overview of political communication research. The edited volume is divided into six sections: Theories and Approaches to Political Communication; Political Messages; News Media Coverage of Politics, Political Issues, and Political Institutions; Political Communication and Public Opinion; International Perspectives on Political Communication; and New Trends in Political Communication Channels and Messages.

Kinder, Donald R. "Communication and Politics in the Age of Information." In *Oxford Handbook of Political Psychology,* ed. David O. Sears, Leonie Huddy, and Robert Jervis. Oxford: Oxford University Press, 2003.

In this chapter, the author provides an excellent review of the media effects literature.

Overholser, Geneva, and Kathleen Hall Jamieson, eds. *The Press.* Oxford: Oxford University Press, 2005.

This outstanding collection of essays examines the media as a critical institution in American democracy. The edited volume covers four topics: The Press and Democracy in Time and Space; The Functions of the Press in a Democracy; Government and the Press: An Ambivalent Relationship; and Structure and Nature of the American Press.

Wilson, Clint C. II, Félix Gutiérrez, and Lena M. Chao. *Racism, Sexism, and the Media: The Rise of Class Communication in Multicultural America,* 3rd ed. Thousand Oaks, Calif.: Sage Publications, 2003.

This compelling text reviews the research on minorities and the media. It is divided into six parts: Majority Rules: "Minorities" and the Media; Racialism in Entertainment Portrayals; Racialism in Public Communication; Women of Color in the Media; Strategies for Dealing with Racially Insensitive Media; and The Rise of Class Communication.

Jacobs, Ronald N. *Race, Media, and the Crisis of Civil Society: From Watts to Rodney King.* Cambridge: Cambridge University Press, 2000.
Rodriguez, América. *Making Latino News: Race, Language, Class.* Thousand Oaks, Calif.: Sage Publications, 1999.
Wolseley, Roland E. *The Black Press, U.S.A.,* 2nd ed. Ames: Iowa State University, 1990.

These books examine the role of the minority media in American society. The Jacobs book compares black and mainstream media coverage of three crucial events in Los Angeles: the Watts uprisings in 1965, the videotaped police beating of Rodney King in 1991, and the events after the police officers were found not guilty of assaulting Rodney King in 1992. The Rodriguez book discusses the history of Latino media and contemporary Latino news. The Wolseley book provides an insightful history of the black press.

FAIR (Fairness & Accuracy in Reporting): www.fair.org
Media Matters for America: http://mediamatters.org

These two groups monitor the media from a progressive perspective.

Accuracy in Media: www.aim.org
Media Research Center: www.mediaresearch.org

These two groups monitor the media from a conservative perspective.

Columbia Journalism Review: www.cjr.org

If you are interested in "Who Owns What," check out this Web site. It provides detailed information on the holdings of major media corporations.

CHAPTER 4

Attitude Stability and Attitude Change

"I DON'T BELIEVE a woman's freedom to live her own life, in all cases, outweighs the fetus's right to life," stated Al Gore when he ran for Congress in the 1970s.[1] While serving in Congress during the 1980s, letters that Gore sent to constituents contained statements consistent with his earlier opinion on abortion, such as, "Let me assure you that I share your belief that innocent human life must be protected and I have an open mind on how to further this goal" and "In my opinion, it is wrong to spend federal dollars for what is arguably the taking of human life."[2] By the time Gore ran for president in 2000, however, his opinion on abortion had changed. Gore had become consistently pro-choice. For instance, in a debate against his opponent, George W. Bush, Gore said the following: "I trust women to make the decisions that affect their lives, their destinies and their bodies. And I think a woman's right to choose ought to be protected and defended."[3]

Gore is not the only politician to have had a change of heart about abortion. As a member of the House of Representatives in the late 1960s, George Herbert Walker Bush was known to support abortion rights and was a strong advocate of family planning services offered by organizations such as Planned Parenthood.[4] Bush's views became more pro-life over the years, however, so much so that the National Right to Life Committee, a conservative group opposed to abortion, endorsed him when he ran for president in 1988.[5] And during his speech at the Republican National Convention that year, Bush said the following: "Is it right to believe in the sanctity of life and protect the lives of innocent children? My opponent says no—but I say yes. We must change from abortion—to adoption."[6]

The reason most commonly given to explain why Gore and Bush altered their attitudes is that they did so for electoral reasons. When representing Tennessee in the Congress, Gore's stated attitudes and voting record were more conservative on the abortion issue, reflecting the opinions of his constituents. As Gore began to consider running for president, his abortion statements became more pro-choice to coincide with the national Democratic Party on this issue. As for Bush, his personally more moderate views toward abortion gave way to Ronald Reagan's pro-life position once Bush agreed to run as Reagan's vice presidential candidate in 1980. Bush was perhaps also thinking about his own future within the

Republican Party, which has a strong pro-life plank in its platform, just as Gore's views changed to coincide with his national party. It is possible, of course, that these two actually did change their minds rather than only changing their public statements as their electoral situations transformed. Gore, for example, has stated that his opinion evolved once he learned more about how abortion rights are exercised in the United States. His early opposition to federal funding of abortions for poor women changed once he realized that holding back federal funding meant that for many women the choice to terminate a pregnancy was not available.[7] As for Bush, he has pointed to family to explain his switch. As he describes it, some of his grandchildren are adopted, yet they would not be members of Bush's family if their birth mothers had chosen to abort when they were pregnant.[8]

Politicians clearly change their minds about political issues, or at least the public pronouncements of their opinions. What about you? Do you find yourself changing opinions on political matters very often? What about the general public? Do you think **attitude change** is common or is **attitude stability** the norm? In chapter 2, we learned how children and adolescents develop their political attitudes. After this early socialization, do political attitudes remain the same throughout one's adulthood? If attitude change occurs, what causes this change? And, from a normative standpoint, what does it say about the public if attitude instability is more common than stability? We address these questions in this chapter, first by examining some evidence for attitude change and some for attitude stability. The remainder of the chapter will overview theories of attitude formation and change from one discipline—psychology—that has prominently influenced the political science study of public opinion.

ARE AMERICANS' ATTITUDES STABLE?

One way to assess whether people's attitudes remain the same over time is to survey people at one point in time about their political opinions and then ask them about the same opinions later. Recall from chapter 2 that this approach, known as a panel study, was the one used by Kent Jennings and Richard Niemi to assess attitudes among high school seniors and their parents at various ages for both groups. Across the years, numerous panel studies been conducted as part of the American National Election Study (ANES) series, allowing researchers to study attitude stability and change among the general public. ANES surveys have been carried out at least every two years, coinciding with presidential and congressional elections, since 1948.[9] While in most years the ANES is a **cross-sectional study**—a survey utilizing a new representative sample of adults—periodically since 1948 panel studies have been conducted whereby previous respondents are reinterviewed.

Individual Attitude Change

One of the very first empirical analyses of political attitude stability was conducted by Philip Converse, using data from ANES's 1956, 1958, and 1960 panel study.[10] This study questioned respondents about salient political issues of the day in each of the three years. These issues included domestic and foreign policy issues such as school desegregation, federal aid to education, the creation of a fair employment practices commission to prevent racial discrimination in employment, and military aid to fight communism. Respondents were also asked their party identification. Comparisons of respondents' political attitudes in 1958 with their attitudes in 1960 are presented in Table 4-1. To measure the degree to which individuals' attitudes were stable, Converse calculated tau-b correlation coefficients, which are presented in the first column of Table 4-1. When tau-b equals 1.0, everyone's attitude was the same in 1960 as it had been in 1958. The smaller the value of tau-b, the more people's attitudes fluctuated over these two years. Another way to compare temporal attitude stability is to determine how many people kept the same opinion at two points in time. We present our results from such an analysis in the second column of the table. Figures here are the percentage of respondents whose opinions stayed on the same side of an issue or their party allegiance was to the same party (or they were politically independent) from 1958 to 1960. Political attitudes are considered stable by this measure even if someone changed from strong to weak agreement or strong to weak partisanship over time. The final column of the table presents the percentage of respondents who expressed no opinion toward the policy issues in either 1958 or 1960, or in both years.

As we see from the results in Table 4-1, party identification was the most stable political attitude over these two years. In fact, the value of tau-b for party identification is significantly higher than the tau-b for any of the other attitudes.

Table 4-1 Stability of Individual Political Attitudes from 1958 to 1960

Political attitude	Correlation between attitudes in 1958 and 1960 (tau-b)	Percentage holding the same attitude in 1958 and 1960	Percentage having no opinion in at least one year
Party identification	.73	85.7	N/A
School desegregation	.43	57.5	15.8
Employment discrimination	.41	60.0	17.9
Guaranteed employment	.41	56.5	15.2
Isolationism	.39	59.6	16.3
Federal aid to education	.38	57.2	13.8
Foreign economic aid	.34	48.0	21.4
Foreign military aid	.32	56.7	24.9
Federal housing	.29	40.7	33.9

Sources: Philip E. Converse, "The Nature of Belief Systems in Mass Publics," in *Ideology and Discontent*, ed. David E. Apter (New York: Free Press, 1964), 240; Analysis of American National Election Studies 1956–58–60 Panel Data File.

For most people, their party affiliation remained the same from 1958 to 1960. Converse attributes this to the fact that attitudes and affect toward groups, such as political parties, help to organize the political opinions of many people. Since party identification was the only attitude surveyed "that touches on pure affect toward a visible population grouping," it came as no surprise to Converse that these attitudes remained quite stable over two years.[11]

In contrast, attitude instability was much more common for the policy issues, with between 40 and 60 percent of the public holding the same opinion over time versus nearly 86 percent for party allegiance. Among the policy issues queried, citizens' attitudes toward racial employment discrimination, isolationist foreign policy, and school desegregation were the least likely to change. Opinions about foreign aid and whether the federal government should be involved in providing housing and electric power were especially likely to fluctuate. To explain why there were these differences in attitude stability across issues, Converse points to the fact that some issues, even domestic ones, were less significant to citizens in the late 1950s.[12] Stable attitudes are more likely toward objects that tend to influence people's everyday lives (such as jobs or schools) or toward salient groups (such as blacks). When issues are more remote, attitude instability is more common.

People's political attitudes could change for a number of reasons. Citizens' opinions are susceptible to change, for instance, in the face of real world events. Current events can provide new information to citizens as well as perhaps new understandings of issues, both of which can produce changes in attitudes. Converse considered this possibility but ruled it out as an explanation for the attitude instability he observed. In the late 1950s, high-profile news events did occur that could have influenced attitudes toward some issues that Converse studied, but not all. The public witnessed standoffs and violence in school desegregation cases in the southern United States, such as the integration of Central High School in Little Rock, Arkansas, in 1957 when Army soldiers were required to escort black students into the formerly all-white high school. News also broke of waste in foreign aid spending during these years. Yet for one of the issues where the public's attitudes were the least stable, the role of the federal government in providing housing, there were no changes in federal policy or other relevant newsworthy items during these years that might have produced public attitude change. Converse also witnessed that the average correlations between people's attitudes were the same, and were similarly low, between 1956 and 1958, between 1958 and 1960, and between 1956 and 1960. One might expect that attitudes would fluctuate more the longer the interval is between measuring the attitudes. This was not the case, leading Converse to turn to explanations for instability other than responses to changing events.

Ultimately, Converse concluded that many citizens' policy opinions are meaningless and might be better characterized as **nonattitudes** than attitudes.[13] Converse argued that "large portions of an electorate do not have meaningful beliefs, even on issues that have formed the basis for intense political controversy among elites for substantial periods of time." [14] If public attitudes were well developed, carefully considered, and based on detailed information, according to Converse, they likely would not change as much as he observed. Converse's statements might seem extreme and unnecessarily harsh, especially when you consider that, according to Table 4-1, a majority of the public did hold opinions on the same side of most issues between 1958 and 1960. Examining temporal attitude stability was only one portion of Converse's research, however, and his conclusions were based on a variety of other analyses. In particular, Converse demonstrated that most people's opinions are not well grounded in broader beliefs (such as liberalism or conservatism) and are not well organized. [15] We will discuss these other conclusions more thoroughly in chapter 5.

Yet, even thinking only about Converse's evidence of attitude change, it is fair to ask how many Americans should have stable attitudes for one to conclude that the public's policy opinions are meaningful. Is our standard 100 percent? If so, then any deviation from this might lead to conclusions similar to Converse's. In fact, it was empirical evidence such as this that fostered the development of the theories of democratic elitism and pluralism. Recall from chapter 1 that these theorists compared empirical research about the public's capabilities with classical democratic theorists' expectations about the public and concluded that the public was not living up to the classical model. By using a different standard, however, perhaps one recognizing that some policy issues are complex and are not central to most people's daily lives, levels of attitude stability apparent in the late 1950s might seem reasonable and not too low.

COLLECTIVE ATTITUDE STABILITY

We turn now to an examination of the stability of **collective public opinion,** that is, the aggregate political opinions of the public. In the most detailed over-time analysis of collective opinion, Benjamin Page and Robert Shapiro analyzed results from public opinion surveys conducted over 50 years. Page and Shapiro's conclusions paint a very different picture than that emerging from studies of individuals. In their own words, "the American public, as a collectivity, holds a number of real, stable, and sensible opinions about public policy and ... these opinions develop and change in a reasonable fashion, responding to changing circumstances and to new information." [16]

Page and Shapiro's evidence for this conclusion consists primarily of comparing responses to survey questions that were asked at least two different times between 1935 and 1990. For 58 percent of these questions, aggregate public opinion did not change significantly over time. For instance, in 1942, approximately 75 percent of the American public believed that the United States should have an active rather than isolationist foreign policy. Fourteen years later, the percentage of Americans holding this attitude was also about 75 percent. Opinions on this topic did fluctuate a bit in the intervening years, but in a narrow range of 72 to 80 percent supporting activism over isolationism.

Turning to domestic matters, Page and Shapiro observed that opinions about government spending on a variety of programs did not fluctuate very much during the 1970s and 1980s. Consistently high percentages of the public (68–77 percent) felt that the government was spending too little to fight crime, while consistently low percentages (12–25 percent) felt that government was spending too little on welfare (see Figure 4-1). Attitudes toward government spending on Social Security were especially stable during the late 1980s (the years for which opinion data are available). The item displayed in Figure 4-1 that shows the most variation is beliefs about education spending. Whereas about 49 percent of the public felt the government spent too little on education in the early 1970s, this percentage gradually increased over the time period, reaching 68 percent in 1989.

While Page and Shapiro did find many examples of collective attitude stability, they did uncover some instances of attitude change. Unlike what we might expect given Converse's results, however, Page and Shapiro observed that collective atti-

Figure 4-1 Opinion toward Government Spending, 1971–1989

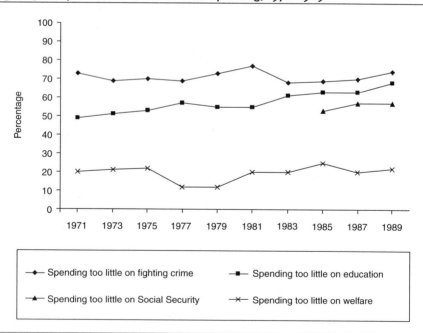

Source: Adapted from Figures 2.2, 4.1, and 4.3 of Benjamin I. Page and Robert Y. Shapiro, *The Rational Public: Fifty Years of Trends in Americans' Policy Preferences* (Chicago: University of Chicago Press, 1992), 49, 120, 126.

tude change was often modest in size and that large attitude swings over short periods of time were not very common. Opinion change was more likely to be gradual (slow, steady shifts in Americans' beliefs, often in response to changes in the broader social or political climate) than to fluctuate (increases in support followed by decreases, or vice versa, over a short period of time). We just observed such a gradual increase with education spending. Americans' opinions have also changed slowly over time for other domestic policy issues, such as racial integration of schools and capital punishment. Only about 30 percent of white Americans supported the integration of schools in 1942, for example, compared with 90 percent in 1985. As for capital punishment, support for the death penalty steadily increased from 47 percent in 1966 to 78 percent in 1985.

Page and Shapiro also explored the prevalence of abrupt opinion changes among the public. Abruptness, or a change of at least 10 percentage points within a year, was especially likely for foreign policy issues. Upon closer examination of these cases, Page and Shapiro concluded that these sudden opinion changes often happened in the wake of real world events: "wars, confrontations, or crises, in which major changes in the actions of the United States or other nations have understandably affected calculations about the costs and benefits of alternative policies."[17] Examples include a decline of 17 points in the percentage of Americans who sympathized with Israel regarding the long-running Arab-Israeli conflict. This decline was registered a few months after the Palestinian intifada (uprising) began in 1987 and the Israelis responded to the intifada with force, force that many felt was too severe.

Collective Public versus Individual Citizens

Throughout their book, Page and Shapiro contrast their image of aggregate public opinion as reasonable, meaningful, and largely stable with those presented in the empirical work of Converse and in the writings of America's founders, most especially James Madison and Alexander Hamilton, who asserted that the public was subject to fits of passion and that public opinion was expected to be volatile. How might we explain these discrepancies? Which view is correct? To answer these questions, we should first consider the differences in examining individual opinions versus the aggregate opinion of the public. Aggregate opinion can appear quite stable even if many individuals change their opinions, provided that the individual changes cancel each other out. Imagine, for example, that we surveyed ten people and six (or 60 percent) support increasing spending for fighting terrorism. One year later, we survey the same ten people and six have changed their minds: three who favored increasing spending now support spending decreases while three who wanted less spending now favor spending more. Even with all of these changes, our aggregate result is the same: 60 percent of our sample supports more money spent to fight terrorism. The same phenomenon can occur when surveying representative samples of the American public. Many over-time changes at the individual level can still result in temporal stability (or near stability) at the aggregate level. Thus, both Converse and Page and Shapiro are correct, in that their conclusions are appropriate for their level of analysis (individual or collective).

In describing the aggregation process, however, these researchers present different assumptions about what the aggregate results are really measuring. Page and Shapiro argue that individual changes, while perhaps frequent, are relatively minor deviations from true, enduring beliefs and values. Converse, in contrast, views the aggregation process as covering up the shallow, fleeting opinions of individual citizens. The sample quotations that follow present these contrasting views, with Page and Shapiro's appearing first:

> [A]t any given moment, the random deviations of individuals from their long-term opinions may well cancel out over a large sample, so that a poll or survey can accurately measure collective preferences as defined in terms of the true or long-term preferences of many individual citizens.[18]

> [I]t is quite possible, thanks to the hidden power of aggregation, to arrive at a highly rational system performance on the backs of voters, most of whom are remarkably ill-informed much of the time.[19]

Normatively, we might wonder whether it is better to think of the public as *individual citizens* or as a *collection of individuals*. Each approach is reasonable and well grounded in democratic theory. Many of these theories highlight the characteristics and capabilities of individual citizens, although theories reach different conclusions as to whether citizens are capable of ruling in a democracy or not. Yet, in positing a role for the citizens to influence public policy, as all democratic theories do, these theories must also focus on aggregate public opinion. Discussions of whether and to what extent the wishes of the public should influence the decisions of elected officials naturally revolve around the wishes of the aggregate public rather than the wishes of an individual citizen. Aggregating individuals' opinions is necessary for representation to occur, whether at the national level, state level, or congressional district level. In other words, if we want to know whether the national government is responsive to the wishes of the public's opinion toward, for instance, counterterrorism policies, we turn to aggregate measures of public opinion toward these policies. So, whether we adopt Converse's conclusions that individual's attitudes are unstable or Page and Shapiro's arguments that the aggregate public holds largely stable opinions depends in part on whether we are concerned about the democratic public as individual citizens or as a collective whose views might influence governmental decisions.

PSYCHOLOGICAL APPROACHES TO ATTITUDES

Psychologists have studied attitudes more thoroughly than scholars in any other academic discipline and have provided important theories and approaches for political scientists who examine political attitudes. In trying to understand attitude formation and change, psychologists place primary emphasis on individuals. Some psychological theories, for instance, focus on the influence of individual characteristics, such as personality traits, mood states, motivations, and core values, on political opinions. Other approaches examine how people learn and process new information, especially persuasive communication meant to change people's attitudes. Psychologists have also postulated many different routes to attitude change. To simplify, we can think of attitude change as occurring because of successful persuasion by another person or as a consequence of a different goal, such as the desire to fit in with one's peers. We provide examples of both of these situations in the following overview of some psychological theories of attitudes. While we do not have space to thoroughly review all of the work on attitudes in psychology, we highlight approaches that are especially relevant to political attitude formation and change.[20]

Functions of Attitudes

One approach to attitudes is to consider the functions they serve for individuals. **Functional theories** of attitudes highlight the motivations people have for holding the attitudes that they do. As one of these theorists put it, "attitudes should be viewed as strategies for meeting personal needs," especially those related to personality characteristics.[21] Of the many purposes that attitudes could serve, Daniel Katz identified four categories of functions.[22] For some people, attitudes serve a **utilitarian function.** People hold positive feelings toward objects that provide benefits, such as support for a tax policy that will increase one's income. Negative attitudes are held toward objects that prevent one from satisfying her needs or that inflict punishment. A second type of function is **ego defense.** Attitudes fulfill this purpose by protecting one's ego or image of himself from threats. These threats could be internal, such as denying certain negative characteristics about oneself. Katz particularly highlighted prejudice as resulting from ego-defense mechanisms. "When we cannot admit to ourselves that we have deep feelings of inferiority," he stated, "we may project those feelings onto some convenient minority group and bolster our egos by attitudes of superiority toward this underprivileged group."[23]

Katz's third attitude function is **knowledge.** Some individuals have a desire to understand the world around them and attitudes can help to fulfill this goal. In particular, our existing attitudes can help us sort through newly encountered information. Imagine, for instance, that someone holds a positive attitude toward Democrats and learns that a Democratic politician is proposing a new policy toward immigration. He can use the knowledge that his attitude toward Democrats provides to arrive at support for the new immigration policy quickly without (or before) learning all of the details of the new policy.

Finally, attitudes that allow individuals to express their core beliefs and values perform a **value-expressive function.** A person who is deeply religious, for example, will feel satisfied and feel that her identity is being actualized if she holds political views that reflect her religiosity. Support for prayer in school or other expressions of religion in public life would be examples of such attitudes. Somewhat related to Katz's value-expressive motivation is **social adjustment**.[24] If social adjustment is an important goal for someone, he will express attitudes that conform to the views and values of peers in his social network. In this case, attitudes do not serve the function of actualizing one's self-concept but rather allow one to express values in order to "easily fit into, and establish smooth interactions with, peer and reference groups."[25]

According to functional theories of attitudes, the reasons why an attitude remains stable or the processes that result in attitude change depend on which function the attitude serves. Attitudes that serve a value-expressive function, for instance, are not very likely to change because they are grounded in one's concept of self. In Katz's own words, "The complacent person, smugly satisfied with all aspects of himself, is immune to attempts to change his values."[26] Attitude change will come about if a person's self-concept does change. Katz provides an example of a pacifist who, in the face of actual instances of unprovoked aggression toward a defenseless group, grows dissatisfied with holding pacifist values. As another example, attitudes that help one make sense of the world will likely change when they cease to provide such knowledge, such as when a person's views toward a group are found to be based on incorrect information. If you believed, for example, that women are not as decisive as men, you would probably evaluate female politicians less positively than male politicians regardless of whether the specific politicians are decisive or not. Repeated encounters with decisive women might cause you to update your stereotype about women, and then alter your attitudes toward female politicians.

Functional approaches to attitudes also suggest when persuasive appeals will succeed. Direct attempts to change someone's attitude will be more successful if the arguments are geared toward the function that the attitude is serving. One series of studies evaluated the success of different messages in persuading people for whom attitudes serve social adjustive versus value-expressive functions.[27] College students were exposed to arguments about the institutionalization of the mentally ill. Some participants were told that 70 percent of college students favored institutionalization. Information such as this resonated more strongly with participants for whom attitudes were presumed to fulfill a social adjustive function. In contrast, those holding attitudes for value-expressive reasons were more persuaded when told that support for institutionalization was based on values that these participants rated highly (particularly loving and responsibility). In other words, messages highlighting cherished values persuade people who hold value-expressive attitudes, whereas messages about the opinions of peer groups persuade people who express social adjustive attitudes.

Learning Theory

Some of our likes and dislikes are acquired through experience. When we are exposed to some stimuli, we receive positive reinforcement, such as feelings of happiness or rewards. Other stimuli provoke negative reactions in us, such as a punishment or fear. A child, for instance, could learn to like spinach if his parents feed him spinach while constantly saying positive things about the food, projecting happiness, and complimenting him when he eats it. In contrast, a sudden scream voiced by one parent when encountering a snake could instill in him negative attitudes toward snakes. Political attitudes can also be passed from parent to child in a similar fashion. A parent's frequent pairing of a political object, such as one of the political parties, with positive adjectives can create a positive attitude toward the party for a child, just as often hearing derogatory words used to describe members of a minority group ("lazy blacks" or "greedy Jews") can cultivate prejudiced attitudes.

With repeated exposure to attitude objects, then, we can learn to like or to dislike these stimuli. This is one basic premise of the **learning theory** of attitudes. More broadly, this theoretical approach assumes that attitudes are obtained much like habits are. In our daily lives, we learn about the attributes of attitude objects and the feelings associated with them; from these cognitions and affect, our attitudes develop. Attitudes are, in this view, a by-product of the learning process and individuals are rather passive actors in the acquisition of attitudes. We are exposed to stimuli, we learn about them, we receive positive or negative reinforcement from them, and along the way we develop attitudes.

Once attitudes are acquired via the learning process, they will tend to remain stable until new learning occurs. One learning opportunity is exposure to persuasive messages meant to change one's attitude. Conducting their research in the late 1940s and 1950s, Carl Hovland, Irving Janis, and Harold Kelley were among the first psychologists to apply the assumptions of learning theory to the topic of persuasion.[28] Their model highlighted the role of incentives in attitude change. Specifically, they argued that hearing a persuasive message is often not enough to change a person's attitude. Instead, the person must have incentives to change from his old to the new attitude suggested by the message. Incentives may be provided by the communicator. For instance, messages delivered by high-credibility or high-status persons are more likely to induce attitude change because people have more of an incentive to win the approval from such sources compared with low-credibility or low-status sources. Hovland et al. also found that certain individuals are more susceptible to persuasive messages. People for whom group memberships are very important, for example, have a stronger incentive to change their attitudes to coincide with persuasive communication delivered by other group members.

Transfer of Affect. According to learning theory, attitudes can also be influenced when the affect that is associated with one attitude object is transferred to a related object. Recall that individuals associate positive feelings toward objects that they like and negative feelings toward disliked objects. These feelings can be passed on to associated objects resulting in either a new attitude or attitude change, depending on whether an attitude already exists for the associated object. In politics, this principle helps us understand why politicians surround themselves with objects that evoke positive feelings for most people, such as the American flag. Politicians hope that the positive feelings citizens have for the flag will transfer to themselves, thus resulting in positive attitudes toward the politicians. Another tactic is for politicians to try to connect their opponents to stimuli that induce negative emotions (fear, disgust, etc.) for most Americans.

The **transfer of affect** from one object to another can happen quite automatically, especially for attitude objects that are relatively unfamiliar. Even affect that is aroused subliminally can be transferred.[29] Researchers conducted an experiment in which participants viewed slides of an unknown woman engaged in a variety of daily activities (shopping, walking into her apartment, washing dishes, etc.). Immediately before each slide, a photo was flashed, but flashed so quickly that the participants were not consciously aware of it. For some participants, these subliminal photos were meant to arouse positive affect, whereas for others all of these photos were meant to arouse negative affect. Examples of the former include pictures of a child with a doll and a pair of kittens. Photos intended to arouse negative affect included a bucket of snakes, a dead body on a bed, and an opened chest during surgery.

After viewing the subliminal photos and the slides, participants were asked their attitudes about the woman whose image appeared in the slides. Participants for whom positive affect was aroused liked the woman more and rated her personality more positively than did those for whom negative affect was aroused. Keep in mind that the study participants did not learn anything about this woman other than what they had seen in the slides, so they had little information on which to base their attitudes. The temporal association between the subliminally presented images and the slides of the woman was sufficient, though, to allow the affect of the former to influence attitudes of the latter.

Communication-Induced Attitude Change

Much attention in psychology has been placed on understanding how and when communication can influence attitudes. Some of this communication is directly designed to change people's attitudes. In contrast to such explicitly persuasive communication, other messages can influence attitudes without necessarily attempting to do so. Examples of the latter include news media stories. By providing new information and understandings of issues, media coverage of current events can influence attitudes even if the journalists' intent is not to do so. Of the many models of communication and attitude change that exist, we highlight two that we feel are especially relevant to understanding communication and political attitudes: Richard Petty and John Cacioppo's elaboration likelihood model of persuasion and John Zaller's receive-accept-sample model.

Petty and Cacioppo's Elaboration Likelihood Model. To understand persuasion, Petty and Cacioppo take a cognitive processing approach.[30] In particular, they consider the situations in which people will actively process persuasive communication versus the situations in which such processing is unlikely. At times individuals are motivated to process thoroughly a persuasive message, such as when the issue is personally relevant to them, they will be held accountable for their decision, or they have a high need for cognition (they enjoy thinking things through). In one study, for example, college students were given a message supporting the university's adoption of comprehensive exams as a graduation requirement.[31] Students who were told that the policy was under consideration for the following year paid much closer attention to the arguments than did those students who were told the policy would not be implemented, if at all, until the following decade. For the former group, the policy proposal was more relevant since it might be enacted while the students were still at the university.

Regardless of motivation, individuals and situations also differ in whether the ability to process a message is present. People are better able to process a message when they hold prior knowledge on the topic, are not distracted, are under no time pressure, and the message is comprehendible. When someone is motivated and able to process persuasive communication, attitude change may come about through what Petty and Cacioppo term the **central route to persuasion.** If motivation or ability or both are lacking, then persuasion may occur via an alternative route, the **peripheral route.** Petty and Cacioppo's approach is called a dual processing model because it posits very different cognitive processes depending on which persuasion route is followed (see Figure 4-2 for an illustration of the model).

In the central route, people attend to the content of persuasive messages, think carefully about the pros and cons of the arguments, and generate thoughts (cognitive responses) to the initial communication. In other words, people engage in substantial elaboration upon the communication in the central route (hence Petty and Cacioppo's choice of **elaboration likelihood** as the name of their model). And it is their internally generated cognitive responses that influence whether people's attitudes change: "If the thoughts are primarily favorable (pro-arguments), persuasion will result: but if the thoughts are primarily unfavorable (counterarguments), resistance will be more likely."[32] Further, if unfavorable cognitions predominate and are more persuasive to a person than are the arguments presented to him, attitudes could even move in a direction counter to the message.

Some key factors affect whether favorable or unfavorable thoughts predominate during elaboration. For one, argument quality is very important. Strong and compelling arguments are more likely to generate cognitive responses that favor the viewpoint presented in the message, whereas weak arguments tend to generate counterarguments. Second, during elaboration, some people might be

Figure 4-2 Petty and Cacioppo's Elaboration Likelihood Model

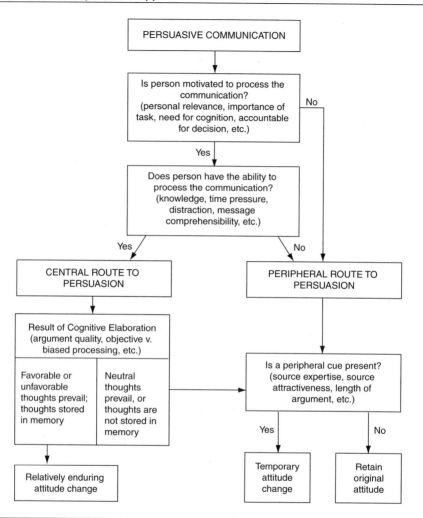

Sources: Adapted from Figure 9.3 in Richard E. Petty and John T. Cacioppo, *Attitudes and Persuasion: Classic and Contemporary Approaches* (Dubuque, Iowa: William C. Brown, 1981), 264, and Figure 1-1 in Richard E. Petty and John T. Cacioppo, *Communication and Persuasion* (New York: Springer-Verlag, 1986), 4.

predisposed to generate either favorable or unfavorable thoughts, regardless of the content of the persuasive arguments. Such biased processing can occur for individuals who possess prior knowledge of the topic or for whom existing attitudes are closely associated with their core values.[33] In the end, and when taking into consideration these and other factors, if exposure to persuasive communication generates largely favorable thoughts or largely unfavorable thoughts that are stored in memory, attitudes will shift in favor of the tenor of these cognitive responses. If primarily neutral responses are generated, or if the cognitive responses are transitory and not stored into memory, peripheral processing will take over.

In contrast to the elaboration that occurs along the central route, the peripheral route to persuasion can result in attitude change "without engaging in any extensive cognitive work relevant to the issue under consideration."[34] Rather than attending to the content of the arguments contained in persuasive messages, individuals' attitudes can be influenced by incidental cues. Such cues include characteristics of the source of the message. Under peripheral processing, if the source is an expert or is attractive, attitudes are more likely to change in favor of the viewpoint of the communication compared with arguments delivered by nonexpert or nonattractive sources. Message length can also provide a peripheral cue: longer messages result in more favorable attitude change. Note that under peripheral processing the message length and the source characteristics influence attitudes regardless of whether the arguments contained in the message are strong or weak. When a cue is present during peripheral processing, attitudes are likely to change, but the resulting attitude will be quite shallow, temporary, and susceptible to change in the future. On the other hand, attitudes that have been influenced by persuasive communication in the central route are much more likely to endure and will be fairly resistant to change because more thought has been devoted to the content of the communication.

Zaller's Receive-Accept-Sample Model. Petty and Cacioppo's model is broad enough to account for the persuasion of a wide variety of attitudes, certainly including political attitudes. John Zaller's receive-accept-sample model, however, was designed more explicitly to account for the formation and change of political attitudes.[35] In building his model, Zaller draws heavily on the work of psychologist William McGuire.[36] McGuire envisioned persuasion to be a multistage process. For people to be persuaded, he argued, they must be *exposed* to a persuasive message, they must *pay attention* to and *comprehend* the message, they *must accept* the communicator's arguments and change their attitude in favor of the advocated position, and they must *store* their new attitude in memory. If any of these steps are missed, the attempt at persuasion will fail. For example, if someone is exposed to and pays attention to persuasive arguments but does not understand the nature of the arguments, her attitudes will not be altered.

McGuire devoted much attention to delineating the factors that are influential at each stage of the persuasion process, including characteristics of both the message and the receiver of the communication. People are more likely to attend to and accept messages that are delivered by credible sources, for example, thus increasing the chance that these messages will induce attitude change. An individual characteristic such as intelligence influences the stages of comprehension and acceptance but in opposite fashion. Those with more intelligence are more likely to understand persuasive messages but are also less likely to accept them because they have a store of knowledge with which to counteract the arguments.

In his model of communication and attitude change, Zaller conceives of communication quite broadly. Rather than isolating discrete persuasive statements, Zaller examines the flow of political information that appears in the mass media. "This coverage," he writes, "may consist of ostensibly objective news reports, partisan argumentation, televised news conferences, or even paid advertisements, as in election campaigns."[37] Collectively, he refers to this communication as **elite discourse,** although he does not always specify whether elites are politicians, candidates, news reporters, or experts quoted in news stories. In fact, he often means to convey that any and all of these types of elites can provide political information to the citizenry—information that may come to influence the public's opinions.

In understanding the dynamics of public opinion formation and change, Zaller borrows from and extends McGuire's model. Of the stages that McGuire proposed, Zaller is primarily interested in exposure, attention, comprehension, and acceptance. He collapses the first three into one stage, **reception.** Since he wants to examine how the flow of elite discourse available in the political environment influences opinions, collapsing these stages made sense. For starters, it is very difficult empirically to measure whether citizens have been exposed to, paid attention to, and understood specific political arguments. Second, Zaller's model highlights an individual characteristic—political awareness—that functions in the same manner for all three stages. More specifically, people who are more politically aware are more likely to be exposed to elite discourse, to pay attention to it, and to understand its content. Thus, for Zaller, separately analyzing these three stages is unnecessary.

More importantly, and here is where Zaller's intellectual debt to McGuire is great, Zaller argues that the effect of elite discourse on attitudes will not be the same for all people. In other words, key individual characteristics mediate the effects of communication on attitudes. Chief among these is **political awareness.** As already mentioned, receipt of political messages is higher for more politically aware citizens. Those who do not follow politics closely are unlikely to receive information generated by political elites. Much as intelligence in McGuire's model, though, political awareness produces the opposite effect at Zaller's second stage of persuasion, **acceptance.** Awareness serves to reduce the likelihood that an individual will accept the premise of an argument that he has received. Simply stated, people who pay more attention to politics are "better able to evaluate and critically scrutinize the new information they encounter."[38]

Given these two relationships between political awareness and reception on the one hand and acceptance on the other, those who possess either low or high levels of awareness are not likely to have their attitudes influenced by elite discourse. Those with low levels of awareness are unlikely to receive political messages, whereas those highly aware are likely to rebut any political arguments they do receive. This means that those with the highest probability of having their attitudes changed by political discourse are people who possess moderate levels of awareness, a pattern displayed visually in Figure 4-3. Moderately aware citizens do receive some political messages but do not possess a large enough store of relevant knowledge with which to resist communication-induced attitude change.

As for other individual attributes that influence whether political messages will result in attitude change, Zaller focuses special attention on people's existing political orientations. These orientations, which he calls **political predispositions,** encompass core values, enduring beliefs, and experiences. Predispositions not only are the ingredients for specific policy opinions (those who value equality will have different political opinions from those who do not value equality, for example) but also mediate whether people accept the premises in elite discourse that they receive. Individuals are not likely to accept a message that is inconsistent with their predispositions. A conservative citizen who encounters a stream of liberal messages, such as arguments in favor of increasing government spending on social welfare policies, is unlikely to adopt the position of these messages because they conflict with her standing political views.

In Zaller's model, then, people are not necessarily passive vessels into which political opinions are poured. Instead, some citizens consider incoming arguments and decide whether to accept them. As Zaller correctly argues, though, the ability of a person to know which messages coincide with and which contradict his

Figure 4-3   Political Awareness in McGuire's and Zaller's Attitude Change Models

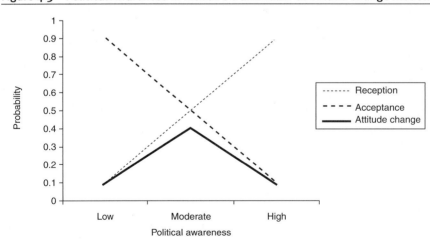

Sources: Based on arguments contained in William J. McGuire, "The Nature of Attitudes and Attitude Change," in *The Handbook of Social Psychology,* 2nd ed., vol. 3, ed. Gardner Lindzey and Elliot Aronson (Reading, Mass.: Addison-Wesley, 1969), and John R. Zaller, *The Nature and Origins of Mass Opinion* (Cambridge: Cambridge University Press, 1992).

predispositions increases with political awareness. In other words, those who are more politically aware are better able to see the connections between elite discourse and their own predispositions, whereas "politically inattentive persons will often be unaware of the implications of the persuasive communications they encounter, and so often end up 'mistakenly' accepting them." [39] Additionally, sometimes cues exist in the elite discourse to facilitate this connection. Such cues provide details regarding the implications of a political argument for one's predispositions. Often these cues are in the form of the partisan or ideological leanings of the source of the message. For example, when a Democratic politician criticizes President George W. Bush's counterterrorism policies, a Democratic citizen is more likely to accept this argument because she can assume, based on the source of the message, that the position advocated therein coincides with her existing political dispositions.

Illustrations of Zaller's Model. An illustration of Zaller's model is supplied by Dennis Chong.[40] Chong wondered if the campaigns on college campuses in the late 1980s and early 1990s to introduce hate speech codes influenced public tolerance toward racists. These codes were created in response to a number of racist incidents on campuses. They were designed to sanction students who directed derogatory speech toward other students based on the targeted students' characteristics, such as race or ethnicity. These codes were supported by some on the grounds that such speech could create a hostile learning environment for the targeted students. Debate about the hate speech codes received attention far beyond the college campuses affected, prompting Chong to examine whether public tolerance was affected. It was, but, as Zaller would have predicted, not among all members of the public.

Chong compared public tolerance of racist comments before 1986 with tolerance after that year. Tolerance of racist comments declined for those who attended college in the mid-1980s or later, the exact set of people who were most likely exposed to debate over hate speech codes (see Figure 4-4). However, tolerance did not decline for people who were not enrolled in college during these years. Further, the declines in tolerance among the college students were greatest for liberals. As Chong argued, liberals were more likely "to accept the argument that restrictions on speech are justified by the pursuit of racial equality and equality of educational opportunities." [41] Conservatives, on the other hand, do not value racial equality as highly as liberals and were thus less receptive to arguments appealing to this goal.

So far, Zaller's approach to communication and attitudes applies the key political traits of attentiveness and predispositions to McGuire's model. From this foundation, Zaller extends McGuire's model in two important directions. First, once people have received and accepted a political message, their political opinions are not necessarily altered at that point. Instead, Zaller argues that individuals accept messages but only update their opinions when they are called

Figure 4-4   Change in Tolerance of Racists among College Students and Others, by Ideology

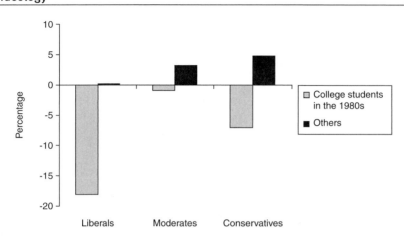

Source: Data from Table 4 of Dennis Chong, "Free Speech and Multiculturalism In and Out of the Academy," *Political Psychology* 27 (2006): 43.

Note: Bars represent the over-time change in percentage of each group that would tolerate a racist holding a teaching position. A negative number indicates a decline in tolerance.

upon to do so, such as when discussing politics with friends or when asked by a polling organization to answer a survey question. At this point, people sample among the considerations that are stored in their memory related to the political issue at hand. **Considerations,** as Zaller defines them, are "any reason[s] that might induce an individual to decide a political issue one way or the other." [42] If, at the time one must state her opinion, there are more considerations at the top of her head that favor the issue, she will indicate support for it. If she gathers more opposing considerations from her memory, however, an opposing opinion will result. This sampling is the final stage of Zaller's **receive-accept-sample model.**

What accounts for the balance of pro- versus anticonsiderations that are accessible in people's minds at any one time? Answering this question provides Zaller's second extension of McGuire. The content of elite discourse at the time influences which considerations come to mind. In particular, Zaller considers environments in which there is elite consensus on an issue so most messages articulated by elites favor the same side of the issue. At other times and for other issues, political elites will disagree over an issue and the flow of political information will contain messages both favoring and opposing the issue. When one message dominates elite discourse, there will be few details to cue citizens as to whether the arguments are consistent with their predispositions. This is because politicians from both dominant political parties and from varying ideological backgrounds will express support for an issue during times of elite consensus.

Therefore, in a one-message environment, more politically aware people will be more likely to receive and, due to the absence of key cueing details, accept the dominant message. Zaller calls this the **mainstream effect.** In contrast, elite disagreement over a policy issue, especially when the disagreement falls along party or ideological lines, results in the **polarization effect.** Attentive Democratic or liberal citizens will hold opinions that coincide with Democratic elites, whereas attentive Republican or conservative citizens will hold the opposing view. The opinions of those with lower levels of political awareness will not differ by political predispositions either because these people are unlikely to receive the countervailing messages or because they accept all received messages (since they are less able to discern the connection between the messages' arguments and their own predispositions).

The mainstream and polarization effects are illustrated in Figure 4-5. During the early years of American involvement in Vietnam, most political elites supported America's role. Consequently, in 1964, citizen support for the Vietnam War increased with political awareness, regardless of whether citizens were liberal or conservative. As the years passed, elite agreement disappeared with more and more Democratic and liberal elites expressing opposition to the war. As a result, liberal citizens began to oppose the war while conservative citizens continued to express support for the war. This division existed, however, among only politically aware members of the public.

Resistance to Persuasion

In recent years, psychologists have begun to examine when people are especially likely to resist persuasive communication. The result of resistance is that attitude change will not occur in the face of persuasive messages. Scholars who explicitly focus on resistance, however, push beyond this outcome-focused definition. Instead, they discuss **resistance** in terms of the *processes* by which people ensure the persuasive communication will fail to change attitudes or individual *motivations* to withstand change.[43] Resistance is more likely (a) for people who consider themselves not easily susceptible to persuasion, (b) for attitudes that are linked to one's core values, and (c) when people have been forewarned that a persuasive message is coming.[44] In contrast, buttering people up before attempting to persuade them can reduce resistance. Why? Because one reason for resisting a persuasive message is a motivation to preserve a positive concept of one 's self. If you have just been told that you possess a positive trait, this motivation is lessened and thus resistance to persuasion is less likely.[45]

How we *think of* our attitudes is also related to whether those attitudes are resistant to persuasion. Imagine for a minute that the 2008 Democratic presidential primary will soon occur in your state and that the only two candidates on the

Public Opinion in Comparative Perspective
BOX 4-1 POLITICAL DISCUSSION IN SOCIAL NETWORKS

There are many forms of communication that can influence people's political attitudes. Persuasive messages transmitted through the mass media are just one example, albeit an important example. Some people also are exposed to political topics and arguments through conversations that occur in their social network. **Social networks** consist of "people with whom a person communicates on a direct, one-to-one basis."[1]

Conversations with family, friends, and others in one's network cover a wide range of topics, of course. How likely is it that politics is discussed? As it turns out, there is substantial variation across nations in how often people discuss politics with other citizens. Political conversations are common in Israel, Norway, the Netherlands, and Greece but much less likely to occur in Great Britain, Singapore, and Canada. The United States falls in between these nations. In comparison with 80 other nations, U.S. citizens engage in political discussions slightly more than average.[2]

Distinct from the frequency of political conversations is the composition of one's social network, particularly the degree to which citizens' social networks include people whose political views differ from their own. Examining survey data from twelve nations, Diana Mutz compared people's political beliefs with those of their conversation partners (excluding spouses).[3] The similarity of views is much higher across discussion partners in the United States compared with other nations. In other words, on a day-to-day basis, Americans are less likely to be exposed to political beliefs and arguments that differ from their own.

Why might there be this political similarity within social networks in the United States? Mutz speculates that Americans' residential choices are a contributing factor. Most people do not select their neighborhood based on the political views of their neighbors, of course. Yet, this decision can be based on core values that are related to political beliefs. For example, some might prefer urban neighborhoods whereas others want a rural setting. Quality of schools, proximity to commercial services, and size of house lot are also factors influencing residential choice. As Mutz puts it, "people are likely to choose environments because they are populated by 'people like me' in the sense of shared lifestyles, values, or even market position."[4]

1. Diana C. Mutz, *Hearing the Other Side: Deliberative versus Participatory Democracy* (Cambridge: Cambridge University Press, 2006), 10.
2. Ibid., chap. 2.
3. Ibid.
4. Ibid., 47.

Figure 4-5   Zaller's Mainstream and Polarization Effects during Vietnam War Era

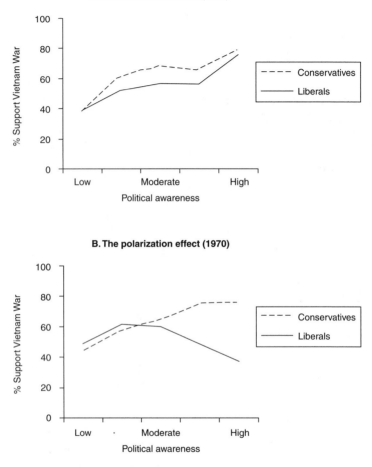

Source: Adapted from Figure 6.1 of John R. Zaller, *The Nature and Origins of Mass Opinion* (Cambridge: Cambridge University Press, 1992), 103.

ballot are Hillary Clinton and Barack Obama. If you prefer Clinton, this preference might exist because you *support* her or because you *oppose* Obama. As it turns out, if you think about your opinion in terms of opposition, it will be more resistant to change. A series of experiments demonstrated this effect.[46] Participants were given information about fictitious candidates and were encouraged to think of their candidate preference in terms of support or opposition. Note that they were not encouraged to prefer a different candidate, but rather to think about their attitude in terms of supporting their preferred candidate or opposing the preferred candidate's opponent. They were then exposed to a counterattitudinal message (such as learning that their preferred candidate had been involved in a scandal) and then asked their candidate preference again. In one study, participants rated candidates separately (for example, do you support candidate Smith?), whereas in another study they were asked for their relative candidate preferences (how much do you support candidate Smith over his opponent?). For both studies, participants who thought of their initial attitude in terms of opposition showed less attitude change after receiving the counterattitudinal message (see Figure 4-6). The researchers argue that this result occurs because negative information (such as opposition) is a more significant contributor to attitudes than are positive details, thus making negatively framed attitudes more resistant to change.[47] In fact, the powerful effect of negative information on evaluations of politicians has been well documented in public opinion research, perhaps helping us to understand why negative campaign advertisements are effective.[48]

Attitudes Follow Behavior

Many people prefer to maintain consistency across their beliefs, attitudes, and attitude-relevant behaviors. Someone who engages in physical exercise, for example, probably has a positive attitude toward exercise and views the attributes of exercise positively (such as believing that exercise is good for cardiovascular health). If inconsistencies exist among these elements, individuals will act to restore order. If someone else has negative attitudes toward exercise but engages in physical activity, she might change her attitude so that it is positive. These examples illustrate

Figure 4-6   Attitude Change When Supporting versus Opposing Candidates

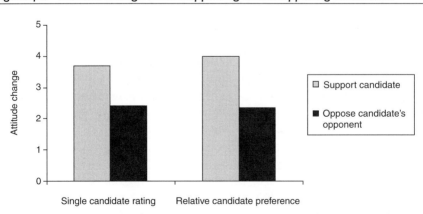

Source: Data from George Y. Bizer and Richard E. Petty, "How We Conceptualize Our Attitudes Matters: The Effects of Valence Framing on the Resistance of Political Attitudes," *Political Psychology* 26 (2005): 558, 563.

key postulates of **cognitive dissonance theory,** presented by Leon Festinger in the 1950s.[49] Festinger argued that when an individual holds cognitive elements (beliefs, attitudes, or knowledge of one's behaviors, for example) that are in opposition, cognitive dissonance exists. This dissonance produces negative arousal and the motivation to either eliminate the dissonance by changing the dissonant cognitive element or reduce the dissonance by adding more consonant elements. The person who exercises but has a negative attitude toward exercise might be unable to change this attitude but could instead reduce dissonance by thinking about the number of positive characteristics of exercise. She might think not only is exercise good for cardiovascular health, but it also improves flexibility, reduces stress, and, when combined with a healthy diet, can lead to weight loss.

Festinger and colleagues conducted a number of studies in which they demonstrated that if people are forced to engage in behavior that contradicts their attitudes, their attitudes can change as a result. Once the behavior is performed, after all, it cannot be unperformed, so attitude change is one way to eliminate the discrepancy between the behavior and the attitude. In one of the more famous of these studies, carried out by Festinger and James Carlsmith, participants were asked to complete a number of tasks that were boring and toward which participants were expected to hold negative attitudes, such as putting objects into a tray, emptying them out, and putting them back in the tray again.[50] Participants were then paid either $1 or $20 to tell the next participant that the tasks were interesting and enjoyable. Finally, the participants were asked to assess the tasks. Those who earned $1 evaluated the tasks more positively than did those who earned $20. Festinger and Carlsmith argued that the cognitive dissonance resulting from stating that the tasks were interesting while actually believing the opposite led to attitude change for those earning $1. Those who earned $20, in contrast, did not experience dissonance. Instead, they attributed their behavior to the compensation they earned: they were paid $20 to say that the tasks were interesting.

In a challenge to cognitive dissonance theory, Daryl Bem proposed a different explanation to account for the findings from cognitive dissonance studies. Bem's approach, called **self-perception theory,** argued that attitude change such as that observed in Festinger and Carlsmith's research was not the result of correcting an unpleasant state of dissonance but rather occurred because people *infer their attitudes* from their behaviors. Bem describes his theory as follows:

> When we want to know how a person feels, we look to see how he acts. Accordingly, it seemed possible that when an individual himself wants to know how he feels, he may look to see how he acts, a possibility suggested anecdotally by such statements as, "I guess I'm hungrier than I first thought." ... Individuals come to "know" their own attitudes, emotions and other internal states partially by inferring them from observations of their own overt behavior and/or the circumstances in which this behavior occurs.[51]

Bem's self-perception theory does not presume that people use their behaviors as a guide to determine all of their attitudes. Instead, he assumed that such self-perception was most likely when attitudes are weak or ambiguous. Because of this, some have argued that self-perception is better at accounting for attitude formation than attitude change.[52] If one is uncertain about his attitude, using his recent behavior as a guide can help to shape a new attitude. If, in contrast, one's attitude is well developed and strong, it is unlikely to change in the face of a contradictory behavior. Perhaps more importantly, the stronger one's attitudes are and the more certain one is about his attitudes, the less likely that he will ever engage in behavior that contradicts them.

Whether through cognitive dissonance reduction or self-perception mechanisms, it seems as if attitudes can follow from behavior. While these theories were not developed specifically for understanding political attitudes, political opinions clearly could be responsive to behavior, as the following examples demonstrate. First, imagine it is the spring of 2003 and a group of friends are discussing the American invasion of Iraq. During this conversation, a woman who had not previously thought very much about her opinion of the invasion finds herself arguing that the U.S. military needed to enter Iraq to remove Saddam Hussein. After she speaks, she realizes that she must support the U.S. invasion, otherwise she would not have made the comments that she did. Second, through their membership in organizations such as churches, fraternities, or sororities, people sometimes agree to volunteer for a variety of activities (at soup kitchens, to clean up a city street, etc.). Such activity is not always motivated by positive attitudes toward volunteerism but rather because one's group expects service from its members. After volunteering, however, positive attitudes toward service activities can develop simply because one has volunteered. As a final example, in some states and localities, people are required to recycle containers and newspapers. After engaging in such recycling, individuals can begin to think of themselves as recyclers and develop positive attitudes toward recycling and its environmental benefits, perhaps even forgetting that they began recycling not out of such attitudes but because of a legal mandate to do so.

CONCLUSION

In summarizing Bem's self-perception theory, psychologists Alice Eagly and Shelly Chaiken write the following:

> In general self-perception theory maintains that people function as relatively superficial information processors who merely generalize their attitudes from currently available external cues. By this account, people look to see what their recent behavior has been and assume that their attitudes are congruent with this behavior.[53]

This view of attitudes—as shallow and changeable—is also present in some of the other approaches that we have reviewed in this chapter. Zaller, for one, assumes that most people, especially those who are not highly politically aware, do not possess stable attitudes but rather hold a mix of attitude-relevant considerations in their heads. People's opinions at any point in time will reflect which of these considerations they bring to mind. For Petty and Cacioppo, attitudes that result from peripheral route processing will be rather ephemeral. Whether individuals engage in this type of processing depends, as you will recall, on individual traits as well as issue characteristics, such as personal relevance. Both of these models thus provide support for elite democratic and pluralistic theorists' assumptions regarding the citizenry, especially their views that the public's political opinions are ill considered and subject to frequent changes. Yet both Zaller's and Petty and Cacioppo's models indicate that these conclusions are not appropriate for all people and for all situations. Reality, in other words, is more complex that some elite democrats and pluralists imply.

Eagly and Chaiken go on to describe another way of understanding attitudes: "a view of attitudes as relatively enduring tendencies suggests instead that people generalize their attitudes from internal data; they have stored their attitudes in memory and retrieve them from this internal source when called upon to make an attitudinal judgment."[54] From this description, we envision attitudes as enduring and stable, as judgments that are well linked to core values and beliefs. Attitudes with these characteristics occur when people process communication in the central route, argue Petty and Cacioppo. Enduring attitudes are also likely if these attitudes serve important functions for individuals. As Katz's work suggests, if people hold attitudes because they serve an ego-defensive or a value-expressive function, they will be fairly resistant to change. Learning theorists remind us that attitudes that have been learned from repeated exposure to attitude objects and that have become habitual are also unlikely to change. While these attitudes might be stable, the functional and learning approaches do not assume, however, that all stable attitudes have been carefully considered. In contrast, learning theorists assume that people rather passively acquire attitudes without thinking through why they might like or dislike an attitude object. Ego-defensive attitudes, such as racial prejudice, provide similar examples of superficial thought. When feeling threatened, Katz argues, some individuals respond by expressing discriminatory attitudes toward members of other racial groups rather than considering the actual source of the threat, which could in fact be their own feelings of inferiority.

Some democratic theorists have assumed and some political scientists have demonstrated empirically that citizen attitudes are quite pliable. One of our goals in this chapter has been to present these arguments and this evidence. We also have presented alternative evidence to encourage you to consider whether attitude instability should be viewed negatively, that is, as evidence that the citizenry is not living up to the model presented by classical democratic theorists. Page and Shapiro, for example, demonstrate that when collective opinion changes it is often in rational response to external cues, such as world events or a changed social climate. Further, we turned to psychology to demonstrate the variety of approaches one can take to understanding the nature of attitudes and the mechanisms by which they can change. Models of communication-induced attitude change are especially relevant for political attitudes. Much of political activity is designed to try to influence the opinions and judgments of political actors, whether they are citizens or politicians. Understanding when and how political communication influences citizens' opinions has been the focus of much public opinion research, so we will continue to pursue this topic throughout the book.

For now, however, perhaps you have some initial thoughts about the following questions: Are citizen attitudes fleeting? If they are, do we care? In particular, does the presence of unstable citizen attitudes undermine the public's ability to evaluate political issues and communicate their preferences to political leaders? Is democratic governance, in other words, threatened by attitude instability?

KEY CONCEPTS

acceptance / 110	nonattitudes / 98
attitude change / 96	peripheral route to persuasion / 107
attitude stability / 96	polarization effect / 114
central route to persuasion / 107	political awareness / 110
cognitive dissonance theory / 118	political predispositions / 111
collective public opinion / 99	receive-accept-sample model / 113
considerations / 113	reception / 110
cross-sectional study / 96	resistance / 114
ego defense function / 103	self-perception theory / 118
elaboration likelihood model / 107	social adjustment / 104
elite discourse / 110	social networks / 115
functional theories / 103	transfer of affect / 106
knowledge function / 103	utilitarian function / 103
learning theory / 105	value-expressive function / 103
mainstream effect / 114	

SUGGESTED SOURCES FOR FURTHER READING

Ajzen, Icek. "The Theory of Planned Behavior." *Organizational Behavior and Human Decision Processes* 50 (1991): 179–211.
LaPiere, Richard T. "Attitudes vs. Actions." *Social Forces* 13 (1934): 230–237.

These two works examine the relationship between attitudes and behaviors, albeit drawing quite different conclusions. LaPiere traveled across the United States with a Chinese couple in the 1930s. In 251 situations when they asked for hotel accommodations or restaurant service, they were denied only once. Yet, when LaPiere sent questionnaires to these establishments after they visited, asking whether they would serve Chinese guests, over 90 percent said they would not. Ajzen's theory of planned behavior, in contrast, posits that behaviors can be predicted from relevant attitudes, provided that you factor in the degree to which one has control over behavior.

Converse, Philip E. "The Nature of Belief Systems in Mass Publics." In *Ideology and Discontent,* ed. David E. Apter. New York: Free Press, 1964.
Converse, Philip E. "Attitudes and Non-Attitudes: Continuation of a Dialogue." In *The Quantitative Analysis of Social Problems,* ed. Edward R. Tufte. Reading, Mass.: Addison-Wesley, 1970.

These are classic studies of individuals' political attitudes, in which Converse concludes that the public's attitudes change frequently and are not well organized.

Eagly, Alice H., and Shelly Chaiken. *The Psychology of Attitudes.* Fort Worth: Harcourt Brace Jovanovich, 1993.

This book provides a detailed overview of attitude theory and research on attitudes in the field of psychology. This literature is extensive, but Eagly and Chaiken cover it well.

Knowles, Eric S., and Jay A. Linn, eds. *Resistance and Persuasion.* Mahwah, N.J.: Erlbaum, 2004.

The essays in this volume discuss when resistance to persuasion is likely to occur. In addition, some of the authors describe how resistance can be overcome.

Page, Benjamin I., and Robert Y. Shapiro. *The Rational Public: Fifty Years of Trends in Americans' Policy Preferences.* Chicago: University of Chicago Press, 1992.

After analyzing public opinion polls conducted between 1935 and 1990, Page and Shapiro conclude that public opinion at the aggregate level is quite stable over time. In addition, their book provides a detailed picture of the public's attitudes toward many important policy issues.

Petty, Richard E., and John T. Cacioppo. *Communication and Persuasion.* New York: Springer-Verlag, 1986.
Zaller, John R. *The Nature and Origins of Mass Opinion.* Cambridge: Cambridge University Press, 1992.

Important insights on the effects of communication on attitudes are contained in these two books. Petty and Cacioppo's elaboration likelihood model and Zaller's receive-accept-sample model have greatly enhanced our understanding of persuasion and attitude change.

PART III

Do Citizens Organize Their Political Thinking?

ARE PEOPLE'S POLITICAL opinions related to one another? That is, is there some consistency across views or does knowing citizens' views on one issue not help you predict their views on other issues? Assessing consistency can be tricky, but one yardstick that has been used is political ideology. With this approach, a person with all conservative views would be considered to have more consistent attitudes than someone with a mixture of liberal and conservative views. But, is ideology the best yardstick? And, if so, what is the best way to measure the degree of ideological thinking and ideological organization of people's political opinions? The first chapter of this section takes up these topics, while the second chapter moves beyond ideology to consider other factors that might shape people's attitudes.

Why should we care whether the public organizes its political thinking? Answering this question brings us back to the normative topic of citizen competence. Can the public function effectively in a democracy if their political views are not well organized? The chapters in this section speak to questions such as these, so we hope you will ponder them as you read the chapter material.

CHAPTER 5

Ideological Innocence and Critiques

IN JUNE 2003, Bill O'Reilly and Al Franken appeared together at Book-Expo America, a convention for book publishers, sellers, and authors. O'Reilly, the host of *The O'Reilly Factor* on the FOX cable channel, and Franken, a former comedian on *Saturday Night Live* turned political commentator, were at Book-Expo to talk about their new books. Franken's book, *Lies and the Lying Liars Who Tell Them: A Fair and Balanced Look at the Right*, criticizes Republicans and right-leaning pundits and journalists, including those on FOX, for bending the truth to fit their aims. Not surprisingly, O'Reilly was annoyed by the arguments contained in as well as the tone of Franken's book. Their appearance at the convention ended in a shouting match. *USA Today* began a news story about the event with this sentence: "Bill O'Reilly, the *conservative* talk show host, first decried political commentators who 'call people names.' Then he called Al Franken, the *liberal* humorist, an 'idiot.'" [1]

O'Reilly and Franken are not the only political figures to be labeled conservative or liberal. Consider, for example, the congressional debate over immigration reform that occurred in the spring and early summer of 2007. The reform plan, proposed by President George W. Bush, called for increased border security, higher fines for employers who hire illegal immigrants, and the creation of a small guest worker program that would admit foreign workers into the United States to work for temporary periods of time. The most controversial aspect of Bush's proposal would have allowed for illegal immigrants already in the United States to apply for legal citizenship. This reform proposal was defeated in the Congress. Opposition to it came from a variety of lawmakers, as described in a CNN.com news story: "Liberals say the bill is unfair because it limits opportunities for unskilled workers. Conservatives oppose what they call 'amnesty' for illegal behavior and say it will encourage more." [2]

Around the same time that Bush's immigration plan was defeated in Congress, the Supreme Court issued decisions over the contentious topics of school desegregation, students' free speech rights, and workplace sex discrimination. The Court ruled that school districts can no longer use a student's race as the primary factor when deciding which public school the student will attend. The free speech case involved a student who displayed a banner with the words "Bong Hits 4 Jesus" outside his high school. Students do not have rights to speech that promotes illegal drug use, a majority of justices concluded. In the sex discrimination case, a female worker sued her employer, alleging that for many years she received lower pay than her male colleagues. The Court ruled against the worker, arguing that she should have submitted her claim within 180 days of the initial discriminatory action rather than years later. For all of these cases, the Court's more conservative justices voted in favor of while the more liberal members opposed the decision. As Nina Totenberg of National Public Radio put it while summarizing a number of the Court's decisions for the 2006–2007 term, "For conservatives, it was pretty close to the best of times, and for liberals it was pretty close to the worst."[3]

While media coverage of these three topics describes key actors as either liberal or conservative, what does it mean to be a liberal or a conservative? Do these terms carry any meaning for you? In particular, do you gain a greater understanding of the topics presented in the news stories if you know them? Liberalism and conservatism are the two dominant ideologies in U.S. politics. A political **ideology** is "an interrelated set of attitudes and values about the proper goals of society and how they should be achieved."[4] Two aspects of this definition are worth emphasizing. First, one's ideology consists of attitudes that are coherent and related to one another.[5] Second, an ideology does not refer to just any set of related attitudes but rather to beliefs about society and especially the proper role of government. In the American context, **conservatives** emphasize order, tradition, individual responsibility, and minimal government intervention, particularly in economic matters. **Liberals**, in contrast, believe that government intervention in the economy is sometimes necessary to combat features of the free market (such as discrimination and low wages). Liberals also value equality, openness to dissenting views, and civil rights.

According to many democratic theorists, citizens and politicians need to communicate effectively with one another, so that, among other reasons, citizens can evaluate the performance of elected officials and so that these officials can know the political preferences of the citizens. Communication between citizens and leaders is enhanced if the two groups talk about politics using the same terms. This does not occur, however, at least according to Philip Converse's classic work on political ideology. Conducting his research in the late 1950s and early 1960s, Converse concluded that political elites are much more likely than citizens to organize the political world ideologically, along a liberal-conservative continuum. Not only are citizens less likely to think about politics ideologically, the terms liberal and conservative carry little meaning for many people. Public understanding of political debates is threatened by such a lack of understanding. As Converse put it, "The more impoverished [a citizen's] understanding of the term [conservative or liberal], the less information [the term] conveys. In the limiting case—if he does not know at all what the term means—it conveys no information at all."[6] Further, low knowledge of ideology and uncommon ideological reasoning among the public is, at least to some, evidence that the public is not capable of democratic citizenship.

Converse's work ignited a firestorm of research, with many scholars trying to resurrect a more respectable view of citizens' capabilities. In this chapter, we review the research that challenges Converse's arguments on theoretical, conceptual, and methodological grounds. First, though, we detail Converse's original argument and the methodology on which his study relies.

CONVERSE'S CLAIM: IDEOLOGICAL INNOCENCE

The overarching goal of Converse's research was to examine the belief systems of citizens and elites. He defined a **belief system** as "a configuration of ideas and attitudes in which the elements are bound together by some form of constraint or functional interdependence."[7] While Converse preferred the term belief system rather than ideology, he does admit that the two are closely related. Further, as we will soon see, to determine whether the public's beliefs are joined in coherent systems, he uses the liberal-conservative ideological dimension as one of his gauges. As for constraint, Converse refers to the degree to which we could predict a specific attitude of someone knowing her attitude toward a different political object. When a belief system is present, "if a person is opposed to the expansion of social security," we can judge that "he is probably a conservative and is probably opposed as well to any nationalization of private industries, federal aid to education, sharply progressive income taxation, and so forth."[8] Constraint, for Converse, meant that people's political attitudes are related to each other because they derive from an overarching worldview (such as a political ideology).

Do People Demonstrate Ideological Thinking?

Converse's overall conclusion, as we already mentioned, was that elites were much more likely to possess belief systems compared with the general public. This conclusion is based primarily on his analyses of the 1956, 1958, and 1960 American National Election Studies (ANES) panel study. To understand and evaluate Converse's conclusions, you need to know what evidence he used to make his arguments. Thus, we summarize Converse's study in depth. For his first analysis, Converse examined the degree to which respondents in 1956 used ideological language in response to questions about the political parties and the two major party candidates for president. This series of questions began with: "Is there anything in particular that you like about the Democratic Party? Is there anything in particular that you don't like about the Democratic Party?" Respondents were then asked for their likes and dislikes of the Republican Party and the candidates (Democrat Adlai Stevenson and Republican President Dwight Eisenhower).

Such **open-ended questions** allow respondents to discuss politics using their own terms and language, thus providing important insight into how people conceive of the political world. From his analysis of the responses, Converse categorized the public into five groups based on the degree to which people used an abstract benchmark, such as the liberal-conservative ideological continuum, to evaluate the parties and politicians.[9] Those individuals who did use this continuum, such as by differentiating the parties based on ideology and correctly linking specific policy positions of the parties to this ideology, were labeled Ideologues.[10] The second group—Near Ideologues—included people who used ideological labels such as liberal or conservative but perhaps did not fully understand the meaning of these terms or did not use ideology as their primary tool for evaluating politics. One example here is a man who liked *both* the "liberalness" of the Democrats and the "conservative element in the Republican Party."[11] All told, only about 11½ percent of the public were classified as either an Ideologue (2½ percent) or a Near Ideologue (9 percent) (see Figure 5-1).

Far more common were people who conceptualized politics in terms other than ideology. The largest category was Group Interest citizens, who comprised 42 percent of the respondents. These individuals tended to discuss the parties and candidates in terms of whether they favor the interests of specific groups, such as the man who disliked Republicans because "[t]hey are more for big business" or the woman who likes that the Democrats "have always helped the farmers."[12] Nature of the Times was the label Converse applied to his fourth level. People in this group (24 percent of the public) linked the parties or candidates with the current state of the nation. Parties in charge during times of peace or prosperity were evaluated more favorably than were those who ruled during war or economic downturns, as the following excerpts from one woman's responses indicate:

> The only thing I associate the Democratic Party with is that it seems to be the party that is in power during a war.

Figure 5-1   Levels of Conceptualization among the American Public, 1956

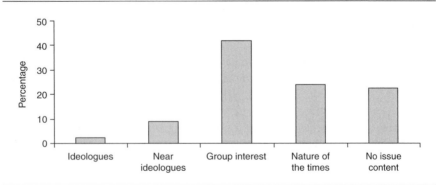

Source: Adapted from Table I of Philip E. Converse, "The Nature of Belief Systems in Mass Publics," in *Ideology and Discontent,* ed. David E. Apter (New York: Free Press, 1964), 218.

I think that the Republican Party has handled the foreign situation—
that is, the cold war—with success, and it is always associated in my mind
with peace and prosperity.[13]

The final group in Converse's classification evaluated the parties and candidates on grounds other than issues. No Issue Content citizens included those who used personal characteristics to evaluate candidates, were not sure what either political party stood for (even when they identified with one of the parties), or did not follow politics closely enough to discuss parties or candidates. This final group comprised 22½ percent of the citizenry, nearly twice that of the Ideologues and Near Ideologues combined. To Converse, these results clearly demonstrated that most members of the public do not think about political parties and candidates ideologically.

Do People Recognize Ideological Terms?

Moving on and mostly moving away from open-ended questions, Converse next assessed the degree to which people could recognize the terms liberal and conservative. Even if ideological reasoning was uncommon among citizens, public understanding of these terms could be more common. To address this possibility, in 1960, Converse asked respondents, "Would you say that either one of the parties is more *conservative* or more *liberal* than the other?" Those answering yes were then asked which party is more conservative and then why they characterized that party as more conservative. Nearly 40 percent of the respondents either did not recognize these terms or were unable to attach any meaning to the terms.

Among those who did identify the ideological leanings of each party and did attempt to discuss the meaning of conservatism, there was variation in the correct use of the terms and in the breadth of ideological thinking apparent in the answers. Converse concluded that about 17 percent did not correctly apply the terms or did not provide a correct meaning for conservatism, whereas 29 percent provided correct meaning but demonstrated only a narrow understanding of the ideologies. Typically, these respondents discussed ideology only in terms of which party spends more money and which saves more. Republicans are more conservative, one person explained, because "they vote against the wild spending spree the Democrats get on."[14] The remaining respondents, about 17 percent, recognized the ideological terms, identified the Democrats as liberal and the Republicans as conservative, and displayed a more thorough understanding of liberalism and conservatism. While this segment of the public is larger than the 11½ percent that displayed ideological thinking in response to the open-ended questions about parties and candidates, it is still a small percentage of the public.

Are Individuals' Attitudes Constrained and Stable?

So far, Converse's analyses suggest that most people do not use the liberal-conservative ideological spectrum to organize their political thinking. This, however, does not mean that the political views of most people are unorganized. Perhaps beliefs are organized along other criteria. **Attitude constraint**, in other words, may exist among the public even though the political worldview that is constraining the attitudes is not liberal or conservative ideology. Converse tested this assumption two separate ways. First, using the 1958 ANES data, he looked at the relationship between a number of issue opinions to see whether opinions toward an issue (such as federal education aid) are correlated with opinions on another issue (such as public housing). Since liberals tend to support federal government spending on education and government provision of public housing and conservatives tend to oppose both, if most of the public organize their issue opinions along this ideological continuum, we would expect that these opinions would be highly correlated among the public. Yet, what if people who support federal education aid also tend to oppose public housing? This would suggest a different organizing framework. If so, we would still see high correlations between the attitudes, albeit in the opposite direction with support on one issue correlated with opposition on the other.

Examining the relationships between four domestic issues and three foreign affairs issues, Converse in fact found very low correlations among the public, leading him to dismiss the possibility that the public's beliefs are constrained along any dimension. Further, he compared the correlations of the public with those for political elites (in this case, congressional candidates) and found that belief constraint is much higher among the elites. See Figure 5-2, which presents average correlations (specifically, gamma coefficients) separately for domestic issues and foreign issues, then for a comparison between all domestic and all foreign issues. You will see that correlations (and thus belief constraint) were higher among elites than the public for all three comparisons.

Second, Converse compared people's issue attitudes in 1956 with their opinions on the same issues in 1958 and again in 1960. This is the analysis we presented at the beginning of chapter 4. As you will recall, levels of **attitude stability** were quite low. The correlation (expressed in this case with tau-b coefficients) between opinions on school desegregation in 1958 and 1960 was .43, while the over-time correlation on the issue of federal housing assistance was .29. In contrast, respondents' party identification was much more stable across these two years (tau-b = .73), demonstrating that party affiliation does not change as much as do issue opinions. Further, Converse found that people's issue opinions fluctuated as much between 1956 and 1958, and between 1958 and 1960, as they did between 1956 and 1960. Given the longer time frame of the latter, we might expect less stability over a four-year time span than over two years. This pattern was not apparent in Converse's data, leading him to conclude that the public "contains significant proportions of people who, for lack of information about a particular dimension or controversy, offer meaningless opinions that vary randomly in direction during repeated trials over time."[15]

Figure 5-2   Relationships between Issue Opinions for the American Public and Political Elites, 1958

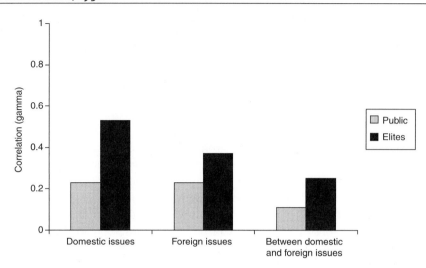

Source: Adapted from Table VIII of Philip E. Converse, "The Nature of Belief Systems in Mass Publics," in *Ideology and Discontent,* ed. David E. Apter (New York: Free Press, 1964), 229.

Groups as Source of Belief Constraint

Although Converse argued that most Americans did not possess an ideologically constrained belief system, he did find one source of belief constraint among the public: attitudes toward social groups. Converse's respondents were asked two policy questions that referenced African Americans (or Negroes, as was the common label in the 1950s). One queried public support for the federal government to ensure public schools are desegregated, whereas the other assessed whether the government should ensure that African Americans are not discriminated against in employment and housing. The correlation between opinions on these two items was .57, much higher than the average relationship among public opinion toward the entire range of domestic policy issues that Converse examined (see Figure 5-2). Further, the correlation between these two items among elites was actually lower than for the public (.31).

   In sum, Converse's conclusions were that (a) the public does not think about political parties and candidates ideologically, (b) recognition and correct use of the terms liberal and conservative are quite rare, (c) constraint across a variety of issue positions is low, and (d) over-time attitude consistency is low. Citizens do appear, however, to organize their political opinions around views of prominent groups. Elites, in contrast, use ideology to organize their political thinking, as is evident by their higher levels of attitude constraint. If these results seem to confirm elite democrats' assumptions that the public is not well equipped for democratic governance, they should. In fact, empirical findings such as Converse's led to the development and refinement of the theory of democratic elitism. Elite democrats assume that the public is neither engaged in nor well informed about politics, which should contribute to their low levels of ideological understanding and use of ideology to organize their thinking. Other theorists, particularly those with a more optimistic view of the public's capabilities, found Converse's work limiting and looked to other explanations to account for his findings.

CRITIQUES OF CONVERSE

Converse's research received much attention at the time of publication, has spurred countless commentaries and studies (some supporting and some opposing his conclusions), and is still influencing public opinion scholars today. His work was referred to as "celebrated" and "influential," but also "notorious" by one scholar,[16] while another described it as an "enduring milestone" and a "millstone," the latter because of the "misleading criteria Converse used to assess political competence and electoral responsibility."[17] As these quotations suggest, Conserve's work was not well received by all. Over the years, critiques have come from many quarters. We summarize and evaluate key counterarguments below. As you will see, each argument provides a somewhat different criticism of Converse, but none provide evidence or reasoning that undermines his entire body of evidence.

The Political Context

Were Converse's results due to the nature of the times? Several people have argued that the 1950s was an especially nonideological time in the nation's politics, thus producing the low levels of ideological thinking measured by Converse. This was a decade of (relatively speaking) **consensual politics**. Disagreements between the political parties were minor, the political environment was not dominated by discussion of conflictual issues, and the public was not very tuned in to politics. Politics during the 1960s and 1970s was much more **ideologically contentious**. Battles raged over civil rights, the United States was involved in what became a controversial war in Vietnam, the economy took a downturn, riots broke out in many cities, and President Richard Nixon was forced to resign as a result of the Watergate burglary. These salient issues increased public attention to political matters and divided the Democrats and Republicans quite publicly as the two parties openly debated their differences over these matters. Did these changed times result in citizen views that were more ideologically grounded? Some early evidence suggested yes.

In their analysis of public attitudes between 1956 and 1976, Norman Nie, Sidney Verba, and John Petrocik concluded that the public's belief systems did become more constrained over time.[18] Much as Converse did, Nie and his colleagues examined the gamma correlations between pairs of issues in each of these years.

These issues included a few domestic (welfare, school integration, etc.) and one foreign policy issue (the Cold War). As we know from Converse's work, the average correlation between the issue pairs was quite low for 1956, 1958, and 1960. Beginning in 1964, however, the average correlation increased substantially, rising to .41 from .13 in 1960 (see Figure 5-3). To Nie et al., this was clear evidence that public beliefs were becoming more organized along a liberal-conservative continuum. As they concluded, "The increase in consistency across issues means that individuals who answer a question on one topic in a liberal direction are now more likely to answer liberally on another topic, and vice versa for conservative answers."[19]

These results seemed to mirror the political context. The 1964 presidential election was notably ideological, with the Republican candidate (Barry Goldwater) running as a self-proclaimed conservative while his opponent (President Lyndon Johnson) tried to portray him as an ideological extremist. Given the nature of the campaign rhetoric, then, it is perhaps not surprising that voters' opinions were more ideologically consistent. This increased consistency then continued through 1976, suggesting that the public's more tightly constrained belief systems were a permanent change. Upon closer examination, however, the increased levels of attitude consistency that Nie et al. documented began to unravel. Higher correlations between issue opinions were not primarily due to the changed political environment after all but to a seemingly minor change in the way the ANES survey

Figure 5-3   Relationship between Issue Opinions, 1956–1976

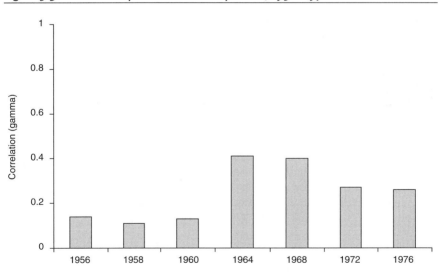

Source: Adapted from Tables 8-1 and 20-1 of Norman H. Nie, Sidney Verba, and John R. Petrocik, *The Changing American Voter,* enlarged ed. (Cambridge: Harvard University Press, 1979), 124, 368.

questions were worded beginning in 1964. We detail the implications of these changed questions below; suffice it here to say that this methodological discovery significantly undercut the argument that Converse's evidence of ideological innocence was due largely to the politically complacent 1950s.

Despite this, there is still some support for the argument that the times do matter, even though the political context has not been as influential as Nie and his collaborators suggested. Some of the increased levels of attitude constraint observed in 1972, for example, were due to the nature of that year's presidential election.[20] The two candidates—Republican President Richard Nixon and Democrat George McGovern—proposed ideologically distinct platforms during their election campaigns. McGovern, in particular, was frequently described as representing the very liberal wing of the Democratic Party. The events of and debate over the Vietnam War also seemed to produce public attitudes that were more stable. In Converse's own words, "the crescendo of political turmoil associated with the later stages of the Vietnam war was producing somewhat firmer opinions on key subjects."[21] More generally, attitude constraint and stability are higher for certain types of issues. Issues that are grounded in religion, morality, or civil rights show less overtime fluctuation and are more tied to ideological principles than are other types of issues (economic, foreign policy, etc.).[22] Importantly, the former issues are more likely to be on the public agenda now than they were in the 1950s. As the issue context changes, then, public belief systems can become more constrained.

The Format of Survey Questions

As we mentioned above, the increased level of public attitude constraint observed by Nie and colleagues has been largely attributed to changes in survey **question wording**. That is, the actual opinions of the public did not become more ideologically organized beginning in 1964; results demonstrating more organization were instead due to the way that these opinions were measured. The ANES changed the format of its issue questions in 1964. Before then, survey respondents were given a statement about a policy issue and asked whether they agreed or disagreed with the statement. This type of question is known as a **Likert question**, named after Rensis Likert, a psychologist at the University of Michigan who developed the format. Beginning in 1964, the Likert questions were changed so that respondents first heard two sides of an issue and then were asked if they favored one side or the other. Table 5-1 presents these two question formats for attitudes about whether the government should ensure that those who want a job can find one. In the early, single-statement version, people were simply asked about whether this should be a goal of the government. The later version, though, provided a counterargument to this position, namely that finding a job should be the responsibility of individuals, not the government. We refer to this question format as the competing-options format.

Table 5-1   Changes in American National Election Studies Survey Questions

Format used before 1964: *Single statement*	*Format introduced in 1964:* *Competing options*
"The government in Washington ought to see to it that everybody who wants to work can find a job. Do you have any opinion on this or not? (If yes) Do you think the government ought to see to it that everybody who wants to work can find a job?"	"In general, some people feel that the government in Washington should see to it that every person has a job and a good standard of living. Others think the government should just let each person get ahead on his own. Have you been interested enough in this to favor one side over the other? (If yes) Do you think that the government:"
Agree strongly	
Agree but not very strongly	
Not sure. It depends	Should see to it that every person has a job and a good standard of living
Disagree but not very strongly	Other, depends, both
Disagree strongly	Should let each person get ahead on his own

Source: Codebooks for 1960 and 1964 American National Election Studies, http://election studies.org/studypages/download/datacenter_all.htm.

Why might different levels of attitude constraint appear across these two versions of the question? The first version promotes agreement with the single stated position because it does not provide respondents with other choices, and, in the case of this specific question, because full employment is considered by most people to be an important goal. Some individuals will know, of course, what options for job provision are available other than the government guaranteeing jobs, but for other people any opposing position will not come easily to mind. The competing policy options version of the question, in contrast, provides an opposing position. When answering questions of this second type, respondents can ponder over which of the two sides comes closest to their own position. Because of this, the questions that were introduced in 1964 are considered more reliable measures of people's actual opinions. And, very importantly for the purposes of studying ideological thinking, these new questions are better assessments of whether people's issue opinions correspond to the liberal-conservative continuum. With its lack of a stated alternative, the single-statement format results in people agreeing that the government should guarantee jobs regardless of whether these individuals are liberal or conservative. The two options presented in the second version of this issue question are balanced between a liberal view (favoring government involvement in providing jobs) and a conservative view (believing that individuals are responsible for finding jobs). Thus, conservatives as well as liberals should have an easier time mapping their ideology to specific issues when they are asked the questions using the competing-options format.

Given these key differences across question wordings, we would expect attitude constraint to be higher when the competing-options version of the survey questions is used. John Sullivan, James Pierson, and George Marcus tested this assumption by conducting an experiment.[23] In 1976, they surveyed a random sample of adults living in the Minneapolis–St. Paul area. One-half of the respondents were asked issue questions using the single-statement wording. The other half were asked about the same issues (welfare, welfare for blacks, the proper size of government, and school integration) but the questions used the competing-options format. Sullivan et al.'s findings confirmed what they expected. Correlations between pairs of issue positions were higher for those people who received the competing-options versus the single-statement format (see Figure 5-4). The correlation between opinions on welfare policy and school integration, for example, was .11 for those receiving the single-statement version of the issue questions, whereas it was .30 for those who responded to questions in the competing-options format.

Because they conducted an experiment in which people were randomly assigned to receive one of the two versions of the survey questions, Sullivan et al. were able to conclude that the differences in attitude constraint that they observed was indeed due to question wording. This finding was a clear blow to the conclusions

Figure 5-4   Correlation between Issue Pairs by Question Format, 1976

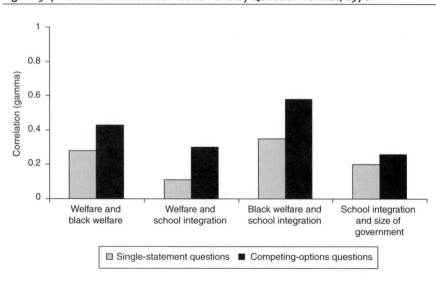

Source: Adapted from Table 3 of John L. Sullivan, James E. Pierson, and George E. Marcus, "Ideological Constraint in the Mass Public: A Methodological Critique and Some New Findings," *American Journal of Political Science* 22 (1978): 241.

reached by Nie, Verba, and Petrocik. Since the ANES changed its question wording in 1964 (the year when Nie and his colleagues saw the largest increase in constraint), and since Sullivan et al. demonstrated that the new questions produce higher levels of attitude constraint, it seems that the large increases in constraint that Nie et al. presented cannot be attributed to the changed political environment, as they argued. Americans had not become substantially more ideological after all. In fact, ideological constraint among the public did not increase significantly *even though* the political context did provide more ideological cues for citizens to use in structuring their own thinking.[24] This is a substantially different conclusion than one positing that Converse's low levels of attitude constraint were due to the political context rather than to individuals.

This specific examination of question wording options raises a broader issue regarding survey research. Survey questions are designed to measure latent attitudes, but the questions do not always correspond well to the actual attitude. Therefore, when trying to determine someone's attitudes using survey questions, some **measurement error** exists. To illustrate this concept, think about measuring a window. Imagine that the actual width of this window is 4 feet. You could measure the window using a digital measuring device or a 6-inch wooden ruler. Your measurement is likely to be more accurate (perhaps even exactly 4 feet) using the former. When moving the 6-inch ruler over the window to measure its width, there will likely be some slippage so that your measured distance might be wider or narrower than 4 feet. In other words, the observed width of the window depends on which measuring instrument was used.

The same is true when measuring attitudes using a survey instrument. Survey questions do not always match up well with people's real opinions on political matters. In some situations, this could be due to the fact that people think of issues on grounds other than those included in the question. Another possibility is that the questions lack precision. If you were asked by an ANES interviewer whether you agree that the government should guarantee everyone a job, your opinion might fall between the offered response choices of "agree strongly" and "agree but not very strongly." To answer the question, you will need to choose one of the options, but neither precisely measures your attitude. For each, there will be some error in the measurement of your attitude. This situation has led some to argue that the over-time instability in attitudes that Converse observed is more likely due to vague questions than to actual change in people's attitudes. Perhaps "respondents will not always respond the same way to the same question even if their attitudes remain unchanged. A subject may say 'strongly agree' one time and 'agree' the next, simply because of the ambiguity of the question asked or because he is uncertain how strong is 'strongly.'"[25]

By now, you might be wondering why any of this matters. Who should care about survey question wording other than those whose job it is to write survey questions? In fact, implications of this discussion reach beyond matters of survey design. At the core of the methodological debate sits the topic of public competence. Are citizens capable of evaluating public policy issues? Your answer to this question will likely depend on your basic view of the democratic public. Responding to the questions that contain competing policy options does make it easier for people to see how their ideology corresponds to the issue at hand. But, is this task too easy? If the public did have meaningful ideologies, shouldn't they be able to figure out on their own what the opposing arguments are when they are asked a one-sided policy question? The fact that attitude constraint is low in response to single-statement questions is ample evidence for some people that citizens do not possess well-formed belief systems. Other people disagree with this conclusion, however. They argue that the task of answering one-sided questions can be too difficult, especially for individuals for whom politics is not their main concern (in contrast with political elites).

Finally, what does this debate over survey question wordings mean for Converse's findings? Should we be skeptical about his conclusions regarding attitude constraint and over-time stability given the type of survey questions he used to measure issue attitudes? General consensus is that the competing-options questions introduced by the ANES in 1964 are more reliable assessments of issue opinions, particularly the degree to which opinions map on to liberal or conservative ideology.[26] This suggests that Converse's findings somewhat understated the degree of attitude constraint and stability that existed in the populace during the late 1950s because of the nature of the questions he analyzed. Yet, even when we examine responses to the more reliable questions, we do not witness very high levels of attitude constraint among the public. Figure 5-5 presents average correlation coefficients (Pearson's r) across pairs of issues for both 1980 and 2004. For each year, relationships between key issues of the day were examined.[27] In 1980, the average correlation between the issue pairs for the public was only .12 whereas it was .22 in 2004.[28]

As for over-time attitude stability, you can see in Figure 5-5 that stability is higher than constraint (Converse also found this). However, similar to what our analysis of attitude constraint demonstrates, levels of attitude stability are not high even when the new ANES questions are used. These results come from analyses of the 1972–1976 and the 2000–2004 ANES panel studies. For the first time period, respondents were asked about three issues using the same question wording in both 1972 and 1976 (abortion, school busing, and defense spending). The average correlation (Pearson's r) between people's responses in these two years was .5.[29] More recently, respondents were asked about several policy issues using the same question wording in both 2000 and 2004. These included preferred levels of government spending on a variety of policies (such as environmental protections, welfare, child care, and aid to blacks) as well as abortion and legal protections against discrimination for homosexuals.[30] Over-time stability across these four years was slightly lower than in the 1970s, with an average correlation of .44.

Figure 5-5   Attitude Constraint and Attitude Stability among American Public and Elites

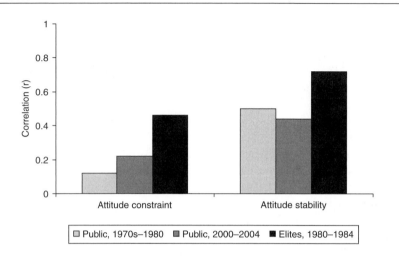

Sources: Attitude constraint for public (1980) and elites (1980) and attitude stability for public (1972–1976) and elites (1980–1984): Adapted from Figures 1 and 5 of M. Kent Jennings, "Ideological Thinking among Mass Publics and Political Elites," *Public Opinion Quarterly* 56 (1992): 426, 432. Attitude constraint for public (2004): Analysis of 2004 American National Election Study Data File. Attitude stability for public (2000–2004): Analysis of American National Election Studies 2000–02–04 Panel Data File.

Recall that Converse compared attitude constraint for the public with that of the elites. Replications of this portion of his analysis have been rare, but one study did examine both elite and public attitude constraint and stability. The results from the public are the ones that we have been looking at in Figure 5-5; the elite results are also presented there. These elite data come from surveys of individuals attending the Democratic and Republican Party conventions in 1980 and 1984. Unfortunately, more recent analyses of elite opinion have not been conducted, so we must rely on this analysis. A quick glance back at this figure demonstrates that elites had higher levels of both constraint and stability than did the public during this time.[31] This result confirms one of Converse's key conclusions: elites possess more ideologically constrained belief systems than do citizens. It also somewhat undermines the argument that Converse's findings among the public were due to poorly worded questions. If poor questions were the cause of low levels of attitude constraint and stability, shouldn't we also see low levels among elites when elites are asked the same questions as the public?

In-Depth Interviewing

Not only have Converse's survey questions been criticized but his chosen method—survey research—has also come under attack. Some argue that asking citizens specific, focused questions does not allow them to reveal the complexity of their political thinking or the connections that they make across policy issues. Furthermore, questions that are designed to assess liberal or conservative ideologies are not likely to pick up the presence of other ideologies among the public. Libertarians, for example, prefer minimal government involvement in the economy but also believe that individual civil liberties need to be protected from government intrusion. These views are thus a mixture of liberalism and conservatism. If we used Converse's method for measuring attitude constraint (and his assumption that ideologies are arrayed along a liberal-conservatism continuum), libertarians would show low levels of constraint even though their attitudes are derived from an overarching ideology.

To better measure other ideologies as well as to examine the process by which people reason about political matters, some researchers prefer **in-depth interviewing** over surveys. During an interview session, a researcher asks someone very broad questions. The questions are designed to allow interviewees to discuss what is important to them rather than pointing them toward specific topics as surveys generally do. Furthermore, interviewing allows an examination of the reasoning process in addition to policy opinions, whereas survey research primarily assesses the latter. As Robert Lane, a contemporary of Converse, argued, political ideology is best gauged through interviewing because this method provides for a contextual analysis of one's thoughts:

> An opinion, belief, or attitude is best understood in the context of other opinions, beliefs, and attitudes, for they illuminate its meaning, mark its boundaries, modify and qualify its force. Even more important, by grouping opinions the observer often can discover latent ideological themes; he can see the structure of thought.[32]

To examine ideology, Lane interviewed 15 working-class and lower-middle-class men from a northeastern U.S. city. He spent several hours with each man, over a few sessions, and asked them questions such as, "What is your understanding of democracy?" "What is your understanding of the phrase 'all men are created equal?'" "What does the word 'freedom' make you think of?" and "What kinds of things do you think the government ought to do? Ought not to do?"[33] In the end, after analyzing the responses to these and hundreds of other questions, Lane concluded that each man possessed an ideology that helped to guide his political views, views that were deeply held. Lane did not attempt to place these ideologies on a liberal-conservative dimension. Instead, he described them as broad premises or themes. Examples apparent across Lane's interviewees include approval of societal inequality, low levels of cynicism toward government, faith that democracy will uphold personal freedom, and disillusionment with representative government. It should be clear from these examples that Lane's definition of ideology is much broader than Converse's belief system. In fact, Lane characterized Converse and his colleagues' research as "examining survey data based upon a five-item 'social welfare' scale and a four-item foreign-policy scale, and labeling the results 'ideology.'"[34] This quotation nicely illustrates the methodological and definitional differences between Lane and Converse.

Lane's approach and results thus present a very different portrait of public ideology. Converse and his supporters respond that whereas Lane uncovered a variety of individual ideologies among the men he interviewed, knowing the prevalence of liberal-conservative thinking is still important. Since elites discuss politics along this dominant dimension, democratic governance might be undermined if the public does not. Second, Converse's research did allow for the possibility that the public's political views were organized along ideological dimensions other than the liberal-to-conservative one. It was this goal, after all, that motivated him to examine over-time attitude stability among the public. Finding low levels of stability, Converse concluded the opinions of many citizens were not grounded in a broader worldview. Finally, on one point, Lane and Converse reached quite similar conclusions. Lane witnessed that many of his interviewees tended to *morselize* events.[35] Rather than tying specific instances, such as being laid off from work or the actions of another nation's government, to a broader context, these are viewed as separate incidents. For some, this morselization is further evidence that most Americans lack a coherent belief system.[36]

Black Political Ideologies

When Converse examined how people answered open-ended questions about political parties and candidates, the most common category of responses referred to groups (refer back to Figure 5-1). These Group Interest citizens did not display ideological thinking, at least according to Converse's standard. Others disagree, arguing that social groups play such a prominent role in American society and politics that group-linked political thinking should be considered ideological. In American society, this is particularly the case with race. As one scholar explains,

> [I]f society is organized around race, and racial conflict is part of everyday life, and if our stories of the world are also organized around race, race is profoundly political and profoundly ideological.... To use Converse's language, there are a number of linking mechanisms between blacks' social locations, their racial identities, and various (generally unsatisfactory) aspects of their social, economic, cultural and political worlds.[37]

Works examining **black political ideology** by Michael Dawson and Melissa Harris-Lacewell exemplify this tradition.[38] They both argue that there is a range of political ideologies among African Americans, ideologies that do not map easily onto the liberal-conservatism dimension, and that these ideologies do influence black opinions. Delineating these ideologies is difficult using national surveys such as the ANES because such surveys are often designed with the political views of majority whites in mind. Thus, Dawson and Harris-Lacewell relied, in part, on surveys of blacks with questions that were created to tap into attitudes and concerns relevant to this community. Dawson also conducted a historical analysis of black ideologies examining how they developed within the black community while also being influenced by one of the dominant ideologies in U.S. society (liberalism). In the end, Dawson identified five political ideologies present among contemporary African Americans whereas Harris-Lacewell argued for four.[39] These ideologies are described in Table 5-2. In contrast to how liberalism and conservatism were defined earlier in this chapter, the black political ideologies encompass views toward the status of blacks in society, the proper strategies for improving this status, whites and other races, and blacks' interactions with the state. Group-based perspectives, in other words, play a prominent role in these ideologies.

Harris-Lacewell's research makes additional contributions to our understanding of political ideology. She argued that ideologies can emerge from the citizenry and are not only those that dominate elite discourse. While elites discuss politics in terms of liberalism and conservatism, for example, the public's views might cover different and more varied ideological terrain. To provide evidence for her conclusions, Harris-Lacewell examined the "everyday spaces" of black people's lives, spaces unlikely to also be occupied by whites.[40] One component of her analysis was **ethnographic research** that was carried out in a black barbershop in Chicago.[41] Because these shops are male spaces, a male colleague of Harris-Lacewell's (Quincy Mills) spent a few months hanging out at a barbershop, listening to and participating in the daily conversations that took place there, as well as taking detailed notes and recording his own impressions of the interactions among men in the barbershop.

Harris-Lacewell and Mills drew a number of interesting conclusions from this research. One is that the barbershop conversations often covered political topics and that the comments made by the men incorporated tenets from black ideological traditions, even though the men's comments are not organized around a liberal-conservative continuum. See Box 5-1 (page 144) for an example of such a conversation among barbershop customers. Another important argument provided by Harris-Lacewell is that one's political ideology is formed, articulated, and updated during daily conversations (what she called everyday talk). To understand the nature and extent of people's political ideologies, then, researchers must continue to engage in research other than opinion surveys and investigate areas other than political arenas.

Table 5-2 Key Components of Black Political Ideologies

Ideology	Central beliefs
Radical egalitarianism (Dawson)/liberal integrationism (Harris-Lacewell)	Believes that racism is widespread in America and that it is spread primarily through racist institutions, but that the nation's ideal of equality for all points toward a colorblind society. Black justice will only be achieved by demanding equality from the state and working across races.
Black nationalism	Views racial categorization and racial oppression as dominant features of society. Whites will oppose attempts by blacks to gain full equality. Proposes a black nation, generally not a separate political unit but instead a community within the broader society with separate cultural traditions and needs. Emphasizes strong unity among blacks.
Black feminism	Opposes the racism of whites and the sexism of white and black men. Race and gender intersect to oppress black women in multiple ways. Will form political alliances with nonblacks, unless racism is present.
Black conservatism	Believes in individual responsibility rather than government to improve the status of blacks. Faith that free markets do not discriminate. Black equality should be achieved through economic progress rather than through programs that provide blacks with special consideration, such as affirmative action.
Disillusioned liberalism (Dawson only)	Views racism among whites as ingrained and unlikely to disappear, so political alliances with whites are discouraged. Racial equality is to be pursued instead by increasing black political and economic power.

Sources: Michael C. Dawson, *Black Visions: The Roots of Contemporary African-American Political Ideologies* (Chicago: University of Chicago Press, 2001), chaps. 1, 3–6; Melissa Harris-Lacewell, *Barbershops, Bibles, and BET: Everyday Talk and Black Political Thought* (Princeton: Princeton University Press, 2004), chap. 1.

BOX 5-1 Black Political Talk in the Barbershop

During my first week at the shop, Damon offered to give me his analysis of the problems facing black America.

"Women these days don't know how to cook and the family structure ain't how it used to be. A big part of the reason that the family structure is messed up is because women don't cook anymore.... Instead, the women are out working and many times makin' more money than the man."

Sherman huffed, "I don't give a shit about that, I can cook!"

In these early weeks Damon was still checking me out, so he asked me what I thought. I responded, "My future wife doesn't have to cook all the time, sometimes I'll cook, sometimes she'll cook. I could give a shit if my wife makes more money than me.... She'll do her thing and I'll do mine and together we'll manage the family."

Jeff, a young brother in his mid-twenties ... responded to my comment by complaining, "Nowadays women think they know everything. They don't understand their roles. You gotta find a woman who knows a bit less than you and mold her."

I replied, "Mold her! I ain't got time to mold nobody. She better be able to stand on her own. I'm not lookin for a child, I'm lookin for a wife!"

...

Damon chimed in to reiterate his point by saying the male and female roles in the black family were ill defined.

But Sherman suggested, "Things have changed and you gotta learn to change with them."

To refute Sherman, Damon said, "Look at these Arab women and these Indian women. Go ask the Arab down the street what his wife does and he'll tell you she takes care of the home. Their family structure has managed to stay intact over the years. It's the black family that has fallen apart."

...

Sherman and I argued that black men and the black community are best served by relationships where African American women are equal partners in finances, home care, and intimacy. Damon and Jeff were arguing that black women should put the needs of the race first. And they were defining the needs of the race in a narrow, patriarchal manner....

Damon's position reflects a long tradition in both Nationalist and Integrationist thought. This position asserts that women should not press concerns about gender equality within the context of racial struggle in order to preserve a unified racial front.

Source: Melissa Harris-Lacewell, *Barbershops, Bibles, and BET: Everyday Talk and Black Political Thought* (Princeton: Princeton University Press, 2004), 182–183.

Summary

Some critics of Converse have chipped away at his conclusions. The levels of attitude constraint and stability that he documented were likely low because of the political environment of the 1950s and the survey questions he used. Better worded questions as well as more ideologically polarizing times reveal more coherent belief systems among the public. The survey method also makes it difficult to uncover idiosyncratic ideologies or ideologies other than the dominant ones of liberalism or conservatism, also likely contributing to Converse's claim of widespread ideological innocence. On the whole, however, many of Converse's key findings have not been substantially undermined.[42] Constraint and stability have increased some over time, but not tremendously so, and public levels fall far short of elite levels for both. There is also little evidence that the public thinks about politics ideologically. Remember that Converse's first attempt at examining ideological reasoning was to analyze responses to open-ended questions about presidential candidates and political parties. Replicating this part of his study in more recent decades has not often been tried by scholars. One attempt, though, demonstrates that in the 1980s more citizens were classified as Ideologues and Near Ideologues than during Converse's time. Overall, however, these two groups comprised only about 22 percent of the population, whereas Group Interest and Nature of the Times individuals were each 30 percent.[43]

Another way to assess the role that ideology plays in the political views of the public is to ask people whether they identify as either liberals or conservatives. The ANES has been asking this question for the past few decades; we present results from 1972 to 2004 in Figure 5-6. This graph presents over-time trends in percentages

Figure 5-6   Over-Time Ideological Identification, 1972–2004

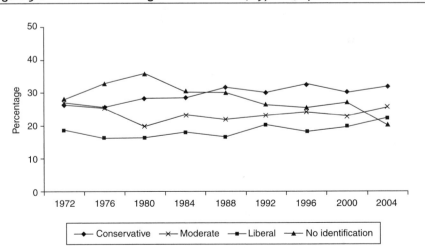

Source: Analysis of American National Election Studies Cumulative Data File, 1948–2004.

of the public identifying as conservative, moderate, or liberal. We ask you to pay particular attention to the fourth line, which demonstrates how many people do not know their political ideology or have not thought enough about it to classify themselves. Between 1972 and 1984 more people chose not to self-identify than did those who claimed an ideological identification. In other words, there were more "Haven't thought much about it" responses than conservatives, liberals, or political moderates during these years, with the number not classifying reaching a high of 35.8 percent in 1980. Beginning in 1988, conservatives began to outnumber those without an ideology, with the number of no identifiers decreasing gradually over time. It was not until 2004, however, that there were more moderates and liberals in the population than nonidentifiers. To us, this is further evidence that a significant portion of the public does not think ideologically. Yet, this situation might be changing. At 20.2 percent, 2004 saw the lowest proportion of the electorate indicating that they were not able to identify an ideology for themselves since the ANES began asking this question.

Public Opinion in Comparative Perspective
BOX 5-2 IDEOLOGICAL THINKING IN OTHER NATIONS

Are United States' citizens unique in displaying low levels of ideological thinking? The short answer is no, although ideological reasoning is more common in some other democracies.

Since Converse's research was conducted, a few studies have applied his methods to studying citizen ideology in other nations. These analyses show that Germans and Italians are more likely than Americans to recognize correctly and to use ideological terms when evaluating political parties.[1] Furthermore, only about 10–20 percent of French citizens do not place themselves on a left-right ideology continuum, compared with significantly higher numbers of Americans who are unable to identify their ideology.[2]

In Great Britain, levels of ideological thinking among the public are similar to those in the United States. Like U.S. citizens, many Britons do not recognize ideological labels and do not think about the parties ideologically.[3] Finally, there is some evidence that ideological constraint is lower in Canada than in the United States. Roger Gibbins and Neil Nevitte compared the correlations among opinions on three types of issues (size of government, income redistribution, and racial minority policies) for Americans, English-speaking Canadians, and French-speaking Canadians from Quebec. They conclude that "French Quebec respondents display much less ideological

(continued)

and attitudinal coherence than do their English-Canadian counterparts, who themselves display much less coherence than was found among US respondents."[4]

What might explain this cross-national variation? National political context seems to play a large role here. In nations where political issues are discussed ideologically or parties distinguish themselves in terms of ideology, ideological thinking is higher among the citizenry. Such is the case in Italy, Germany, and France.[5] In contrast, parties in Britain and the United States tend to contain multiple ideological strains, thus resulting in party platforms that do not demonstrate consistent ideological principles. Gibbins and Nevitte suggest that the lower ideological constraint in Canada occurs because many pressing issues of the day are not debated along a traditional liberal-conservative divide. Instead, regional divides are apparent for many important issues, such as the role of Quebec in the Canadian political structure.[6]

1. Russell J. Dalton, *Citizen Politics: Public Opinion and Political Parties in Advanced Western Democracies,* 2nd ed. (Chatham, N.J.: Chatham House, 1996), chap. 2.
2. Christopher J. Fleury and Michael S. Lewis-Beck, "Anchoring the French Voter: Ideology versus Party," *Journal of Politics* 55 (1993): 1100–1109.
3. Dalton, *Citizen Politics,* chap. 2.
4. Roger Gibbins and Neil Nevitte, "Canadian Political Ideology: A Comparative Analysis," *Canadian Journal of Political Science/Revue Canadienne de Science Politique* 18 (1985): 597.
5. Dalton, *Citizen Politics,* chap. 2; Fleury and Lewis-Beck, "Anchoring the French Voter."
6. Gibbins and Nevitte, "Canadian Political Ideology."

RELATED EVIDENCE?

The critiques we assessed above were related directly to Converse's research. Many other people have examined public ideology since Converse's work first appeared, and these studies have proceeded in many different directions.[44] We briefly overview some of that work here. Specifically, we focus on research whose conclusions could be interpreted to undermine Converse's conclusions, even though the research itself does not replicate his analyses. In other words, while this research has progressed somewhat outside of the bounds of the argument that the public is ideologically innocent, its conclusions can be applied to the debate that Converse's work began.

Ideological Identification Is Related to Issue Opinions

During the same decades that scholars were examining whether people's issue opinions hang together in an ideological fashion, others were demonstrating that you can predict someone's opinion on a specific issue by knowing her self-identified ideology. Conservatives are more supportive of increased spending on defense and crime, tax cuts, and the death penalty, whereas liberals are more likely to approve of social welfare policy, environmental protection, abortion, and gay rights.[45] One's ideology has also been found to influence which issues concern him; conservatives focus more on terrorism whereas liberals are more concerned about the economy, poverty, and global warming.[46]

While the public might not have tightly constrained belief systems across a variety of issues and might not think about politics ideologically, their ideology appears meaningfully related to a range of political opinions. How could this be? A couple of possibilities have been suggested. One explanation for the relationship between ideology and issue opinions is that people rely on ideological cues that are available in the political environment. When a prominent conservative politician, for example, is described as such and also described as favoring the death penalty, matching your own ideology to opinions on this issue becomes easier than when this type of information is not available. Using such shortcuts, or **heuristics**, enables people to make reasonable policy choices absent detailed information or ideological thinking.[47] The second explanation is that ideological self-identification and issue opinions are both rooted in evaluations of social and political groups. Whether one is liberal or conservative is tied to his assessment of business people, the police, minorities, and people on welfare, just as opinion toward issues can be influenced by feelings toward these groups.[48] Thus, with both ideology and issue opinions related to group attachments, it is not surprising that ideology and opinions are also related to one another. Finally, we need to keep in mind that seeing a connection between someone's ideology and issue positions is possible only for those members of the public who are able to identify their own ideology. For 20–35 percent of the public, such self-identification does not occur (recall Figure 5-6), so they are excluded from such analyses. Including them would likely weaken the relationship between ideological orientation and issue opinions since these members of the public had admittedly not thought much about their own ideology.

Ideological Identification Tied to Personality Characteristics

Look around your dorm room or apartment (or, if you are not in your living space now, imagine its contents). Do you see calendars, an iron, and a laundry basket? What about books and music—are there many types of books and CDs, or are your book and music collections rather homogeneous? Do you have any art supplies in your room or evidence of travel (such as an airline ticket, travel books, or souvenirs)? Are your living quarters neat or messy? Well lit or quite dark? According to recent psychological research, your answers to these questions are likely related to whether you are conservative or liberal.[49] A study of college students and recent graduates demonstrates that conservatives tend to have neater, better lit, and better organized (hence the presence of calendars and laundry supplies) residences. Liberals, on the other hand, live in messier and darker rooms that contain a wider variety of books, music, and artistic supplies as well as travel literature and souvenirs.

This intriguing work demonstrates that one's ideological leanings can be related to nonpolitical factors. Specifically, ideology seems to be tied to personality traits. Psychologists have identified five core personality traits of individuals: openness, conscientiousness, extraversion, agreeableness, and neuroticism. For each of these, people can possess the trait or not; in other words, some people are clear extraverts while others are somewhat extraverted and still others are the opposite of extraverted (introverted). Of the "big five," it turns out that political ideology is related to the first two. Liberals tend to be more open-minded whereas conservatives are more conscientious.[50] Since we generally think of political views following from personality traits, rather than the reverse, these results provide a framework for explaining why some people are liberal and some are conservative. Converse would likely argue in response to this that no matter how permanent an individual's ideology is, there is still little evidence that ideology helps to provide attitude constraint or that people use their ideology to make sense of the political world. True enough, but connecting ideology to core personality traits suggests a permanence (our personalities do not change that much throughout our lives, after all) and foundation for one's ideology that Converse's claims of ideological innocence do not.

Growth of Liberal and Conservative Media

Compared with prior decades, ideologically oriented news outlets are today more common. Whether it be cable television stations, talk radio, or Internet blogs, citizens now have many choices for strictly liberal or strictly conservative news.[51] The growth in ideological news has especially occurred on the conservative side, with Rush Limbaugh's talk radio program and *The O'Reilly Factor* on FOX News channel as salient examples, but liberal news programming is also on the rise. A notable example is the Air America radio network that was launched in 2004. Not only do these liberal and conservative media sources exist, but people's choice of news sources is related, at least in part, to their ideology. Compared with the general public, for example, *The O'Reilly Factor*'s viewers and Limbaugh's listeners are significantly more likely to be conservative (36 percent versus 72 percent and 77 percent, respectively).[52] This evidence suggests that one's ideology influences her choice of news and that people choose to be exposed to information that supports their own ideology, perhaps reinforcing it. We do need to be careful not to overstate this news influence, however, particularly because audiences for liberal or conservative outlets are still smaller than for mainstream news. Whereas 28 percent of the public regularly watch the nightly news on ABC, NBC, or CBS, only 20 percent regularly listen to political talk radio and 9 percent regularly watch *The O'Reilly Factor*.[53]

CONCLUSION

Few, if any, works have influenced public opinion scholarship to the extent that Converse's "The Nature of Belief Systems in Mass Publics" has. The piece has been called the "foundation stone of political-behavior research"[54] and a veritable cottage industry of research on public ideology arose after its 1964 publication. Some of that research confirmed Converse's findings, whereas other studies, including many that we discussed in this chapter, presented alternative conclusions. Our goal has been to present this work, while also providing counterarguments to specific points throughout the chapter to help you sort through the claims and counterclaims as you think about whether you support Converse or his critics. Our own view, with which you might disagree, is that many of Converse's core conclusions have stood the test of time. Chief among these is that members of the public tend not to see the political world in ideological terms. When asked to evaluate candidate and parties, after all, ideologically oriented responses are still fairly rare. And, recall that when asked whether they consider themselves to be liberal or conservative, significant portions (as high as 35 percent at one point) of the public respond that they have not thought enough about this topic to classify themselves. The proportion of the public self-identifying has increased of late as has the attractiveness of ideologically oriented media, perhaps suggesting that ideological thinking is on the rise. Time will tell whether this is indeed a new trend.

One of Converse's key concerns, and the topic with which we began this chapter, was the degree to which citizens and elites think about and discuss politics using the same terms. Converse found that elites are much more likely to possess ideologically constrained belief systems. Elite constraint has rarely been studied since Converse's work was published, but research examining this topic has confirmed Converse's finding. As one public opinion scholar writing a recent review of belief systems research put it, "Subsequent work has tended to confirm Converse's picture of a tiny stratum of well-informed ideological elites whose passionate political debates find little echo, or even awareness, in the mass public."[55]

What are the implications of this disconnect between the public and its leaders? For one, it is more difficult for citizens to evaluate and constrain, if necessary, elite behavior if they do not understand the nature of elite policy decisions. This undermines democratic governance, certainly the type of governance assumed by participatory democrats who hope that citizens will fairly routinely monitor the actions of leaders. Even elite democrats believe that the public should hold elected officials accountable during election time, a task that becomes difficult if these two groups do not think about and discuss politics using the same terms. Governing may also become difficult for leaders. With their belief systems more ideologically constrained, "it presumably becomes more difficult for [elites] to fashion agendas and priorities that can appeal to large swaths of a more variegated, unconstrained rank and file."[56]

Finally, if the public tends not to think ideologically and if many members of the public do not organize their beliefs along an ideological continuum, is it fair to conclude that public attitudes are fleeting and not well reasoned? We are not prepared to draw that conclusion, and we hope you will wait as well. In the next chapter, we describe other sources of people's political beliefs, including personality, values, self-interest, group attitudes, and historical events. Whether these alternative sources are as or more politically meaningful as ideology and whether they revive a view of the public as more competent for democratic politics than Converse concluded are topics that we encourage you to consider as you read chapter 6.

KEY CONCEPTS

attitude constraint / 130	ideologically contentious / 132
attitude stability / 130	ideology / 126
belief system / 127	in-depth interviewing / 140
black political ideology / 141	liberals / 126
consensual politics / 132	Likert question / 134
conservatives / 126	measurement error / 137
ethnographic research / 142	open-ended questions / 127
heuristics / 148	question wording / 134

SUGGESTED SOURCES FOR FURTHER READING

Converse, Philip E. "The Nature of Belief Systems in Mass Publics." In *Ideology and Discontent,* ed. David E. Apter. New York: Free Press, 1964.

This is Converse's classic study, in which he outlines his argument for ideological innocence and presents survey data as evidence to support his conclusions.

"Is Democratic Competence Possible?" Special issue of *Critical Review* 18 (2006).
MacKuen, Michael B. and George Rabinowitz, eds. *Electoral Democracy.* Ann Arbor: University of Michigan Press, 2003.

The special issue of the journal *Critical Review* contains a republication of Converse's 1964 "Nature of Belief Systems" paper (which is currently out of print) along with twelve essays that comment on research conducted on this topic since 1964. The issue ends with an interesting response essay by Converse in which he addresses some of the arguments of his critics. *Electoral Democracy* is also a collection of essays that explore themes related to Converse's work, including factors that influence people's opinions and interactions between the public and elites.

Dawson, Michael C. *Black Visions: The Roots of Contemporary African-American Political Ideologies.* Chicago: University of Chicago Press, 2001.

Harris-Lacewell, Melissa. *Barbershops, Bibles, and BET: Everyday Talk and Black Political Thought.* Princeton: Princeton University Press, 2004.

Lane, Robert E. *Political Ideology: Why the American Common Man Believes What He Does.* New York: Free Press, 1962.

The authors of these books discuss and examine political ideology in ways quite different from Converse. Lane and Harris-Lacewell argue that ideology is best uncovered using methods other than surveys, such as interviews or ethnographic research. The latter two books further demonstrate that group-based thinking should indeed be considered political ideology.

"Beyond Red vs. Blue: The 2005 Political Typology," Pew Research Center for the People and the Press, http://typology.people-press.org/.

This Web site presents the results of the Pew Research Center's efforts to classify the American public into one of nine political typologies. Their typologies include some ideologically based ones (Social Conservatives and Pro-Government Conservatives, for example). For a fun exercise, click on the "Where Do You Fit?" link, answer the questions that appear, and find out your political type.

Campaigns and Elections Political Blog Directory: www.campaignsandelections.com/blogs/ index.cfm?navid=53.

ETALKINGHEAD: An Online Political News Magazine: http://directory.etalkinghead.com/.

These two Web sites provide extensive lists of online political blogs. The blogs are organized by ideological leaning, among other criteria.

CHAPTER 6
Pluralistic Roots of Public Opinion

AFTER THE PUBLICATION of Philip Converse's path-breaking research in 1964, which we discussed at length in the previous chapter, much of the debate among public opinion scholars was driven by his findings regarding the public's lack of ideological sophistication. In fact, some observers argued that too much attention was paid to this debate over ideology, distracting scholars from how citizens really do think about politics.[1] In this chapter, we move beyond Converse and his critics to address this question: if ideology doesn't organize citizens' opinions, what does? Donald Kinder has offered an answer to that question. He encourages scholars to consider the **pluralistic roots** of public opinion.[2] Specifically, he suggests five factors that might influence citizens' attitudes: personality, self-interest, values, group attitudes, and historical events.

The research on the public's lack of ideological sophistication leaves us with a view of citizens as not competent enough to play an active role in governance, which bolsters the elite democratic theorists' argument that citizens should be removed from the policymaking process. In contrast, the research on the pluralistic roots of public opinion resurrects a more positive view of the average citizen. From this perspective, citizens are capable of holding reasoned, complex opinions derived from meaningful political factors, such as values and group identity. Pluralists are especially pleased by the reliance on group-based thinking. Participatory democratic theorists are also encouraged that citizens' opinions have some logic underlying them, yet we will see they are not always thrilled by the particular logic that drives public opinion.

In this chapter we discuss the five factors—personality, self-interest, values, group attitudes, and historical events—that shape public opinion. Each section focuses primarily on one of the factors, but you will quickly notice that these forces are not mutually exclusive. In many instances, more than one of the factors influence public opinion on a particular issue.

PERSONALITY

Let's begin with a discussion of a personality trait that influences public opinion: authoritarianism. In 1950, Theodor Adorno and his colleagues introduced the concept of an "authoritarian personality."[3] They defined authoritarianism as a set of personality traits, including submissiveness to authority, a desire for a strong leader, general hostility and cynicism toward people, strict adherence to convention, and a belief that people should be roundly punished if they defy those conventions.[4] These traits appear most often in people exposed to strict and rigid child-rearing practices. In other words, children whose parents dole out a "relatively harsh and threatening type of home discipline" are more likely to have authoritarian personalities as adults.[5]

This harsh upbringing leads to frustration among children, which ultimately gets redirected toward outgroups; anger and resentment toward parents becomes displaced onto people who are considered weak and inferior. As a result, authoritarians demonstrate high levels of intolerance for outgroups. This theory was developed shortly after World War II as a way to make sense of anti-Semitism. Over the years, Adorno et al.'s work on the authoritarian personality has been challenged on a number of theoretical and methodological fronts.[6] Nevertheless, the concept has continued to be a compelling one for social scientists.

More than fifty years after the publication of Adorno's research, Karen Stenner's recent work has reinvigorated the study of authoritarianism.[7] According to Stenner, "authoritarianism is an individual predisposition concerned with the appropriate balance between group authority and uniformity, on the one hand, and individual autonomy and diversity, on the other."[8] She labels people who value sameness and conformity to group norms as **authoritarians** and people who value diversity and individual freedom as **libertarians**.

Stenner takes pains to point out that the differences between authoritarians and libertarians are not simply a matter of political ideology.[9] In earlier research, some scholars had conflated conservatism and authoritarianism. But there is an important distinction. For example, people whom Stenner labels as "status quo conservatives" do not mind diverse viewpoints, as long as that diversity is stable over time. In contrast, authoritarians are bothered by the diversity in and of itself. Another way to think of the distinction is that status quo conservatives do not like change, whereas authoritarians are pleased with change as long as it moves people toward greater "oneness and sameness."[10] (Also note that we briefly discussed libertarians in chapter 5. There we were discussing libertarianism as a political ideology, whereas here Stenner is using the term to refer to a personality predisposition.)

Stenner argues that authoritarianism and libertarianism constitute very broad, normative worldviews about the way society should function, and these worldviews influence citizens' opinions across a wide range of political, racial, and moral issues. Because authoritarians value conformity and obedience to authority, they favor policies that stifle diversity and enforce sameness across citizens. On the other end of the continuum, libertarians value freedom and difference and thus oppose coercive government policies or policies that discourage individuality.

Stenner provides evidence of the impact of authoritarianism on public opinion by analyzing national survey data from the General Social Survey (GSS). But before we dive into Stenner's research findings, we must first discuss how she measures the concept of authoritarianism. Stenner argues that the best way to determine whether someone is an authoritarian is to examine his or her beliefs about child-rearing practices. Child-rearing values "can effectively and unobtrusively *reflect one's fundamental orientations* toward authority/uniformity versus autonomy/difference."[11] The GSS asks respondents to rank child-rearing values by indicating which qualities are "most desirable" for a child to have and which ones are "least important" (see Table 6-1). According to Stenner, authoritarians place a high value on obedient, neat, and well-mannered children, whereas libertarians are partial to inquisitive and responsible children with good judgment.[12]

Stenner examined data from surveys conducted by the GSS between 1990 and 2000; she focused her attention solely on white respondents.[13] Her analysis showed that authoritarians are significantly more likely than libertarians to be racially, morally, and politically intolerant. In terms of race, authoritarian citizens tend to oppose interracial marriage, support housing segregation, and say they would not vote for a black presidential candidate. When it comes to moral issues, authoritarians oppose homosexuality, believe in compulsory school prayer, and think that pornography should be banned. Citizens who are authoritarian are also opposed to civil liberties for groups from both the left and right side of the ideological spectrum. For example, authoritarians do not think that homosexuals or racists should be allowed to teach in a college or university. In addition, authoritarians are more punitive than libertarians. Authoritarians are more likely to

Table 6-1   Measuring Authoritarianism

Authoritarian child-rearing values	Libertarian child-rearing values
"That a child obeys his or her parents well"	"That a child is interested in how and why things happen"
"That a child is neat and clean"	"That a child has good sense and sound judgment"
"That a child has good manners"	"That a child is responsible"

Source: Karen Stenner, *The Authoritarian Dynamic* (New York: Cambridge University Press, 2005), Appendix D, www.karenstenner.com/AD3_appendix%20D.pdf.

Note: The General Social Survey asks respondents to rank order thirteen child-rearing values using a series of questions: (a) "Which three qualities listed on this card would you say are the most desirable for a child to have?" (b) "Which one of these three is the most desirable of all?" (c) "All of the qualities listed on this card may be desirable, but could you tell me which three you consider least important?" (d) "And which one of these three is least important of all?" Stenner constructed her authoritarianism scale based on the ranking of the six values presented in this table.

support the death penalty, believe that courts are too soft on criminals, support wiretapping, and own a gun. Taken as a whole, Stenner provides strong evidence that white authoritarian citizens abhor difference and diversity and believe people should be harshly punished for disobedience.

Our discussion of Stenner's research has probably raised an important question in your mind: what about authoritarianism among non-white Americans? Presumably some African American, Hispanic, Asian American, and Native American citizens value oneness and sameness over diversity and difference just as some whites do. And if authoritarianism is a basic and universal personality predisposition, as Stenner suggests, then wouldn't we expect it to influence the policy opinions of nonwhite citizens as well?[14] Perhaps authoritarian blacks would not see voting for a black presidential candidate as a violation of oneness and sameness (or perhaps they would given that the political system is dominated by whites and therefore a black presidential candidate might be seen as disruptive), but it seems likely, for example, that authoritarian blacks would be more opposed to homosexuals and racists in the classroom than libertarian blacks. Unfortunately, Stenner's research does not shed light on authoritarianism among minority citizens in the United States.

In addition to analyzing national survey data, Stenner conducted a fascinating experiment to gain a better understanding of the authoritarian predisposition. Stenner randomly assigned black and white interviewers to conduct in-depth interviews with white subjects who were either extremely authoritarian or extremely libertarian (based on their answers to an earlier mail survey conducted in Durham, North Carolina, in 1997). For each interview, there was a primary interviewer and an interview partner. Note that the interviewers were unaware that the people they were interviewing had been selected based on their authoritarianism scores, nor did the interviewers know which people were highly authoritarian and which people were highly libertarian. Further, the subjects themselves did not know they had been chosen for the interviews based on their levels of authoritarianism. Twenty-two authoritarians and eighteen libertarians were interviewed.[15]

After each interview, the interviewers were asked to answer a series of questions about their interactions with the subject. For example, the interviewers rated how reluctant the subject was to participate in the study once the interviewers were on the doorstep and how hostile the subject was during the interview session. Authoritarians were significantly more reluctant to participate than libertarians in general, but this was especially the case when the primary interviewer was black. Authoritarians were also more hostile than libertarians to the interviewers, but again this was exacerbated when the interviewers were black. Stenner argues that these behaviors illustrate how authoritarians do not like strangers (especially black strangers) coming into their homes, whereas libertarians are much more open to different others.

Authoritarians and libertarians also differed in a number of ways when it came to the content of their discussions with the interviewers.[16] During the in-depth interviews, the interviewers asked the participants several questions about racial issues. The transcripts of the interviews were analyzed by a coder who was unaware of the purpose of the study and had no idea that some subjects were authoritarian and others were libertarian. Based on this coding, Stenner found that authoritarians were more likely than libertarians to say that blacks and whites should not mix and to blame blacks themselves for inequality in society. But, quite interestingly, Stenner also showed that authoritarians clearly understood that what they were saying was politically incorrect. When interviewed by a black interviewer, authoritarians were no more likely to say racist things than libertarians, but when interviewed by a white interviewer, authoritarians let their racist beliefs shine through.

Stenner's research also examined the effect of **normative threats** on citizens with authoritarian predispositions. To authoritarians, a normative threat is a situation in which oneness and sameness is called into question. It is worth quoting Stenner at some length on her definition of normative threats:

> In diverse and complex modern societies, the things that make us *one and the same* are common authority and shared values. The conditions most threatening to oneness and sameness, then, are questioned or questionable authorities and values: that is, disrespect for leaders or leaders unworthy of respect and lack of conformity to or consensus in group values, norms, and beliefs.[17]

Stenner argues that when citizens are faced with normative threats, authoritarianism becomes activated and thus has a stronger effect on intolerance of difference. In other words, those citizens with an authoritarian bent become even more intolerant when they are in a situation in which "diversity and freedom 'run amok.'"[18]

In a series of experiments, Stenner provides evidence to support this interaction between authoritarianism and normative threats. For example, Stenner embedded an experiment in a national telephone survey to examine the reaction of authoritarians to normative threats.[19] In the Belief Diversity condition, interviewers read subjects a (fictitious) news story about how public opinion in the United States is increasingly divided on a number of important political issues and then asked the subjects how they felt about the story. This story represents a normative threat to authoritarians because of its focus on violations of oneness and sameness. In the Good Leadership condition, interviewers read subjects a (fictitious) news story about how strong and trustworthy U.S. presidents have been and how citizens can expect high-quality presidential candidates in the future and then asked the subjects how they felt about the story. This story is a normatively reassuring one to authoritarians because it emphasizes authority. There was also a control condition in which subjects were not exposed to a news story.[20] Later on in the survey, subjects were asked their opinion about whether whites have a right to keep blacks out of their neighborhoods.

In the control condition, authoritarians were more likely than libertarians to say that whites can keep blacks out of their neighborhoods. Furthermore, authoritarians became even more intolerant and libertarians more tolerant in the Belief Diversity condition. In other words, authoritarians reacted to the normative threat by becoming even more opposed to difference, whereas libertarians responded to the normative threat by becoming even more open to difference.

When exposed to the normative reassurance of the Good Leadership news story, however, authoritarians and libertarians became very similar in terms of their levels of racial tolerance. This convergence occurred because authoritarians became less intolerant and libertarians became more intolerant (than in the other two conditions) in response to the normative reassurance of the Good Leadership news story. As Stenner puts its, "They each let down their defenses in the wake of such reassurance, rendering authoritarians calmed and libertarians complacent, the latter fairly characterized as 'asleep at the wheel'" in this condition.[21]

Stenner also examined the interaction of authoritarianism with normative threats in other domains (i.e., political and moral) and found the same pattern of results: normative threats activated authoritarianism and thus led people with authoritarian leanings to be more intolerant and people with libertarian predispositions to be more tolerant. These research findings are problematic for participatory democratic theorists. Recall that participatory democratic theorists believe that citizens can come together to discuss political issues in a productive way. Citizens can learn from one another, which will help them look beyond their self-interest and gain an understanding of what is best for the nation as a whole. Stenner's research, however, pokes a big hole in this argument. Her findings suggest that if authoritarians are exposed to diverse viewpoints during conversations with their fellow citizens, they would view that as normatively threatening and thus become even more intolerant; however, participatory democratic theorists can take some solace from Stenner's results showing that libertarians exposed to diverse viewpoints become more tolerant.

Public Opinion in Comparative Perspective
BOX 6-1 AUTHORITARIANISM ACROSS THE WORLD

In her book, *The Authoritarian Dynamic,* Karen Stenner argues that the concept of authoritarianism helps us understand intolerance of difference not just in the United States but across the world "from Switzerland to China to Nigeria to Azerbaijan."[1] She analyzed the World Values Survey, which includes survey data collected from over 110,000 people in fifty-nine nations between 1990 and 1998. She measured authoritarianism based on people's evaluation of child-rearing practices. Citizens who cherish obedient and well-mannered children more than they value children who are tolerant of other people, independent, and imaginative are considered authoritarian.[2] Stenner demonstrated that authoritarians are more likely to be intolerant across a range of racial, political, and moral issues. For example, authoritarian people are more opposed to homosexuality, abortion, divorce, and racial integration than libertarians. Further, authoritarians are more likely to believe that jobs should be reserved for the native-born, that maintaining order is more important than free speech, and that fighting crime is more important than progressing toward a humane society.

What is so fascinating about Stenner's work is that she demonstrates the linkage between authoritarianism and intolerance in a wide variety of countries across the globe. This is noteworthy because conflict within countries is often attributed to factors specific to that country. So, for example, when observers try to explain the breakup of Yugoslavia during the 1990s, they often point to long-standing ethnic hatreds that were unleashed after the death of Tito, the country's powerful and charismatic communist leader, in 1980. In France, conflict surrounding the assimilation of North African immigrants is most often explained by cultural and religious factors unique to that country and those particular immigrants. But Stenner argues that regardless of the particular groups involved or whether difference is based on culture, religion, race, ethnicity, or tribes, the primary factor that explains intolerance is authoritarianism. Why? Because authoritarianism is a universal personality predisposition. Stenner concludes, "authoritarianism rather consistently produces a predictable cluster of sociopolitical stances varying in target and form, but never in function: the animating spirit throughout is to limit difference in people, beliefs, and behaviors."[3]

1. Karen Stenner, *The Authoritarian Dynamic* (New York: Cambridge University Press, 2005), 129.
2. Ibid., 91.
3. Ibid., 116.

SELF-INTEREST

It seems incredibly intuitive that **self-interest** would have an important effect on our policy attitudes. When considering human nature, it certainly seems as if people are looking out for number one. Indeed, James Madison argued that a representative form of government is the best form of government because citizens are too focused on their narrow self-interest, whereas representatives have the wisdom to "best discern the true interest of their country."[22] Elite democratic theorists have used this argument to justify why elites (rather than citizens) should have central decision-making roles in politics.

Despite the intuitive—even compelling—nature of the claim that citizens follow their self-interest, there is actually quite limited evidence to support the proposition. On policy opinions ranging from government spending to race and gender issues to foreign policy, scholars have found only weak or nonexistent effects of self-interest.[23] For example, several studies showed that white nonparents were as likely to oppose school busing as a means to achieve racial integration as white parents with school-age children.[24] Instead of self-interest, racial prejudice was a key factor influencing attitudes on school busing: prejudiced citizens were more opposed to busing, whereas nonprejudiced citizens were more supportive of the policy (regardless of whether the citizens had kids or not). Other research indicates that citizens' evaluations of the nation's economy are more important than their own personal economic circumstances when assessing the political party in power.[25] In other words, general concerns about society—what political scientists call **sociotropic concerns**—trump **pocketbook issues** when citizens evaluate their government.

There are a few instances, however, when self-interest does influence citizens' policy attitudes. For example, homeowners are more likely to favor property tax cuts than nonhomeowners.[26] Smokers are more opposed to cigarette taxes and bans on smoking than nonsmokers.[27] And gun owners are less supportive of gun restrictions than people who do not own guns.[28] These examples suggest that self-interest plays a meaningful role when the effects of a policy are *visible, tangible, large, and certain.*[29]

In an innovative study, Dennis Chong, Jack Citrin, and Patricia Conley examined the conditions under which self-interest matters.[30] They defined self-interest as the "tangible, relatively immediate, personal or family benefits of a policy."[31] They conducted an experiment to examine when self-interest has a stronger effect on citizens' attitudes. Specifically, they collected data by embedding an experiment in a telephone survey of a national representative sample of 1,067 U.S. citizens. The survey was conducted between June 21, 1998, and March 7, 1999. Respondents were randomly assigned to one of three conditions: No Prime, Self-Interest Prime, or Sociotropic Prime. In the No Prime condition, subjects were asked to indicate their preference regarding two possible reforms of the Social Security system: reducing benefits to wealthier retired people or increasing taxes on people who are working. In the Self-Interest Prime condition, subjects were first prompted (or primed) to consider how the policy changes would affect them personally and then asked the question about which reform they would prefer. In the Sociotropic Prime condition, subjects were first asked to consider which policy change would be better for future generations and then asked to indicate which change they would prefer. See Table 6-2 for question wordings.

Table 6-2 The Influence of Self-Interest on Social Security Attitudes

"There is a lot of discussion about the possible ways to change Social Security to make sure that all people who retire can get their Social Security benefits. One proposal is to reduce the amount of money paid to retired people who have additional sources of income. Another proposal is to keep the amount of money paid to retired people the same as it is now, but increase Social Security taxes for people who are currently working."

	Reduce retiree benefits	Raise Social Security taxes
No prime:		
"Which proposal do you think should be adopted?"		
Under 60	56%	45%
60 and over	32	68
Self-interest prime:		
"Which proposal do you think would be financially better for you personally—reducing the amount of money paid to retired people who have additional sources of income, or keeping the amount of money paid to retired people same as it is now, but increasing Social Security taxes for people who are working?"		
"Which proposal do you think would be financially better for other members of your family?"		
"Which proposal do you think should be adopted?"		
Under 60	52	49
60 and over	28	72
Sociotropic prime:		
"Which proposal do you think would do more to ensure that the Social Security fund will have enough money to provide for future generations?"		
"Which proposal do you think should be adopted?"		
Under 60	45	55
60 and over	42	58

Source: Dennis Chong, Jack Citrin, and Patricia Conley, "When Self-Interest Matters," *Political Psychology* 22 (2001): 555, 565–566.

Chong et al. compared the responses of people age 60 and over with those under 60 in these three conditions. If self-interest is at work, then older people should lean toward raising taxes on folks who are working, whereas those under 60 should favor cutting benefits for retirees. That is the pattern we see in the No Prime and Self-Interest conditions: a strong majority of the older group support raising taxes, while a small majority of those under 60 prefer to reduce retiree benefits (see Table 6-2). But when citizens were primed to think about sociotropic considerations—which proposal will be best for future generations—opinions varied little by age. In the Sociotropic Prime condition, the younger group became more supportive of raising Social Security taxes and the older group became more open to reducing benefits. Overall, these results suggest that self-interest influences how citizens think about Social Security, yet the extent to which self-interest matters depends heavily on how the issue is presented.

VALUES

Values are "general and enduring standards."[32] They are abstract beliefs about how the world *should* work. As such, values constitute citizens' core principles, guiding their understanding of right and wrong. Thus, it makes sense that citizens' values would influence their specific policy positions.[33]

Scholars have identified two fundamental values that influence public opinion: egalitarianism and individualism.[34] **Egalitarianism** is the belief that citizens should be equal regardless of their personal characteristics.[35] In the U.S. context, egalitarianism emphasizes equality of opportunity, not necessarily equality of results. In other words, egalitarianism is the belief that all citizens should have the *chance* to achieve rather than the belief that all citizens should be guaranteed equal outcomes. **Individualism** is the belief that citizens should get ahead by virtue of their own hard work; people should "pull themselves up by their own bootstraps" and rely on their own ingenuity.

Egalitarianism and individualism are abstract concepts and therefore difficult to measure. Nevertheless, political scientists have devised a set of survey questions to assess these concepts. In particular, Stanley Feldman analyzed citizens' levels of agreement with several statements that were included on a pilot study for the 1984 American National Election Study (ANES) to come up with the best way to measure egalitarianism and individualism.[36] He identified three statements that provide a valid measure of egalitarianism (see Table 6-3 for the wording of these items). The first two items seem to focus on support for equal opportunity, while the third is more ambiguous. Some people might infer that treating people "more equally" means ensuring equal results, whereas others might think the statement simply refers to providing people with equal opportunities. Feldman also identified five statements that provide a valid measure of individualism (again, see Table 6-3 for the wording of these items). These statements emphasize the personal effort that is needed for someone to get ahead in life. (Note that agreeing with the

Table 6-3   Measuring Egalitarianism and Individualism

"I am going to read several statements. After each one, I would like you to tell me whether you agree or disagree. I would also like to know whether you agree or disagree strongly or not strongly."	
Egalitarianism	*Individualism*
"Our society should do whatever is necessary to make sure that everyone has an equal opportunity to succeed."	"Any person who is willing to work hard has a good chance of succeeding."
"One of the big problems in this country is that we don't give everyone an equal chance."	"If people work hard, they almost always get what they want."
"If people were treated more equally in this country, we would have many fewer problems."	"Most people who don't get ahead should not blame the system; they really have only themselves to blame."
	"Hard work offers little guarantee of success."
	"Even if people try hard, they often cannot reach their goals."

Source: Stanley Feldman, "Structure and Consistency in Public Opinion: The Role of Core Beliefs and Values," *American Journal of Political Science* 32 (1988): 421.

first three statements is the individualistic response, whereas disagreeing with the last two statements is the individualistic response.) What do you think—do these statements do a good job measuring individualism and egalitarianism?

Feldman analyzed the impact of egalitarianism and individualism on citizens' policy attitudes. He demonstrated that egalitarianism is closely related to citizens' opinions on a wide range of policies. For example, egalitarian citizens are more likely to support welfare programs, increased government spending on health and education, and government efforts to improve the societal position of African Americans, women, and the poor. Thus, across many different policy areas, egalitarianism leads to more progressive political views. In contrast, individualism has an effect in only a few policy areas; nevertheless, its influence is still noteworthy. Individualistic citizens are more likely to oppose welfare spending and prefer a more limited role for the federal government (as compared with state governments) in handling social and economic problems.

Donald Kinder and his colleagues also examine support for egalitarianism, with a particular focus on the differing levels of support among black and white citizens.[37] They demonstrated that blacks are substantially more likely to endorse egalitarian statements than whites (see Figure 6-1). For example, three-fourths of African Americans believe that our society should take whatever steps are necessary to ensure equal opportunity, whereas two-thirds of whites support that view. There is an even more staggering racial gap—more than 25 percentage points—in agreement on the two statements that tap into how serious of a problem inequality is in our society.[38]

Figure 6-1   Egalitarianism among Blacks and Whites

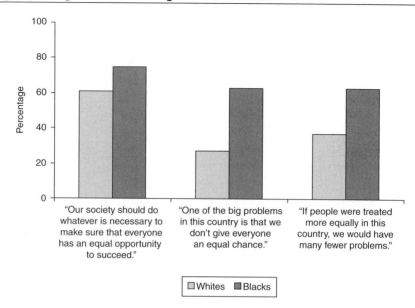

Source: Donald R. Kinder and Lynn M. Sanders, *Divided by Color* (Chicago: University of Chicago Press, 1996), 134.

Note: Bars represent the percentage of respondents who indicated they "agree strongly" with each statement.

This racial difference in support for egalitarianism is extremely important because it translates into differences in policy opinions between blacks and whites. For example, blacks are more likely than whites to support federal spending on education, college financial aid, the poor, the homeless, the unemployed, and programs that assist blacks. To illustrate the extent of the racial gap in issue opinions, let's examine opinion toward federal spending for the unemployed: two-thirds of blacks favor increased government expenditures in this area, whereas just over one-third of whites take that position.[39] There are several factors that create this racial gap in opinion, but egalitarianism is a key factor. Higher levels of egalitarianism among blacks lead them to be more supportive than whites of a wide variety of social welfare programs.[40]

Political values also influence public opinion in the domain of gay rights. Analyzing ANES data from 1992, 1996, and 2000, Paul Brewer demonstrated that egalitarianism has a strong effect on support for gay rights. Specifically, citizens who are more egalitarian tend to favor laws that protect homosexuals against job discrimination and believe that homosexuals should be allowed to serve in the military. Furthermore, the influence of egalitarianism on support for gay rights is consistently strong in all three years.

Brewer also highlights another influential value: moral traditionalism. **Moral traditionalism** refers to citizens' "underlying predispositions on traditional family and social organization." [41] Moral traditionalists prefer stable, two-parent—one male and one female, that is—families and are opposed to changing norms regarding family structure and acceptable lifestyles. See Table 6-4 for the statements used to measure moral traditionalism. [42] (Note that agreeing with the first and third statements is the morally traditional response, whereas disagreeing with the second and fourth statements is the morally traditional response.)

Brewer found that citizens who are moral traditionalists are more likely to oppose laws to protect homosexuals from job discrimination and to think that homosexuals should not be allowed to serve in the armed forces. This held for all three years under study, but moral traditionalism was a more influential factor explaining attitudes toward gay rights in 1992 and 1996 than in 2000.

Although the primary focus of this section is on values, we would be remiss if we failed to discuss Brewer's other important findings regarding support for gay rights. First, Brewer suggests that moral traditionalism had less of an impact on citizens' views in 2000 because of people's reactions to *historical events*. He points to the brutal murder of Matthew Shepherd as an event that likely shaped how citizens thought about gay rights. Matthew Shepherd was a college student at the University of Wyoming. In 1998, he was kidnapped, viciously beaten, tied to a fence, and left to die. His death received extensive media coverage. Why would this tragedy influence public opinion on gay rights? Because Matthew Shepherd was

Table 6-4 Measuring Moral Traditionalism

"Now I am going to read several statements. After each one, I would like you to tell me whether you agree strongly, agree somewhat, neither agree nor disagree, disagree somewhat, or disagree strongly with this statement. The first statement is ... "

"The newer lifestyles are contributing to the breakdown of our society."

"The world is always changing and we should adjust our view of moral behavior to those changes."

"This country would have many fewer problems if there were more emphasis on traditional family ties."

"We should be more tolerant of people who choose to live according to their own moral standards, even if they are very different from our own."

Source: Paul R. Brewer, "The Shifting Foundations of Public Opinion about Gay Rights," *Journal of Politics* 65 (2003): 1218.

gay. Brewer speculates that this repugnant act might have led some people to question whether their traditional moral views should be linked to opposing gay rights.

Second, Brewer shows that *attitudes toward gays and lesbians* are an important predictor of opinion on gay rights. Citizens who have negative feelings toward gays and lesbians are more likely than those who have positive feelings to oppose employment rights for the group. This was true each year, although attitudes toward homosexuals became a less important predictor of gay rights opinion across the time period. Again, Brewer links this decrease in the importance of attitudes toward gays and lesbians to the public responding to historical events. As gays and lesbians became more visible on television (think *Ellen* and *Will and Grace*, for example), Brewer argues that people became more familiar with homosexuals, therefore breaking down stereotypes and reducing hostility. Citizens began to see gays and lesbians as individual people rather than an undifferentiated mass. As a result, citizens were less likely to derive their opinions on gay rights from their feelings toward gays and lesbians as a group.

In sum, several scholars have demonstrated the important role of values in shaping citizens' issue attitudes. Individualism, egalitarianism, and moral traditionalism are all abstract, enduring standards that influence public opinion. Brewer's research on attitudes toward gay rights also points toward two additional factors that are key to understanding public opinion: group attitudes and historical events. We discuss these forces in more detail in the next two sections.

GROUP ATTITUDES

Many public policies can be thought of in terms of the groups that are affected by the policy.[43] Here are some examples: equal pay policy has clear implications for women; welfare policy has a direct effect on poor people; and Social Security policy has an impact on elderly people. In each of these instances, attitudes toward the groups involved play an important role in shaping issue opinions.[44] In this section we demonstrate that prejudice toward, stereotypes about, and identification with social groups have a strong influence on policy opinions. Much of the research on the role of **group attitudes** has focused on racial attitudes. As a result, we highlight several such studies below. We also touch on party identification in this section because political parties are one of the most important reference groups in American politics. We demonstrate the fundamental role party identification plays in shaping citizens' political views.

Racial Prejudice and Race-Targeted Policy Opinion

One of the most controversial areas of public opinion research is the study of racial prejudice and its impact on policy attitudes. Racial prejudice is a complex concept, and thus debates over its definition and measurement have raged for several decades. One school of thought among public opinion scholars is that racism is significantly different today from what it once was. Researchers from this camp argue that there is a distinction between old-fashioned racism and new racism. **Old-fashioned racism** is a set of beliefs about the innate inferiority of black Americans. These beliefs served as a justification, for instance, for segregating blacks and whites. Old-fashioned racism led to separate blood supplies for blacks and whites, white fears of miscegenation, the segregation of public accommodations (such as restrooms, hotels, restaurants, etc.), and legal discrimination against black Americans. Over time, these beliefs about black inferiority were discredited by scientific research (which is ironic because for many years "scientific" arguments were used to justify old-fashioned racism). Consequently, citizens are much less likely to endorse old-fashioned racism these days compared with forty years ago. For example, today a large majority of Americans oppose laws against racial intermarriage, whereas only 40 percent opposed such laws in 1964 (also see Figure 9-4 in chapter 9).[45] Furthermore, young adults are less likely to endorse old-fashioned racism than older Americans (see Box 9-1 in chapter 9).[46] Thus, as generational replacement occurs, levels of old-fashioned racism should continue to decline.

Although old-fashioned racism has decreased, many scholars contend that a new, more subtle, form of racial prejudice has emerged.[47] Donald Kinder and Lynn Sanders argue that a "new form of prejudice has come to prominence, one that is preoccupied with matters of moral character, informed by the virtues associated with the traditions of individualism. At its center are the contentions that blacks do not try hard enough to overcome the difficulties they face and that they take what they have not earned."[48] Kinder and Sanders label this new form of prejudice **racial resentment**.[49] Instead of blaming biological or genetic factors for black inferiority as old-fashioned racism does, racial resentment blames a lack of work ethic for the continued inequality between blacks and whites in our society.

Kinder and Sanders make the case that racial resentment developed among whites in response to the success of the civil rights movement. As discriminatory laws were knocked down by the Supreme Court and Congress passed civil rights legislation, white Americans began to think that racial problems were solved. Yet, five days after the 1965 Voting Rights Act was signed by President Lyndon B. Johnson, riots broke out in Watts, a South Central neighborhood in Los Angeles. The uprising went on for days, and other riots followed in major cities across the country over the next few years. This social disorder appalled Americans across the racial divide, although many blacks understood the uprisings as legitimate protests based on long-standing grievances, whereas many whites saw the riots as inexcusable criminal behavior. Many whites felt that blacks should be grateful for government efforts on their behalf and should take advantage of the opportunities now open to them rather than continue to complain about past discrimination.

Kinder and Sanders argue that racial resentment is fairly widespread among white citizens and that it has a strong influence on policy opinions dealing with race. Before we discuss the impact of racial resentment on policy attitudes, we need to review the way Kinder and Sanders measured racial resentment. They used four survey statements (included on the ANES) to tap into this concept (see Figure 6-2 for the wording of these survey items). Because racial resentment is a subtle form of prejudice, Kinder and Sanders asserted that a "roundabout" approach is the most appropriate way to measure the concept.[50] Thus, their survey statements did not require whites to agree that blacks are outright lazy or that blacks are simply hucksters trying to con white America into giving them something they don't deserve. No, nothing of the sort. Instead, the statements used subtle language to get whites to reveal their bias. And indeed, many whites demonstrate racial resentment, according to Kinder and Sanders's research.

In 1986, for example, roughly 60 percent of whites endorsed racially resentful responses when asked whether (a) blacks should work their way up without special favors, (b) blacks should try harder to be as well off as whites, and (c) blacks have gotten less than they deserve (see Figure 6-2). The only question on which a majority of whites did not give the resentful response was with regard to the lin-

Figure 6-2 Racial Resentment among Whites

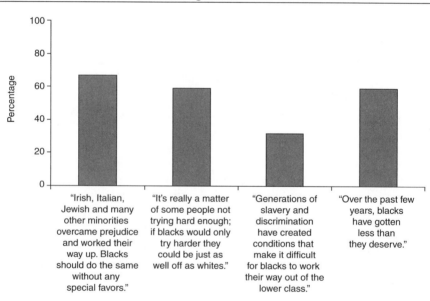

Source: Donald R. Kinder and Lynn M. Sanders, *Divided by Color* (Chicago: University of Chicago Press, 1996), 107.

Note: Bars represent the percentage of white respondents who gave racially resentful responses. For the first two statements, the racially resentful response is agreeing "strongly" or "somewhat" with each statement. For the last two statements, the racially resentful response is disagreeing "strongly" or "somewhat" with each statement.

gering effects of slavery and discrimination. Just over 30 percent were resentful on that question.[51]

Now let's turn to the impact of racial resentment on white citizens' policy attitudes. Specifically, we are interested in the effect of racial resentment on white citizens' attitudes toward race-targeted policies. **Race-targeted policies** are those designed to specifically aid black Americans, such as affirmative action and the government taking steps to ensure fair treatment in employment. Kinder and Sanders analyzed the influence of racial resentment on race-targeted policy attitudes using ANES data from 1986, 1988, and 1992. They found that white citizens who were more racially resentful were more opposed to a variety of race-targeted policies. For example, racially resentful whites were significantly more likely to oppose affirmative action in college admissions and employment than whites who did not hold such attitudes.[52] The relationship held between racial resentment and policy opinions even though other important variables were taken into account, such as self-interest, individualism, egalitarianism, and demographic characteristics.

Ultimately, it is not that surprising that attitudes toward blacks influence white citizens' opinions on race-targeted policies. Pluralists, in particular, would view this as entirely appropriate given the emphasis these theorists put on groups as the primary organizers of political life in the United States. Participatory democratic theorists, in contrast, would not be thrilled with the way in which *prejudicial* group attitudes drive the policy positions of whites. Because the participatory democratic theorists care a great deal about equality, they would be very concerned about the level of racial resentment among whites and the extent to which racial resentment influences white policy opinions. What is even more troubling to participatory democratic theorists is the power of racial prejudice to shape attitudes on policies beyond those directly tied to African Americans. We turn to research on that topic in the next section.

Race-Neutral Policy Opinion, or Race-Coded?

A distinction is often made between social policies that are race-targeted and social policies that are race-neutral. As we just discussed, race-targeted policies are ones that directly affect African Americans.[53] In contrast, **race-neutral policies** are ones that affect citizens regardless of race. For example, government assistance to help blacks is a race-targeted policy, whereas government assistance to help poor people is a race-neutral policy. Research by Martin Gilens, however, leads us to consider another possibility: **race-coded policies**.[54] Race-coded policies are race-neutral, yet have become linked with black Americans in the minds of white citizens. Gilens argues that welfare is an example of such a policy.[55] Gilens maintains, "Although political elites typically use race-neutral language in discussing poverty and welfare, it is now widely believed that welfare is a 'race-coded' topic that evokes racial imagery and attitudes even when racial minorities are not explicitly mentioned."[56] Thus, because welfare is linked to race,

Gilens hypothesizes that opposition to welfare policy among whites largely stems from their racial attitudes.

To test this hypothesis, Gilens analyzed data from the 1991 National Race and Politics Study, a national representative survey. To measure attitudes toward welfare spending, Gilens used this question, "Suppose you had a say in making up the federal budget, would you prefer to see more spent, less spent, or the same amount of money spent on welfare as it has been?"[57] To measure racial attitudes, Gilens focused on the stereotype that blacks are lazy. Specifically, Gilens asked respondents to assess the work ethic of blacks by indicating whether terms like *lazy* and *hardworking* characterize the group. Gilens found that white citizens who endorsed the view of blacks as lazy and not hardworking were significantly more opposed to welfare spending than white citizens who rejected that stereotype. The relationship between racial stereotypes and welfare attitudes held even when taking into account other variables that might influence welfare attitudes, such as perceptions of welfare recipients as undeserving, individualism, party identification, ideology, and demographic characteristics.[58]

How did a race-neutral issue like welfare become a race-coded issue? Gilens argues that news media coverage of poverty and welfare disproportionately focuses on black Americans, which leads to this linkage of race and poverty in the minds of white citizens.[59] To provide evidence to support this contention, Gilens analyzed newsmagazine stories on poverty between 1950 and 1992. He identified every poverty-related story in *Time, Newsweek,* and *U.S. News & World Report* during this time period. Then, he examined every picture within the poverty stories. He coded whether the race of each poor person pictured was black, non-black, or undeterminable; he also coded whether the topic of the poverty story was sympathetic (such as old-age assistance) or unsympathetic (such as the underclass, which refers to people who belong to the lowest socioeconomic class and who are often stereotyped as deviant).

Gilens found that whites were the dominant image of poverty in the 1950s and early 1960s. In 1965, however, the racial makeup of the poor in these magazine stories on poverty changed quite dramatically. The representation of blacks jumped from 27 percent of the poor in 1964 to 72 percent in 1967. From 1967 on, blacks tended to dominate the coverage of poverty, averaging 57 percent of the poor portrayed by these newsmagazines between 1967 and 1992. To illustrate the skewed nature of this media coverage, Gilens compared the true percentage of blacks among the poor (based on data from the U.S. Census Bureau) with the racial makeup of the poor depicted in the newsmagazines. In reality, blacks only made up about 29 percent of the poor during this time period. Thus, the magazines' depiction essentially doubled the proportion of blacks among the poor. Gilens also found that the overrepresentation of blacks became even more extreme when unsympathetic topics were covered. For example, blacks made up 100 percent of the poor people pictured in stories on the underclass and 84 percent of the poor in stories on urban problems. In contrast, there were no blacks pictured in stories on old-age assistance, and only about one-quarter of the poor were black in stories on hunger and medical care.[60]

Rosalee Clawson and Rakuya Trice updated and extended Gilens's study by examining the representation of poverty in five newsmagazines between 1993 and 1998.[61] They analyzed the same three magazines as Gilens, as well as two additional newsmagazines, the *New York Times Magazine* and *Business Week*. They found that blacks continued to be grossly overrepresented in pictures of the poor, making up 58 percent of the poor during this time period.[62]

Group Consciousness

Group attitudes also shape the opinions of minority citizens. Here the research has primarily focused on the effects of group consciousness on black public opinion.[63] **Group consciousness** refers to an awareness of how membership in a particular group shapes the "lives and fortunes" of individuals.[64] Most scholars agree that group consciousness is made up of several components, including group identity and perceived discrimination.[65]

In separate studies, two prominent scholars, Michael Dawson and Katherine Tate, provide insight into the critical role of racial group identity in shaping black public opinion. They demonstrated that **racial identity** is an important determinant of policy opinions. Blacks who have high levels of racial identity, as measured by the extent to which they perceive their fate is directly tied to the fate of their race, are more likely to support redistributive policies and government programs to assist blacks.[66] In addition, another study by Tate showed that blacks with strong racial identification are more likely to favor the drawing of congressional districts in such a way that increases the likelihood a minority will be elected.[67]

Unfortunately, public opinion researchers have paid less attention to the role of group consciousness in shaping Latino public opinion. A study by Gabriel Sanchez, however, provides insight into this topic.[68] He analyzed data from a nationally representative survey of 2,417 Latinos conducted in 1999. He examined whether group consciousness influenced attitudes on two issues particularly salient to Latinos, immigration and bilingual education, and two issues not connected directly to Latinos, abortion and the death penalty. Sanchez found that an important component of group consciousness, **perceived discrimination**, was an influential factor shaping attitudes on issues salient to Latinos but not on abortion and the death penalty. Specifically, Sanchez demonstrated that citizens who thought that discrimination against Latinos was a big problem in society were more likely to support increased immigration to the United States and to believe that children of immigrants should be able to take some classes in their native language.

One question that arises with the study of group consciousness is whether minorities with high levels of consciousness are hostile toward whites. Some observers argue that race consciousness leads to separatism and a pursuit of divisive politics by minority citizens, whereas others argue that race consciousness is empowering to minorities and has very little to do with their attitudes toward whites. Mary Herring, Thomas Jankowski, and Ronald Brown put these contradictory propositions to the test by investigating the relationship between African Americans' racial identification and their attitudes toward whites. Herring et al. analyzed the 1984 National Black Election Study (NBES), a national representative survey of black Americans. The NBES included a set of questions about racial identity and evaluations of whites. They examined several measures of racial identity and found little evidence to support the claim that high levels of racial identification are closely associated with hostility toward whites. For example, Herring et al. demonstrated that there was no relationship between blacks feeling close to their racial group and the belief that whites keep blacks down.

Party Identification

Party identification is one of the most important political attitudes that individuals hold. As we discussed in chapter 1, party identification refers to a person's allegiance with a political party or identification as independent of a party. Not surprisingly, party identification is the best predictor of which party a person will vote for in an election. But party identification has effects that extend far beyond that: party identification also colors how citizens view political candidates and public policies.[69] For example, research shows that when citizens know a candidate's party identification, they rely on that knowledge to evaluate the candidate rather than relying on information about the candidate's issue positions, even when those positions are inconsistent with the party label.[70]

An interesting study by Brian Gaines, James Kuklinski, Paul J. Quirk, Buddy Peyton, and Jay Verkuilen demonstrates the powerful influence of party identification in shaping public opinion.[71] Gaines et al. conducted panel surveys with University of Illinois students between October 2003, which was roughly six months after the U.S. invasion of Iraq, and December 2004, which was soon after the United States turned authority over to the Iraqis. They examined whether partisanship influenced (a) citizens' factual beliefs about the situation in Iraq, (b) the interpretation of those facts, (c) opinions about President George W. Bush's handling of the war in Iraq, and (d) the relationship among facts, interpretations, and opinions about President Bush.

First, Gaines et al. asked participants to identify their party affiliation. Next, they examined whether factual beliefs varied by party identification. For example, they analyzed whether some partisan groups were more accurate than others when asked how many troops had been killed in Iraq. They found that citizens of all partisan stripes were fairly accurate in assessing the number of casualties. Moreover, as the number of troops killed in action increased over time, citizens updated their estimates accordingly, regardless of their party identification. Gaines et al. noted that this was an especially interesting finding for strong Republicans, because they were the group who would be most motivated to distort reality since it was a Republican president who led the country into war.

Despite the accuracy of their beliefs about the number of troop casualties, citizens' opinions on President Bush's handling of the war diverged a great deal based on partisanship. Strong Republicans were the most approving of President Bush, with weak Republicans the next most supportive group. At the other end of the continuum, strong Democrats were the most disapproving of the president, with weak Democrats not too far behind.

Now, since all groups basically agreed on the number of casualties, why did their opinions of President Bush differ so much? To answer that question, Gaines et al. examined how the partisan groups *interpreted* the factual information about casualties. Specifically, they asked, "When you think about [the number of] U.S. troops being killed in the military action in Iraq since the May announcement that major combat operations had ended, do you think of that number as very large, large, moderate, small, or very small?"[72] An overwhelming proportion of strong Democrats indicated that the number of casualties was either very large or large. Weak Democrats generally agreed with strong Democrats, although they were a bit more likely to say the number was moderate. In sharp contrast, approximately 80 percent of strong Republicans saw the casualties as moderate, small, or very small. Even as casualties rose across time, strong Republicans did not change their interpretation of the number of casualties. Weak Republicans demonstrated a different pattern. They were more likely than strong Republicans to see the number of casualties as large or very large at the beginning of the study (although not as high as Democrats viewed them), and as more deaths occurred, an even greater percentage of weak Republicans interpreted the number killed in action as large or very large. Therefore, the views of weak Republicans were more responsive to the facts on the ground than the views of strong Republicans. Overall, the results clearly suggest that citizens' party affiliations shaped how they interpreted the number of casualties.

Thus far, the results we have discussed compare the beliefs, interpretations, and attitudes of different partisan *groups*. Gaines et al. also conducted an *individual-level* analysis to sort out whether it was the factual beliefs or the interpretation of those beliefs that influenced citizens' attitudes toward President Bush's handling of the war. They found that factual beliefs about the number of casualties had no effect on citizens' evaluations of the president, whereas people's interpretation of how large the casualties were had a substantial influence on their views of the president. This was the case for all partisan groups (although the effect just missed statistical significance for weak Democrats). "In other words, the meanings that people gave to their factual beliefs about troop losses, not the beliefs themselves, drove their opinions toward the war."[73] Notably, these meanings were heavily influenced by party identification.

HISTORICAL EVENTS

In addition to personality, self-interest, values, and group attitudes, **historical events** also shape citizens' political attitudes. For example, public opinion toward the president is influenced by events, particularly international crises.[74] When a president gets a boost in popularity as a result of an international crisis, political scientists call it the "rally-round-the-flag" effect. The most obvious example of this phenomenon is when President George W. Bush's approval ratings skyrocketed after the al-Qaeda attacks of September 11, 2001. At the end of August 2001, President Bush's approval rating was sitting at 55 percent according to a Gallup poll, but his approval jumped to 90 percent in a Gallup poll conducted on September 21 and 22, a record high according to the polling organization.[75] It is clear that citizens' attitudes toward President Bush were influenced by the events of 9/11.

Another political attitude that responds to historical events is party identification. Although party identification tends to be a stable political attitude, there are times when it is influenced by events. Before the civil rights movement, for example, the South was often referred to as the Solid South because of its steadfast commitment to the Democratic Party. But as the national Democratic Party became the party of civil rights during the 1960s, many white southerners began to shift their party allegiance away from the Democrats toward independence, with some citizens even making a switch to the Republican Party.[76] By 2000, the South had become solidly Republican with every southern state supporting the Republican presidential candidate, George W. Bush, rather than the Democratic candidate, Al Gore.[77] Gore even lost his home state of Tennessee.

The partisanship of African Americans was also influenced by the civil rights movement. African Americans as a group tend to support the Democratic Party, but African Americans who came of age during the civil rights movement have the strongest identification with the Democrats. Younger cohorts of African Americans who were socialized after the civil rights movement have demonstrated a small, yet significant, move toward identification with the Republican Party.[78]

The civil rights movement also influenced political attitudes beyond party identification. In a ground-breaking study, Taeku Lee demonstrated the impact of **social movements** on public opinion.[79] Specifically, Lee argued that events initiated by social movements can have a more powerful effect on public opinion than events initiated by political elites. He argued that too often public opinion research focuses on how attitudes are shaped by elite actions and not enough attention is dedicated to the influence of non-elites, such as movement activists. Furthermore, Lee made the case that political scientists rely too heavily on public opinion polls to assess citizens' attitudes. He maintained that public opinion polls are not well suited for the task of distinguishing between elite and non-elite influences on the public.

To illustrate the effect of non-elite events on public opinion, Lee conducted an in-depth analysis of the civil rights movement between 1948 and 1965. Lee showed that political events initiated by movement activists galvanized the black public, which then led to a backlash from white southerners who opposed the goals of the civil rights movement. This, in turn, led to national elites reacting to the events on the ground in the South, as well as racially liberal white citizens from across the country responding sympathetically to the plight of black citizens.

Lee tracked this chain of events not by monitoring public opinion data from polls but by examining letters written to the president of the United States during this time period. Lee argued that constituency mail measures **activated mass opinion**, which is "beliefs and sentiments that are at once *salient* in the mind and *impel* one to political action."[80] He showed that letter writing to the president increased in response to events initiated by civil rights activists. For example, the Montgomery bus boycott, Freedom Summer, and especially Bloody Sunday in Selma stimulated an outpouring of letters from citizens.[81] In contrast, the passage of the Civil Rights Act of 1964, the presidential election of 1964, and the Voting Rights Act of 1965—all elite-driven events typically considered watershed moments in the push for civil rights—did not inspire citizens to write the president.[82]

Lee also examined the race of the correspondent, which was identifiable in about 47 percent of the letters, and the timing of the letter writing.[83] He found that blacks, who were universally sympathetic to the civil rights activists, were the first to be activated by movement events. This was followed by sympathetic northern whites who wrote to the president outraged by the extremely violent backlash of white southerners against blacks participating in the civil rights movement. Next, white southerners were motivated to write the president in strong opposition to elite actions at the national level to end racial segregation. Finally, racially liberal whites from across the nation (except the South) wrote to the president in support of integration. Based on this pattern of letter writing, Lee does not dismiss the importance of elite events entirely but concludes that a "movement-initiated, movement-elite interaction" model best describes the events that influenced public opinion on racial issues during this period.[84] In other words, citizens' opinions were affected by movement events, *and* their opinions were shaped by elite activities *in response* to movement events.

Lee's research speaks to one of the most important debates within the study of public opinion: the capability of citizens to function effectively in a democratic society. Elite democratic theorists, of course, argue that citizens do not have the ability or the desire to participate in the rough and tumble of politics. But Lee's important work suggests that is not always the case. Lee concludes that "ordinary citizens, under appropriately compelling circumstances, *will* take an active part in crafting politics rather than merely consuming the political outputs of elite actors."[85] These are heartening words to the ears of participatory democratic theorists.

CONCLUSION

Do citizens organize their political attitudes in any kind of coherent way? Yes, the research we have discussed in this chapter suggests that public opinion is derived from several factors. Therefore, instead of a single ideological dimension underlying public opinion (a la Converse), it is more appropriate to think in terms of the pluralistic roots of public opinion. The research on authoritarianism provides compelling evidence that personality influences a wide range of attitudes on moral, political, and racial issues. Self-interest, in contrast, has a much more limited effect on public opinion. In certain circumstances, however, self-interest does matter. When the effects of a policy are clear and salient, self-interest can kick in and influence public opinion. In addition, citizens' values play an important role in shaping political attitudes. Egalitarianism, in particular, influences public opinion on a number of social issues. Group attitudes also drive citizens' opinions. Racial prejudice is a key determinant of white attitudes on both race-targeted and race-coded issues, whereas group consciousness affects the policy opinions of minority citizens. Party identification is arguably the most important political attitude that individuals hold, because it fundamentally shapes how citizens view political candidates and issues. Moreover, party identification influences how citizens interpret facts, which has a dramatic effect on their political judgments. Finally, public opinion is molded by historical events. The civil rights movement, in particular, affected citizens' political attitudes.

What would democratic theorists make of the pluralistic roots of public opinion? Pluralists would be drawn to the research on group attitudes and would view the extensive effect of such attitudes on public opinion as evidence of the importance of groups in society. Pluralists believe that groups are fundamental to the practice of politics in the United States; consequently, it is completely reasonable that citizens' animosity toward and identification with groups would influence their political attitudes.

Elite democratic theorists would be surprised by the limited role that self-interest plays in shaping public opinion. Their justification for the centrality of elites in the political system is based at least in part on the argument that citizens are too self-interested to be intimately involved in decision making. The research suggests, however, that their argument is more of a rationalization than a justification. Taeku Lee's research also delivers a body blow to the elite democratic theorists. His research shows quite convincingly that elite actions are not always central to the lives of citizens. Instead, events initiated by social movement activists have an important effect on public opinion.

Participatory democratic theorists are delighted that the studies discussed in this chapter demonstrate that citizens are capable of holding reasoned opinions derived from important political factors. The research on the pluralistic roots of public opinion revives an image of citizens as more sophisticated than the one suggested by Converse's research. This research, however, does not put participatory democratic theorists completely at ease. The powerful effects of racial prejudice on white citizens' political attitudes is particularly troubling, and the intolerant reaction of authoritarians to diverse viewpoints undermines the faith that participatory democratic theorists have in citizens coming together to work on political problems in a constructive way.

KEY CONCEPTS

SUGGESTED SOURCES FOR FURTHER READING

Adorno, T. W., Else Frenkel-Brunswik, Daniel J. Levinson, and R. Nevitt Sanford. *The Authoritarian Personality.* New York: Harper & Brothers, 1950.
Altemeyer, Bob. *Enemies of Freedom: Understanding Right-Wing Authoritarianism.* San Francisco: Jossey-Bass, 1988.
Stenner, Karen. *The Authoritarian Dynamic.* New York: Cambridge University Press, 2005.

In these three books, the authors grapple with the concept of authoritarianism. Adorno and his colleagues argue that authoritarianism is a deeply rooted personality trait stemming from exposure to harsh child-rearing practices, whereas Altemeyer asserts that authoritarianism develops through social learning. Stenner emphasizes that authoritarianism has a stronger effect on attitudes when citizens are faced with normative threats.

Brewer, Paul R. *Value War: Public Opinion and the Politics of Gay Rights.* Lanham, Md.: Rowman & Littlefield, 2008.

In this book, Brewer uses a variety of methods (surveys, experiments, and content analysis) to examine how the public debate over gay rights has shaped citizens' attitudes. In particular, he highlights the importance of values in molding citizens' beliefs about gay rights.

Dawson, Michael. *Behind the Mule: Race and Class in African-American Politics.* Princeton: Princeton University Press, 1994.

In this book, Dawson argues that many black Americans see their own interests as closely tied to the interests of their racial group because of historical and current experiences with discrimination. Thus, blacks feel a sense of linked fate with other black citizens. Dawson shows that this racial identity influences policy positions among black Americans (even when taking into account class differences).

Nelson, Thomas E., and Donald R. Kinder. "Issue Frames and Group-Centrism in American Public Opinion." *Journal of Politics* 58 (1996): 1055–1078.

In a series of experiments, Nelson and Kinder show that group attitudes have a stronger effect on policy opinion when issues are framed in such a way that highlights the beneficiaries of the policy. For example, attitudes toward the poor have a stronger impact on citizens' support for spending on the poor when the emphasis is on whether poor people actually need the money rather than whether the government can afford the spending.

Sears, David O., and Jack Citrin. *Tax Revolt: Something for Nothing in California*, enlarged ed. Cambridge, Mass.: Harvard University Press, 1985.

This classic book examines citizens' opinions on taxes and government spending in California during the "tax revolt" of the late 1970s. The authors demonstrate that both self-interest and symbolic racism influence support for the tax revolt.

Walsh, Katherine Cramer. *Talking about Race*. Chicago: University of Chicago Press, 2007.

In this innovative study, Walsh uses participant observation to analyze how citizens talk about racial issues while participating in community programs designed to foster dialogue among citizens from different racial groups. She finds that participants seriously grapple with how to balance a desire for unity with respect for racial differences.

Project Implicit: www.implicit.harvard.edu

This is a fascinating Web site on which you can complete tasks to assess whether you have hidden biases. The Implicit Association Test was developed by social scientists as a way to measure implicit attitudes, that is, those attitudes that people are either unable or unwilling to report in a survey. For example, to examine whether you have unconscious associations between African Americans and violence, click on "Demonstration Tests." Read the information and then click on "Go to the Demonstration Tests." Read the information and then click on "I wish to proceed." Click on "Weapons IAT" and follow the directions from there. At the end of the task, you will be provided with an assessment of whether you have an unconscious bias. There are also tasks dealing with gender, age, disability, weight, sexuality, race, and skin tone.

PART IV

Do Citizens Endorse and Demonstrate Democratic Basics?

CERTAIN FEATURES OF a democratic society place expectations on the citizenry. Popular sovereignty, for example, puts some decision making in the hands of the citizens. To exercise this duty, must democratic citizens be knowledgeable about and attentive to politics? Other important characteristics of a democratic society are the ability of citizens to express their views without governmental suppression and the openness of its political system to citizens from many different walks of life. These are known, respectively, as civil liberties and civil rights. How important, though, is it in a democracy for citizens to support civil liberties and civil rights?

Not surprisingly, the answers to these two questions differ depending on which type of democratic theorist is responding. The normative debates over these key democratic basics (knowledge and attentiveness, support for civil liberties, and support for civil rights) are profiled in this section. In the chapters that follow, we also pay particular attention to whether citizens endorse these democratic basics in the abstract and demonstrate them in practice.

CHAPTER 7

Knowledge, Interest, and Attention to Politics

DO YOU KNOW who Harry Reid is? How about Robert Gates? Peyton Manning? If you are like many Americans, you have no clue that Harry Reid is the Senate Majority Leader or that Robert Gates is the Secretary of Defense, but you know Peyton Manning is the star quarterback for the Indianapolis Colts, the Super Bowl XLI champion. According to a Pew Research Center poll conducted in February 2007, only 15 percent of Americans could identify Harry Reid and 21 percent could identify Robert Gates. In contrast, 62 percent knew Peyton Manning, 64 percent could identify the singer and actress Beyoncé Knowles, and 93 percent could correctly describe Arnold Schwarzenegger.[1] See Table 7-1 for data on citizens' knowledge of various politicians and celebrities.

Does it matter that citizens are not highly knowledgeable about key political figures? Participatory democratic theorists say yes. "Political information is to democratic politics what money is to economics: it is the currency of citizenship."[2] Thus, without knowledge, citizens cannot function effectively. From this perspective, democracy *requires* informed citizens, as well as interested and attentive ones.

Other scholars argue that citizens can make reasonable decisions without being knowledgeable about or particularly interested in and attentive to politics. By using heuristics (i.e., shortcuts), citizens can still perform well in a democratic society.[3] Citizens can use informational shortcuts, such as cues from individuals or groups they trust, to form their political opinions. Thus, "people can be knowledgeable in their reasoning about political choices without necessarily possessing a large body of knowledge about politics."[4] Since many of the cues citizens rely on come from elites, this perspective assigns a central role to elites. Thus, this argument is in line with the thinking of elite democratic theorists.

A more extreme position taken by some elite democratic theorists is that citizen ignorance actually allows democracies to flourish. Elite democratic theorists, of course, envision a limited role for citizens. Consequently, there is no need for citizens to be knowledgeable about, interested in, or attentive to politics. Indeed, democracy works better when citizens stay out of day-to-day political happenings.[5]

Table 7-1 Knowledge of Politicians and Celebrities, February 2007

"Now I would like to ask you about some people who have been in the news recently. Not everyone will have heard of them. If you don't know who someone is, just tell me and I'll move on. Can you tell me who _____ is?"

Politician/ celebrity	Answered correctly	Answered incorrectly	Never heard of (volunteered)	Don't know/ refused to answer
Hillary Rodham Clinton	93%	3%	2%	2%
Harry Reid	15	4	44	37
Nancy Pelosi	49	4	20	27
Robert Gates	21	16	26	37
Condoleezza Rice	65	8	9	18
Barack Obama	61	3	18	18
Lewis "Scooter" Libby	29	4	34	33
Arnold Schwarzenegger[a]	93	4	1	2
Peyton Manning	62	2	19	17
Beyoncé Knowles	64	1	20	15

Source: Public Knowledge of Current Affairs Little Changed by News and Information Revolutions (Pew Research Center for the People and the Press, Washington, D.C., April 15, 2007), 23; http://people-press.org/reports/display.php3?ReportID=319.

[a] Counted correct if identified as California governor or a former action-movie star.

"Limited participation is not only unavoidable, but preferable, in that it assures that conflict is managed, that political demands are limited, and, thus, that economic and social order is maintained."[6] Clearly, elite democratic theorists and participatory democratic theorists have very different views on how engaged the public should be.

In this chapter, we discuss the competing visions of elite democratic theorists and participatory democratic theorists regarding levels of citizen knowledge, interest, and attention to politics. Next, we examine how knowledgeable citizens actually are about politics. As with so many concepts, there is controversy over how to measure political knowledge; we will discuss that debate. Then we turn to an analysis of why some citizens are more knowledgeable than others. We consider the effect of individual characteristics and political context on knowledge. We also examine the consequences of political knowledge and ignorance. Finally, we discuss whether citizens are interested in politics, and we examine attention to politics by focusing on citizens' attentiveness to and knowledge of the war in Iraq. We conclude the chapter by considering whether citizens are knowledgeable enough, interested enough, and attentive enough to function effectively in a democracy.

HOW KNOWLEDGEABLE, INTERESTED, AND ATTENTIVE SHOULD CITIZENS BE IN A DEMOCRACY?

Democratic theorists debate about how much knowledge, interest, and attention to politics is necessary for citizens to function effectively in a democracy.[7] Participatory democratic theorists argue that citizens should have high levels of knowledge and be actively engaged in the political world so they can hold elites accountable. Citizens should be well informed so they can (a) figure out their interests, (b) recognize which policies serve those interests, and (c) identify which political parties, interest groups, and politicians are pursuing those policies. These theorists argue that citizens need to be on the ball because elites may try to misrepresent the facts or may not even know the facts to begin with.

Participatory democratic theorists assume that all citizens have the ability to understand what is going on in the political arena. Thus, if citizens are *not* knowledgeable, interested, and attentive, there must be barriers that keep citizens from engaging. For example, participatory democratic theorists might point to the media's tendency to focus on a game schema rather than a governing schema (as we discussed in chapter 3) as an obstacle to citizens acquiring the knowledge they need to successfully evaluate elite behavior.

Elite democrats, on the other hand, are not particularly concerned about levels of citizen knowledge, interest, and attention to politics. In fact, some scholars argue that it is *irrational* for citizens to spend time on politics.[8] Why is that the case? First, there are substantial costs to acquiring information about politics. It takes significant time for citizens to arm themselves with the knowledge necessary to form opinions, evaluate policy proposals, and understand the political process. Staying informed also requires financial resources. Buying newspapers or traveling to public meetings, for example, entails a monetary commitment on behalf of citizens. Second, citizens can expect very little in return for becoming knowledgeable. The voice of a citizen would be just one of many; thus, it is extremely unlikely that a single person could influence the adoption of a particular policy or the outcome of an election. If citizens were assured a payoff from becoming informed, it would be rational for them to invest in gathering information. But since that is not the case, it does not make sense for them to spend time and money becoming knowledgeable. In the words of acclaimed rational choice theorist Anthony Downs, "In general, it is irrational to be politically well-informed because the low returns from data simply do not justify their cost in time and other scarce resources."[9]

Even though it is irrational to become knowledgeable about politics, citizens can still function in a democracy because they can rely on cues in their environment to make reasonable political judgments.[10] Citizens can use heuristics, such as party identification and ideology, to figure out where they stand on issues. They can take cues from trusted groups and individuals to determine which politicians best represent their interests. Scholars refer to this as **low-information rationality.**

From this perspective, citizens can get by with fairly minimal levels of knowledge. As long as they know enough to take cues from political parties, interest groups, and other elites, citizens can function effectively. Note that taking cues from interest groups is consistent with the pluralist vision of a democratic society.

Other scholars emphasize that citizens use heuristics not because it is irrational to become informed but because it is *impossible* for citizens to become fully informed. The political world is extremely complex, and citizens are **limited information processors.** They simply do not have the cognitive abilities to systematically process the vast amounts of political information out there. Instead they rely on whatever shortcuts are available to simplify complex material and thus function efficiently, if not always accurately.[11]

Hard-core elite democrats make a different argument about citizen knowledge, interest, and attention to politics. They believe that democratic nations are actually better off when citizens are apathetic and ignorant. From this perspective, elites do the heavy lifting, and citizen engagement would just complicate matters. These theorists remind us that many features of the U.S. government, such as the Electoral College and the Supreme Court, were specifically intended to keep citizens at bay. Moreover, since the institutions of government were designed to check and balance each other, it is not necessary for citizens to hold elites accountable. Some citizens might be political junkies, but most people are not interested in, and many are even turned off by, the conflict and compromise that is part and parcel of democratic decision making.[12] And that's a good thing according to some elite democratic theorists.

ARE CITIZENS KNOWLEDGEABLE ABOUT POLITICS?

"Nothing strikes the student of public opinion and democracy more forcefully than the paucity of information most people possess about politics."[13] In this section, we discuss the empirical evidence that speaks to this claim. Is it the case that citizens are uninformed about politics? Also, are citizens misinformed about politics? Have citizens become more or less knowledgeable over time? Are citizens informed (or uninformed) about politics in general or do they specialize in specific areas?

Are Citizens Informed or Uninformed?

As we briefly discussed in the introduction to this chapter, citizens are not particularly well informed about politics. Almost everyone knows politicians with celebrity appeal such as Hillary Rodham Clinton and Arnold Schwarzenegger, but knowledge drops off sharply after that. In early 2007, only 49 percent of citizens could correctly identify Nancy Pelosi and 20 percent admitted they had never heard of her, despite the fact that she was in the news quite a bit at the time as the first female Speaker of the House. Refer back to Table 7-1. This poll by the Pew Research Center suggests that citizen knowledge is rather limited.

To delve into this topic more deeply, we turn to the classic research of Michael X. Delli Carpini and Scott Keeter. They define **political knowledge** as "the range of factual information about politics that is stored in long-term memory."[14] To be knowledgeable about politics, Delli Carpini and Keeter argue citizens should be well informed in three areas: (a) the rules of the game, (b) the substance of politics, and (c) the people and players (including parties and groups).[15] To assess citizen knowledge in these areas, Delli Carpini and Keeter pulled together 54 years worth of national survey data. They examined numerous polls conducted between 1940 and 1994, which included over 2,000 questions regarding factual knowledge of politics.

Overall, Delli Carpini and Keeter found a mixed bag when it comes to levels of citizen knowledge.[16] On the one hand, citizens clearly do not live up to the standards set out by participatory democratic theorists. "Only 13 percent of the more than 2,000 questions examined could be answered correctly by 75 percent or more of those asked, and only 41 percent could be answered correctly by more than half the public."[17] Furthermore, many citizens do not even know enough to use heuristics. For example, bare majorities of the public could identify party positions on key issues. Thus, for those who don't know, it would be impossible to use party as a cue. On the other hand, citizens are not as ignorant of politics as suggested by some observers. Most citizens are aware of some basic facts, such as the length of a presidential term (96 percent), the name of their governor (86 percent), that there is no religious test for political candidates (81 percent), that Cuba is a communist country (82 percent), and that Social Security does not provide job training (89 percent).

Citizens do best at answering questions about the **rules of the game**. This is probably due to the fact that the institutions and processes of politics rarely change over time. Further, this is the type of knowledge citizens are exposed to in high school civics classes. Turn to Table 7-2 for some examples of what citizens know and don't know. In 1985, virtually everyone knew that the United States was a member of the United Nations, but hardly anyone could name two Fifth Amendment rights in 1989. Before you make fun of the public, can you name two Fifth Amendment rights?

Citizens are a bit less knowledgeable when it comes to the **substance of politics** and the **people and players.** Again, Table 7-2 contains several examples. Citizens were well informed about the steel dispute back in 1952 but shockingly uninformed about Watergate in 1972. In terms of foreign affairs, only about one-half of the public knew that black South Africans could not vote in 1985, and a mere 11 percent could describe Glasnost—a Soviet policy of openness—in 1987. Basically everyone could identify Ronald Reagan as president in 1986, but only 3 percent could name the president of Mexico in 1991.

It is a bit disturbing that in the 1990s more people could name the judge in the O. J. Simpson criminal trial, Lance Ito (64 percent), than could name the

Table 7-2   Examples of Political Knowledge and Ignorance, 1940–1994

Knowledge of	Answered correctly
Rules of the game	
U.S. is a member of the UN (1985)	96%
Accused are presumed innocent (1983)	50
Name all three branches of government (1952)	19
Name two Fifth Amendment Rights (1989)	2
Substance of domestic politics	
What is the steel dispute about (1952)	96
What is greenhouse effect (1988)	50
What is Watergate about (1972)	22
Percentage of population that is black (1990)	8
Substance of foreign affairs	
Ozone damage affects whole world (1988)	94
Black South Africans can't vote (1985)	51
Number of U.S. soldiers killed in Vietnam (1965)	17
Describe Glasnost (1987)	11
People and players	
U.S. president (1986)	99
Andrew Young (1977)	48
Republican party stance: Pro-life amendment (1980)	21
President of Mexico (1991)	3
Nonpolitical facts	
Who is Bill Cosby (1988)	93
Who wrote Huck Finn (1990)	51
Old Testament prophet (1954)	19
How many liters in a gallon (1977)	1

Source: Michael X. Delli Carpini and Scott Keeter, *What Americans Know about Politics and Why It Matters* (New Haven: Yale University Press, 1996).

Chief Justice of the Supreme Court at the time, William Rehnquist (12 percent).[18] But as Delli Carpini and Keeter point out, citizens are not uniformly knowledgeable about popular culture and other nonpolitical facts either (see Table 7-2). Almost everyone knew Bill Cosby in 1988, but only 19 percent could name an Old Testament prophet in 1954, and a mere 1 percent knew how many liters were in a gallon in 1977. This suggests that knowledge—political and otherwise—is not simply a function of ability and motivation but also opportunity. If a Supreme Court case were covered as obsessively in the media as the Simpson trial, we are quite sure most people would be able to name the Chief Justice.

Public Opinion in Comparative Perspective
BOX 7-1   CROSS-NATIONAL KNOWLEDGE OF FOREIGN AFFAIRS, 1994

Knowledge of foreign affairs	Germany	Italy	France	United Kingdom	Canada	United States	Spain
Percentage who answered four or five questions correctly	58	34	25	18	19	15	10
Percentage who answered none correctly	3	18	23	22	27	37	32
Mean number correct	3.55	2.49	2.13	2.01	1.92	1.53	1.35

Source: Michael X. Delli Carpini and Scott Keeter, *What Americans Know about Politics and Why It Matters* (New Haven: Yale University Press, 1996), 90.

How does the United States compare with other Western democracies when it comes to knowledge of foreign affairs? Not favorably, according to a 1994 survey.[1] This cross-national survey asked respondents to identify Boutros Boutros Ghali and to name the president of Russia, the country threatening to withdraw from the nonproliferation treaty, the ethnic group that had conquered much of Bosnia, and the group with whom Israelis had recently reached a peace accord. The United States had the second lowest percentage of citizens who answered at least 80 percent of the questions correctly and the highest proportion of citizens who answered none of the questions correctly. The average American got 1.53 questions right, whereas the average German answered 3.55 correctly.

We should be cautious about interpreting these results, according to research conducted by Jeffery Mondak and Damarys Canache.[2] They analyzed knowledge of science and the environment in a cross-national survey of twenty nations. The United States ranked sixth based on the average number of correct responses. Mondak and Canache argue, however, that people in different nations have different levels of tolerance for uncertainty. People in cultures that feel threatened by uncertainty will be less likely to guess compared with people in cultures that embrace uncertainty. When people

(continued)

guess, they are at least occasionally going to guess correctly. Thus, the level of political knowledge in a country is driven by both true knowledge and the propensity of the people to guess. To obtain a more precise measure of political knowledge, Mondak and Canache argue that survey questions should be designed to strongly discourage "don't know" responses. We will discuss this issue further in the "Measuring Political Knowledge" section.

1. Michael X. Delli Carpini and Scott Keeter, *What Americans Know about Politics and Why It Matters* (New Haven: Yale University Press, 1996), 90.
2. Jeffery J. Mondak and Damarys Canache, "Knowledge Variables in Cross-National Social Inquiry," *Social Science Quarterly* 85 (2004): 539–558.

Are Citizens Misinformed?

James Kuklinski, Paul Quirk, Jennifer Jerit, David Schwieder, and Robert Rich make an important distinction among people who are **informed**, **uninformed**, and **misinformed**.[19] They explain the differences this way:

> To be *in*formed requires, first, that people have factual beliefs, and second, that the beliefs be accurate. If people do not hold factual beliefs at all, they are merely *un*informed. They are, with respect to the particular matter, in the dark. But if they firmly hold beliefs that happen to be wrong, they are *mis*informed—not just in the dark, but wrongheaded.[20]

Using survey data from a representative sample of Illinois residents, Kuklinski et al. demonstrated that citizens are largely misinformed about welfare policy.[21] For example, citizens were asked what percentage of the federal budget is spent on welfare. The survey used a multiple choice format and provided the following options: 1 percent, 5 percent, 8 percent, 11 percent, or 15 percent. The correct answer is 1 percent, but a whopping 90 percent of the respondents selected one of the other options. Although citizens were the most misinformed about this fact, more than a majority of citizens demonstrated they were "not just in the dark, but wrongheaded" on five other questions regarding welfare. Furthermore, when asked how confident they were of their answers, a majority of citizens said they were very or fairly confident about their responses. Thus, many citizens were not just wrong, they were quite confident in their wrongheadedness.

In general, citizens tended to be misinformed in an antiwelfare direction. For example, believing that a much higher percentage of the budget is spent on welfare than actually is would probably make people less supportive of welfare. Indeed, Kuklinski et al. found that misinformation leads people to be more opposed to welfare spending than they otherwise would be. Since Kuklinski et al.'s survey respondents are from Illinois, the authors were careful not to generalize their findings to American citizens in general. Nevertheless, their research raises significant concerns about the public's ability to understand and evaluate important public policies.

Have Levels of Political Knowledge Changed over Time?

Are citizens more knowledgeable about politics today than they were fifty years ago? There are certainly reasons to believe that citizens might be significantly more informed today.[22] First, citizens' ability to understand politics should have increased since levels of formal education have risen dramatically over the years. "In 1940 the median number of years of education was 8.6, three-fourths of the public had not finished high school, and only 10 percent had some college experience. By the early 1990s the median number of years of education had risen to 12.7, with less than one-fourth not having finished high school and 43 percent having had college experience."[23] Second, citizens' motivation to understand politics should have increased since the government has become significantly "bigger" over the last few decades. Both domestically and on the world stage, the U.S. government plays a much larger role today than it did in the 1940s. Thus, citizens should be more concerned with all the ways the government affects their daily lives and how U.S. power is wielded around the world. Third, citizens should have more of an opportunity to learn about politics given the huge leaps in communication that have occurred over the last fifty-plus years. Virtually every citizen owns a television today, and most citizens have access to cable television news at any time of the day or night.

But let's not get too far ahead of ourselves. There are also reasons to suspect that citizens may be less knowledgeable today than in the 1940s.[24] Although levels of formal education have increased, that does not necessarily mean a corresponding increase in civics education. Moreover, some observers have lamented the low quality of education in today's schools. More students may be graduating, but with fewer skills and knowledge than once was the case. As for motivation, it may be that a larger and more visible government turns citizens off rather than encourages engagement. And certainly television provides citizens greater access to news, but it also provides greater access to entertainment programming that draws attention away from the politics of the day. Further, television presents news as entertainment, which has severe negative effects on levels of political knowledge, according to some critics.[25] "Our politics, religion, news, athletics, education and commerce have been transformed into congenial adjuncts of show business, largely without protest or even much popular notice. The result is that we are a people on the verge of amusing ourselves to death."[26]

So, there are arguments in both directions regarding whether citizens are more knowledgeable today than fifty years ago, but ultimately this is an empirical question. Therefore, Delli Carpini and Keeter collected national survey data from 610 randomly selected respondents in 1989 to answer this question.[27] The survey included political knowledge questions matching those asked on surveys from the 1940s and 1950s. Thus, Delli Carpini and Keeter were able to compare levels of political knowledge across time. They found that "the level of public knowledge has remained remarkably stable."[28] For example, over 90 percent of the public knew that a presidential term lasts four years and roughly two-thirds of citizens knew which party controlled the House in both 1947 and 1989. There were some questions on which people demonstrated significant increases or decreases in knowledge, but many of these changes seem understandable given varying patterns of media coverage and elite emphasis over time.

Almost twenty years have passed since Delli Carpini and Keeter conducted their 1989 study, and during that time period the Internet revolution has occurred, providing citizens with unprecedented access to information. With a few keystrokes, citizens can hunt down political information in a quick, efficient way. Have citizens become more knowledgeable as a result? Perhaps Delli Carpini and Keeter's conclusions about the stability of political knowledge are **timebound.**

We turn to survey data collected by the Pew Research Center to address this issue. Pew conducted knowledge surveys in 1989 and 2007 that included nine identical or comparable questions. The Pew data do not show that citizens have become markedly more knowledgeable in recent years; instead, citizens were more knowledgeable about some topics in 2007 but less informed about others (see Table 7-3). Citizens were less likely to correctly name the vice president, their state's governor, the president of Russia, and an administration official involved in a scandal (i.e., Scooter Libby in 2007, who was in the midst of a trial for perjury and obstruction of justice in the case involving the outing of CIA agent Valerie Plame, and John Poindexter in 1990, who was in the midst of a trial for involvement in the Iran-Contra scandal). They were also less likely to know the United States has a trade deficit. On the upside, the public was more aware of which party controlled the House and the ideology of the Chief Justice. They were also more likely to identify the Speaker of the House and the Secretary of Defense. Overall, the Pew surveys suggest citizens have not become more knowledgeable as a result of technological changes making information easier to access. Therefore, it seems that Delli Carpini and Keeter's research findings are not timebound: levels of citizen knowledge have stayed roughly the same from the 1940s until the present.

Are Citizens Generalists or Specialists?

When it comes to political knowledge, are citizens generalists or specialists? A **generalist** would be knowledgeable across all political topics. For example, a generalist would be able to name the Secretary of State, identify the U.S.'s largest trading partner, know the minimum wage, and identify two Fifth Amendment rights. In contrast, a **specialist** would have knowledge on some topics but not

Table 7-3   Political Knowledge, 1989–2007

Political knowledge	1989	2007	Difference
Percentage who could correctly name:			
The current vice president	74%	69%	−5
Their state's governor	74	66	−8
The president of Russia[a]	47	36	−11
Percentage who knew:			
U.S. has a trade deficit	81	68	−13
The party controlling the House	68	76	+8
The chief justice is conservative	30	37	+7
Percentage who could correctly identify:			
Tom Foley/Nancy Pelosi	14	49	+35
Richard Cheney/Robert Gates	13	21	+8
John Poindexter[b]/Scooter Libby	60	29	−31

Source: Public Knowledge of Current Affairs Little Changed by News and Information Revolutions (Pew Research Center for the People and the Press, Washington, D.C., April 15, 2007), http://people-press.org/reports/display.php3?ReportID=319.

[a]Data from 1994.
[b]Data from 1990.

others. For example, a specialist might be well informed about foreign affairs but pay little attention to domestic politics. To use a basketball analogy, generalists would know Lisa Leslie and Kobe Bryant, and they would know the difference between traveling and double dribbling. Specialists, on the other hand, might know star players like Leslie and Bryant but not be familiar with the rules of the game.

If it is the case that people specialize, then measuring political knowledge would be quite difficult. It would require lots of survey questions covering a wide range of political topics. Survey researchers would need to include multiple questions on the substance of domestic and foreign policy, rules of the game (both domestic and foreign), and people and players (again both domestic and foreign). If, on the other hand, citizens are generalists, then a relatively small set of survey questions will provide a valid and reliable measure of political knowledge.

Delli Carpini and Keeter analyzed a variety of survey data to determine whether citizens are generalists or specialists.[29] They found that citizens can best be characterized as generalists.[30] In other words, the same person who can name the vice president also tends to know the president of Russia, which party controls the House, who declares war, what a recession is, and whether the United States has a trade deficit. As a result, Delli Carpini and Keeter argued it is possible to successfully measure political knowledge using a small set of items. Based on their extensive analyses, they recommended using five questions to measure political knowledge.[31] Those items, as well as the introduction they suggested, are presented in Table 7-4.

There are two noteworthy exceptions to the argument that citizens are generalists. First, Delli Carpini and Keeter's research shows that some people specialize in state or local politics.[32] These citizens are knowledgeable about political events and issues in their states or in their local communities but are not as aware of national politics. Consequently, Delli Carpini and Keeter's measure of political knowledge may classify some people who are highly informed about state and local politics as ill informed. Thus, their measure is not a good indicator of state and local political knowledge.

Second, some people may specialize in knowing about issues and people particularly pertinent to them or groups to which they belong. Delli Carpini and Keeter's research, for example, shows that blacks have lower levels of political knowledge than nonblacks in general but are just as knowledgeable on race-related issues.[33] A study conducted a few months after the al-Qaeda attacks on the World Trade Center and the Pentagon shows that citizens living in the Northeast were more knowledgeable about the events of 9/11 than people living in other parts of the country but not better informed about politics in general.[34] Overall then, the research demonstrates that some citizens have domain-specific knowledge in areas that are particularly important to them.

Table 7-4 Measuring Political Knowledge

"Last, here are a few questions about the government in Washington. Many people don't know the answers to these questions, so if there are some you don't know just tell me and we'll go on."

"Do you happen to know what job or political office is now held by [insert name of current vice president]?"

"Whose responsibility is it to determine if a law is constitutional or not … is it the president, the Congress, or the Supreme Court?"

"How much of a majority is required for the U.S. Senate and House to override a presidential veto?"

"Do you happen to know which party had the most members in the House of Representatives in Washington before the election this/last month?"

"Would you say that one of the parties is more conservative than the other at the national level? Which party is more conservative?"

Source: Michael X. Delli Carpini and Scott Keeter, *What Americans Know about Politics and Why It Matters* (New Haven: Yale University Press, 1996), 305–306.

Measuring Political Knowledge

Delli Carpini and Keeter's method of measuring political knowledge has greatly influenced how political scientists study the concept. Not all scholars agree, however, that their measurement technique is the best. Indeed, recent research conducted by Jeffery Mondak and Belinda Creel Davis suggests that levels of citizen knowledge may be underestimated by the Delli Carpini and Keeter method.[35] Another scholar, Doris Graber, argues that Delli Carpini and Keeter's emphasis on factual knowledge is misplaced. We will discuss both critiques below.

Political Knowledge and the Propensity to Guess

Mondak and Davis argue that Delli Carpini and Keeter's measure of political knowledge is problematic because it encourages respondents to answer "don't know." Refer back to Table 7-4. Notice the introduction informs respondents that "many people" can't answer these questions and encourages them to say don't know if they are one of those people. In addition, the question wording on three of the items welcomes don't knows with the phrases "Do you happen to know ..." and "Would you say...." Further, survey interviewers are instructed not to probe respondents when they say don't know. Citizens who might be willing to guess with a little coaxing are not encouraged to do so. As a result, Delli Carpini and Keeter's method measures two things: political knowledge and the **propensity to guess.**

Imagine two citizens participating in a telephone survey. Let's call them Alonzo and Sadie. They are asked which party controls the House of Representatives. Both feel 80 percent confident they know the correct answer, but Alonzo decides to go ahead and guess, while Sadie decides not to do so. In this situation, assuming Alonzo does guess correctly, he will appear more knowledgeable than Sadie when in reality there is no difference. Thus, Mondak and Davis conclude this often-used measure of political knowledge is not **valid.** In other words, the items designed to measure political knowledge are not measuring what they are supposed to measure.

To demonstrate their point, Mondak and Davis analyzed a **split-half survey** of political knowledge included on the American National Election Studies (ANES) 1998 Pilot Study. A split-half survey is an experiment embedded in a survey whereby one-half of the respondents are randomly assigned to one condition and the other one-half are randomly assigned to another condition. In this case, respondents received question wordings that either encouraged don't know responses or discouraged don't know responses (see Table 7-5). As you can see, respondents appear more knowledgeable when don't knows are discouraged. For example, 61.5 percent of citizens understand judicial review when don't knows are discouraged compared with 54.3 percent when such responses are encouraged. Also note the dramatic drop in don't know responses across the two conditions. Overall, these

Table 7-5   The Perils of Measuring Political Knowledge: Encouraging versus Discouraging Don't Know Responses

	Introduction encourages don't knows	Introduction discourages don't knows
	"Here are a few questions about government in Washington. Many people don't know the answers to these questions, so if there are some you don't know, just tell me and we'll go on."	"Here are a few questions about government in Washington. Many people don't know the answers to these questions, but even if you're not sure I'd like you to tell me your best guess."
Question	Answered correctly (answered don't know)	Answered correctly (answered don't know)
"Who has the final responsibility to decide if a law is constitutional or not? Is it the president, Congress, or the Supreme Court?"	54.3% (11.5%)	61.5% (0.81%)
"And whose responsibility is it to nominate judges to the federal courts? The president, Congress, or the Supreme Court?"	47.3% (16.7%)	53.2% (1.9%)
"[Do you happen to know] which party has the most members in the House of Representatives in Washington?"	66.3% (22.2%)	72.1% (9.5%)
"[Do you happen to know] which party has the most members in the U.S. Senate?"	57.2% (31.4%)	64.6% (10.7%)

Sources: Jeffery J. Mondak, "Developing Valid Knowledge Scales," *American Journal of Political Science* 45 (2001): 227; Jeffery J. Mondak and Belinda Creel Davis, "Asked and Answered: Knowledge Levels When We Will Not Take 'Don't Know' for an Answer," *Political Behavior* 23 (2001): 216.

findings demonstrate that some people do know correct answers but hesitate to respond if they are not completely sure. Thus, the Delli Carpini and Keeter method measures both true political knowledge and the propensity to guess; as a result, it underestimates levels of public knowledge.

Encouraging don't know answers on political knowledge questions has another pernicious effect on the measurement of this concept: it exacerbates the **gender gap in political knowledge**.[36] Studies of political knowledge commonly show that men are significantly more knowledgeable about politics than women. As one example, skip ahead to Table 7-7 and note that 37 percent of citizens knew Chief Justice John Roberts was conservative in 2007, but there was a notable 8 percentage point gender gap on this question, with 41 percent of men knowing the correct answer and only 33 percent of women knowing it. The introduction to the Pew question says, "Next I would like to ask about some things that have been in the news. Not everyone will have heard about them." Further, when the interviewers read the question, they do not prompt the respondents to guess. Thus, the measurement of political knowledge in this Pew survey encourages don't know responses.

Jeffery Mondak and Mary Anderson argue this is a problem because men are more likely to guess than women. This propensity to guess has nothing to do with underlying levels of knowledge. Think back to our Alonzo and Sadie example. Remember both were equally confident about the response to a knowledge question, but Alonzo went ahead and threw out an answer, while Sadie said she didn't know. As a result, Sadie was guaranteed not to get the question right, while Alonzo at least had a chance of being correct. Mondak and Anderson's analysis shows that roughly 50 percent of the gender gap is due to men guessing at higher rates than women. Thus, the 8 percentage point gender gap on knowledge of the Chief Justice's ideology is probably closer to a 4 percentage point difference.

Another concern with the measurement of political knowledge is the use of **short answer questions**.[37] People are more likely to say don't know to these questions than to **multiple choice questions**. People who are semiconfident may not be willing to toss out an answer with a short answer question but will articulate a response once they hear the option mentioned in a multiple choice format. So again, the short answer questions are measuring two things: political knowledge and the propensity to guess. Further, multiple choice questions may jog people's memories, allowing them to select the correct answer.

Table 7-6 presents survey data from the Pew Research Center that illustrate the differences between short answer and multiple choice questions.[38] Note the data presented here are not from a split-half survey. Instead, they are drawn from two national representative surveys, one conducted in February and the other in March 2007. Thus, it could be the case that other factors besides the question format affected levels of political knowledge. We should be cautious in interpreting these results; nevertheless, the data suggest that format matters. On all three items, citizens appear more knowledgeable with a multiple choice question. And notice the dramatic difference on the question about the president of Russia: citizens go from being fairly ignorant to fairly well informed with the switch in format.

Table 7-6   The Perils of Measuring Political Knowledge: Short-Answer versus Multiple-Choice Questions

Answer	Short answer format February 1–13, 2007	Multiple choice format March 9–12, 2007
	"Do you happen to know which political party has a majority in the U.S. House of Representatives?"	"Do you happen to know which political party has a majority in the U.S. House of Representatives? Is it the Democratic Party? The Republican Party?"
Democratic Party	76%	82%
Republican Party	10	13
Don't know/refused	14	5
	"Can you tell me who Robert Gates is?"	"Is Robert Gates the U.S. Secretary of Defense? A senator from Michigan? The chairman of General Motors? OR is he something else?"
U.S. Secretary of Defense	21%	37%
Anything else/don't know/ refused	79	63
	"Can you tell me the name of the president of Russia?"	"Can you tell me who is the president of Russia? Is it Boris Yeltsin? Vladimir Putin? Mikhail Gorbachev? Or is it someone else?"
Vladimir Putin	36%	60%
Anything else/don't know/ refused	64	40

Source: Public Knowledge of Current Affairs Little Changed by News and Information Revolutions (Pew Research Center for the People and the Press, Washington, D.C., April 15, 2007), 23–33; http://people-press.org/reports/display.php3?ReportID=319.

In reaction to the research by Mondak and his colleagues, the most recent surveys conducted by the ANES discourage don't know responses.[39] The introduction to the knowledge section reads, "Now we have a set of questions concerning various public figures. We want to see how much information about them gets out to the public from television, newspapers and the like." If a respondent volunteers don't know, the interviewer probes by asking, "Well, what's your best guess?" And none of the questions include phrases such as "Do you happen to know ..." But, the ANES does continue to use the short answer format. The 2004 survey asks, for example, "Dick Cheney—what job or political office does he now hold?" Overall then, the ANES has improved its measurement of political knowledge, but changing to a multiple choice format might also be a wise move.

Too Much Emphasis on Factual Knowledge?

Doris Graber raises an even more fundamental concern with Delli Carpini and Keeter's measure of political knowledge.[40] She argues that political scientists should focus on what citizens *need to know* to function in a democracy rather than emphasize "precisely remembered factual knowledge about historically important past and current events."[41] Why? Because citizens are limited information processors. Graber reviews research by communication scholars, psychologists, biologists, and neuroscientists and concludes that it is simply not possible for citizens to remember every little detail about politics because our brains are not designed to do so.[42]

This does not mean, however, that citizens are clueless about politics. Instead, they pay attention to issues that are relevant to them. People are interested in understanding the impact of political events on their lives and on the well-being of the country, not on memorizing the names of politicians or constitutional rights. Citizens want *useful* information, not factoids. Graber argues, for example, "There may be areas of knowledge where the poor, trained in the school of hard knocks, may excel. But scores of streetwise knowledge are not usually gathered and reported."[43]

To substantiate her claims, Graber analyzed transcripts of nine **focus groups** conducted in the Chicago area.[44] The ninety-eight focus group participants ranged from suburban voters to city voters to young people to homeless people. The focus groups began with the moderator asking, "What are the issues that are most important to you in your community, however you define that? What would you tell an elected official?"[45] Graber coded for whether participants' responses were "simple," such as statements of fact or description, or "complex," such as statements that showed understanding of a variety of perspectives and drew connections among different ideas.

Here is an example of a black voter discussing economic problems using complex statements: "I would like to hear a political person say that one of the viable alternatives to crime in our neighborhoods is really lobbying for minimum wage standards ... not just talking about minimum wage but how do we get people who have smaller stores to expand and employ more people.... How do we talk to Sears about having part-time staff with no benefits?"[46] Overall, Graber found that people often made complex statements or a mix of complex and simple statements when talking about political topics. Simple statements dominated the discussion in only 18 percent of the issue areas discussed by the focus groups.

Graber admits these people would not score well on Delli Carpini and Keeter's measure of political knowledge, but she does not expect them to given the inherent limitations of the brain. Instead, Graber argues that the focus group participants "possess reasonably sophisticated, politically useful knowledge about current problems that confront them and that the issue areas covered by this knowledge are generally quite well suited to carrying out the actual tasks of citizenship that most Americans perform." [47] Participatory democratic theorists would prefer, of course, that American citizens perform a wider variety of citizenship tasks than they currently perform and thus would argue that citizens need substantially greater political information than what Graber thinks is necessary.

Why Are Some Citizens More Knowledgeable than Others?

Thus far, we have focused primarily on overall levels of political knowledge among the public. Here we turn our attention to understanding why some citizens are more informed than other citizens. Citizens vary in political knowledge based on their abilities, motivations, and the opportunities available. We begin with a discussion of the relationship between demographic characteristics and political knowledge. Next we examine the role of motivation. Then we turn to a discussion of contextual factors that affect political knowledge.

Demographic Groups and Political Knowledge

Several studies have demonstrated substantial differences in political knowledge across demographic groups.[48] We discussed the gender gap in knowledge above but will briefly expand on the phenomenon here. Women tend to be less informed than men, with a couple of important exceptions. First, women are as knowledgeable about local politics as men. For example, a study of citizens in Richmond, Virginia, found that women were as informed about how the mayor and city council were elected as their male counterparts.[49] Second, women are as knowledgeable as men on issues particularly pertinent to them, such as suffrage and abortion rights.[50]

There is also a **racial gap in political knowledge.** In general, whites are more knowledgeable about politics than racial minorities. But, as we mentioned briefly above, blacks and whites are comparable when it comes to knowledge of issues particularly important to blacks. For example, the Pew Research Center finds that blacks can identify Barack Obama and Condoleezza Rice at the same level as whites, but blacks are less informed than whites in other areas.[51]

The racial and gender gaps in adult political knowledge extend to young people. A study of students at six middle schools in Maricopa County, Arizona, shows that white adolescents were significantly more knowledgeable about politics than African American, Latino, and Native American adolescents.[52] Further, a national, representative survey of high school seniors demonstrates that boys have slightly more civics knowledge than girls and whites have substantially more civics knowledge than Hispanics and African Americans.[53]

Levels of political knowledge also differ across age groups. In general, older folks are better informed than younger ones. This appears to be due to both life cycle and generational effects. As people progress through the life cycle, they are simply exposed to more political information. Older citizens have experiences, such as buying a house and paying property taxes, that younger people are less likely to have. These experiences result in an increase in political knowledge. Also, older people were raised in a more politically engaged era than today's young people. Accordingly, this early socialization put the older generation on a track to pay attention to, and thus be knowledgeable about, politics throughout their lives.

Income and education also matter. Wealthy citizens are better informed than their poorer counterparts. Similarly, citizens with higher educations are substantially more knowledgeable than those with a minimal education. Education is critical, of course, because it improves citizens' cognitive abilities to learn about politics. But it also boosts interest in politics, which motivates citizens to become more knowledgeable. In addition, education affects the opportunities citizens have to become informed: formal education allows people to obtain jobs in which politics matter on a regular basis (such as lawyers, business executives, and political science professors) and places people in social networks that value political knowledge. Indeed, "formal education is the single most important factor differentiating those who know more about politics from those who know less. Citizens who spend more years in school simply know a lot more about politics."[54]

In Table 7-7, we illustrate demographic differences in political knowledge by examining citizens' familiarity with Chief Justice John Roberts's political ideology. The February 2007 poll conducted by the Pew Research Center asked respondents whether Roberts is generally considered a liberal, a moderate, or a conservative.[55] We see that 37 percent of citizens correctly identified the Chief Justice's political ideology as conservative. There is striking variation, however, across sex, race, age, education, and income. Men, whites, older citizens, wealthier people, and those who are better educated were more likely to know Roberts's ideology. Notice in particular the large impact of education on political knowledge.

Motivation and Political Knowledge

People also differ in how motivated they are to learn about politics. Citizens who are interested in and attentive to politics are significantly more knowledgeable than those who just don't care.[56] This finding extends to young people. Among high school seniors, students who expressed an interest in studying government were substantially more likely to have a grasp of civics knowledge than other students. Political discussion is also a factor. A study of citizens in the United States and Great Britain found a significant link between discussing politics with family and friends and being well informed about politics.[57]

Motivation is also important when it comes to learning from the news media. Jonathan S. Morris and Richard Forgette analyze the effect of "news grazing" on

Table 7-7   Demographic Differences in Political Knowledge

"*The Chief Justice of the Supreme Court is John Roberts. Can you tell me if he is generally considered a liberal, a moderate, or a conservative?*"

Characteristics	Answered correctly
Total	37%
Sex	
Male	41
Female	33
Race	
White	39
Black	28
Hispanic (white or black)	29
Age (in years)	
18–29	29
30–49	39
50–64	41
65+	35
Family income	
<$20,000	23
$20,000–$29,999	22
$30,000–$49,999	37
$50,000–$74,999	38
$75,000–$100,000	48
$100,000+	53
Education	
High school or less	23
Some college	38
College graduate	61

Source: Public Knowledge of Current Affairs Little Changed by News and Information Revolutions (Pew Research Center for the People and the Press, Washington, D.C., April 15, 2007), 19; http://people-press.org/reports/display.php3?ReportID =319.

levels of political knowledge.[58] **News grazers** "tend to follow the news on television with their remote control in hand, flipping to other channels when they become disinterested."[59] Morris and Forgette's investigation shows that news grazers are less likely than non–news grazers to know which political party controls the House of Representatives and the name of the terrorist organization responsible for the September 11 attacks but are just as likely to know that Martha Stewart was found guilty in court. Thus, it seems that news grazers are motivated to stop flipping the channel when news of Martha Stewart comes on. Another study demonstrates that citizens who prefer entertainment over news become less knowledgeable about politics when they have access to cable and the Internet.[60] But, at the same time, citizens who prefer news over entertainment become better informed as a result of cable and Internet access. Again, it seems that motivation influences whether or not citizens use the media to become more or less knowledgeable about politics.

Context and Political Knowledge

Political knowledge is not simply a function of individual characteristics and motivation. To become knowledgeable about politics, citizens must also have the opportunity to do so.[61] Some political contexts offer greater opportunities for citizens to become informed than others. Richard Niemi and Jane Junn emphasized the influence of **civic education** on political knowledge.[62] They analyzed survey data from a national, representative sample of high school seniors and found that students who had more civic classes and more recent civics instruction were more knowledgeable than others. Furthermore, the particular type of curriculum mattered: students who were exposed to a wide variety of topics and discussed current events in their classes were more likely to be knowledgeable about politics.

The **political structure** also influences citizens' levels of political knowledge. For example, voters in states that regularly use ballot initiatives are more knowledgeable than voters in states without such direct political participation.[63] The ballot initiatives have no effect, however, on nonvoters. Thus, those citizens who take the opportunity to vote on ballot initiatives derive benefits from doing so: they gain in political knowledge. Political structures also differ across nations, which provide scholars with the chance to compare the effects of different institutional arrangements and electoral systems on political knowledge cross-nationally.[64] For example, in a nation with competitive elections, parties are motivated to provide information to citizens and citizens find the information useful. In such a political context, citizens are more knowledgeable about politics.

The political context in the United States is dominated by men, which has an effect on levels of political knowledge among women. A study by Nancy Burns, Kay Schlozman, and Sidney Verba asks the question, "What if politics weren't a man's game?"[65] Burns et al. found that women living in states with a female senator or a female Senate candidate are substantially more knowledgeable about politics than women living in states without those characteristics. Specifically, only 51 percent of women from male-dominated states could name one of their U.S. senators, whereas 79 percent of women could do so when the political context included powerful female politicians.[66] This is a huge difference and suggests that the knowledge gap between men and women could close if more women served in elective office.

Jennifer Jerit, Jason Barabas, and Toby Bolsen examined another aspect of the political context: how the **information environment** affects citizens' political knowledge.[67] They hypothesized that citizens will be better informed about politics when the information environment is rich. In other words, when the media pay a great deal of attention to political issues, the public will become more knowledgeable as a result. An information-rich environment, however, will help the better educated more than it will help their less-educated counterparts. Instead of information leveling the playing field, the well educated will be better equipped to integrate new knowledge into their existing stores of information, which will allow them to move even further ahead of those who are less educated. Thus, the knowledge gap between the less educated and better educated will be exacerbated by an information-rich environment.

To test these hypotheses, Jerit et al. analyzed media coverage and public knowledge of the 1998 tobacco settlement with U.S. states. Certain features of the tobacco settlement received significantly more media coverage than others. The settlement required tobacco companies to pay states billions of dollars; it also retained the right of individuals to sue the tobacco industry. The financial aspect of the settlement received substantial media coverage: twenty-eight stories by the Associated Press (AP) during the six-week time period under study. The right to sue, however, was only covered in four AP stories during the same time period. If Jerit et al. are correct that media attention to an issue leads to greater knowledge, then citizens should be more knowledgeable about the payment of billions of dollars to the states than about the right to sue. That was indeed the case. Polling data collected shortly after the settlement showed that roughly 70 percent of Americans knew the payment to the states was part of the settlement, but only 25 percent knew the settlement allowed individuals to sue tobacco companies.

Jerit and colleagues also predicted that better educated citizens would benefit more from an information-rich environment than less educated ones. Again, they found evidence to support their hypothesis. To illustrate, they compared a typical respondent with a high school degree with a typical respondent with at least some college. Both respondents had a 23 percent chance of correctly answering the right to sue question. A different pattern emerged, however, for knowledge about the payment to the states. The typical low education person had a 65 percent chance of knowing the correct answer, whereas the typical high education person had a 77 percent chance of answering correctly. Thus, both benefited from the media attention, but the educated gained more.

Does it matter whether the information-rich environment is created by news stories in print or on television? Yes, it does. In a second study, Jerit et al. examined the relationship between different types of media coverage and political knowledge of forty-one issues, ranging from understanding how the West Nile virus is spread to knowledge of the Supreme Court's ruling on partial-birth abortion to knowing about President George W. Bush's drug plan. Replicating the results of their first study, the researchers found that on issues with low levels of media attention (such as Bush's drug plan), highly educated people are only slightly more likely to answer questions correctly than those with low education, whereas there is a large knowledge gap on issues receiving a great deal of media attention (such as how the West Nile virus is spread). Furthermore, this knowledge gap is exacerbated when the issue receives extensive coverage in the print media. In contrast, for issues receiving extensive television coverage, both low-education and high-education people gain. A knowledge gap remains, of course, but the important point is that the gap is not increased by the television coverage.[68] While media critics have complained about the simplicity and inanity of television news compared with print, these findings suggest that television presents information in a way that benefits those who are least knowledgeable.

Overall, these studies suggest the political context matters a great deal. Citizens are more knowledgeable when the political context is a favorable one. This is consistent with the views of participatory democratic theorists. If you are interested in boosting levels of political knowledge, as participatory democratic theorists are, then it makes sense to structure the political environment in a way that encourages and enables citizens to easily and efficiently acquire information.

WHAT ARE THE CONSEQUENCES OF POLITICAL KNOWLEDGE?

Does it matter whether citizens are politically knowledgeable or ignorant? This is a normative question to be sure. As we have already discussed, different democratic theorists have different views on the consequences of political ignorance. But it is also an empirical question. By examining the differences between those who are knowledgeable and those who are not, we can get a handle on the consequences of political ignorance.

Delli Carpini and Keeter identify a number of ways in which knowledgeable citizens differ from others.[69] First, well-informed citizens are more likely to demonstrate political tolerance, a fundamental norm in a democratic society. Second, knowledgeable citizens participate at higher rates than their counterparts. Third, knowledgeable citizens are more likely to have stable issue opinions and structure their opinions along a liberal-conservative continuum. Fourth, informed citizens are more likely to recognize their interests, bring their issue positions in line with their party identification, and vote accordingly. Fifth, knowledge begets knowledge. In other words, knowledgeable citizens are able to handle new information with ease. Existing knowledge allows citizens to efficiently incorporate new tidbits into their beliefs systems. All of these things are critical in a democracy, according to Delli Carpini and Keeter. "Because so many of these differences bear on the issue of political power, a key implication of these findings is that the maldistribution of political knowledge has consequences: it threatens the basic democratic principle of political equality among citizens."[70] Delli Carpini and Keeter find this maldistribution particularly alarming because those who are already less powerful in society (i.e., women, minorities, the poor, the less educated, young people) are the ones who are less knowledgeable.

Political ignorance also has an effect on policy attitudes and vote choice. Recall the study about misinformation by Kuklinski et al. we discussed earlier in the chapter.[71] Kuklinski et al. found that citizens were more opposed to welfare spending than they otherwise would be because of the incorrect beliefs they held about welfare. Another study used an experimental design to show that when citizens were provided with accurate information about the decrease in crime in recent years, they were more likely to say the government was spending too much money on building prisons.[72] Other scholars have demonstrated that uninformed citizens would vote for different candidates if they were fully informed.[73] Thus, this research highlights the important policy and electoral impact of citizens' lack of knowledge.

ARE CITIZENS INTERESTED IN AND ATTENTIVE TO POLITICS?

Are citizens interested in politics and political campaigns? Do they pay attention to political news? These are important questions because citizens who are interested in and attentive to politics tend to have higher levels of political knowledge than citizens who are not engaged.[74] And, as we just discussed, knowledge has important political consequences.

Interest in Public Affairs and Political Campaigns

Citizens are modestly interested in politics, according to ANES surveys.[75] In 2004, 26 percent of citizens said they "follow what's going on in government and politics most of the time." Another 41 percent indicated they were interested "some of the time" (see the solid lines in Figure 7-1). Over time, the proportion of citizens highly interested in politics has decreased. In the 1960s and 1970s, roughly one-third of the public said they were following politics most of the time. From the 1980s until the present, it was only about one-quarter.

What about interest in political campaigns? In 2004, citizens were quite interested.[76] Forty percent said they were "very much interested" and another 44 percent said they were "somewhat interested" (see the dotted lines in Figure 7-1). This was the highest level of interest in political campaigns recorded since the survey's inception in 1952. It probably reflects the anger many on the left felt about the Iraq war and the effective mobilization of the right by the Bush White House. As Figure 7-1 shows, there is quite a bit of variation over time. Like 2004, citizens indicated significant interest in 1992, but they were less engaged in 1996 and 2000. Nevertheless, in every presidential election year since 1964, at least 70 percent of the public have said they were somewhat or very much interested in political campaigns. Overall then, citizens seem to perk up during the presidential campaign season but are somewhat less engaged when it comes to the day-to-day of politics.

As with political knowledge, levels of interest vary across demographic groups.[77] Men and whites are generally more interested in politics. Likewise, those

Figure 7-1   Interest in Public Affairs and Current Campaign, 1964–2004

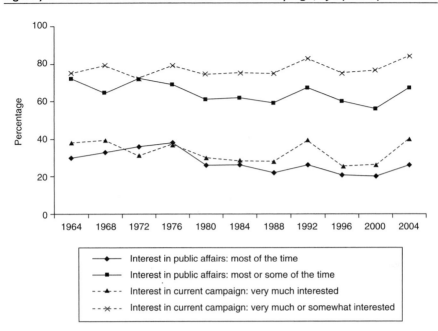

Source: The American National Election Studies (www.electionstudies.org). *The ANES Guide to Public Opinion and Electoral Behavior.* Ann Arbor: University of Michigan, Center for Political Studies (producer and distributor).

Note: Interest in Public Affairs question wording: "Some people seem to follow (1964: think about) what's going on in government and public affairs most of the time, whether there's an election going on or not. Others aren't that interested. Would you say you follow what's going on in government and public affairs most of the time, some of the time, only now and then, or hardly at all?"

Interest in Current Campaign question wording: "Some people don't pay much attention to the political campaigns. How about you, would you say that you have been/were very much interested, somewhat interested, or not much interested in following the political campaigns (so far) this year?"

with more education and higher incomes are more concerned with political happenings. Age, in particular, has a strong relationship with political interest. Thirty-eight percent of citizens between the ages of 62 and 77 said they follow public affairs most of the time in 2004, whereas only 13 percent between the ages of 18 and 29 said the same. Partisans and ideologues are also much more likely to follow politics than independents or moderates.

The political context also matters. In states where females hold statewide offices (such as senator or governor), women are significantly more interested in politics than in states without such female representation.[78] Similarly, women in states with competitive female candidates are more likely to discuss politics and try to convince others to support a political candidate than women in states without viable female contenders.[79] The political context is also important for adolescents. Girls, for example, are more likely to anticipate future political involvement when they see women run high-profile, viable political campaigns.[80]

What do democratic theorists have to say about variation in levels of political interest? Participatory democratic theorists would be concerned with the demographic differences in political interest, and they would argue that changes in the political context are necessary to ensure all citizens are interested in politics. Some elite democrats, on the other hand, would wonder why so many citizens are interested in politics. From their point of view, it is irrational for citizens to spend time on politics. The likelihood that a citizen, even an interested and informed one, could make a difference is so small that it simply doesn't make sense for him or her to devote resources to such an endeavor.

Attention to the War in Iraq

Since U.S. military action in Iraq began in 2003, over 3,700 U.S. soldiers have died, another 35,000 have been wounded, and tens of thousands of Iraqis have been killed.[81] The Iraq war has lasted longer than World War II and cost taxpayers billions of dollars. Among elites, it is the most controversial and agonizing issue of our times. So, are citizens paying attention to the events in Iraq? And do they have the basic knowledge necessary to evaluate the situation?

Most citizens are attentive to the war in Iraq, according to weekly surveys conducted by the Pew Research Center.[82] "In the first six months of 2007, the Iraq war has captivated the public's interest and eclipsed most of the year's other major news stories, including the 2008 presidential election, two major Washington political scandals, and news from other international trouble spots. Iraq has been the most closely followed news story in eighteen of the twenty-two weeks that Pew has been tracking public attentiveness to the news."[83] Between January and June of 2007, at least two-thirds of Americans indicated they were following the news about Iraq "very closely" or "fairly closely" (see Figure 7-2). Although citizens were not paying as much attention to the events in Iraq as they did the first few months of the war (when over 80 percent said they were following very or fairly closely), it is still the news story that holds the attention of most citizens. The Pew survey also finds that Democrats are consistently more likely to pay attention to the war than Republicans or Independents. In June 2007, for example, 35 percent of Democrats said they were paying close attention to the news about Iraq, while 28 percent of Republicans and Independents said they were doing so.

Given the life-and-death importance of the war, participatory democratic theorists would argue there is a heightened need for citizens to hold leaders ac-

Figure 7-2   Attention to News about Iraq, 2007

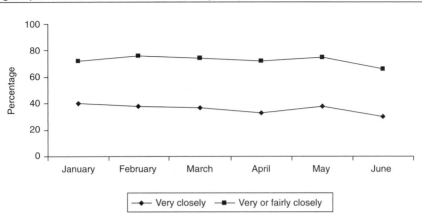

Source: Iraq Dominates News Landscape in First Six Months of 2007 (Pew Research Center for the People and the Press, Washington, D.C., June 28, 2007), http://people-press.org/ reports/display.php3?ReportID=340.

Note: The Pew Research Center conducts weekly surveys on the public's interest in major news events. The data in the figure are from the first survey taken each month. Question wording: "As I read a list of some stories covered by news organizations this past week, tell me if you happened to follow each news story very closely, fairly closely, not too closely, or not at all closely: News about the current situation in Iraq (January through March)/News about the current situation and events in Iraq (April through June)."

countable for their war-related decisions. Thus, citizens should not just be attentive to the news about Iraq, they should also be highly knowledgeable about the situation. The evidence is mixed in this regard, according to a June 2007 Pew Research Center survey.[84] On the one hand, more than 60 percent of Americans knew that the number of casualties was higher in 2007 than the year before and that the number of troops in Iraq had gone up recently (see Table 7-8). Forty-nine percent knew that the deaths of U.S. troops numbered around 3,500, with another 20 percent saying 2,500 and 12 percent guessing 4,500. Overall, these data suggest the public has a general understanding of what is happening in Iraq.

When it comes to the details, however, the public is not nearly as informed. Most Americans are either uninformed or misinformed about which group is the largest in Iraq. Only 41 percent can identify the Shia as the group with the largest population (see Table 7-9). And most Americans could not name either the U.S. Commander in Iraq—General David Petraeus—or the head of the Iraqi government—Nouri al-Maliki. These are not unimportant facts; they capture fundamental aspects of the conflict in Iraq. The sectarian violence between the

Table 7-8   General Knowledge of the War in Iraq, June 2007

Answer	*"Now I'd like to ask you about some things that have been happening in Iraq recently. Not everyone will have heard about them."*
	"What's your impression about what's happened in Iraq so far this year? Has the number of American military casualties since January been higher, lower, or about equal compared to the same period last year?"
Higher (correct)	66%
Lower	4
About equal	22
Don't know/refused	8
	"In recent months, has the number of U.S. troops serving in Iraq gone up, gone down, or stayed about the same?"
Gone up (correct)	61
Gone down	5
Stayed the same	28
Don't know/refused	6
	"Since the start of military action in Iraq, about how many U.S. soldiers have been killed overall? To the best of your knowledge, have there been around 1,500, around 2,500, around 3,500, or around 4,500 military deaths in Iraq?"
Around 1,500	9
Around 2,500	20
Around 3,500 (correct)	49
Around 4,500	12
Other (volunteered)	3
Don't know/refused	7

Source: Iraq Dominates News Landscape in First Six Months of 2007 (Pew Research Center for the People and the Press, Washington, D.C., June 28, 2007), http://people-press.org/reports/display.php3?ReportID=340.

Shia and the Sunni has not allowed U.S. troops to "stand down"; General Petraeus, a counterinsurgency expert, was put in charge to quell the violence; and al-Maliki was the leader counted on by the United States to take the necessary political steps to create a functioning government.

Given the high stakes in Iraq, participatory democratic theorists would expect more from the public. Paying attention to the conflict is a good first step for cit-

Table 7-9   Knowledge of Key People and Groups in Iraq, June 2007

Answer	*"Now I'd like to ask you about some things that have been happening in Iraq recently. Not everyone will have heard about them."*
	"There are three major groups that live in Iraq: the Sunni, the Shia, and the Kurds. As far as you know, which group has the largest population?"
The Sunni	30%
The Shia (correct)	41
The Kurds	8
Don't know/refused	21
	"Do you happen to know the name of the U.S. Commander in Iraq? Is it ..."
General David Petraeus (correct)	30
General Peter Pace	13
General John Abizaid	14
Don't know/refused	43
	"Do you happen to know the name of the Prime Minister of Iraq? Is it ..."
Nouri al-Maliki (correct)	27
Muqtada al-Sadr	19
Mahmoud Abbas	15
Don't know/refused	39

Source: Iraq Dominates News Landscape in First Six Months of 2007 (Pew Research Center for the People and the Press, Washington, D.C., June 28, 2007), http://people-press.org/reports/display.php3?ReportID=340.

izens, but having the knowledge to monitor, evaluate, and hold elites accountable is crucial in a democracy. Elite democratic theorists, on the other hand, would be satisfied by citizens' general understanding of what is happening in Iraq. They would point to the Democratic takeover of Congress in 2006 as evidence that the public was knowledgeable enough to express its concern about the war by voting Republicans out of office. Since voting is the main expectation elite democrats have for citizens, extensive knowledge of the conflict is unnecessary.

CONCLUSION

Are citizens highly knowledgeable about politics? No, many people are not particularly well informed, and some citizens are outright misinformed about important political issues. Yet, people are not as ignorant about politics as some observers have suggested. Further, citizens have not become more ignorant over time:

levels of political knowledge have been remarkably stable over the last fifty years. There is controversy about how to measure political knowledge, with several scholars arguing that Delli Carpini and Keeter's method underestimates citizen competence. Indeed, Graber argues that citizens do know useful political information but do not have the brain capacity to deal with every little detail.

Why are some citizens more knowledgeable than others? Citizens differ in ability, motivation, and opportunity. Formal education, for example, provides citizens with the cognitive ability to become informed about politics. Other demographic characteristics matter as well: men, whites, higher income, and older people are more likely to be knowledgeable. Motivational factors, such as interest, attention, discussion, and how people use the media, lead citizens to be informed. The political context also acts as either a facilitator or inhibitor of political knowledge.

Are there consequences of political knowledge? Yes, indeed there are. Citizens who are knowledgeable are more likely to endorse democratic values and participate in political activities. They have issue opinions that are more stable and more closely linked to their ideology and party identification. In addition, knowledgeable citizens are capable of dealing with new information in an efficient manner, making it easier for them to learn even more about politics. And perhaps most importantly, informed citizens hold different issue opinions than they otherwise would. Thus, political knowledge has significant ramifications for policy preferences among the public.

Are citizens interested in and attentive to politics? Citizens demonstrate modest interest in politics and fairly high interest in political campaigns. They are paying quite a bit of attention to the war in Iraq and are fairly well informed about what is happening generally with the war. In terms of details, however, people are not nearly as knowledgeable.

Overall, do people live up to the democratic ideal of knowledgeable, engaged citizens? Participatory democratic theorists would say no. They would argue that citizens should be more knowledgeable so they can play an active role in the democratic process. Informed and engaged citizens are at the heart of a democracy. They are necessary to influence elite behavior and hold elites accountable. Participatory democratic theorists find the demographic differences in political knowledge especially troubling since they are concerned with inequalities in society. These theorists do not blame individuals for their lack of political savvy and interest, however. Instead, they point to the barriers that limit citizen engagement and knowledge.

In sharp contrast, some elite democratic theorists are curious why citizens are interested and knowledgeable at all given the low odds that their voices will be influential. In their minds, the puzzle is not why so many people lack knowledge, but why so many people are informed. Elite democrats who think government works best when the public interferes least would probably be satisfied with the low levels of knowledge and modest levels of political interest. Scholars who emphasize that citizens can make sensible political decisions by using heuristics would be troubled by the lack of knowledge about such things as party stances on issues. Some citizens can use cues to effectively muddle their way through, but many people do not even have those basic insights.

You are an expert now on political knowledge, interest, and attention. You understand the different normative approaches to citizen competence, and you have a good grasp of the empirical research findings. So, what do you think? Are citizens knowledgeable enough, interested enough, and attentive enough to function effectively in a democracy?

KEY CONCEPTS

civic education / 201
focus groups / 197
gender gap in political knowledge / 195
generalist / 190
information environment / 202
informed / 188
limited information processors / 184
low-information rationality / 183
misinformed / 188
multiple choice questions / 195
news grazers / 200
people and players / 185

political knowledge / 185
political structure / 201
propensity to guess / 193
racial gap in political knowledge / 198
rules of the game / 185
short answer questions / 195
specialist / 190
split-half survey / 193
substance of politics / 185
timebound / 190
uninformed / 188
valid measure / 193

SUGGESTED SOURCES FOR FURTHER READING

Bennett, Stephen E. "Why Young Americans Hate Politics, and What We Should Do about It." *PS: Political Science & Politics* 30 (1997): 47–53.

This short article examines the disconnect of young citizens from politics. It also explains why we should care about this disconnect and steps we can take to combat it.

Davis, Darren W., and Brian D. Silver. "Stereotype Threat and Race of Interviewer Effects in a Survey on Political Knowledge." *American Journal of Political Science* 47 (2003): 33–45.
McGlone, Matthew S., Joshua Aronson, and Diane Kobrynowicz. "Stereotype Threat and the Gender Gap in Political Knowledge." *Psychology of Women Quarterly* 30 (2006): 392–398.

These scholars argue that stereotype threat explains at least part of the racial and gender gap in political knowledge. Stereotype threat occurs when blacks and women feel pressure to perform well on political knowledge questions because they are aware of negative stereotypes about their intellectual abilities. As a result of stereotype threat, blacks and women do worse on political knowledge tests— not because they are less knowledgeable but because the stress of the situation interferes with their ability to answer correctly.

Delli Carpini, Michael X., and Scott Keeter. *What Americans Know about Politics and Why It Matters.* New Haven: Yale University Press, 1996.

This classic book discusses the conceptualization and measurement of political knowledge, examines levels of political knowledge, and analyzes the causes and consequences of political knowledge.

Galston, William A. "Political Knowledge, Political Engagement, and Civic Education." *Annual Review of Political Science* 4 (2001): 217–234.
Niemi, Richard G., and Jane Junn. *Civic Education: What Makes Students Learn.* New Haven: Yale University Press, 1998.

The Galston article reviews the literature on the connection between civic education and political knowledge. Galston discusses recent research (including Niemi and Junn's book) that shows civic education in high schools can bolster political knowledge. If you are an education major, you will find these pieces particularly interesting.

Graber, Doris A. *Processing Politics: Learning from Television in the Internet Age.* Chicago: University of Chicago Press, 2001.

In this book, Graber challenges the method political scientists typically use to measure political knowledge. She also contends that television, because of its audiovisuals, can play an important role in helping citizens learn about politics.

Prior, Markus. "Political Knowledge after September 11." *PS: Political Science & Politics* 35 (2002): 523–529.

This brief article examines the increase in political knowledge that occurred after 9/11.

Pew News IQ Quiz: http://pewresearch.org/newsiq/

Check out this Web site for an online news quiz. Take the quiz and then compare your performance with other American citizens.

The American National Election Study Guide to Public Opinion and Electoral Behavior: www. electionstudies.org/nesguide/nesguide.htm

This Web site provides public opinion data from national, random samples of U.S. citizens. See the "Political Involvement and Participation in Politics" section for a set of questions that measure citizens' levels of engagement in politics. Question wording and response choices are included. Both tables and graphs present the data. There are also tables that show how different demographic groups respond to the questions.

CHAPTER 8

Support for Civil Liberties

AS LEADER OF the National Socialist Party of America (Nazis), Frank Collin requested permission for his group to demonstrate in Skokie, Illinois, in 1977. They had been planning to protest against racial integration in Chicago, but a policy there required them to have a $250,000 insurance bond before they would be given a permit to demonstrate. Since they were not able to post this bond, the Nazis turned to a number of Chicago suburbs, including Skokie. Collin indicated that the Nazis would carry signs expressing their white supremacist beliefs (such as "Free Speech for the White Man") and that they would be wearing uniforms that would include swastikas.

Response to Collin's request was swift and negative. Skokie was home to thousands of Jewish residents, including survivors of the World War II Nazi concentration camps. Many of these survivors spoke out publicly against the Nazis' march and tried to influence public officials to prevent the march. The mayor of Skokie was persuaded to fight against the Nazis' request after a Holocaust survivor told him that a concentration camp guard had killed his two-year-old daughter in front of him. By recounting this episode, the man hoped to convince the mayor of the "emotional reaction ... [he] might have to the sight of a group of men marching in [this] community wearing the swastika symbol."[1] The survivor was successful; the mayor agreed to fight strongly against the Nazi march.

Shortly thereafter, village leaders in Skokie unanimously adopted a number of ordinances designed to prevent the Nazis from marching. These new policies required demonstrators to have $350,000 worth of insurance and allowed village officials to deny a permit to any group that promoted hostility toward individuals based on their race, ethnicity, or religious affiliation. A further ordinance, even more clearly directed toward the Nazi party, banned anyone from participating in a demonstration "as a member or on behalf of any political party while wearing a military-style uniform."[2] The American Civil Liberties Union (ACLU), representing the Nazi party, filed suit, declaring that the Skokie ordinances were unconstitutional in that they were designed to restrict free speech. By working to protect the Nazis' freedom of expression, the ACLU received much negative publicity and suffered significant membership declines. Some ACLU members felt that they could no longer support an organization that would stand up for the rights of a group with views as distasteful as the Nazis. In the end, however, the federal courts agreed with the ACLU's legal arguments and nullified the village ordinances. Meanwhile, the Chicago requirement of insurance for demonstrators was also declared unconstitutional, paving the way for the Nazis to hold their demonstration there, which they did in 1978, thus ending one of the most notable free speech controversies of the past few decades.

Alongside the principle of majority rule, democracies guarantee the political rights of those individuals or groups holding unpopular viewpoints. In fact, this protection of minority views is one key characteristic of democratic nations and is the principle that the courts upheld during the Skokie controversy. Because of the courts' decisions, "even though an overwhelming majority of the citizens of Skokie opposed the Nazi march and even though every member of the Village government and a host of community leaders were actively involved in the effort to prevent the Nazis from marching, the march very nearly took place."[3]

In the United States, the rights of freedom of speech, freedom to assemble, freedom of religion, and freedom to petition the government are protected by the First Amendment of the Constitution. These rights are also known as **civil liberties,** which are defined as rights granted to citizens that are protected from government suppression. Public support for civil liberties is known as **political tolerance.** Yet, we do not commonly refer to someone as tolerant if she supports the exercise of civil liberties only for those who share her political beliefs. More typically, tolerance refers to extending freedoms to individuals or groups with whom one disagrees: "a willingness to 'put up with' those things that one rejects. Politically, it implies a willingness to permit the expression of those ideas or interests that one opposes."[4] Or, in the more direct phrasing of Samuel Stouffer, the author of a ground-breaking book on political tolerance, "if I am tolerant, there are rights which I will grant, within the law, even to those whom I most condemn."[5]

For classical and participatory democratic theorists, a key characteristic of democracy is the active engagement of the public. Citizens should debate issues and share their preferences with politicians, and the policy that results should reflect the wishes of the people. Political equality is also important to these theorists; all citizens should be able to share their views in the public forum regardless of the content of these views. Equality is important because, among other matters, only when there is a free **marketplace of ideas** will leaders be able to discern what is in the public's interest. For such equality to exist in practice, support for freedom of expression must be high among the public. While these theorists do not necessarily assume that everyone will be tolerant, high levels of public intolerance would seem to be counter to the democratic principles they espouse. Participatory democratic theorists have focused particularly on the importance of civil liberties for democracy. They further believe that with more formal education, greater involvement in politics, and more exposure to democratic principles, citizens can learn to tolerate the political expressions of all, even those with whom they vehemently disagree. Thus, participatory democrats value educational and political opportunities for the public to learn key democratic norms.

In contrast, elite democrats are not nearly as optimistic about the citizenry. In fact, given these theorists' beliefs that the public is uninformed about and uninterested in politics and their assumption that when citizens do participate they only do so to further their own interests, democratic elitists expect the public to be intolerant of political viewpoints that differ from their own. How, then, can a democracy that values minority rights continue to function given high levels of public intolerance? To answer this question, democratic elitists, and also pluralists, turn to elites. Elites, they argue, strongly support minority rights and ensure that these rights are upheld. The elites, these theorists contend, are aware of the importance of civil liberties and further understand the consequences to democracy were civil liberties to be eroded. Democratic regimes will be stable, even in the face of widespread public intolerance, as long as the political elites support civil liberties and ensure that the principle of minority rights is applied to all.

Not all variants of these theories have such faith in the good judgment of elites, however. In particular, James Madison, at the time of the writing and ratification of the U.S. Constitution, made a forceful case that all people, elites included, could not be trusted to welcome the political expression of all viewpoints.[6] Madison's remedy to this problem was the creation of a political system that, first, divided power among three branches of government and, second, ruled over such a large population that diverse interests would be represented in the national government. These characteristics would ensure that leaders would need to compromise with others—others who were representing a multitude of different interests—in the policymaking process. Interacting with one's opponents repeatedly would instill in these leaders an appreciation for the value of tolerating diverse viewpoints. Occasionally, elites might even need to join in coalition with individuals who hold very different views than they do. Madison's was thus a pragmatic approach to ensuring that in America civil liberties would be ensured, rooted as they were in the **constitutional framework** rather than in the natural virtue of either the public or the elites.

In this chapter, we discuss attitudes toward civil liberties and tie this evidence back to the normative debates about support for civil liberties in a democracy. More specifically, we discuss levels of tolerance in the United States, sources of tolerance, and differences between elites and citizens in their support for civil liberties. Much of our attention will be on views toward the freedoms of expression contained in the First Amendment, as this has been the topic of most public opinion research on civil liberties. The first ten amendments of the Constitution (the **Bill of Rights**) list a number of other civil liberties, however, such as the right to bear arms and some rights of those accused of crimes, including the rights against self-incrimination and unreasonable searches and seizures. Historically, less scholarly attention has focused on public support for these liberties, but in the wake of the September 11, 2001, al-Qaeda attacks and increased national attention on how to effectively capture terrorists, more focus has been placed on these particular rights. The national debate has largely swirled around the proper balance between protecting civil liberties and promoting national security. The implications of this changed climate on public support for civil liberties since the 9/11 attacks will be discussed later in the chapter.

ARE AMERICANS TOLERANT?

Public support for many civil liberties principles in the abstract is very high. In the late 1930s and early 1940s, for example, over 95 percent of survey respondents answered yes to the following question: "Do you believe in freedom of speech?"[7] In more recent years, similarly high percentages of citizens have agreed that "[p]eople in the minority should be free to try to win majority support for their opinions" and that "[no] matter what a person's political beliefs are, he is entitled to the same legal rights and protections as anyone else."[8] Yet, support for the application of these principles in specific circumstances tends to be lower, sometimes substantially so.[9] As one scholar put it, "Americans believe in free speech in theory, but not always in practice. Many would like to see controversy limited and the Bill of Rights tailored to the times and to the occasion. Very few have ever accorded complete freedom of expression to political extremists."[10] In other words, tolerance for the practice of civil liberties, especially among those with unpopular viewpoints, tends not to be very high. Furthermore, the public is not equally tolerant of all types of political acts. Support for certain acts, such as blocking entrances to government buildings or violent demonstrations, is quite low.[11] Have levels of public tolerance changed over time? This question is not so easy to answer. As we will see, specific conclusions as to whether levels of tolerance among the citizenry have changed across the decades depend, in part, on how tolerance is assessed.

Stouffer's Classic Study

In one of the very first empirical analyses of public support for civil liberties, Samuel Stouffer assessed tolerance toward individuals holding unconventional political views.[12] It was the 1950s and Stouffer was interested in probing a variety of public attitudes toward communism. A primary goal of his analysis was determining levels of tolerance toward **communists** and two other groups, **socialists** and **atheists.** During this time, political leaders, at both the national and state levels, prominently led by U.S. Senator Joseph McCarthy, had taken actions to restrict the rights of communists. During this era, known as the Red Scare, suspected communists were jailed, blacklisted, and, in some cases, deported. Stouffer wanted to explore whether the public was intolerant of communists and, if so, what measures might be taken to increase public tolerance.

Stouffer's conclusions are based on results from two public opinion polls conducted in 1954. Survey respondents were selected from a national probability sample. Their responses, therefore, can be generalized to the entire nation. For each of the three nonconformist groups under study, Stouffer queried respondents' willingness to tolerate specific activities performed by group members. The survey questions used by Stouffer to assess tolerance toward these groups have been repeated over the years by many others researching civil liberties. The questions have also come under criticism, as we will soon see. Thus, it is important that we consider how these questions were worded (see Table 8-1). A few aspects of these questions are noteworthy. First, these questions assessed tolerance for three specific activities of these nonconformists: making a speech, keeping a published book in the public library, and teaching at a university. The first two are clearly examples of freedom of expression, a civil liberty protected by the Bill of Rights. Second, Stouffer described the views of atheists (those against churches and religion) and socialists (those favoring government ownership) rather than using the group name. In contrast, he referred to communists directly by name, presumably because citizens were more familiar with communists than with the other two groups, given the national attention devoted to communism during the 1950s. Asking the public about socialists or atheists directly might have been unproductive if people did not know the opinions of these groups.

Levels of public tolerance toward these groups in 1954 are presented in Figure 8-1. The bars represent the percentage of the public who would tolerate the specific act for each group. At first glance, it is clear that levels of tolerance toward these groups were not very high. In fact, the public might best be described as intolerant, especially toward communists and atheists. At most, only about a quarter of the public would support any of the three rights for communists, with only 6 percent of the citizens feeling that communists should not be fired from college teaching. Public support for civil liberties toward atheists was somewhat higher, with just over one-third feeling that atheists should be able to make speeches or have their books kept in the local library. Only 12 percent of the public, however, would support the right of atheists to teach college courses. Tolerance was highest for socialists, with a slight majority of the public expressing support for two of the rights. As with communists and atheists, though, the public was much less supportive of socialists teaching compared with the other two acts.

Overall, then, while public tolerance was quite low in 1954, citizens did make distinctions across the political groups. Support for the civil liberties of socialists was highest, followed by atheists and communists, possibly because the latter two groups' opinions were further from the mainstream than socialists were perceived to be and also because communism was viewed by many to be a threat to the American way of life. Levels of tolerance also varied across the specific acts, with tolerance consistently higher for the two freedoms of expression than for holding a teaching job. University teaching, with its potential to indoctrinate young adults,

Table 8-1 Assessing Public Tolerance: Stouffer's Survey Questions

Questions gauging tolerance of atheists:

"There are always some people whose ideas are considered bad or dangerous by other people. For instance, somebody who is against all churches and religion."

> "If such a person wanted to make a speech in your city (town, community) against churches and religion, should he be allowed to speak, or not?"

> "Should such a person be allowed to teach in a college or university, or not?"

> "If some people in your community suggested that a book he wrote against churches and religion should be taken out of your public library, would you favor removing this book, or not?"

Questions gauging tolerance of socialists:

"Or consider a person who favored government ownership of all the railroads and all big industries."

> "If this person wanted to make a speech in your community favoring government ownership of all the railroads and big industries, should he be allowed to speak, or not?"

> "Should such a person be allowed to teach in a college or university, or not?"

> "If some people in your community suggested that a book he wrote favoring government ownership should be taken out of your public library, would you favor removing the book, or not?"

Questions gauging tolerance of communists:

"Now, I should like to ask you some questions about a man who admits he is a Communist."

> "Suppose he is teaching in a college. Should he be fired, or not?"

> "Suppose this admitted Communist wants to make a speech in your community. Should he be allowed to speak, or not?"

> "Suppose he wrote a book which is in your public library. Somebody in your community suggests the book should be removed from the library. Would you favor removing it, or not?"

Source: Samuel A. Stouffer, *Communism, Conformity, and Civil Liberties: A Cross-Section of the Nation Speaks Its Mind* (Garden City, N.Y.: Doubleday, 1955), 252, 258.

Figure 8-1   Tolerance of Political Minorities, 1954

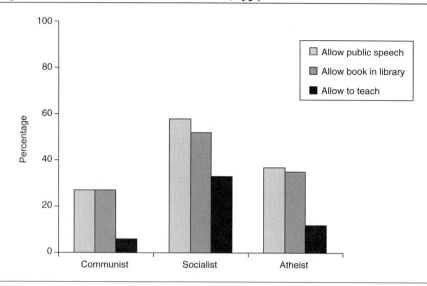

Source: Data from Samuel A. Stouffer, *Communism, Conformity, and Civil Liberties: A Cross-Section of the Nation Speaks Its Mind* (Garden City, N.Y.: Doubleday, 1955), chap. 2.

was thought to be more risky for society than speechmaking or book publishing, hence it was less tolerated.

Trends in Political Tolerance

Have Americans become more or less tolerant since the 1950s? Fortunately, we can directly compare levels of tolerance in that decade with more recent years, as Stouffer's tolerance questions have appeared on the General Social Survey many, many times since this survey began in 1972. Every year at first, then biennially since 1994, a national sample of adults have been asked their attitudes toward a variety of social and political objects.[13] The GSS is a cross-sectional study, which means that different people are surveyed each year. Many of the same questions have been asked over the years, so we can compare the responses of one year with responses in other years to determine if the attitudes of Americans have changed. Keep in mind that the GSS is not a panel study; in other words, the same people are not surveyed every time. Instead, each time the GSS is conducted, a new national probability sample of adults is contacted. Based on this sampling design, we can assume that the results for a given GSS represent the opinions of all American adults for the year of the specific study.

By using Stouffer's questions, tolerance of the speechmaking rights of a variety of political minority groups has been assessed. Figure 8-2 presents results from these surveys for selected years. First, let's consider the three groups that Stouffer examined. Public levels of tolerance toward these groups were much higher in 1972 compared with 1954 and, for communists and atheists, have steadily increased since.[14] It is very possible that tolerance of socialists has also increased, but since the GSS stopped asking questions about this group in 1974, we cannot be certain about this. Throughout these decades, the public has consistently been more tolerant of atheists than communists.

Beginning in the 1970s, the GSS also queried the public about its tolerance of three other groups: **racists** ("a person who believes that blacks are genetically inferior"), **militarists** ("a person who advocates doing away with elections and letting the military run the country"), and male **homosexuals.** The first two of these groups hold opinions on the political right, unlike Stouffer's three groups who are all leftists. A comparison of tolerance for these two groups with that for the groups on the left suggests that increases in public tolerance were primarily restricted to leftist groups (refer to Figure 8-2).[15] More specifically, tolerance of racists remained fairly level between 1973 and 2004. The public is more supportive of civil liberties for militarists now than was the case in 1973, but the tolerance gains for this group have been smaller than have the gains for communists. Finally, although homosexual men are more accurately categorized as a social-political group rather than purely a political group, the political attitudes of homosexuals tend to

Figure 8-2   Tolerance of Speechmaking, 1954–2004

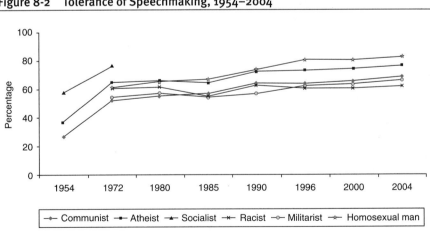

Sources: Data for 1954 from Samuel A. Stouffer, *Communism, Conformity, and Civil Liberties: A Cross-Section of the Nation Speaks Its Mind* (Garden City, N.Y.: Doubleday, 1955), chap. 2. Data for all other years from the General Social Survey.

Note: 1972 data for racist and militarist are actually from 1976; 1972 data for homosexual are actually from 1973.

be ideologically liberal. Thus, we classify this group as leftist. And, similar to the other leftist groups we examined, we see that the public has become significantly more tolerant of homosexual men than was the case in the 1970s. In fact, by 2004, citizens were more likely to support speechmaking by homosexual men than by members of the other groups.

It is now the case that majorities of citizens, sometimes more than 70 percent, support the practice of civil liberties for individuals professing views that are outside of the political mainstream. Yet, for no group or act do Americans unanimously support civil liberties. Would it be thus accurate to conclude that United States' citizens are generally a tolerant lot? Certain democratic theorists, especially participatory democrats, would be reluctant to offer such a rosy conclusion. They would be pleased to see the increasing levels of tolerance toward these groups but would likely prefer even more citizens to possess tolerant attitudes. Furthermore, the empirical evidence demonstrating increases in tolerance since Stouffer's original analysis has come under criticism, most notably by John Sullivan, James Piereson, and George Marcus. The changes in public responses to Stouffer-type questions do not confirm a more tolerant public, they argue, but instead reflect changes in attitudes toward the groups that have been the focus of these questions.

Sullivan, Piereson, and Marcus: Tolerance of "Least Liked" Groups

To be tolerant, one must allow the behavior of those whom one opposes. To Sullivan, Piereson, and Marcus, this is a crucial component of tolerance, yet it is one that is not captured by Stouffer's survey questions.[16] While many Americans probably disagree with communists or atheists, Stouffer's questions do not directly probe for attitudes toward communism or atheism. It is thus impossible to know whether the public dislikes these groups. To compensate, Sullivan et al. used an alternative method for assessing public tolerance, one that they argued more faithfully represents a definition of tolerance as support for the rights of those holding repugnant political views.

Sullivan et al.'s measures of tolerance have come to be called the **"least liked" group** approach based on the wording of their survey questions. Rather than listing specific groups that they assumed the public would not support, they asked survey respondents to identify which political group they liked the least from a list of potentially unpopular groups. Individuals were also allowed to suggest a group that was not on the list, in the hope that everyone would select the group that they most strongly disliked. The specific wording read by the survey interviewers to elicit each respondent's least liked group follows. These statements were read as the respondents perused a printed list of the groups.

> I am giving you a list of groups in politics. As I read the list please follow along: socialists, fascists, communists, Ku Klux Klan, John Birch Society, Black Panthers, Symbionese Liberation Army, atheists, pro-abortionists, and

anti-abortionists. Which of these groups do you like the least? If there is some group that you like even less than the groups listed here, please tell me the name of that group.[17]

In addition to those groups analyzed by Stouffer, included in this list are groups from the political left (Black Panthers and Symbionese Liberation Army) and right (fascists, Ku Klux Klan, and John Birch Society), as well as two groups on opposite sides of the abortion debate. This question was first used by Sullivan and colleagues in 1976, so the groups selected are ones that were salient at that time. For example, the Symbionese Liberation Army, perhaps best known for kidnapping Patty Hearst in 1974, combined urban guerilla tactics with calls for a black revolution. On the other end of the political spectrum, the John Birch Society is a very conservative organization that promotes individual freedom and a limited government and that was formed to protect the Constitution from communism. While still active today, the John Birch Society does not garner as much attention as it once did. More contemporary research contains a somewhat different list of groups, such as racists, religious fundamentalists, and feminists.[18]

Which groups does the American public like the least? Sullivan et al. included their original list of groups on a national survey of the American public in 1978; Table 8-2 presents their results. The most commonly disliked group was communists, yet most people chose a different group as the one they liked the least. Indeed, less than 40 percent selected any one of the three groups Stouffer analyzed. Nearly one-quarter disliked the Ku Klux Klan the most, while 14 percent selected one of the two leftist groups that were especially politically active in the 1970s (Black Panthers or Symbionese Liberation Army). If tolerance is best understood as supporting freedom of expression for those individuals whose speech you strongly dislike, then focusing only on tolerance for communists, atheists, and socialists might overestimate levels of public tolerance since these three groups are especially disliked by only a minority of the public.

While this examination of which groups Americans dislike most is interesting, the heart of Sullivan et al.'s research focused on whether the public is *tolerant* of those groups that they dislike. Thus, after being asked which group they disliked most, survey respondents were asked whether they would support certain activities being performed by members of the selected group, such as holding rallies and making speeches. In the same 1978 survey, participants were also asked to respond to the Stouffer items regarding tolerance for communists and atheists making speeches and having their books in the library. This clever research design allows us to compare public levels of tolerance toward their least liked group versus toward two of the groups that were the focus of Stouffer's, and more recent, research. Results to facilitate such a comparison are presented in Figure 8-3.

Focusing first on the one activity that was asked of all groups—making a speech—we see that public tolerance is higher for communists and atheists than

Table 8-2   Least Liked Political Groups, 1978

Political group	Percentage selecting group as their least liked
Stouffer's groups	
Communists	29
Atheists	8
Socialists	1
Other groups on political left	
Symbionese Liberation Army	8
Black Panthers	6
Groups on political right	
Ku Klux Klan	24
Fascists	5
John Birch Society	1
Abortion groups	
Pro-abortionists	4
Anti-abortionists	2
Other group	2
Don't know	10

Source: Data from John L. Sullivan, James Piereson, and George E. Marcus, "An Alternative Conceptualization of Political Tolerance: Illusory Increases 1950s–1970s," *American Political Science Review* 73 (1979): 790.

it is for people's self-selected least liked group. Regardless of which group was selected, only 50 percent of the public would support speechmaking for their least liked group, whereas 63 percent and 65 percent would support such rights for communists and atheists, respectively. Responses to other questions confirm that levels of tolerance toward least liked group members are indeed very low. Only about one-third of the public would allow members of a group they disliked to hold a public rally. Further, when asked whether such a group should be outlawed, only 29 percent provided a tolerant response. In other words, 71 percent of the public felt that their most disliked group should not be able to exist.

Sullivan et al.'s new measures of tolerance significantly altered research on political tolerance and changed many people's conclusions about how tolerant Americans are. Their results seem to indicate that the public has not become significantly more tolerant over time, in contrast to the conclusions of those who updated Stouffer's analysis beginning in the 1970s. Such apparent increases in tolerance were misleading, argue Sullivan and colleagues, and were the result of less negative attitudes toward the groups under study rather than the result of more support for civil liberties among the public. During the Cold War of the 1950s, the **political times** produced especially high levels of intolerance toward communists

Figure 8-3   Tolerance of Least Liked Groups, Communists, and Atheists, 1978

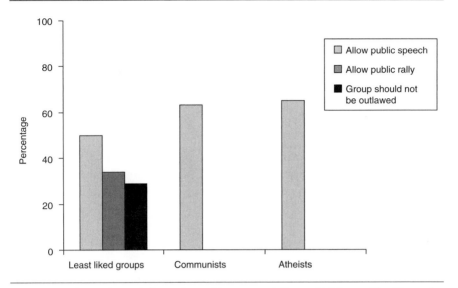

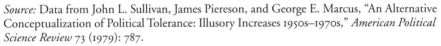

Source: Data from John L. Sullivan, James Piereson, and George E. Marcus, "An Alternative Conceptualization of Political Tolerance: Illusory Increases 1950s–1970s," *American Political Science Review* 73 (1979): 787.

and groups with similar ideologies. Yet, as time passed and the threat of communism receded in many people's minds, the public was more likely to support freedom of expression for these groups. Concurrently, other political groups became the focus of public intolerance. By assessing public attitudes toward a variety of groups, and especially by allowing individuals to select which groups they strongly disliked, Sullivan et al. were able to pick up public intolerance that other researchers missed.

These high levels of intolerance would certainly disappoint classical democratic and participatory democratic theorists, as the results indicate majorities of the public would restrict the rights of those individuals whose opinions they oppose, a clear majority even agreeing that these disliked groups should not exist. Democracy, these theorists argue, requires the free exchange of ideas and the opportunity for political minorities to have their views represented in public forums. On the other hand, Sullivan et al. did not view their findings quite as pessimistically for the prospect of democracy. Rather than leveling intolerance toward only one group, they concluded that intolerance in America is *pluralistic,* that the public selects a number of groups to not tolerate. With intolerance spread around as it is, it is not the case that only one group's rights are undermined by the tyranny of the majority. In other words, "the diversity of the targets selected works against and mitigates to some extent the rather high levels of intolerance."[19] These authors recognized, however, that the conditions could exist for public intolerance to be directed toward one group, thus undermining the democratic rights of such a group. When the political climate directs attention toward one group whose political views are especially threatening to many Americans, as was the case with communists in the 1950s or is perhaps the case with al-Qaeda members and sympathizers today, the civil liberties of these group members could come under direct attack.

Sources of Tolerant Attitudes

There are many reasons why some people are more tolerant than others. Chief among these is education. Just as theorists of participatory democracy hope and predict, the more years of formal education one has, the more likely he will be tolerant toward people with unpopular political views. This relationship between education and tolerance has been uncovered by many researchers, beginning with Stouffer's study and continuing since.[20] Furthermore, some researchers have even concluded that education is the strongest predictor of how tolerant a person is.[21] While there has been the rare challenge to this consensus, the overwhelming evidence is that more education leads to greater tolerance.[22] Why would this be? It is generally assumed that one outcome of more education is greater exposure to ideas and people that are different from oneself. With this exposure often comes greater acceptance of diversity, as manifested in greater levels of tolerance.[23] Another line of reasoning highlights the cognitive development that often accompanies formal education. More years of education can result in "greater acquaintance with the logical implications of the broad democratic principles."[24] Similarly, some suggest that education promotes "knowledge, a flexible cognitive style, and a broadened cultural sophistication."[25] In one of the few analyses to directly examine this assumption, people with more years of education were found to be more cognitively sophisticated (more intellectually engaged and more able to reason about complex concepts) and thus more tolerant of diverse viewpoints.[26]

Other demographic characteristics have also been found to be related to political tolerance. Younger Americans tend to be more tolerant than older citizens. Men are more tolerant than women. Those living in cities are more tolerant than rural residents. People from the southern United States are less tolerant than are those living in other regions of the nation.[27] Stouffer attempts to bring together these disparate findings under one umbrella explanation: the more contact people have with others unlike them, the more tolerant they become. For example, as to why rural citizens are less tolerant of political nonconformity than urban dwellers, Stouffer has the following to say:

> There is something about life in a small community that makes it less hospitable to divergent opinions than is the case in our urban centers. In the

anonymity of city life it is much easier for deviant behavior to flourish than in the goldfish bowl of a small community. In the large community there are sometimes so many goldfish that nobody bothers to look at them. In the small town a lone exotic specimen can be viewed with careful, critical and occasionally devastating attention.[28]

As for regional differences in political tolerance, Stouffer suggests that "movement into new environments exposes people to values different from those they learned at home, and shows that the difference is not necessarily bad or that if it is bad there are ways of handling it without complete intolerance." He goes on to note that the Western states are more tolerant than the South because the former contain many more migrants (from within and outside the United States) than the latter, "so many of whose people have never lived anywhere else."[29]

In one update of Stouffer's research, his assumption that group differences in levels of tolerance were due to **exposure to diversity** was tested.[30] Using survey data from 1973, researchers found that, as predicted, urban dwellers, white-collar workers, and people in the West were more tolerant than their counterparts (rural residents, blue-collar employees, and Southerners, respectively). However, gender differences in tolerance appeared not to be related to exposure to diversity. Stouffer's assumption was that women were less tolerant than men because they were more isolated from others (keeping in mind that women were significantly less likely to work outside the home in the 1950s). The 1973 research, however, found that while women continue to be less tolerant, **social isolation** does not appear to account for the gender differences. Specifically, the level of tolerance among women who worked at home versus those who worked outside the home did not differ; both groups of women were less tolerant than men.[31]

So, to explain why women are less tolerant, we must consider factors other than social isolation. As it turns out, many characteristics other than the demographic categories described above predict whether one will be tolerant. These include psychological features, most especially personality traits. People with low levels of self-esteem tend to be less tolerant, presumably because such negative attitudes toward self interfere with the learning of social norms, tolerance being among them. Further, dogmatic individuals are less likely to be tolerant, especially when compared with those who are more open-minded. In the words of Sullivan and his colleagues, "Persons with flexible, secure and trusting personalities are much more likely to be tolerant."[32] Certain political attitudes, such as support for democratic norms, are also related to tolerance. People who tend to support civil liberties in the abstract (such as the principle of freedom of speech) and to support democratic procedural norms, such as majority vote, are more tolerant toward specific groups or for specific acts.[33] **Political expertise** is also relevant. The more knowledgeable about and interested in politics one is, the more tolerant she will be.[34]

Last but by no means least, **threat perceptions** are a particularly strong predictor of tolerance. Many researchers, beginning with Stouffer, have found that the more a person believes that a particular group is threatening, the less tolerant she is toward the group.[35] She might feel that the group threatens the American way of life and would threaten the stability of the government if the group becomes too powerful, engages in violent tactics and thus could threaten people and property, or is personally threatening to her because of the nature of the group's political views. Regardless of the exact nature of the threat, however, perceiving that a particular group is threatening can significantly reduce one's support of civil liberties for group members.

These other predictors of tolerance can help us to understand why women are less tolerant than men, as Ewa Golebiowska demonstrates.[36] Analyzing GSS data collected in 1987, Golebiowska compared the sources of women's tolerance judgments with the sources of men's. She found that women display lower support for democratic norms and are more likely to feel threatened by disliked groups, both attributes that produce lower levels of tolerance. Probing even deeper, Golebiowska posited two separate explanations to account for the gender differences she uncovered. The first relates to political learning. Relative to men, women are less likely to be politically knowledgeable and engaged, factors which contribute to their lower support for democratic norms. The second explanation highlights women's role as caregivers. In their desire to protect their children and families, women can be hesitant to support groups with extremist views, even to the point of believing these groups are more threatening than men believe. The desire to preserve family life could also account for women's greater attachment to traditional moral values, which also tends to make women less tolerant than men of unpopular political groups.

CONTEXTUAL INFLUENCES ON TOLERANCE JUDGMENTS

You have just learned that there are many individual-level attributes and attitudes that influence one's tolerance for political diversity. Certain features of the **context** also affect whether one is tolerant or not. Contemporary events, both national and global, are relevant, as nicely illustrated by an examination of tolerance for communists.[37] Shortly before World War II, at a time of alliance between the Nazis in Germany and the communist-led government of the Soviet Union, tolerance for communists was fairly low in the United States. This was likely due to Americans feeling their democracy was especially threatened by both the Nazis and the Soviets. During the war, the Nazi-Soviet pact collapsed and the Soviets became an ally of the United States, and tolerance for communists increased. Once the war ended, tensions between the Soviets and the United States escalated. The public began then to display lower support for civil liberties for communists, because of the external threat that the Soviets posed to America and because of the internal threat of communists in the United States. As national attention, from both politicians and the news media, to domestic communism faded in the 1960s and 1970s, tolerance for expression of communist beliefs increased.

One of the most systematic analyses of the influence of context on public tolerance was conducted by George Marcus, John Sullivan, Elizabeth Theiss-Morse, and Sandra Wood, results of which were published in their book *With Malice Toward Some.*[38] Marcus and his colleagues carried out a series of experiments in 1989 and the early 1990s, in which they manipulated various features of the context surrounding civil liberties controversies to determine which of these features influence people's tolerance. Experimental participants first selected their "least liked" group, using the tolerance measures created by Sullivan, Piereson, and Marcus. Two weeks later, the participants read a scenario about a hypothetical political group, but a group that had similar views as the participants' least liked group. So, for example, those who most disliked feminists read about Women for Justice and their goals for eliminating male dominance in the United States. Anyone who most disliked either racists or the Ku Klux Klan was presented with the platform of the White Supremacist Faction, including this group's desire "to restrict the economic and political rights of Blacks and perhaps even Catholics."[39]

Regardless of which hypothetical group the participants were presented with, however, their vignette began with a description of the group's beliefs. The key experimental manipulations appeared next. Marcus and his research collaborators wanted to examine whether either of two specific contextual features influences tolerance judgments. The first was whether the group violated norms regarding appropriate political activity. Was the group respectful and law-abiding or reckless and violent? Some scenarios described the group as the former (cooperating with police, following designated parade routes) whereas others portrayed the group as more threatening (tangling with police, history of violence at rallies). Second, the likelihood of gaining political power by the group was also manipulated. About half of the participants read that the group was likely to gain power (due to their ability to raise a lot of money from supporters and win a few elections) and the other half learned that such prospects were remote (because of, among other things, a lack of public support for the group).

Following rigorous experimental procedures, participants randomly received either the threatening or the reassuring norm violation information. Separately, participants were randomly assigned to either the high or low probability of gaining political power condition. That is, all combinations of these experimental conditions were possible: threatening-high, threatening-low, reassuring-high, and reassuring-low (see Table 8-3). Such a design, coupled with random assignment to experimental conditions, allows researchers to draw conclusions about whether the information received by participants influences their attitudes.

In this case, Marcus and colleagues wanted to know whether either characteristic of the hypothetical group influenced participants' tolerance for the group. They found that participants were influenced by the normative violation manip-

Table 8-3   Conditions for Marcus, Sullivan, Theiss-Morse, and Wood's Experiments

Probability of gaining political power condition	Violation of norms condition	
	Threatening	Reassuring
High probability	Condition 1: Threatening-high	Condition 2: Reassuring-high
Low probability	Condition 3: Threatening-low	Condition 4: Reassuring-low

Source: George E. Marcus et al., *With Malice Toward Some: How People Make Civil Liberties Judgments* (Cambridge: Cambridge University Press, 1995), chap. 4.

ulation: those who learned that the group was likely to violate key norms expressed lower levels of tolerance compared with those who were reassured that the group would conduct its rallies peacefully and lawfully. The probability of power manipulation did not influence tolerance judgments, however. Participants' levels of tolerance toward the group did not depend on whether the group was likely to gain significant political power. In the end, then, Marcus and his coauthors demonstrate that some features of the context surrounding a civil liberties controversy can influence tolerance. They do not conclude, though, that tolerance is related only to this contextual information. In fact, their model of tolerance judgments considers the roles that both individual predispositions (such as support for abstract democratic principles) and contextual information play. In the end, they conclude that "Some people *tend* to be tolerant while others *tend* to be intolerant, but contemporary information … can elicit judgments that differ from people's standing decisions."[40] In other words, people who are predisposed to be tolerant can become less tolerant when presented with certain types of information.

Support for freedom of expression is an important value in democratic societies, but it is not the only one. This value can come in direct conflict with others, such as a desire for public order. Individual people can differ in which of these two they regard more highly, with consequences for their tolerance. A survey of members of the Houston Gay Political Caucus, for example, shows that caucus members who opposed the right of the Ku Klux Klan to march in opposition to homosexuality in a Houston gay neighborhood did so largely because they feared violence would break out at the march. Supporters of the Ku Klux Klan's right to march, however, were not so worried about potential violence and instead strongly supported freedom of expression for all.[41]

Importantly, the broader context can, at times, influence which of these competing values is most dominant. One source of this influence is the news media. Recall the Nelson, Clawson, and Oxley study about media framing of a Ku Klux

Klan rally that we discussed in chapter 3. That study demonstrated the effects of different media frames on levels of tolerance for the KKK. To briefly summarize, Nelson et al. conducted an experiment and showed that subjects exposed to a media frame emphasizing the disorder that might result from a KKK rally were significantly more intolerant of the Klan than subjects exposed to a media frame emphasizing freedom of speech for the KKK. This research demonstrates that journalists' choices regarding how to present the news can influence support for civil liberties. A steady stream of stories stressing groups' free speech rights would likely increase tolerance levels. Given the media's proclivity for airing stories that highlight violence and public disruption, however, a more likely outcome is lower levels of public tolerance toward all types of groups in the political minority.

Methods to Increase Tolerance

What contextual features can increase tolerance? Among adolescents, exposure to a **tolerance curriculum,** particularly one designed to link democratic principles and the American legal system with specific examples of speech by unpopular groups, such as a case study of the Nazi-Skokie controversy, has been found to create stronger support for civil liberties in practice. In contrast, curricula that highlight only abstract democratic norms tend not to change students' levels of tolerance.[42]

Being reminded of the ideals of free expression can also increase tolerance. In addition to Marcus and his colleagues' experiments described above, they also conducted a study whereby they controlled whether the participants were exposed to information extolling the virtues of free expression. Recall that each participant read about a hypothetical group whose views were similar to the participants' least liked group. In this new study, some participants' scenarios included statements that were meant to remind them of the **value of free expression,** such as "no matter how much I dislike these jerks [the hypothetical group], I feel strongly that they should have the freedom to say what they want to" or "[p]eople should have access to a variety of ideas, so that they can make up their minds based on full information."[43] Being exposed to such statements resulted in higher levels of tolerance. While this conclusion was drawn from a laboratory experiment, Marcus and his coauthors conclude that in real life civil liberties controversies, such as that which occurred when the Nazis wanted to march in Skokie, political elites could discuss these democratic principles more often: "Framing the issues in terms of a marketplace of ideas, stressing the positive role of dissent, and noting historic freedoms in the United States can increase support for tolerance, even when the group involved is extremely unpopular."[44]

ARE ELITES MORE TOLERANT?

Do elites express greater support for civil liberties than citizens do, as assumed by the theory of democratic elitism? Yes, according to a number of empirical analyses of this topic, beginning with Stouffer's important work. In addition to his public opinion poll of adults across the nation, Stouffer surveyed 1,500 local community leaders from cities with populations between 10,000 and 150,000. For this portion of his research, he selected political elites (such as mayors, chairs of county Democratic and Republican party committees), community activists (president of the women's club, president of the Parent-Teachers' Association, for example), and people holding other top positions in these communities (Chamber of Commerce president, publisher of the local newspaper, etc.).[45] The community leaders responded to the same tolerance questions contained on the public opinion poll. Results of the comparison between these elites and the mass public are clear: the leaders are much more tolerant of political nonconformists.[46] For example, whereas 84 percent of the leaders supported the right of a socialist to make a speech in the community, only 58 percent of the public did. Similarly, 51 percent of elites supported communists' speechmaking rights, whereas only 27 percent of the public expressed such support. Stouffer's study was also replicated in 1973. The conclusions of this more recent study were essentially the same as Stouffer's: elites continue to express more tolerant attitudes than citizens do.[47]

This greater support for civil liberties among elites is a very robust finding, as it has also been demonstrated a number of other times, as well as when different types of elites have been studied. One study focused on political party activists, interviewing delegates to the 1956 Republican and Democratic national conventions. Compared to responses provided by citizens surveyed in a national poll, these party elites were more tolerant. Whereas, for example, only 18 percent of the party activists agreed that "A book that contains wrong political views cannot be a good book and does not deserve to be published," 50.3 percent of the public agreed with this statement.[48] Differences between elites and the public were smaller in regard to support for abstract civil liberties (such as "I believe in free speech for all"), yet the elites were more tolerant of these principles as well.

The tolerance of national elected officials has also been compared with public attitudes. In 1987, ninety-nine members of the House of Representatives were interviewed and a national representative public opinion poll was conducted. Both the elites and the public answered questions regarding tolerance toward their least liked groups. Members of Congress were 60 percentage points more supportive than the public of allowing their most disliked group to hold a public rally (93 percent versus 33 percent favored this right, respectively) and, by 43 percentage points, more in favor of the speechmaking rights of their least liked group (93 percent versus 50 percent, respectively).[49]

Explanations for Higher Elite Tolerance

Why would elites be more tolerant of minority viewpoints than citizens? One possible explanation focuses on differences in demographic characteristics of leaders versus the mass public. In general, political elites tend to possess characteristics, such as higher levels of education, that are related to higher levels of tolerance. A nice illustration of this pattern comes from research conducted by Robert Jackman.[50] Using Stouffer's data, Jackman compared the community leaders with those who responded to Stouffer's public opinion poll. He found that the former were more educated, more male, and less likely to live in the South. Forty-five percent of the leaders possessed a college degree, for example, whereas only 7.5 percent of the public did. Further, a majority of the leaders were men (77 percent), whereas only 47 percent of the survey respondents were male. Since men, those with more education, and those living outside of the South are more tolerant than their counterparts, differences in these characteristics of the two samples accounted for their differing levels of support for civil liberties. When comparing leaders with members of the public with similar characteristics, Jackman noticed no sizable differences in levels of tolerance. In other words, community leaders who were male, non-Southern, and college graduates expressed similar levels of tolerance as members of the public with the same characteristics. Similarly, female, Southern leaders with a high school diploma displayed roughly equivalent support for civil liberties as did female, Southern citizens with a high school diploma.

A second explanation for elite-public disparities posits that elites have higher levels of tolerance because of their direct involvement in politics. Early proponents of this view included V. O. Key, Robert Dahl, and Herbert McClosky.[51] Leaders experience specific adult socialization effects through their political activity, learning to become more tolerant. This increased tolerance occurs for a number of reasons:

> [G]reater and more intimate contact with ideological diversity decreases authoritarianism and increases tolerance; the necessity to compromise with individuals who disagree strongly with oneself can lead to a more realistic and less dramatic view of the threat presented by nonconformist groups and their ideas; the great responsibility of having actually to govern, of seeing the consequences of one's view enacted into policy and of shaping others' lives can lead to a "sober second thought" about the consequence of one's own intolerance.[52]

Support for this political socialization explanation was found in an examination of attitudes of politicians in four nations: Britain, Israel, New Zealand, and the United States. The elites in the study, all members of their national legislature, displayed more tolerance than would be expected given their levels of education, support for democratic norms, and personality traits such as dogmatism. In other words, the reason why elites are more tolerant is not only because they differ from the general public in certain characteristics that we know to be related to tolerance (such as having more education or being less dogmatic), but also because their engagement with politics socializes them differently than other adults. This general pattern was evident in all nations, with a few exceptions, as mentioned in Box 8-1. Note also that this finding contradicts Jackman's, but that is likely because of the different types of elites that were studied. While Jackman's elites were local community leaders who were engaged in political activity to some degree, politics was not the primary career for many of these leaders, and they were certainly devoting less time and attention to politics compared with the national legislators of Sullivan et al.'s study. This suggests that the differential adult socialization of elites versus citizens will only emerge for elites who are very actively involved in politics.

Public Opinion in Comparative Perspective
BOX 8-1 POLITICAL TOLERANCE IN OTHER NATIONS

Examining public tolerance in other nations can provide insights into the dimensions of tolerance that are harder to uncover when only studying the United States, with its specific history and culture. Tolerance in a nation transitioning toward democracy is likely quite different from tolerance in a stable democracy, for example. In their analyses of tolerance in South Africa, James Gibson and Amanda Gouws uncover some of these differences.[1] Society in South Africa is characterized by deep divisions among people from different racial, ethnic, and class backgrounds, with cleavages existing across as well as within races. Racial classification was instituted by and group animosities were fueled by the apartheid regime. The apartheid system mandated that people from different racial groups keep separate from one another. Whites and blacks, for instance, lived in different towns, attended different schools, rode on different buses, and ate in different restaurants. Furthermore, blacks were denied citizenship and political rights, such as the right to vote, and faced legal discrimination in employment.

In the transition from apartheid to democracy that began in the mid-1990s, many opposing groups competed for political power. The long history of conflict among particular groups coupled with the desire of all to hold power in the new regime has produced a situation in which political competition often turns violent with death a not uncommon result. Further, the newly created democratic institutions are not strong enough to protect South African citizens from such violence. Thus, people in South Africa feel very threatened by their political enemies.

What are the implications for political tolerance? For one, when asked to identify their least liked group, a South African is much more likely to se-

(continued)

lect a group that she views as a competitor for political power, whereas an American would be more likely to select "a marginal, fringe group" that has little chance of wielding significant power.[2] Not surprisingly, then, levels of intolerance are high in South Africa, with citizens being quite unwilling to support political rights for their most disliked group. This intolerance is also fairly intractable. It is very difficult, for example, to convince South Africans that their most disliked group would conduct a rally lawfully and without violence; many simply will not believe this information. Thus, unlike Americans, South Africans cannot easily be moved in a more tolerant direction when exposed to positive details about a disliked political group.

Realistic group threat also influences the sources of political tolerance among elites. One of the key conclusions from an analysis of tolerance in Britain, Israel, New Zealand, and the United States is that elite tolerance is less dependent on threat perceptions than is public tolerance.[3] While elites feel threatened by unorthodox political groups just as citizens do, elites are able to set aside these concerns when deciding whether to support the groups' rights to engage in the political process. This conclusion, however, holds only when none of the groups in question poses a real threat to the nation. At the time of this research, the mid-1980s, a political party on the extreme right of Israeli politics, Kach, had won one seat in the Israeli parliament. Kach advocated removal of Arabs from Israeli and the creation of a religious state among the remaining Israeli Jews. These antidemocratic beliefs in combination with Kach's electoral success, albeit minor, heightened the sense of threat some Israeli elites felt toward the group. Additionally, for those elites who selected Kach as their least liked group, threat perceptions were strongly related to support for civil liberties for Kach members. Among those elites not selecting Kach, perceptions that their least liked group posed a threat did not influence tolerance toward the group. Finally, in nations, such as the United States, where there was not a group that posed a realistic threat, threat perceptions were not related to tolerance among any elites, regardless of which group they selected as their least liked.

1. James L. Gibson and Amanda Gouws, "Making Tolerance Judgments: The Effects of Context, Local and National," *Journal of Politics* 63 (2001): 1067–1090; James L. Gibson and Amanda Gouws, *Overcoming Intolerance in South Africa: Experiments in Democratic Persuasion* (Cambridge: Cambridge University Press, 2003).
2. Gibson and Gouws, "Making Tolerance Judgments," 1072.
3. John Sullivan et al., "Why Politicians Are More Tolerant: Selective Recruitment and Socialization among Political Elites in Britain, Israel, New Zealand and the United States," *British Journal of Political Science* 23 (1993): 51–76.

CIVIL LIBERTIES POST-9/11

Not surprisingly, in response to the September 11, 2001, al-Qaeda attacks on New York City and Washington, D.C., national leaders made some significant changes to policies designed to identify and capture suspected terrorists. These changes have had implications for the practice of civil liberties and for public support of civil liberties. One notable new policy is the **USA Patriot Act** (Uniting and Strengthening America by Providing Appropriate Tools Required to Intercept and Obstruct Terrorism). This legislation, passed by Congress in October 2001, made it easier for federal authorities to issue telephone wiretap orders, conduct searches, and obtain records (financial, library, Internet usage, etc.) of individuals. In some cases, the authorities are no longer required to demonstrate probable cause that a wiretap or search will uncover evidence of criminality or are not required to obtain judicial approval (such as a warrant) before acting.

Depending on your perspective, the Patriot Act either provides law enforcement officials with additional tools for apprehending terrorists or unnecessarily restricts the civil liberties of all, including law-abiding citizens. The debate about the Patriot Act is thus often cast as being between protecting the homeland and upholding civil liberties. For example, Viet Dinh, former Assistant Attorney General in the George W. Bush administration, justifies new laws such as the Patriot Act by stating that "We cannot afford to wait for [terrorists] to execute their plans; the death toll is too high, the consequences too great. We must neutralize terrorists *before* they strike."[53] Jay Stanley and Barry Steinhardt of the ACLU, in contrast, describe the Patriot Act as "an overnight revision of the nation's surveillance laws that vastly expanded the government's authority to spy on its own citizens and reduced checks and balances on those powers, such as judicial oversight."[54]

The public has been somewhat divided over the Patriot Act since its enactment. According to polls conducted by Fox News and Opinion Dynamics between July 2003 and January 2006, slight majorities (53–57 percent) of the public felt that the Patriot Act has been good for the United States (see Table 8-4). At the same time, close to one-third of the public thought that the Patriot Act has been bad, while less than 20 percent were either unsure or believed the Patriot Act has been somewhat good and somewhat bad for the United States. Further, these attitudes remained fairly static during this time period.

The Pew Research Center for the People and the Press has also gauged public attitudes toward the Patriot Act, with somewhat different results. In both December 2004 and January 2006, just under 40 percent of the public felt that this act has gone too far and is threatening civil liberties. While roughly the same percentage of the public believe the Patriot Act is necessary to fight terrorism, more people thought this act necessary in 2006 compared with in 2004 (39 percent versus 33 percent). Compared with the polls conducted for Fox News, respondents to the Pew polls were more likely to indicate they did not know their opinion or refused to answer the question. This could be because the question used by Fox

Table 8-4   Public Opinion: The Patriot Act and Civil Liberties versus National Security

Support for the Patriot Act

"After the 9/11 terrorist attacks, Congress passed the Patriot Act which, in part, gives federal officials wider authority to use wiretaps and other surveillance techniques. Some people say the Patriot Act is a necessary and effective tool in preventing terrorist attacks, while others say the act goes too far and could violate the civil liberties of average Americans. Which comes closer to your view? Overall, would you say the Patriot Act is a good thing for America or a bad thing for America?"[1]

	Good thing	Bad thing	Mixed	Unsure
July 2003	55%	27%	9%	9%
April 2004	54	28	11	7
June 2005	57	30	NA	13
January 2006	53	30	13	4

"Which comes closer to your view ... Is the Patriot Act a necessary tool that helps the government find terrorists or does it go too far and pose a threat to civil liberties?"[2]

	Necessary tool	Goes too far	Don't know/ refused to answer
December 2004	33%	39%	28%
January 2006	39	38	23

Support for civil liberties versus national security

"Which comes closer to your view? The government should take all steps necessary to prevent additional acts of terrorism in the U.S., even if it means your basic civil liberties would be violated. OR, The government should take steps to prevent additional acts of terrorism, but not if these steps would violate your basic civil liberties."[3]

	Take all steps necessary	Don't violate basic liberties	Unsure
January 2002	47%	49%	4%
June 2002	40	56	4
September 2002	33	62	5
November 2003	31	64	5
December 2005	31	65	4

Sources:

1. Fox News/Opinion Dyamics polls, www.pollingreport.com/terror3.htm.
2. Pew Research Center for the People and the Press polls, http://people-press.org/reports/display.php3?ReportID=267.
3. CNN/*USA Today*/Gallup polls, www.pollingreport.com/terror4.htm.

News and Opinion Dynamics contained more information about the Patriot Act than did the question contained on the Pew polls. These details could have reminded or informed respondents about the content of the Patriot Act, thus making them more likely to answer the question.

One explanation for public approval of the Patriot Act and other government measures to fight terrorism is that Americans are generally more willing to sacrifice civil liberties when they feel threatened than when they feel secure. This was the case, for example, after Timothy McVeigh bombed the Oklahoma City federal building in 1995, purportedly in retaliation for federal authorities raiding the compound of a religious group, the Branch Davidians, near Waco, Texas. The Oklahoma City bombing resulted in the deaths of 168 people, making it the deadliest domestic terrorist act in the United States. Shortly after the Oklahoma City bombing, nearly one-half of the public felt that giving up some civil liberties would be necessary to fight terrorism. Two years later, however, during which time no other acts of terrorism occurred on U.S. soil, only 29 percent of the public were willing to sacrifice their liberties.[55] We see a similar trend in the years since the 9/11 attacks. In early 2002, 47 percent of the public were willing to let the government take whatever actions they deemed necessary to fight terrorism (refer to Table 8-4). In the years since, the percentage of the public holding this view has steadily declined while more and more citizens believe the government should not violate civil liberties in the hunt for terrorists. More specifically, in December, 2005, 65 percent of the public prioritized civil liberties over fighting terrorism while only 31 percent would give the government authority to take any necessary steps to prevent terrorism.

Individual Differences in Opinions

Which Americans are most willing to trade off civil liberties for protecting the nation from terrorism? We read earlier in the chapter of the close connection between personal threat and support for civil liberties, so it comes as no surprise that people who feel most threatened by terrorism are most likely to favor national security over civil liberties. As Darren Davis and Brian Silver explain, "the 9/11 attacks ... caused widespread anxiety and concern among Americans. One emotional response to threat is to try to reduce the discomfort by increasing personal security, increasing physical and psychological distance, or eliminating the threatening stimuli."[56]

In probing post-9/11 attitudes toward civil liberties, however, Davis and Silver reveal that threat perception is only one piece of the puzzle. Trust in government, especially law enforcement, is also relevant. Considering only those people who place a lot of trust in the government, support for civil liberties is lowest for citizens who are very concerned that another terrorist attack might occur. However, people who display little trust in government demonstrate stronger support for civil liberties whether they fear another terrorist attack or not. In other words, for people who are distrustful of government, this distrust overrides their concern about future terrorist activity, and they are less willing to trade off civil liberties for security. Finally, Davis and Silver conclude that personal characteristics, especially political ideology and race, also influenced how citizens responded to the 9/11 attacks. Liberals were consistently less willing to support restrictions in civil liberties than were conservatives, and African Americans expressed stronger pro–civil liberties positions than either whites or Latinos. Davis and Silver attribute this latter finding to African Americans' "struggle for civil rights and … distrust of government. As a result, African Americans may be reluctant to concede rights that they have worked hard to achieve or to empower a government in which they have little confidence, even for the sake of personal security." [57]

Other Counterterrorism Policies

Even though times of threat increase the likelihood that citizens favor government restrictions on civil liberties, not all possible **counterterrorism policies** are strongly supported by the public in the post-9/11 era.[58] Of the three policies presented in Figure 8-4, for example, the public is most supportive of the requirement that citizens carry a national identity card at all times. Support for government monitoring of people's credit card purchases is lower, and support for monitoring individuals' telephone calls and e-mail activity is lower still. In fact, by early 2006,

Figure 8-4 Public Support for Specific Counterterrorism Policies

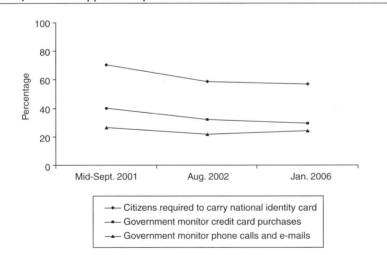

Source: Data from *Americans Taking Abramoff, Alito and Domestic Spying in Stride* (Pew Research Center for the People and the Press, Washington, D.C., January 11, 2006), http://people-press.org/reports/display.php3?ReportID=267.

Note: Data points are the percentage of the public favoring each policy.

opposition to these latter two hypothetical government activities was strong, with only about a quarter of the public voicing support for them.

Opinion surveys have also queried public support for actual Bush administration counterterrorism policies that were originally kept secret from the public. In particular, the news media reported in late 2005 that the National Security Agency (NSA) had been listening in on telephone conversations between American citizens and suspected terrorists living abroad without obtaining proper judicial warrants for this wiretapping. Shortly after this news broke, the public also learned that the Bush administration had authorized the collection of phone calls to examine the calling patterns of most Americans. Lists of phone numbers were checked for the numbers of suspected terrorists in order for officials to determine which Americans had been calling those suspects. The public was fairly divided over these two government policies. For example, in a poll conducted in 2006, 44 percent of the public felt that the wiretapping of phone calls without a warrant was the right thing to do, whereas 50 percent thought it was wrong. Just over one-half (54 percent) of respondents to the same poll felt that it was right to gather and analyze phone call information, whereas 39 percent believed this collection of phone numbers was wrong.[59] Thus, support was higher for the collection of phone records than for the NSA warrantless wiretapping program, perhaps because concerns over violating individual privacy were lower since no conversations were listened to for the former.

Public support for government policies that are more obviously directed toward those suspected of terrorism or those with the same racial or religious characteristics as the 9/11 hijackers tends to be a bit higher than for policies that might restrict the civil liberties of a broader range of citizens. For instance, the Bush administration has classified some individuals suspected of committing terrorist acts as **enemy combatants.** Enemy combatants, according to Bush administration policies, can be held without being charged with a specific crime and can be tried by a military commission without the civil liberties afforded to citizens who are accused of committing crimes. Many of these enemy combatants are being held at a U.S. military prison in Guantanamo Bay, Cuba. In 2003, 65 percent of the public supported holding these individuals at Guantanamo without trials, with only 28 percent opposing. Three years later, 57 percent supported this policy, with 37 percent in opposition.[60]

Racial profiling involves selecting someone for questioning or extra scrutiny on the basis of race or ethnicity. Historically, racial profiling has been used most commonly in the United States to target African Americans. More recently, though, it has been used in an attempt to identify suspected terrorists. Specifically, airport personnel have been accused of screening passengers who appear to be Middle Eastern or Muslim more thoroughly.[61] Nearly 60 percent of the public supports these airport policies, according to surveys conducted by the Pew Research Center in 2002 and 2006.[62] More broadly, between November 2001 and September 2003, between 61 and 73 percent of the public felt that the U.S. government protected the rights of Arab Americans and American Muslims well enough.[63] So, we see that clear majorities of the public seem to support the enemy combatant and racial profiling policies that are directed toward specific groups of people, yet policies that might impinge on the civil liberties of all Americans tend to receive less support (refer back to Table 8-4 and Figure 8-4). Given the history of American citizens displaying lower levels of tolerance for the civil liberties of unpopular groups, these results were not unexpected.

CONCLUSION

Are Americans tolerant of nonconformity? Is the public more or less tolerant than elites? What are the sources of tolerance and intolerance? Does public support for civil liberties change as political times do? These questions motivated Samuel Stouffer to write *Communism, Conformity, and Civil Liberties* 50 years ago. Although the answers have changed somewhat and certainly have become more complex since, these questions continue to be the focus of most political tolerance research today. Stouffer was also worried about the implications of public intolerance for the nation and therefore proposed solutions for increasing levels of tolerance. Discussing whether the level of tolerance is high or low enough in a polity is, of course, at the heart of democratic theorists' writings on civil liberties. It is to democratic theory that we now turn, particularly evaluating the assumptions of both elite and participatory theories of democracy in light of conclusions drawn from political science studies of tolerance.

Elite Democracy

Elite democrats expect the public to be intolerant toward those whose views they reject, especially because of the public's self-interested proclivities and disengagement from political forums where opposing views are aired. Thus, these theorists would not be terribly surprised by Stouffer's findings of widespread public intolerance, the similar conclusions drawn by Sullivan and colleagues, and post-9/11 public support for restricting civil liberties of those who are thought to be sympathetic to or engaged in terrorist activities. Moreover, democratic elitists argue that the leaders of a nation will display more support for civil liberties than the public, a point that is also supported by the empirical political science research. Recall that these theorists went one step further, arguing that the leaders' support for civil liberties would ensure that these liberties are protected, even in the face of much public intolerance. Yet, while elites do profess more attitudinal support for civil liberties than the citizens do, in reality the actions of elected officials do not always coincide with their expressed support for civil liberties in the abstract. When the Nazi party requested permission to march in Skokie, for example, it was the city's politicians who enacted local laws designed to prevent the march. After the 9/11 attacks, it has been the actions of the Bush administration that have restricted civil liberties, most notably of those suspected of committing terrorist acts. Further, it was members of Congress who passed and President Bush who signed the USA Patriot Act of 2001, which allowed the federal government more latitude in collecting information on citizens.

These examples remind us that elite democratic theory has perhaps overstated its case that elites will ensure the maintenance of civil liberties in a democracy. Before settling on this conclusion, however, we must consider the role of the courts. It is not unusual for the courts to rule in favor of upholding civil liberties and against the decisions of legislatures and executives. The Skokie and Chicago ordinances that were designed to prevent the Nazi party from demonstrating in 1978 were declared unconstitutional by federal courts, allowing the Nazis to exercise their freedom of expression.

More recently, the U.S. Supreme Court has invalidated some of the Bush administration's counterterrorism policies. In a 2006 decision (*Hamdan v. Rumsfeld*), the Court ruled that using military tribunals to try enemy combatants held at Guantanamo is improper. For one, the Court held that the tribunals violate the treatment of captured combatants as dictated by the **Geneva Conventions,** an international treaty signed by the United States. According to this international law, detainees shall be tried only by "a regularly constituted court affording all the judicial guarantees which are recognized as indispensable by civilized people." [64] The Bush administration's proposed military tribunals failed to reach this standard in a number of ways, including by not guaranteeing that the detainees could attend their own trials and by allowing into the tribunal evidence that would not be permissible in a civilian court, such as hearsay evidence. The other primary reason why the Court invalidated the military tribunals is because they were created by President Bush without the authority of Congress. In response to this ruling, Congress passed legislation establishing rules for the military tribunals, yet this legislation does not protect all of the legal rights of the detainees that the Court argued was necessary.[65] Here then we have another case where the actions of elected elites attempt to restrict civil liberties, seemingly contradicting the theories of elite democrats.

Participatory Democracy

Beyond their faith in elites, there is another reason why elite democrats do not worry themselves very much about high levels of public intolerance. Since, according to these theorists, citizens are generally too apathetic to engage in political activity, the likelihood that the public will engage in any behavior to actually limit the civil liberties of others is low. "[A]pathy ... furnishes its own partial corrective by keeping the [intolerant] from acting upon their differences. In the United States, at least, their disagreements are *passive* rather than active, more the result of political ignorance and indifference than of intellectual conviction." [66]

Such a viewpoint maddens theorists of participatory democracy. A nation's continued commitment to support for minority rights and other civil liberties should not be predicated upon the apathy of a segment of the citizenry, argue participatory democrats. Among the key democratic goals for these theorists is the full involvement of the citizenry, so they find any argument that applauds the political uninvolvement of the public worrisome.

In contrast, participatory democrats want the public to be more involved in politics, believing that one can learn to become more tolerant through political activity. Thus, participatory democrats are quite pleased with the empirical evidence that formal education leads to more tolerant attitudes and the conclusion that political leaders are more tolerant than the public because of the leaders' exposure to political activity, especially bargaining and compromising with one's opponents. These two findings are promising for increasing citizen tolerance in that they suggest two routes to pursue this goal. The fact that specific types of high school curricula can increase tolerance is especially relevant to participatory democrats' arguments and demonstrates the role that the educational system could play: "if civic education were to include a systematic examination of the role of dissent in a democratic society, young people might develop a commitment to protect civil liberties that would ultimately engender a more fully democratic citizenry."[67]

As should be clear, most participatory democrats assume that high levels of public tolerance are ideal for a democracy. It is worth considering, however, whether supporting the free expression rights of some groups might actually undermine tolerance. Take a group that preaches hatred toward another group, such as the Ku Klux Klan's denigration of blacks. If the KKK speaks out in favor of curtailing the political rights of blacks, and if this speech then reduces the participation of blacks or removes the viewpoints of blacks from the marketplace of ideas, is it tolerant to support the views of the KKK? What of groups that advocate the overthrow of a democratic government? In other words, are "the citizens of a democracy obliged to tolerate those who, if they prevailed, would destroy the practice of tolerance? If tolerance is among the highest values in democratic regimes, does it make sense to tolerate those who threaten this very principle?"[68]

These questions suggest that tolerance might not require supporting the political expression of all viewpoints in a democracy, that some viewpoints are "uniquely undeserving of First Amendment protection."[69] To some people, however, particularly those for whom the freedom of expression of all groups is an absolute necessity, raising such questions is downright intolerant. This debate, which, by the way, was prevalent during the Skokie-Nazi controversy, will exist as long as differing understandings of tolerance and intolerance exist in society.

Key Concepts

atheists / 217

Bill of Rights / 216

civil liberties / 215

communists / 217

constitutional framework / 216

context / 228

counterterrorism policies / 239

enemy combatants / 240

exposure to diversity / 227

Geneva Conventions / 242

homosexuals / 221

"least liked" group / 222

marketplace of ideas / 215

militarists / 221

political expertise / 227

political times / 224

political tolerance / 215

racial profiling / 240

racists / 221

social isolation / 227

socialists / 217

threat perceptions / 228

tolerance curriculum / 231

USA Patriot Act / 236

value of free expression / 231

Suggested Sources for Further Reading

Barnum, David G. "Decision Making in a Constitutional Democracy: Policy Formation in the Skokie Free Speech Controversy." *Journal of Politics* 44 (1982): 480–508.

Gibson, James L., and Richard D. Bingham. "Skokie, Nazis, and the Elitist Theory of Democracy." *Western Political Quarterly* 37 (1984): 32–47.

These two articles discuss the Skokie free speech controversy and its implications for the theory of democratic elitism.

Darmer, M. Katherine B., Robert M. Baird, and Stuart E. Rosenbaum, eds. *Civil Liberties vs. National Security in a Post-9/11 World.* Amherst, N.Y.: Prometheus Books, 2004.

This collection of timely essays discusses the state of civil liberties post-9/11. A variety of viewpoints is presented, including both individuals who worry that civil liberties have been curtailed too severely in the fight against terrorism and those who argue that national security concerns warrant some restrictions on civil liberties.

Gibson, James L., and Amanda Gouws. *Overcoming Intolerance in South Africa: Experiments in Democratic Persuasion.* Cambridge: Cambridge University Press, 2003.

Gibson and Gouws study public tolerance in a nation, South Africa, transitioning toward a stable democracy. Their insightful and detailed analysis illuminates cultural, historical, and individual-level factors that produce high levels of intolerance among South Africans. Prospects for a more tolerant South African public are also addressed by the authors.

Marcus, George E., John L. Sullivan, Elizabeth Theiss-Morse, and Sandra L. Wood. *With Malice Toward Some: How People Make Civil Liberties Judgments.* Cambridge: Cambridge University Press, 1995.

In a series of experiments, the authors demonstrate that new information about unpopular political groups (such as whether they intend to hold a rally that will be violent) can interact with people's existing beliefs (such as whether they support freedom of expression in the abstract) to influence tolerance judgments.

Stouffer, Samuel A. *Communism, Conformity, and Civil Liberties: A Cross-Section of the Nation Speaks Its Mind.* Garden City, N.Y.: Doubleday, 1955.

In this classic study, Stouffer thoroughly examines Americans' tolerance toward nonconformists. More broadly, the book provides a portrait of the public's views toward communism, communists, and the communist threat in the 1950s.

Sullivan, John L., James Piereson, and George E. Marcus. "An Alternative Conceptualization of Political Tolerance: Illusory Increases 1950s–1970s." *American Political Science Review* 73 (1979): 781–794.
Sullivan, John L., James Piereson, and George E. Marcus. *Political Tolerance and American Democracy.* Chicago: University of Chicago Press, 1982.

In this article and book, the authors present their "least liked" group measure of tolerance and explain why it is a better measure than others. The book also discusses many sources of political tolerance.

American Civil Liberties Union: www.aclu.org

One of the nation's leading organizations supporting civil liberties, the ACLU aims, in a variety of ways, to ensure the individual protections provided for in the U.S. Constitution are upheld. Their Web site details the organization's activities as well as presents a wealth of information about many civil liberties issues, such as free speech, religious liberty, the death penalty, and immigrants' rights.

www.Tolerance.org

A program of the Southern Poverty Law Center, this Web site provides many free resources, including teaching tools, for people who wish to fight bias and promote respect for diversity in their communities. A guide for college students ("10 Ways to Fight Hate on Campus") is one of the featured documents.

CHAPTER 9

Support for Civil Rights

DURING THE SUMMER of 2007, Senators Hillary Clinton and Barack Obama were the leading candidates for the 2008 Democratic presidential nomination. On the Republican side, Mitt Romney was raising substantial sums of money and leading in the polls in Iowa, the first caucus state. If any of these three candidates were to win his or her party's nomination, let alone win the presidency, history would be made. A woman, a black, or a Mormon has never won a major party nomination. What does the public think of this turn of events? How supportive are citizens of candidates who break the mold?

One marker of a democratic society is the openness of its political system to citizens from many different walks of life. If elected officials only come from a narrow stratum of society, it raises questions about how representative the institutions of government truly are. In the United States, the institutions of government do not accurately reflect the diversity of the citizenry. Take gender for example. Currently, the U.S. Congress is 16 percent female. Obviously that is low given the proportion of women in society. It is also low in comparison with many other legislatures around the world, yet it is the highest percentage female in the history of the U.S. Congress.[1] Furthermore, only two women have served on the Supreme Court throughout its history, with just one currently sitting on the High Bench. And of course the presidency is the ultimate bastion of male dominance. No woman has ever been elected president, and only one woman has run as vice president on a major party ticket. Certainly there are no laws on the books that stop women and minorities from seeking political office, so why is there this inequality in officeholding? Are citizens' attitudes toward women and minorities partially to blame for the lack of diversity in our institutions?

In this chapter, we discuss how supportive citizens are of political rights for women and minorities, specifically holding the office of president. If even a small segment of society is biased against women and minorities, it can have huge electoral implications. Over the last two decades, presidential elections have been decided by differences in the popular vote of less than 10 percentage points. In 2000, the difference between Al Gore and George W. Bush was one-half of 1 percentage point; in 2004, the difference between John Kerry and George W. Bush was

2.5 percentage points.[2] Given such a closely split electorate, any hesitation on the part of citizens to vote for someone due to a particular characteristic could spell disaster for that candidate.

Political rights are a specific type of civil right we discuss in this chapter, but we also examine support for other **civil rights.** "Civil rights are government guarantees of equality for people in the United States with regard to judicial proceedings, the exercise of political rights, treatment by public officials, and access to and enjoyment of the benefits of government programs."[3] In particular, we examine public opinion concerning civil rights policies geared toward two groups: African Americans and homosexuals.

We focus on African Americans because they are an important group in the United States, both historically and in contemporary society. African Americans have had to fight for their civil rights since the founding of this nation, and the struggle has been a long and hard one. Still today, African Americans battle to preserve the civil rights they have gained and work to expand them. In addition, we highlight opinion toward policies dealing with African Americans for practical reasons. Social scientists have collected extensive public opinion data on issues dealing with African Americans; unfortunately, other racial minority groups have not received nearly as much attention.[4]

In comparison with African Americans, the movement for gay and lesbian rights is a more recent phenomenon. Over the last few decades, gay and lesbian issues have been quite prominent. In the 1980s, fear of AIDS led to concerns about job discrimination against gays and lesbians; in the early 1990s, the "Don't Ask, Don't Tell" policy that allowed gays and lesbians to serve in the military as long as they did not reveal their sexual orientation was an extremely divisive issue; and in recent years, gay marriage has been one of the most heated issues in the United States.

Controversies over civil rights concern participatory democratic theorists a great deal. Participatory democratic theorists worry about equality in the political sphere, and thus are concerned when the path to leadership is not open to all citizens. To these theorists, opposition to civil rights reflects the fact that many citizens are not actively involved in politics. If all citizens participated in political decision making, then women and minorities would have more power within the political system and thus would be able to successfully push for civil rights. Furthermore, participatory democratic theorists believe that participation in and of itself produces better citizens. That is, political interactions with many different types of people allow citizens to see beyond their narrow worlds and to gain a better understanding of what's good for other citizens and for the nation as a whole. As a result, citizens would probably demonstrate greater support for civil rights.

In contrast, elite democratic theorists are not particularly concerned with equality in society. Indeed, some elite democratic theorists *expect* that certain inequities will exist in the political system. Thus, they would not be surprised that our institutions of government do not reflect the diversity of society. Other elite democratic theorists are not concerned about opposition to civil rights among the public because these theorists emphasize that elites are the key political players. Because the elites appreciate and support the rights of minorities, the public's views on the subject don't really matter.

PUBLIC OPINION AND PRESIDENTIAL CANDIDATES

There are very few formal qualifications to run for president of the United States. A person must be a natural-born citizen, at least 35 years of age, and a resident of the United States for 14 years to be eligible for the presidency. That's it. In practice, however, the story is much different. The youngest president ever elected was John F. Kennedy at 43 years old, and the oldest was Ronald Reagan at 69. The majority of presidents have been between the ages of 50 and 59 when elected. Only one president has been Catholic, while two have been Quakers. And, of course, no women or racial minorities have ever been elected president of the United States. What explains why presidents have come from such a limited pool of citizens? We turn to some fascinating public opinion data to help answer this question.

Religion and Presidential Candidates

For several decades, the Gallup organization has asked citizens whether they would vote for particular types of candidates if nominated by their party.[5] Let's first examine support for candidates of different religious faiths (see Figure 9-1). Support for Baptist presidential candidates has been high since the question was first asked in 1958.[6] In contrast, support for a Catholic was modest in 1937 but has climbed steadily since then. Support for a Jewish candidate was under 50 percent in 1937 but has also increased over time. In 2007, over 90 percent of citizens said they would vote for a well-qualified Catholic or Jew if nominated by their party.

Support for a Mormon president has stayed fairly constant over time. The question was first asked in 1967 when George Romney (Mitt Romney's father) ran for the Republican presidential nomination. At that time, three-fourths of Americans said they would vote for a Mormon nominated by their party. Forty years later, support for a Mormon is still stuck down in the 70 percent range. Thus, there is significant opposition to a Mormon becoming president of the United States, which does not bode well for Mitt Romney's bid for the presidency. His chances for the presidency look good, however, compared with an atheist's chances. In the late 1950s, support for an atheist presidential candidate was very weak, and while it has doubled since then, it is still anemic. In July 2007, only 45 percent of Americans said they would vote for a well-qualified atheist if nominated by their political party.

Another way to examine this is to ask citizens whether they would be *more or less likely* to support a candidate with particular characteristics. The Pew Research Center conducted a poll in February 2007 that did just that (see Table 9-1). This

Figure 9-1   Support for Presidential Candidates, 1937–2007: Religion

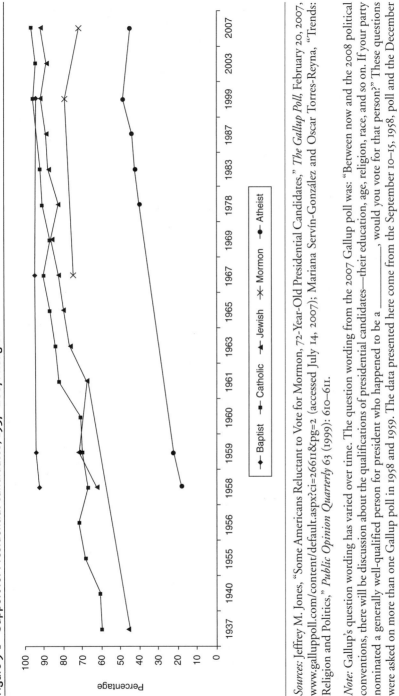

Legend: ◆ Baptist   ■ Catholic   ▲ Jewish   ✕ Mormon   ● Atheist

Sources: Jeffrey M. Jones, "Some Americans Reluctant to Vote for Mormon, 72-Year-Old Presidential Candidates," *The Gallup Poll,* February 20, 2007, www.galluppoll.com/content/default.aspx?ci=26611&pg=2 (accessed July 14, 2007); Mariana Servín-González and Oscar Torres-Reyna, "Trends: Religion and Politics," *Public Opinion Quarterly* 63 (1999): 610–611.

Note: Gallup's question wording has varied over time. The question wording from the 2007 Gallup poll was: "Between now and the 2008 political conventions, there will be discussion about the qualifications of presidential candidates—their education, age, religion, race, and so on. If your party nominated a generally well-qualified person for president who happened to be a _____, would you vote for that person?" These questions were asked on more than one Gallup poll in 1958 and 1959. The data presented here come from the September 10–15, 1958, poll and the December 10–15, 1959, poll.

poll asked about support for Christian, Mormon, Muslim, and atheist presidential candidates. For 56 percent of people, whether a candidate is a Christian wouldn't matter; when it does matter, being a Christian is more likely to help the person than hurt him or her. Similarly, 64 percent of people said it wouldn't matter if a candidate was a Mormon, but when it does matter, it works strongly against the candidate. Thirty percent said they would be less likely to support a Mormon, while only 2 percent said they would be more likely to support a Mormon (which perhaps not coincidentally is the percentage of Mormons in the United States). Just less than one-half of Americans indicated that a candidate being Muslim wouldn't matter to them, but 46 percent said they would be less likely to support a Muslim. Still, being a Muslim puts you at an advantage over an atheist. Almost two-thirds of Americans said they would be less likely to support a candidate who does not believe in God. Given these current levels of public opposition, it seems unlikely that the United States will have either a Muslim or an atheist president any time soon.

Citizens might be leery about answering survey questions regarding what types of candidates they prefer. These are personal preferences that people might not want to reveal to a survey interviewer. Indeed, many citizens probably recognize that it is politically incorrect—or **socially undesirable** as survey researchers would put it—to say they wouldn't vote for a candidate just because of his or her religious beliefs; however, people might be more forthcoming when asked whether

Table 9-1 Religion and Likelihood to Vote for a Presidential Candidate, 2007

| Response | *"Regardless of the specific candidates who are running for president, we'd like to know how you generally feel about some different traits. Would you be more likely or less likely to support a candidate for president who is _____, or wouldn't this matter to you?"* | | | |
	Christian	*Mormon*	*Muslim*	*Does not believe in God*
More likely to support	39%	2%	1%	3%
Less likely to support	4	30	46	63
Wouldn't matter	56	64	49	32
Don't know/ refused	1	4	4	2

Source: Survey by Pew Research Center for the People & the Press and Princeton Survey Research Associates International, February 7–February 11, 2007. The iPOLL Databank, The Roper Center for Public Opinion Research, University of Connecticut, www2.lib.purdue.edu:4076/ipoll.html (accessed September 23, 2007).

their *fellow citizens* are ready to elect a particular type of candidate. In a September 2006 survey, the Gallup organization asked citizens, "Generally speaking, do you think Americans are ready to elect a Jew as president, or not?" Forty-two percent of citizens said that Americans are not ready to elect a Jew.[7] This implies much higher levels of opposition than suggested by citizens' own responses regarding whether they would vote for a Jew for president (refer back to Figure 9-1). Citizens are also skeptical about whether Americans are ready to elect a Mormon or an atheist. Sixty-six percent said the country is not ready for a Mormon president, and 84 percent said Americans are not ready for a president who is an atheist.[8] Again, these numbers suggest more opposition than when citizens are asked directly about their opinions (refer back to Figure 9-1 and Table 9-1). Of course it could simply be the case that citizens believe their fellow Americans are more prejudiced than they really are, and thus greatly underestimate the openness of the public to elect an atheist or a candidate from a minority religion. Nevertheless, these data raise red flags about the electability of a non-Protestant candidate.

Race and Presidential Candidates

What about racial minorities? Are citizens willing to support a black candidate, such as Senator Barack Obama, or a Hispanic candidate, such as Governor Bill Richardson, for the presidency? Since 1958, the Gallup poll has been asking citizens whether they would support a well-qualified black candidate nominated by their party for the presidency. Less than 50 percent of Americans said they would support a black candidate in the late 1950s (see Figure 9-2). This percentage has increased steadily over time. Seventy-nine percent of Americans said they would support a black candidate in 1987. The question was not asked again until 1997, by which time support had jumped to 93 percent. For the last ten years, support has remained in the low-to-mid 90 percent range.

When citizens were asked in 2007 whether they would be more or less likely to support a black candidate, the vast majority said it would make no difference and only 4 percent said less likely (see Table 9-2). A different picture emerges, however, when citizens were asked whether other Americans are ready to elect an African American or black candidate as president. In 2006, 40 percent of respondents said that Americans are not ready.[9] As with religion, this may suggest that more people are opposed to electing a black president than are willing to admit it openly.

In 2007, the Gallup poll asked citizens for the first time whether they would vote for a well-qualified Hispanic for president if nominated by their party. Eighty-seven percent said they would do so (see Figure 9-2). When respondents were asked whether they would be more or less willing to support a Hispanic presidential candidate, 80 percent said it wouldn't matter, but 14 percent said they would be less likely to support such a candidate (see Table 9-2). Further, 58 percent of citizens said that Americans are not ready to elect a Hispanic president. Similarly,

Figure 9-2 Support for Presidential Candidates, 1937–2007: Gender, Race, and Sexual Orientation

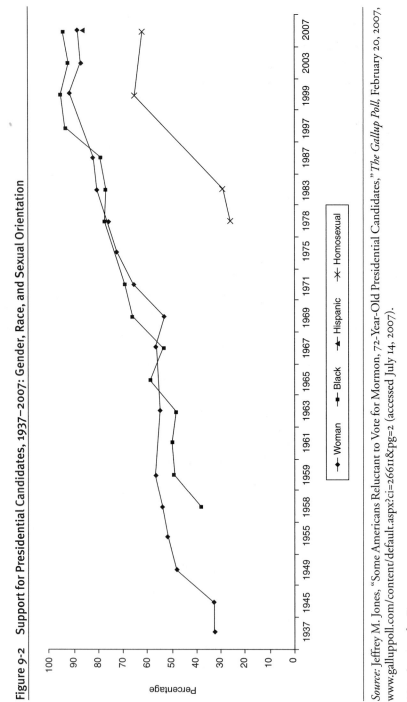

Source: Jeffrey M. Jones, "Some Americans Reluctant to Vote for Mormon, 72-Year-Old Presidential Candidates," *The Gallup Poll,* February 20, 2007, www.galluppoll.com/content/default.aspx?ci=26611&pg=2 (accessed July 14, 2007).

Note: Same as for Figure 9-1.

Table 9-2 Race, Gender, Sexual Orientation, and Likelihood to Vote for a Presidential Candidate, 2007

Response	"Regardless of the specific candidates who are running for president, we'd like to know how you generally feel about some different traits. Would you be more likely or less likely to support a candidate for president who is _____, or wouldn't this matter to you?"			
	Black	*Hispanic*	*Woman*	*Homosexual*
More likely to support	7%	4%	13%	1%
Less likely to support	4	14	11	46
Wouldn't matter	88	80	75	51
Don't know/ refused	1	2	1	2

Source: Survey by Pew Research Center for the People & the Press and Princeton Survey Research Associates International, February 7–February 11, 2007. The iPOLL Databank, The Roper Center for Public Opinion Research, University of Connecticut, www2.lib.purdue.edu: 4076/ipoll.html (accessed September 23, 2007).

64 percent said Americans are not ready for an Asian president.[10] Perhaps this hesitancy about a Hispanic or Asian candidate stems from anti-immigrant sentiment. Immigrants in recent years have come heavily from Mexico and from countries in Asia (such as China and India), so some citizens' negative views of immigrants may spill over into dislike for native-born Latinos and Asian Americans who might run for the presidency. On the whole, these public opinion data raise questions about whether a nonwhite candidate can win the presidency.

Gender and Presidential Candidates

Since 1937, the Gallup organization has asked citizens whether they would vote for a well-qualified woman nominated by their party for the presidency. Only one-third of Americans said they would do so in 1937 (see Figure 9-2). During the 1950s and 1960s, support for a woman candidate hovered in the 50 percent range. Coinciding with the women's movement, support for women candidates increased significantly in the 1970s. By 1975, 73 percent of citizens said they would support a well-qualified woman for the presidency. This percentage increased to 92 percent by 1999, only to fall back a few percentage points in recent years.

Why has support for a woman candidate dropped since the late 1990s? It is difficult to answer that question by examining the Gallup data because the organization did not ask the question between 1999 and 2003. Another polling organization, however, did ask the question of a representative sample of citizens in

August and September of 2002. In that poll, only 65 percent of respondents said they would vote for a qualified woman candidate nominated by their party for the presidency. Seven percent said they would not do so, while 28 percent said they were unsure.[11] What led to all this uncertainty about a woman candidate? What happened between 1999 and 2002 that might have led citizens to be hesitant about electing a woman as president?

On September 11, 2001, terrorists struck the World Trade Center and the Pentagon, a tragic event that is etched in the minds of most Americans. Since that fateful day, foreign policy issues, especially the war on terrorism, have dominated American politics. Why would this influence whether citizens would be willing to support a woman candidate? Because many citizens believe male politicians are more competent than female politicians when it comes to issues relating to the war on terror. For example, in the 2002 poll just mentioned, 35 percent of citizens said that men would be more competent to punish the people responsible for the September 11 attacks and 40 percent indicated that men were more capable of protecting the homeland from future attacks. Virtually everyone else said that women and men would be equally competent to deal with these issues, with only a tiny percentage indicating women would be more competent. It turns out that the same citizens who doubted the competency of women were the ones more likely to indicate they would not vote for a woman candidate or were unsure whether they would do so.[12]

Thus, these data suggest that in an atmosphere focused on the war on terror, women candidates are at a severe disadvantage because of the endorsement of **gender stereotypes** by a significant minority of the American people. These results help explain why Senator Hillary Rodham Clinton has taken such tough stances on foreign policy issues during her presidential election campaign: she knows she must campaign in a way that will undermine citizens' gender stereotypes and thus make them comfortable voting for a woman. The good news for Senator Clinton is that the Gallup polls indicate support for a woman candidate has bounced back from the low number in the aftermath of September 11; however, given the closeness of recent elections, Clinton will have an uphill battle even if only a small percentage of the electorate is biased against her on the basis of gender. Indeed, when citizens were asked in 2006 whether their fellow Americans are ready to elect a woman president, 38 percent said no.[13]

Sexual Orientation and Presidential Candidates

In 1978, the Gallup organization asked citizens for the first time about voting for a homosexual presidential candidate. Only 26 percent of Americans said they would vote for such a candidate (refer back to Figure 9-2). By 2007, that percentage had more than doubled, with 55 percent indicating they would vote for a homosexual nominated by their party for the presidency. When asked if it would matter whether a candidate was homosexual, just over one-half of citizens said it wouldn't matter, yet 46 percent said it would make them less likely to support the candidate (see Table 9-2). How do citizens think their fellow Americans would react to a gay or lesbian candidate? Not well: a whopping 91 percent of respondents said that other Americans were not ready to elect such a candidate.[14] Overall, these polling data suggest an openly gay or lesbian candidate has little chance of winning the White House any time soon.

Other Demographics and Presidential Candidates

In addition to religion, race, gender, and sexual orientation, there are a number of other candidate characteristics that citizens might consider relevant when evaluating potential candidates. In February 2007, the Pew Research Center conducted a survey in which respondents were asked whether they would be more or less likely to support candidates with a variety of traits. In terms of a candidate's educational background, nearly one-half of respondents said they would be less likely to support a candidate who did not attend college. In contrast, 22 percent said they would be more likely to support someone who attended a prestigious university (see Table 9-3). As for age, many citizens demonstrated a bias against older candidates. Forty-eight percent said they would be less likely to support a candidate in their 70s, whereas 18 percent said they would be more likely to support a candidate in their 40s. The vast majority of Americans, 86 percent, said that a candidate with a physical handicap wouldn't make a difference to them, yet 7 percent indicated it would make them less likely to back the candidate. A divorced candidate wouldn't matter to most people; however, if the divorce was a result of an extramarital affair, the candidate might be in big trouble. Thirty-nine percent of Americans said they would be less likely to support a philandering candidate. These data are particularly interesting given the diverse crop of presidential hopefuls who pursued the 2008 nomination, including candidates with prestigious university degrees, older candidates, younger candidates, divorced candidates, and philanderers.

SUPPORT FOR CIVIL RIGHTS POLICIES

"Equal Justice Under Law" are the words majestically incised above the entrance of the U.S. Supreme Court building. This simple phrase captures the essence of civil rights, as suggested by the more detailed definition of civil rights that we presented at the beginning of the chapter. In this section, we discuss public support for African American rights and how support for those rights has changed over time. We also examine public attitudes toward gay and lesbian rights and how those attitudes have changed since the 1970s.

Support for Civil Rights for African Americans

Are citizens supportive of civil rights for black Americans? In principle, the answer is yes. Both white and black Americans overwhelmingly endorse **principles of equality**. In practice, however, the answer is much more complex. Support drops

Table 9-3 Various Demographics and Likelihood to Vote for a Presidential Candidate, 2007

"Regardless of the specific candidates who are running for president, we'd like to know how you generally feel about some different traits. Would you be more likely or less likely to support a candidate for president who _____, or wouldn't this matter to you?"

Response	Did not attend college	Attended a prestigious university	Is in their 70s	Is in their 40s	Has a physical handicap	Has been divorced	Had an extramarital affair in the past
More likely to support	3%	22%	5%	18%	4%	3%	1%
Less likely to support	46	5	48	8	7	9	39
Wouldn't matter	49	72	45	73	86	86	56
Don't know/refused	2	1	2	1	3	2	4

Source: Survey by Pew Research Center for the People & the Press and Princeton Survey Research Associates International, February 7–February 11, 2007. The iPOLL Databank, The Roper Center for Public Opinion Research, University of Connecticut, www2.lib.purdue.edu:4076/ipoll.html (accessed September 23, 2007).

significantly among whites when it comes to the **implementation** of civil rights policies, especially if the implementation means that blacks will receive preferential treatment or redress for past harms.[15] Blacks also demonstrate less support for civil rights in practice than in principle, but a majority still supports the enforcement of civil rights policies.

Support for Equality in Principle.   Let's first discuss attitudes toward school integration and interracial marriage to illustrate support for the principles of equality. When the white public was first asked in 1942 whether they thought Negro and white students should go to the same or separate schools, only one-third supported integration (see Figure 9-3). White opinion on this issue has shifted dramatically over time, with virtually all whites supporting integration in 1995. Some scholars have characterized this change in attitudes as a "revolution."[16] Indeed, the General Social Survey has stopped asking the question since support for equality is so high. Regrettably, this question was not asked of blacks until 1972. Black support for integration was nearly universal at that time and has remained so ever since.

Support for the legality of interracial marriage follows the same general pattern as support for integration. In the 1970s, two-thirds of whites opposed laws against interracial marriage (i.e., two-thirds supported the legality of such marriages) (see Figure 9-4). Over time, this has increased substantially, with 89 percent supporting the legality of interracial marriage in the 2000s. Still, one out of ten white Americans think there should be a law against such marriages. What about the attitudes of black citizens? Unfortunately, blacks were not asked this question until the 1980s. Ninety-two percent supported the legality of such marriages at that time; today, virtually all blacks support these marriages.

Support for Implementation of Civil Rights Policies.   In sharp contrast to their support for equality in principle, whites show much less support for the implementation of civil rights policies. Given high levels of racial segregation in residential patterns, it was rare (and continues to be rare to this day) that white and black students attended the same neighborhood schools. Thus, to achieve school integration, several communities enacted busing plans during the 1970s. In other words, some cities bused white children to schools in black neighborhoods and black children to schools in white neighborhoods as a way to end segregation. These policies were highly unpopular with white citizens. When asked whether they favored or opposed "the busing of Negro and white school children from one school district to another," only 14 percent of white Americans supported the policy in the 1970s (see Figure 9-5). Over time, white support for busing has doubled, but it is still quite low at 30 percent. Compare these low levels of support for busing with the high levels of support white Americans voiced for whites and blacks going to the same schools (refer back to Figure 9-3). Clearly, there is a huge gap between how whites think about equality in theory versus in practice.

Blacks also demonstrate lower levels of support for the implementation of school integration policies than they do for integration in principle. During the

Figure 9-3   Support for Same Schools, by Race

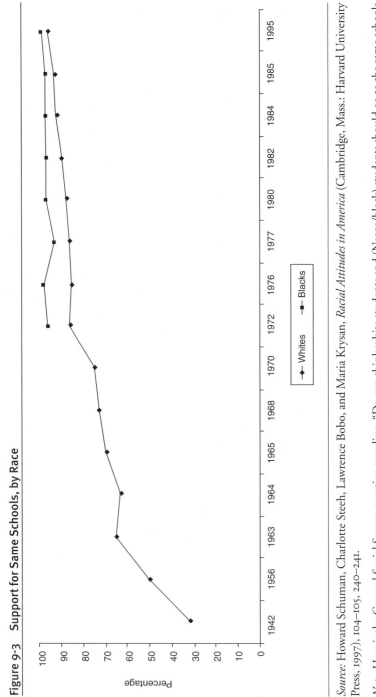

Source: Howard Schuman, Charlotte Steeh, Lawrence Bobo, and Maria Krysan, *Racial Attitudes in America* (Cambridge, Mass.: Harvard University Press, 1997), 104–105, 240–241.

Note: Here is the General Social Survey question wording: "Do you think white students and (Negro/black) students should go to the same schools or to separate schools?"

Figure 9-4   Support for the Legality of Interracial Marriage, by Decade and Race

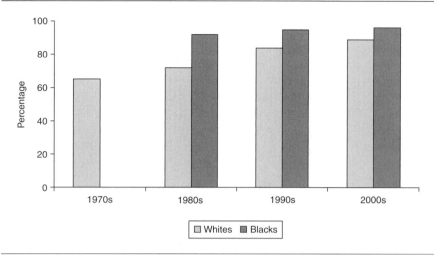

Source: Analysis of General Social Survey Cumulative Data File, 1972–2004.

Note: Here is the General Social Survey question wording: "Do you think there should be laws against marriages between (Negroes/blacks/African-Americans) and whites?" Bars represent the percentage opposing laws against interracial marriage.

1970s, 53 percent of blacks supported school busing (see Figure 9-5). By the 1990s, black support for busing had increased to 61 percent. While this percentage is lower than the almost universal support among blacks for the abstract notion of the two groups attending school together (refer back to Figure 9-3), black support for busing is still double the level of white support.

Support for Affirmative Action.   **Affirmative action** is an umbrella term for a variety of policies that ensure equal treatment of minorities and whites in education and employment. Affirmative action policies range from a job advertisement that includes a declaration that the company is an equal opportunity employer to a business taking race into account when making hiring decisions to a college considering race as a factor in admissions. Some affirmative action policies ensure equal opportunity, while other policies take special steps to turn the principle of equal opportunity into practice by encouraging equal outcomes.[17]

Affirmative action policies have been justified primarily on two grounds. First, they are intended to make up for past and continuing discrimination against racial minorities in our society. And second, they are designed to ensure that the diversity of the United States is reflected in our colleges and universities, government institutions, and workplaces. Policies to ensure equal treatment between men and women are also referred to as affirmative action policies.

Figure 9-5   Support for School Busing, by Decade and Race

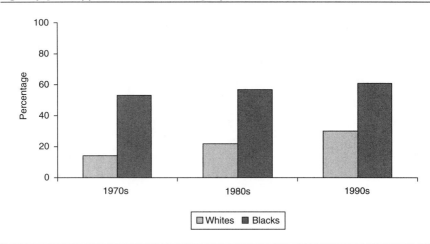

Source: Analysis of General Social Survey Cumulative Data File, 1972–2004.

Note: Here is the General Social Survey question wording: "In general, do you favor or oppose the busing of (Negro/black/African-American) and white school children from one school district to another?"

As with other civil rights policies, whites and blacks support affirmative action in principle more than they do in practice. In 1995 and again in 2007, the Pew Research Center asked citizens whether they supported "affirmative action programs designed to help blacks, women and other minorities get better jobs and education." This question focuses on the principle of enhancing opportunities rather than providing special treatment. As a result, a majority of whites and almost all blacks support the policy. Specifically, 53 percent of white citizens favored such programs in 1995.[18] By 2007, the level of support had increased to 65 percent. Among blacks, support for this type of affirmative action policy was nearly universal in both 1995 and 2007 (94 percent and 93 percent). The fact that the question refers to both blacks *and* women may also boost support for the policy.

Citizens' support for affirmative action falls dramatically when the policies refer to specific steps to ensure the equal treatment of blacks. Since 1986, the American National Election Study has asked whether "blacks should be given preference in hiring and promotion." At that time, only 14 percent of white Americans supported such policies. White levels of support have varied little over time, and a mere 12 percent favored preferential treatment in 2004 (see Figure 9-6). Among blacks, we also see less support for affirmative action policies designed to put equality into practice. Nevertheless, two-thirds of blacks supported these policies in 1986, and a majority continues to favor these types of policies today.

Figure 9-6   Support for Preferences in Hiring and Promotion for Blacks

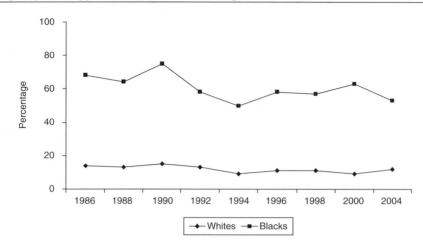

Sources: Howard Schuman, Charlotte Steeh, Lawrence Bobo, and Maria Krysan, *Racial Attitudes in America* (Cambridge, Mass.: Harvard University Press, 1997), 174–175, 268–269; Analysis of American National Election Studies Cumulative Data File, 1948–2004.

Note: Here is the American National Election Study question wording: "Some people say that because of past discrimination, blacks should be given preference in hiring and promotion. Others say that such preference in hiring and promotion of blacks is wrong because it gives blacks advantages they haven't earned. What about your opinion—are you for or against preferential hiring and promotion of blacks?"

Support for Reparations.   Since 1989, Congressman John Conyers has proposed the "Commission to Study Reparation Proposals for African Americans Act" in every Congress and says he will continue to do so until the bill is passed into law. The bill would establish a commission to examine the effects of slavery on African Americans living today and make recommendations regarding appropriate remedies to address slavery's harmful effects. Such remedial policies are referred to as **reparations**.

Are black citizens supportive of reparations? During the summer of 2003, Rosalee Clawson, Katherine Tate, and Eric Waltenburg conducted a national survey of black Americans.[19] The survey included several questions asking blacks about various issues related to reparations. There was overwhelming support for the beliefs that slavery is a crime against humanity and that blacks still suffer negative consequences from the enslavement of their ancestors (see Table 9-4). There was somewhat less support when the survey questions suggested actions on the part of the government. Nevertheless, nearly three-quarters of blacks agreed that the government should apologize for slavery. Similarly, almost three-quarters disagreed with the statements that blacks are not owed anything or that blacks had already been compensated. Overall then, blacks demonstrate widespread support for reparations.

Another survey conducted by the Gallup organization in 2002 also sheds light on black support for reparations. A small, yet representative sample of black respondents was informed that several companies still around today made money from slavery. Respondents were then asked whether they supported specific types of reparations. A majority of black Americans supported cash payments to slave descendants from both the government and corporations (see Table 9-5). Sixty-eight percent supported an apology from the companies who benefited from the slave trade, and fully three-quarters supported scholarship funds for black Americans who are descendants of slaves. These statistics are consistent with the picture provided by the larger sample of black Americans in Clawson et al.'s study.[20]

What about white Americans? Do they support reparations for the descendants of black slaves? No, they do not. The 2002 Gallup poll interviewed a national sample of white respondents. White citizens overwhelmingly opposed the government or corporations making cash payments to slave descendants (see Table 9-5). At 34 percent, whites were somewhat more supportive of corporations making an apology to black Americans; similarly, roughly one-third of whites supported corporations setting up scholarship funds to benefit black Americans who are descendants of slaves. Overall, whites have strikingly different views than black Americans on the subject of reparations for slave descendants.

Table 9-4   Black Support for Reparations, 2003

Statement	Percentage who agree
"Slavery is a crime against humanity like the Holocaust."	92
"Black Americans still suffer negative psychological and economic consequences from the enslavement of their ancestors."	83
"The U.S. government should apologize to the descendants of African American slaves."	73

	Percentage who disagree
"The government has already compensated for the injuries of slavery through other government programs, including affirmative action."	73
"Slavery happened a long time ago. Blacks today are not owed anything."	71

Source: Data from Rosalee A. Clawson, Katherine Tate, and Eric N. Waltenburg, *Blacks and the U.S. Supreme Court Survey,* 2003.

Table 9-5   White and Black Support for Reparations, 2002

"As you may know, several companies in business today made profits from slavery prior to the civil war..."	Percentage supporting reparations	
	Whites	Blacks
"Do you think the government should or should not make cash payments to Black Americans who are descendants of slaves?"	6	55
"Do you think corporations who made profits from slavery in the United States should or should not make cash payments to Black Americans who are descendants of slaves?"	11	57
"Do you think corporations who made profits from slavery in the United States should or should not apologize to Black Americans who are descendants of slaves?"	34	68
"Do you think corporations who made profits from slavery in the United States should or should not set up scholarship funds for Black Americans who are descendants of slaves?"	35	75

Source: Peter Viles, "Suit Seeks Billions in Slave Reparations," *CNN.com,* March 27, 2002, http://archives.cnn.com/2002/LAW/03/26/slavery.reparations (accessed August 25, 2007).

Philip J. Mazzocco and his colleagues conducted a fascinating study to examine *why* whites oppose reparations for black Americans who are the descendants of slaves.[21] One possible reason for people to oppose reparations is that the crime of slavery happened long ago and neither the perpetrators of the crime nor the victims of the crime are alive today. Thus, reparations are not fair because they would benefit people who were not directly harmed and penalize people who had nothing to do with slavery. If this reasoning explains white opposition to reparations, then it makes sense that whites would oppose reparations for *any type* of crime that happened long ago, not just reparations for slavery. Is this the case?

To answer this question, Mazzocco et al. asked sixty-six white college students to read a scenario in which someone had done significant harm to their great, great grandfather, including gaining financial advantage at the expense of their relatives. After reading the scenario, participants were asked whether they would join in a class action suit to try and recover some of their great, great grandfather's assets. Here is the scenario:

Imagine that about 150 years ago, in the mid 1800s, your great, great grandfather was kidnapped by Fineus Jones. Jones demanded a million dollars from your great, great grandfather's shipping business. The family borrowed the money and paid the ransom and your great, great grandfather was released. Jones escaped to Europe and was apprehended, but none of the

BOX 9-1 The Racial Attitudes of Young White Adults

Are young white Americans more supportive of civil rights than older white Americans? The evidence is mixed in this regard. On the one hand, young people are less likely to endorse old-fashioned racism than older citizens. **Old-fashioned racism** refers to the beliefs that blacks are innately inferior to whites and therefore should be kept separate from whites. Old-fashioned racism is the ideology that was used to justify "Jim Crow" laws in the South— laws that among other things kept blacks from drinking from the same water fountains, using the same restrooms, and attending the same schools as whites. As you can see in the table below, young adults are less likely than older Americans to endorse beliefs consistent with old-fashioned racism. Specifically, young people are less likely to endorse the notion that blacks are unintelligent and less likely to think that blacks differ from whites due to inborn abilities. These differences are statistically significant.[1]

On the other hand, young people are just as likely as middle-aged citizens and only slightly less likely than those 50 or older to endorse beliefs consistent with symbolic racism. **Symbolic racism** refers to the beliefs that blacks do not work hard enough and that black disadvantage cannot be explained by racial discrimination. One-quarter of young adults endorse the stereotype that blacks are lazy and deny the effect of discrimination on black-white differences; almost one-half believe that racial differences are due to a lack of motivation on the part of blacks. These views are shared by middle-aged and older citizens. The differences between the younger citizens and the older two groups are not statistically significant.[2]

White Support for Old-Fashioned Racism and Symbolic Racism by Age

Type of racism	18–29	30–49	50+
Old-fashioned racism			
Blacks are unintelligent	8%	14%	21%
Differences between blacks and whites due to inborn ability	2	7	11
Symbolic racism			
Blacks are lazy	25	23	31
Differences between blacks and whites are due to lack of black motivation	46	48	53
Differences between blacks and whites are not due to discrimination	26	29	31

Scott Blinder argues that this mixed pattern of prejudice among young white people is the result of a two-tracked process of socialization.[3] On one track, children are explicitly taught about principles of equality by their parents, through the media, and in the school system. As a result, children learn to accept antiracist norms. On another track, children pick up implicit messages—also from their parents, the media, and the schools—about differences among racial groups. "For example, it is easy to imagine—or even recall from personal experience or observation—White American parents telling their children to treat everyone equally regardless of race but balking at the thought of passing through a so-called 'bad' neighborhood where Black people live."[4] Consequently, young whites no longer accept beliefs consistent with old-fashioned racism, yet some continue to endorse racial stereotypes consistent with symbolic racism.

1. Scott B. Blinder, "Dissonance Persists: Reproduction of Racial Attitudes Among Post–Civil Rights Cohorts of White Americans," *American Politics Research* 35 (2007): 325.
2. Ibid., 325.
3. Ibid., 303–306.
4. Ibid., 304–305.

million dollars was found. Your great, great grandfather lost his business to pay back the ransom loan and died in poverty. Recently it was proven that the lost money had been transferred to one of Fineus Jones's sons who started a successful banking company with a successor firm now worth 100 million dollars. Your cousins have found a respected attorney who will press a claim on the successor firm and will do the work on a contingency basis, that is, the attorney will receive a portion of the amount awarded by the court. If all costs are included in the claim, the amount awarded to each claimant will be about $5,000.00. Your cousins have asked if you would wish your name to be included on the list of claimants.[22]

What would you do? Would you allow your name to be included in the class action suit? Of the participants in the study, 61 percent said they would want their name to be listed in the lawsuit. Thus, it seems that many whites are not opposed to the notion of reparations in principle; rather, they are opposed to reparations for black Americans who are the descendants of slaves.

Mazzocco et al. argue that this opposition to reparations for blacks stems from white Americans underestimating racial disparities in the United States. Across many areas of society—health care, criminal justice, education, the economy—blacks are at a disadvantage relative to whites. But since many whites do not seem to understand or appreciate the cost of being black in our society, they do not support reparations.

The research by Mazzocco et al. was not conducted on a random sample of white citizens. Thus, we should be cautious about generalizing these results to whites in general. Nevertheless, it is striking how similar the level of white support for reparations based on the scenario is to the percentage of blacks who supported cash payments to the descendants of slaves in the 2002 Gallup poll. Ideally, future research will examine the reaction of a representative sample of whites to these types of scenarios.

Support for Civil Rights for Gays and Lesbians

Do citizens support civil rights for gays and lesbians? It depends on which type of right. Citizens largely oppose discrimination in employment but are less supportive of gay rights when it comes to the legality of intimate relationships between homosexuals. Furthermore, support for gay rights has increased significantly over time, although it seems to have stalled in recent years.

Support for Equality in Employment. Let's begin with a discussion of attitudes toward equality for gays and lesbians in the workplace. Since 1977, the Gallup organization has been asking citizens whether they think "homosexuals should or should not have equal rights in terms of job opportunities." A majority of Americans, 56 percent, supported such rights in 1977 (see Figure 9-7). By the mid-1990s, support for equal job rights had jumped to over 80 percent. As of 2007, almost 9 out of every 10 Americans supported equal job opportunities for gays and lesbians. This is a large shift in public opinion over time.[23]

Despite widespread public support for gay rights in employment, there is no federal or constitutional ban against employment discrimination based on sexual orientation. In other words, federal law and the U.S. Constitution allow employers to fire employees simply because they are gay or lesbian. To ensure this does not happen, some states, localities, universities, and corporations have instituted bans on discrimination based on sexual orientation. As a result, whether gay rights are protected depends on where you live and where you work in the United States. We will use ourselves to illustrate this point. Zoe Oxley lives in a state—New York—which has a law that bans employment discrimination based on sexual orientation. In contrast, Rosalee Clawson lives in a state that does not ban such employment discrimination, yet the city she lives in, Lafayette, Indiana, does have a gay rights ordinance barring job discrimination. Both Clawson and Oxley work at universities in which discrimination based on sexual orientation is prohibited.

A particular type of employment has gotten a great deal of attention: gays and lesbians serving in the U.S. military. Since 1977, the Gallup poll has asked citizens whether they thought homosexuals should or should not be hired for the armed forces. Just over one-half of citizens believed gays and lesbians should be allowed to serve in the military at that time (see Figure 9-7). Over the past three decades, support for gays and lesbians in the armed forces has risen steadily. By 2003, support had reached 80 percent. In 2005, the last time the question was asked by Gallup, support had declined a bit, with 76 percent of Americans saying they would support the right of gays and lesbians to serve in the military. It is too early to tell whether this is just a statistical blip or a sign that support for gay rights in the military is declining. We will have to wait until Gallup asks the question a few more times to determine if there is a trend.

Again, despite three-fourths of Americans supporting the hiring of gays and lesbians in the armed forces, the U.S. military has a policy against gays and lesbians serving openly in their ranks. In 1994, the "Don't Ask, Don't Tell" policy was implemented that allows homosexuals to serve as long as they do not reveal they are gay or lesbian. The policy states that supervisors are not allowed to ask service members about their sexual orientation, but if gay and lesbian soldiers or marines disclose their orientation, they will be discharged. This policy was a compromise after President Bill Clinton met a great deal of resistance from the military when he called for lifting the ban on gays and lesbians early in his presidency. The "Don't Ask, Don't Tell" policy is still in effect today, although all the candidates who ran for the 2008 Democratic nomination for president called for its repeal. For example, Senator Hillary Clinton has quoted Barry Goldwater saying, "You don't have to be straight to shoot straight." In contrast, all the Republican candidates who ran for the presidency supported leaving the policy as it currently stands, with some arguing that such a policy should not be changed during war time.[24]

Support for Equality in Intimate Relationships.   Although most people are opposed to discrimination in employment, public opinion is much more divided when it comes to support for intimate relationships between gays and lesbians. Since 1977, the Gallup poll has asked citizens whether they think "homosexual relations between consenting adults should or should not be legal." Only 43 percent of citizens supported the rights of gays and lesbians to have sexual relations at that time (see Figure 9-7). The level of support dropped even lower in the mid-1980s when merely 33 percent of the public supported such rights. This drop in support might have been a reaction to the Supreme Court ruling on gay sex in 1986. In *Bowers v. Hardwick*, the Supreme Court ruled that the U.S. Constitution does not protect homosexual relations between consulting adults even in the privacy of their own homes.[25] Thus, the Court ruling might have given "permission" to citizens who were hesitant about gay rights to decide it was acceptable to oppose the legality of gay and lesbian sexual relationships. This was also a period during which people's fears of AIDS may have influenced their attitudes toward gay and lesbian rights.

By the late 1980s, support for homosexual relationships had gone back up and was at 47 percent. An all-time high of support for gay and lesbian relationships was

Figure 9-7   Support for Gay Rights, 1977–2007

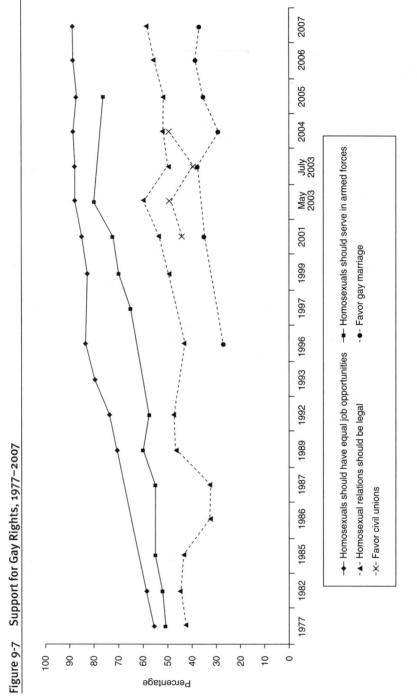

Homosexuals should have equal job opportunities   —■— Homosexuals should serve in armed forces
- ▲ - Homosexual relations should be legal   —●— Favor gay marriage
-X- Favor civil unions

Sources: Homosexual Relations (The Gallup Poll, Washington, D.C., 2007), www.galluppoll.com/content/default.aspx?ci=1651&pg=1; Hope Lozano-Bielat and David Masci, *Same-Sex Marriage: Redefining Marriage around the World* (The Pew Forum on Religion and Public Life, Washington, D.C., July 11, 2007), http://pewforum.org/docs/?DocID=235; and Alan S. Yang, "Trends: Attitudes toward Homosexuality," *Public Opinion Quarterly* 61 (1997): 477–507.

Note: The solid lines indicate employment policies, while the dashed lines indicate policies concerning intimate relationships. There have been some minor variations in question wording over time. Most recent question wordings:

Job Opportunities (Gallup): "As you may know, there has been considerable discussion in the news regarding the rights of homosexual men and women. In general, do you think homosexuals should or should not have equal rights in terms of job opportunities?"

Serve in Armed Forces (Gallup): "Now, I'd like to ask you about the hiring of homosexuals in specific occupations. Do you think homosexuals should or should not be hired for the following occupations: The Armed Forces?"

Relations between Consenting Adults (Gallup): "Do you think homosexual relations between consenting adults should or should not be legal?"

Marry Legally (Pew): "As I read some programs and proposals that are being discussed in the country today, please tell me whether you strongly favor, favor, oppose, or strongly oppose each … Allowing gays and lesbians to marry legally."

Civil Unions (Gallup): "Would you favor or oppose a law that would allow homosexual couples to legally form civil unions, giving them some of the legal rights of married couples?"

Public Opinion in Comparative Perspective
Box 9-2 Support for Gay Rights across the World

In 2006, the European Union commissioned a study of attitudes toward same-sex marriage. Forty-four percent of the people in the European Union favored gay marriage, while 49 percent opposed it. Support for gay marriage varied a great deal across countries within the European Union, ranging from 82 percent of citizens supporting it in the Netherlands to only 12 percent supporting it in Latvia. The survey question asked whether "Homosexual marriage should be allowed throughout Europe." The percentage of citizens in each country who agreed is presented in this table.[1]

Percentage Who Agreed that Homosexual Marriage Should be Allowed in Europe

Country	%	Country	%
The Netherlands	82	Ireland	41
Sweden	71	Italy	31
Denmark	69	Slovenia	31
Belgium	62	Portugal	29
Luxembourg	58	Estonia	21
Spain	56	Slovakia	19
Germany	52	Hungary	18
Czech Republic	52	Malta	18
Austria	49	Lithuania	17
France	48	Poland	17
United Kingdom	46	Greece	15
Finland	45	Cyprus	14
European Union	**44**	Latvia	12

In many other countries around the world, same-sex marriage is not even on the agenda. Instead, the acceptability of homosexuality itself is the issue. In 2002, the Pew Research Center conducted a Global Attitudes survey in forty-four nations. The survey asked respondents whether "homosexuality is a way of life that should be accepted by society." People in Middle Eastern and African countries were particularly opposed to homosexuality. As in the United States, attitudes in many Latin American countries were fairly split on this question.[2]

(continued)

Should Homosexuality be Accepted by Society?

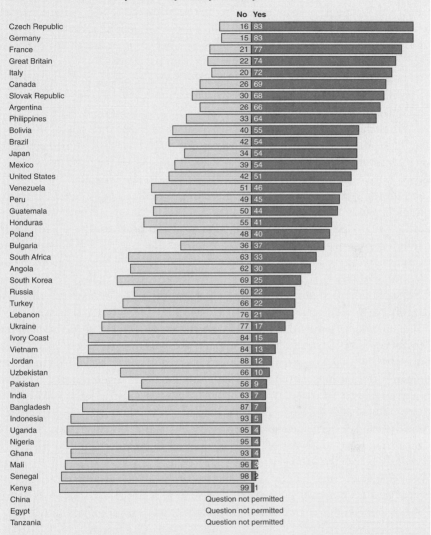

	No	Yes
Czech Republic	16	83
Germany	15	83
France	21	77
Great Britain	22	74
Italy	20	72
Canada	26	69
Slovak Republic	30	68
Argentina	26	66
Philippines	33	64
Bolivia	40	55
Brazil	42	54
Japan	34	54
Mexico	39	54
United States	42	51
Venezuela	51	46
Peru	49	45
Guatemala	50	44
Honduras	55	41
Poland	48	40
Bulgaria	36	37
South Africa	63	33
Angola	62	30
South Korea	69	25
Russia	60	22
Turkey	66	22
Lebanon	76	21
Ukraine	77	17
Ivory Coast	84	15
Vietnam	84	13
Jordan	88	12
Uzbekistan	66	10
Pakistan	56	9
India	63	7
Bangladesh	87	7
Indonesia	93	5
Uganda	95	4
Nigeria	95	4
Ghana	93	4
Mali	96	3
Senegal	98	2
Kenya	99	1
China	Question not permitted	
Egypt	Question not permitted	
Tanzania	Question not permitted	

Note: Some responses do not sum to 100 percent because of refusals or "don't knows." In some countries, this constitutes a significant minority of the responses.

1. Hope Lozano-Bielat and David Masci, *Same-Sex Marriage: Redefining Marriage Around the World* (The Pew Forum on Religion and Public Life, Washington, D.C., July 11, 2007), http://pewforum.org/docs/?DocID=235.
2. The Pew Global Attitudes Project, *Views of a Changing World* (The Pew Research Center for the People and the Press, Washington, D.C., June 2003), http://people-press.org/reports/pdf/185.pdf.

reached in May 2003 at 60 percent. Again however, public opinion seemed to react to a Supreme Court decision on gay and lesbian rights, although this time the Court was in support of such rights. On June 26, 2003, the Supreme Court reversed its earlier decision on gay sex and ruled in *Lawrence v. Texas* that the U.S. Constitution protects consensual sexual relationships between two people of the same sex.[26] This ruling caused an immediate outcry from conservative activists, especially because many argued this ruling was the logical precursor to the legalization of gay marriage. As a result, public support for homosexual relations between consenting adults dropped to 50 percent in a July 2003 Gallup poll. Over the last few years though, citizen support for gay rights has crept back up to 59 percent.[27]

That brings us to the most controversial gay rights issue of our times: **gay marriage**. In 1996, the Pew Research Center asked citizens for the first time whether they favored or opposed "allowing gays and lesbians to marry legally." Only 27 percent said they supported gay marriage at that time (see Figure 9-7). When the question was asked again in 2001, 35 percent of Americans said they would support gay marriage. Support has hovered around that point for the last few years, remaining entrenched below the 40 percent mark. There is somewhat higher support for civil unions, however. Between 2001 and 2005, support ranged between 40 and 49 percent, according to polls conducted by the Gallup organization. Thus, civil unions seem to be a bit less threatening to some Americans, but still roughly one-half of citizens prefer to deny gays and lesbians this right.

Public policy across the United States reflects this divide in public opinion. Most states have constitutional amendments or state laws that restrict marriage to one man and one woman, yet some of those same states allow civil unions or domestic partnerships. For example, Vermont and California have state laws that prohibit same-sex marriage; at the same time, both provide state-level spousal rights to gay and lesbian couples within their states.[28] We expect that sooner or later the issue of same-sex marriage will end up before the Supreme Court. Since Supreme Court rulings are consistent with public opinion roughly two-thirds of the time, how the Court will rule on gay marriage may depend largely on what citizens think about the issue at the time.[29] Given that 56 percent of young people between the ages of 18 and 29 support gay marriage, it seems quite possible that marriage rights will be extended to gay and lesbian Americans at some point in the future.[30]

CONCLUSION

Are citizens hesitant about supporting women and minority candidates? Well, it depends. If you are a Muslim, an atheist, or gay, you might as well forget about running for president any time soon. The public is not predisposed to favor such a candidate. If you are a woman, a Jew, a Mormon, or a racial minority, you would also have an uphill battle, especially because many citizens believe their fellow Americans are not ready to elect such a candidate. The good news is that over time citizens have become increasingly likely to say they would vote for a woman or minority candidate, with one exception. The public is no more likely to say they would support a Mormon today than they were forty years ago. Now, these survey questions ask about hypothetical candidates; perhaps an actual flesh and blood person who happens to have one of these characteristics will be able to break down stereotypes and overcome prejudices to win the presidency.

What about citizens' support for civil rights for black Americans? When it comes to equality for blacks, citizens' attitudes depend heavily on two factors. First, support varies based on whether the policy at hand refers to equal rights in principle or equal rights in practice. People tend to support the goals of equal rights, yet support drops when the focus is on implementation. Second, levels of support for civil rights differ a great deal between black and white citizens. Both racial groups support the principle of equal rights more than specific policies designed to achieve those rights, yet support for civil rights in principle is basically universal among blacks, and typically a strong majority support policies to implement civil rights. In contrast, a majority of whites support civil rights in principle (in some cases, a very large majority), yet support drops precipitously when it comes to putting the principle into action.

What about public support for gay rights? Citizens demonstrate strong support for equal job opportunities for gays and lesbians. Further, three-fourths of Americans think that gays and lesbians should be able to serve in the military. There has been a sea change in attitudes toward employment rights for gays and lesbians over the last three decades. Citizens are less supportive, however, when it comes to supporting gay and lesbian sexual relationships. Still, support for such relationships has increased over time, with a majority saying those relationships should be legal in 2007. Citizens are most reluctant to extend marriage rights to gays and lesbians. Slightly over one-third of citizens support gay and lesbian marriage, and that percentage has not increased in the 2000s. Support for civil unions is slightly higher but doesn't yet reach the 50 percent mark.

Overall, these findings certainly provide some encouragement to participatory democratic theorists. That citizens have become more supportive of women and minorities holding office and that citizens' support for several civil rights policies has increased over the years are heartening to theorists who worry about inequality in society. But, the news is not all good for participatory democratic theorists. A meaningful minority (especially given the closeness of presidential races) still oppose women and minorities running for the highest office in the land. Further, the hesitancy to support the implementation of civil rights policies on the part of whites and the opposition to the legality of gay and lesbian intimate relationships raise serious doubts about whether our society provides "equal justice under law" as proclaimed by the words on the Supreme Court building.

Because elite democratic theorists expect some inequality in society, they are not shocked by opposition to women and minority candidates or by the lack of support among white Americans for implementing civil rights policies or by the opposition to gay and lesbian marriage. As we have discussed earlier, elite democratic theorists emphasize that it is fine if the public doesn't support civil rights because elites hold the power. Because elites are more sophisticated, they appreciate the importance of civil rights in a democratic society and are therefore better equipped to protect the rights of marginalized or unpopular groups. Political theories, however, do not always accurately capture the practice of politics. Take the issue of gay rights. Many (although certainly not all) elites in both the Republic and Democratic parties oppose marriage rights for gays and lesbians. Clearly these elites are no more protective of this particular civil right than the public.

KEY CONCEPTS

affirmative action/259	old-fashioned racism/264
civil rights/247	principles of equality/255
gay marriage/272	reparations/261
gender stereotypes/254	socially undesirable/250
implementation/257	symbolic racism/264

SUGGESTED SOURCES FOR FURTHER READING

Golebiowska, Ewa A. "When to Tell? Disclosure of Concealable Group Membership, Stereotypes, and Political Evaluation." *Political Behavior* 25 (2003): 313–337.
Sanbonmatsu, Kira. "Gender Stereotypes and Vote Choice." *American Journal of Political Science* 46 (2002): 20–34.

These two studies examine how stereotypes influence the evaluation of political candidates. Golebiowska investigates the effect of gay and lesbian stereotypes on responses to candidates, and Sanbonmatsu analyzes the influence of gender stereotypes.

Bolce, Louis, and Gerald De Maio. "Religious Outlook, Culture War Politics, and Antipathy Toward Christian Fundamentalists." *Public Opinion Quarterly* 63 (1999): 29–61.
Panagopoulos, Costas. "Trends: Arab and Muslim Americans and Islam in the Aftermath of 9/11." *Public Opinion Quarterly* 70 (2006): 608–624.

These articles examine attitudes toward two religious groups in our society. Bolce and De Maio show that many citizens who are not Christian fundamentalists are not particularly fond of those who are. Similarly, Panagopoulos demonstrates that many Americans have reservations about Muslim Americans.

Schuman, Howard, Charlotte Steeh, Lawrence Bobo, and Maria Krysan. *Racial Attitudes in America*, rev. ed. Cambridge, Mass.: Harvard University Press, 1997.

This classic book examines trends in racial attitudes since the early 1940s. The authors analyze the racial attitudes of both blacks and whites.

Human Rights Campaign: www.hrc.org

The Human Rights Campaign is the largest civil rights organization working for gay, lesbian, bisexual, and transgender (GLBT) equality. This Web site contains information about GLBT issues, such as marriage, adoption, and workplace discrimination. You can look up GLBT policies in your state and community on this site.

National Association for the Advancement of Colored People (NAACP): www.naacp.org

Founded in 1909, the NAACP is the nation's oldest civil rights organization. Their Web site contains both historical and contemporary information about civil rights issues. The site includes a "Youth & College" section that students will find of particular interest.

National Council of La Raza: www.nclr.org

The National Council of La Raza is the largest national Latino civil rights organization in the United States. This Web site contains information about civil rights, including racial profiling, criminal justice issues, and voting rights.

PART V

What Is the Relationship between Citizens and Their Government?

DO UNITED STATES' citizens trust the government? Do they support the institutions of government and the people who occupy key political offices? Does the government respond to the policy preferences of the public? If so, do all citizens' opinions weigh equally or do the views of some matter more? Alternatively, is policy not related to public opinion but rather influenced by the wishes of others, such as interest groups or elected officials' own goals?

All of these questions point, in one way or another, to the relationship between citizens and their government, the focus of this section. In addition to these empirically oriented questions, we also consider many normative ones. How important to democratic governance is citizen trust in government? Can a democracy survive without it? What if citizens display little support in the institutions of government? Are there worrisome implications that arise under this situation? Finally, why does it matter whether public opinion influences public policy? Are there some circumstances where the public should have a large influence? A small one? No influence?

CHAPTER 10

Trust in Government, Support for Institutions, and Social Capital

> A democratic political system cannot survive for long without the support of a majority of its citizens. When such support wanes, underlying discontent is the necessary result, and the potential for revolutionary alteration of the political and social system is enhanced.[1]

AS THIS QUOTATION implies, one important feature of democratic public opinion is citizen assessment of government. Democratic citizens are expected to not only evaluate their government and their political leaders but also have the means to enact change if they are dissatisfied. Citizens can hold elected officials accountable by voting for their opponents on Election Day. Severe dissatisfaction with the government could lead to calls for changing governmental procedures or even for replacing the structure of government with a new one. This type of citizen control is one key characteristic of democracies, as so clearly stated by Thomas Jefferson in the Declaration of Independence. "[W]henever any Form of Government becomes destructive of these ends [securing individual rights]," wrote Jefferson, "it is the Right of the People to alter or abolish it, and to institute new Government."[2] Furthermore, a belief that one's government is legitimate is related to citizen obedience to authorities and to laws, whereas alienation from government may suppress involvement in political activities.[3] Not surprisingly, then, given the importance to democratic functioning, public opinion scholars have long been interested in whether citizens demonstrate support for their government.

There are, of course, many aspects of government toward which the public holds attitudes, including constitutional principles, day-to-day functioning, governmental institutions, governmental decisions, and the performance of elected and appointed officials. One useful way to categorize these various attitude objects was presented by political scientist David Easton in the 1960s.[4] Easton suggests there are two types of public support for political systems: diffuse support and specific support. **Diffuse support** refers to public opinions about the political system, such as contentment with the form of government and attachment to the norms and structure of the regime. In contrast to this broad attitude, the public also holds attitudes toward the performance of incumbent political leaders and governmental outputs, such as public policies. This is what Easton calls **specific support,** which "flows from the favorable attitudes and predispositions stimulated by outputs that are perceived by members to meet their demands ... [such as] a tariff, minimum wage, high economic growth rate, or publicly financed medical care."[5] As for diffuse support, "its one major characteristic is that since it is an attachment to a political object for its own sake, it constitutes a store of political good will. As such, it taps deep political sentiments and is not easily depleted through disappointment with outputs."[6] In other words, if citizens are unhappy with governmental policy decisions, specific support for the government will be low, but diffuse support can remain high.

In this chapter, we discuss attitudes tapping both diffuse and specific support for government. We first examine public trust in government, which encompasses characteristics of diffuse and specific support. We demonstrate that public trust in government has declined over time, present explanations to account for changing levels of trust, and discuss the implications of lower trust levels. Second, we examine confidence in particular governmental institutions—the executive branch, Congress, and the Supreme Court. Public faith in those institutions is also a function of both diffuse and specific support. Support for the three institutions of government has been low and fairly stable over the last 35 years. Of the three institutions, confidence in the Supreme Court is highest, trailed by the executive branch, and then Congress. We also consider whether attitudes toward the *members* of the institutions are distinct from attitudes toward the *institutions* themselves. Indeed, they are: citizens give substantially higher approval ratings to institutions than to members of those institutions. In the final section we move away from an assessment of public evaluations of government to explore citizen interaction with other citizens. Social capital, or the degree to which people connect with and trust other citizens and engage in civic activities, is related to both trust in government and support for government institutions. As we will see, though, social capital has other important consequences for the public and for democratic governments. Also, as with trust in government, the stock of social capital in America has declined of late, a trend we will examine. Finally, to help us think through the importance and implications of public trust in government, support for national institutions, and social capital, we turn to relevant democratic theories throughout the chapter.

TRUST IN GOVERNMENT

Although a number of different definitions of **trust in government** have been proposed, scholars generally agree that trust refers to "the public's basic evaluative orientation toward the government in Washington."[7] As such, trust seems to be a measure of diffuse support for government. Consider, however, the more focused definition provided in the 1970s by Arthur Miller, a leading researcher of public trust: "the belief that the government is operating according to one's normative expectations of how government should function."[8] More recently, trust has been described "as a pragmatic running tally of how people think the government is doing at a given point in time."[9] These definitions suggest that public trust involves assessing the performance of government. The attitude of trust therefore can also be classified as a measure of specific support, since it involves some evaluation of governmental outputs. The lack of trust is commonly referred to as cynicism or distrust.[10] Following from Miller's definition of trust, **cynicism** "reflects the belief that the government is not functioning in accordance with individual expectations of efficiency, honesty, competence and equity."[11]

Many democratic theorists agree that public trust in government is important for democratic societies. Citizens place governing duties in their elected representatives and appointed officials. Given their distance from government and their lack of knowledge regarding the many complex policy matters that leaders must address, citizen trust in leaders and governing institutions is a salient feature of democratic decision making.[12] If citizens trust their government, they will accept and comply with its decisions, leading to a stable democracy. If, on the other hand, citizens do not trust their government, it will be difficult for government to enforce the law, leading to political and social disruption.[13]

Proponents of participatory democracy and related variants, such as deliberative democracy, further emphasize that citizen trust in government reacts to the political environment. Trust can be increased the more that government procedures are transparent and the more that citizens become involved in debating issues. "Deliberative arenas—unlike, say, those of the mass media—provide opportunities to explain oneself, one's group, one's problems," leading to greater understanding of the views of others and perhaps engendering trust in others' motives.[14] An obvious extension of this view is that declines in public trust could be indicative of too little involvement of the public in decision making.

Elite democratic theorists have a more nuanced view of trust in government. One key feature of liberal democracy, a theoretical precursor to contemporary elite democracy, is a presumption that citizens should distrust the people in government.[15] After all, the Federalists designed the complex checks and balances of the U.S. political system with the presumption that political leaders would not pursue the public good but would rather look out solely for their own interests. Yet, the founders wanted citizens to trust the representative institutions of government so that people would not feel it necessary to pursue direct democracy, which was anathema to the founders.[16] Thus, elite democrats would expect the public to place less trust in government leaders than in the institutions and procedures of government that were established to hold leaders in check.

Measuring Public Trust

To measure public trust in government, survey researchers working on the American National Election Studies (ANES) developed four specific questions in the early 1960s.[17] These questions are the ones most commonly used to examine trust, so it is worth considering the content of the survey items in detail. Complete wording of these questions appears in Table 10-1. The first question asks respondents directly how often they trust the national government. The next two items query people about the behavior of politicians, specifically whether they waste taxpayer money and whether they work for "the benefit of all the people" or only a "few big interests." The final question requires respondents to assess whether politicians are crooked. As for specific criteria that these items were intended to assess, Donald Stokes, one of the creators of the questions, lists the following:

> The criteria of judgment implicit in these questions were partly ethical, that is, the honesty and other ethical qualities of public officials.... But the criteria extended to other qualities as well, including the ability and efficiency of government officials and the correctness of their policy decisions.[18]

Despite the varied nature of these qualities, Stokes's analysis indicated that public responses to the individual questions correlated strongly with each other to form a general evaluation of government, usually referred to as the trust in government scale.

Although the ANES questions are often used by scholars, many acknowledge they are not perfect measures of trust. The first item, with its explicit focus on trusting "the government in Washington," most closely resembles the notion of trust as a characteristic of the political regime. The other items, however, appear to tap

Table 10-1   Assessing Public Trust: Survey Questions from the American National Election Studies

"How much of the time do you think you can trust the government in Washington to do what is right—just about always, most of the time, or only some of the time?"

"Do you think that people in government waste a lot of money we pay in taxes, waste some of it, or don't waste very much of it?"

"Would you say the government is pretty much run by a few big interests looking out for themselves or that it is run for the benefit of all the people?"

"Do you think that quite a few of the people running the government are crooked, not very many are, or do you think hardly any of them are crooked?"

Source: American National Election Studies Cumulative Data File, 1948–2004.

specific attitudes toward politicians (whether they are crooked), their motives (whether they represent all of the people), or their actions (whether they waste tax-payer money). Because of this, argued Jack Citrin, an early critic of the ANES measures, the survey questions register "mere disapproval of incumbent political leaders" rather than "alienation from the political regime."[19] This seems especially likely since the attitude objects that are the focus of these questions alternate between the general government and politicians ("the government in Washington" versus "the people running the government," for example). In place of these survey items, Citrin preferred questions asking respondents whether they favored changing the form of government or whether they were proud about the form of government. For Citrin, such questions "appear to be on their face more valid indicators of a basic attachment to the political regime than most of the items comprising the Trust in Government scale."[20] In contrast, because the ANES questions specifically mention politicians, Citrin viewed these as measures solely of specific support. Unlike Citrin, however, most public opinion researchers recognize that the ANES items tap a combination of diffuse and specific support.[21]

In response to Citrin, Arthur Miller presents a forceful defense of the ANES trust measures. Recall that Miller defines trust as matching one's expectations for government to the actual functioning of government. Elaborating on this definition, Miller discusses what distrust in government means for citizens. Some who distrust government might prefer that a new political system replace the current one, but for other people distrust might "be associated with the partisan hopes of 'voting the rascals out'; for others, it may indicate a sense of enduring inequities in government decisions and outputs."[22] Miller's view of trust is thus broader and more complex than Citrin's, encompassing not only an assessment of the political system but also evaluations of how responsive politicians are to the public. Since the ANES measures tap these two aspects of people's attitudes, they are, for Miller, valid assessments of public trust. It is clear that Citrin and Miller disagree over what the ANES items seem to be measuring based on the content of the questions. Perhaps more important, as we will see later in this chapter, they also disagree over how to *interpret* public attitudes toward government measured using these survey questions.

Decline in Public Trust

One benefit of the ANES trust questions is that they have been asked of the American public since 1964, allowing us to examine levels of public trust over a forty-year time span. The graph in Figure 10-1 displays public responses to the four ANES items in presidential election years since 1964. The most obvious conclusion to be drawn from this figure is that public trust has declined considerably over the past four decades. Nearly 80 percent of the public felt that government could be trusted to do the right thing most of the time or just about always in 1964. This percentage steadily declined until 1980, when it registered a low of 25.7 percent.

Public trust increased somewhat in 1984 with 44.9 percent of the public trusting the government, then declined in 1988 and 1992. Since 1992, slightly and steadily increasing percentages of the public demonstrate trust in the government, although this percentage was only 46.6 in 2004, far lower than in 1964. The precise level of trust depends on the particular question. For example, the public is more likely to think the government wastes money than to think politicians are crooks. Nevertheless, the overall trend of public opinion toward all four items in the trust scale is very similar. Significant increases in negative evaluations occurred between 1964 and 1980, followed by somewhat more positive assessments in the mid-1980s and since 1992.

What explains this over-time variation in public trust? The large and steady decline in trust that ended in 1980 began, in part, with tumultuous events that occurred during the 1960s and 1970s. U.S. involvement in and ultimate withdrawal from Vietnam demonstrated the inability of the American military to succeed in this conflict. The urban uprisings of the late 1960s were visible manifestations that the government was incapable of preventing social unrest. The Watergate scandal further quickened the pace of decreasing public trust. The burglary of the Democratic National Committee headquarters in the Watergate complex occurred in 1972. This was followed two years later by President Richard Nixon resigning his office among allegations of abuse of power and trying to cover up his involvement in the burglary. Thus, it is perhaps not surprising that the largest four-year decline in the trust-in-government item occurred between 1972 and 1976, when the percentage of the public believing government could be trusted always or most of the time fell from 54.2 percent to 34.5 percent.

Figure 10-1 Public Trust in Government, 1964–2004

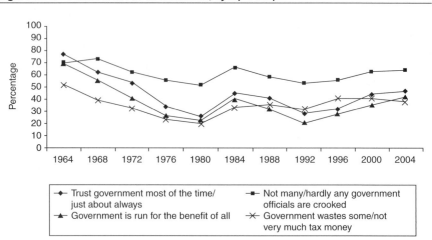

Source: Analysis of American National Election Studies Cumulative Data File, 1948–2004.

Public Opinion in Comparative Perspective
BOX 10-1 LEVELS OF PUBLIC TRUST IN OTHER NATIONS

Declining levels of public trust are not a uniquely American phenomenon. In fact, across many advanced industrial democracies, trust in government has declined over the past decades. Across a number of nations, including Japan, Australia, New Zealand, and many in Europe, public beliefs that the government is run by a few big interests rose from the 1970s to the 1990s. In Germany, for example, about 33 percent of the public held this view in the 1970s, but twice that many did twenty years later.[1] To explain these cross-national declines, Russell Dalton points to three key factors. First, contemporary democratic publics have higher expectations for government and the democratic process than their governments are meeting. Second, the expansion of governments' policy agendas and increased interest group activity provide multiple opportunities for public dissatisfaction with government. As a government tries to address more societal problems, some groups of the public will inevitably be unhappy with the resulting solutions. Further, interest groups are "unrelenting critics of government ... often highlight[ing] how governments and legislation fall short of the group's ideal."[2] With more active interest groups, the public is exposed to more antigovernment rhetoric. Finally, Dalton points to the increased tendency of the mass media and the public to hold political officials accountable for their unethical behavior as another contributor to rising levels of distrust.

The fact that many democracies have witnessed declines in public trust could be good news for those in the United States who worry about public distrust and wonder what is wrong in America for trust to have dropped. Yet, Dalton reminds us of an alternative, less sanguine interpretation: "the commonality of these trends suggests that no one has found a way to restore public confidence in politicians, parties and political institutions ... which implies that low levels of support may be a continuing feature of advanced industrial democracies."[3]

1. Russell J. Dalton, *Democratic Challenges, Democratic Choices: The Erosion of Political Support in Advanced Industrial Democracies* (Oxford: Oxford University Press, 2004).
2. Ibid., 196.
3. Ibid., 208.

Presidential scandals are also cited to explain later trust declines, such as those witnessed between 1984 and 1988 and again at the beginning of Bill Clinton's first term in office.[23] (While not plotted on the graph in Figure 10-1, trust in government declined from 1992 to 1994, then increased by 1996.) In 1986, the public became aware that members of President Ronald Reagan's administration had sold arms to Iran to help fund a group (the Contras) fighting the communist government in Nicaragua. Details relating to these events, known as the Iran-Contra scandal, dogged Reagan for the rest of his time in office. Clinton was embroiled in a number of scandals shortly after assuming office, including allegations that he and his wife Hillary were involved in a shady real estate deal (the Whitewater development), the firing of the entire White House travel office, and continued rumors of his marital infidelities.

Quite notably, public trust in government did not drop during President Clinton's biggest scandal—the Monica Lewinsky affair. Why might that be the case? According to one political scientist, President Clinton's approval ratings withstood the scandal because the economy was strong, the country was at peace, and Clinton pursued moderate policies.[24] Perhaps these factors also kept trust in government from declining. We have already mentioned how military involvement lowers trust, and below we will discuss how good economic times and moderate policies might increase trust among the public.

Other explanations for the long-term decline in trust include **changes in public expectations of government.** In particular, Jane Mansbridge focuses on broader societal and cultural changes to explain why government increasingly does not meet public expectations.[25] Societal changes force new problems onto government's agenda, problems that the public expects government to address but that the government might not necessarily be equipped to solve. Mansbridge identifies two issues that emerged since the 1960s that fit these criteria: increasing crime rates and childhood poverty. The sources of these problems are varied, including increasing violence in popular culture for the former and higher divorce rates for the latter. Regardless of the causes of the problems, however, Mansbridge argues that the steady expansion of government involvement in the economic sector after the depression of the 1920s coupled with the sustained economic prosperity witnessed after World War II increased the public's expectations about the government's ability to solve a wide range of social problems. When the problems persist over time, government is perceived as being unable to solve problems, and public distrust results.

The increase in public trust during the 1980s has been attributed to two factors: President Reagan and an improved national economy. As Reagan took over the White House from Jimmy Carter, public trust in government increased, in large part due to the differing personas of these two presidents. Reagan was viewed by many as a strong leader and as inspiring. Further, his "apparent self-assurance, good humor, decisiveness and ... communicat[ion of] a sense of pride in the nation and its past" contrasted strongly with Carter, who was perceived as weak and lacking in the self-confidence that Reagan possessed.[26] Improved assessments of the president and his abilities led directly to increasing faith in the government. The decline in public trust during this time was also reversed because the economy improved. The high inflation and high unemployment rates of the 1970s turned around in the 1980s. Public perceptions of government handling of the economy became more favorable, leading to increased trust in government.[27] Economic performance and the public's evaluations of the government's economic policies have been correlated with public trust at other times as well. Declines in trust often accompany a poorly performing economy, as was the case in the 1970s and during President George H. W. Bush's term in office (1988–1992), whereas trust rebounds when the economy improves (such as between 1992 and 2000).[28]

Having said this, the state of the national economy and public perceptions of the economy worsened in 2000, yet public trust in government continued the increase that began in the mid-1990s. This was largely because of the September 11, 2001, attacks and the attention placed on terrorism, foreign policy, and domestic security that has resulted. In a detailed analysis of public trust since 2000, Marc Hetherington demonstrates that upsurges in trust have followed events that have placed public attention squarely on terrorism and foreign affairs, such as the 9/11 attacks themselves or the 2002 congressional resolution giving President George W. Bush authority to begin the war in Iraq.[29] Hetherington attributes this to the propensity of the public to rally around the president during times of crisis and to the public's positive evaluation of the United States' military. In contrast, when media attention drifted away from national security and toward other issues (such as the poor state of the economy or the bankruptcy of Enron and other corporate accounting scandals), public trust declined. Thus, while the overall trend since 2000 has been a slight increase in public trust (refer to Figure 10-1), Hetherington is not optimistic that this upward movement will continue. "[U]nless foreign and domestic security permanently takes center stage in the coming decades," he writes, "trust in government is unlikely to remain very high. . . . The elements that people typically use to evaluate the government, such as traditional welfare state programs, will again take center stage, which will almost certainly lead to lower sustained levels of political trust absent another exogenous shock."[30]

Sources of Trust

Citizens' trust in government arises from a variety of sources. Some of these were encountered in the preceding discussion of over-time variation in public trust, such as real world events and government activities (U.S. military involvement abroad and presidential scandals, for example), evaluations of the personal characteristics of the president, the state of the economy, and assessments of governmental economic policy performance. Public trust is also related to evaluations of governmental policymaking across many other domains. In other words, people's *assessments of the products of government* (especially public policies) influence whether they trust the government. Generally speaking, distrust rises for citizens whose policy preferences are furthest from policy decisions enacted by leaders or the platforms of the parties. Between 1964 and 1970, this meant that people with strongly liberal or strongly conservative views were the most distrusting because government policy was increasingly centrist, or moderate, rather than either liberal or conservative.[31] During this time, liberal cynics expected the government to address forcefully and quickly a number of social problems (such as poverty, inflation, and unemployment), but policymakers enacted more moderate policies instead. Conservative cynics also felt let down by government, because they believed the policies favored by both the Republican and Democratic parties were too liberal (such as not using substantial police force to stop urban riots). By the 1990s, however, both parties had become more ideologically extreme. The Democratic Party platform was more liberal than it had been, while the Republican platform was more conservative. During this time, however, the ideological and policy preferences of the citizens did not change substantially. So, as the parties drifted more to the extremes, centrist citizens were the ones who felt removed from the parties' goals and who trusted government less.[32]

Public attitudes toward government are also shaped by messages from the political environment. When news media coverage becomes more cynical toward leaders and more questioning of politicians' motives, as has been the case over the past few decades,[33] public trust declines. Not all news outlets present the same level of cynicism toward politics, of course, but people who read more critical newspapers are less trusting of government.[34] The media are not the only source of negative statements about government. Political leaders themselves also communicate such sentiments to the public. It is not uncommon for candidates, especially newcomers to national politics, to run for office by criticizing the government and portraying themselves as outsiders. This was the successful strategy pursued by Jimmy Carter, former governor of Georgia, when he ran for president in 1976. Sitting presidents have also been known to speak harshly about government, as did Ronald Reagan when during his first inaugural address he stated, "Government is not the solution to our problems; government is the problem."[35] Similarly, during his 1996 State of the Union speech, President Bill Clinton declared, "The era of big government is over."[36]

With such attacks on government delivered by politicians, it is perhaps not surprising that public trust is low. Could a more positive tone toward government increase trust? An experiment conducted by Shmuel Lock, Robert Shapiro, and Lawrence Jacobs suggests that it could. During the course of a telephone survey, Lock, Shapiro, and Jacobs asked all of their respondents, "how much confidence do you have in the federal government's ability to run its national programs?"[37] For half of the respondents, questions about the government's ability to run specific programs (the military, Social Security, environmental protection, and Medicare) were asked before the general confidence item appeared in the survey. These respondents displayed greater confidence in government than did those for whom the specific policy questions appeared after the general item (see Table 10-2). For example, whereas 44 percent of the people who answered the general

Table 10-2   Effects of Communication on Confidence in Government

Survey question	Confidence in the government's ability to run its programs		
	Great deal of confidence	Some confidence	Hardly any confidence
Survey Version 1: General confidence question asked before questions about confidence for specific programs (e.g., Social Security, military)	9%	47%	44%
Survey Version 2: Questions about confidence for specific programs (e.g., Social Security, military) asked before general confidence question	8	55	36

Source: Data from Shmuel T. Lock, Robert Y. Shapiro, and Lawrence R. Jacobs, "The Impact of Political Debate on Government Trust: Reminding the Public What the Federal Government Does," *Political Behavior* 21 (1999): 247.

question first had "hardly any" confidence in the federal government, only 36 percent who answered the general question last held this attitude. Lock et al. attribute this difference to the fact that those receiving the questions about government policy in specific domains were reminded about government programs that are generally regarded as successful. With thoughts of successful government activities at the forefront of their minds, people displayed greater confidence in government. This research suggests that if elite and media communication more often contained details of well-regarded government policies, levels of trust among the public could rise.

One factor that is not strongly related to people's trust attitudes is their demographic characteristics. Beginning with initial analyses of the ANES trust items and continuing on to more recent times, many scholars have found that levels of trust do not differ substantially across subgroups of people.[38] As you can see from Figure 10-2, in 2004 levels of trust in government were almost identical for women and men. Trust also was quite similar for people of various ages and income levels. Differences across education levels are also not that large, with the exception that those with at most a grade-school level of education are less trusting than those with more years of formal schooling.

Racial differences in trust are apparent, however. Beginning in 1968, blacks have generally been less trusting of government than whites.[39] Most explain these differences using the **political reality model**.[40] Blacks have less political power

Figure 10-2 Trust in Government for Specific Demographic Groups, 2004

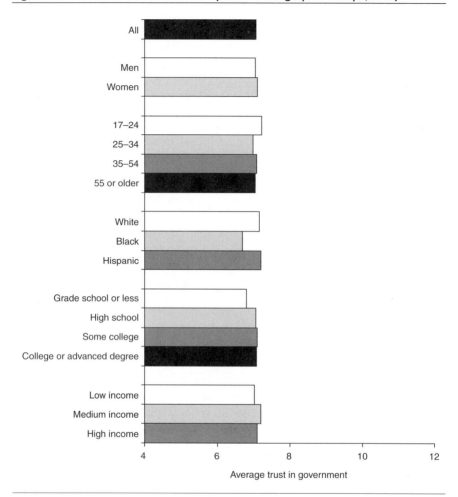

Source: Analysis of American National Election Studies Cumulative Data File, 1948–2004. For these comparisons, we constructed an index of trust by adding up people's responses to the four ANES trust items. The possible range of the index was 4 to 12, with higher numbers indicating more trust. The average for all respondents was 7.06.

than whites in the United States, and blacks find the government less responsive to their needs than do whites. Thus, blacks display more distrust of government. An illustration of this was evident in a comparison of public trust among all Americans with New Orleans citizens in 1984. New Orleans had been governed by a black mayor and black administration since 1976, contributing to higher levels of trust among blacks in New Orleans than among blacks nationally. Furthermore, levels of trust among whites were the same in New Orleans as for the entire national population. Thus, the researchers concluded, "a black city administration changes black attitudes about their political position."[41] A more recent study of citizens from over 100 cities found mixed support for the political reality model. On the one hand, having a black mayor and greater black representation on the city council did not increase black levels of trust in local government, but having a higher proportion of blacks on the police force led to significantly higher levels of trust in the police.[42] Given these nuanced findings, additional research is needed to fully understand when the political reality model holds and when it does not.

Implications of Declining Public Trust

What are we to make of the decline in public trust since the 1960s? Answers to this question depend, in part, on what you think the trust survey questions are measuring. Thus, we return to the debate between Arthur Miller and Jack Citrin. Recall that Miller believed the ANES questions tap into system-level attitudes toward government. For him, then, a sustained decline in public trust suggests an unhealthy democracy. On this point, it is worth quoting him at length:

> Democratic theory emphasizes voluntary consent as the basis of political obligation and legitimacy. Democratic government assumes—indeed, requires—widespread participation, political equality, the accountability of leaders and protection of the individual citizen's constitutional guarantees. The full attainment of these values is only possible when the relationship between the leaders and the public is based on mutual understanding and reciprocal trust rather than on the use of coercive and arbitrary authority.[43]

Miller also worries that a long-term decline in trust might lead citizens to demand radical change to the democratic political system.[44]

According to Citrin, such consequences are unlikely to result from declines in trust as measured by the ANES because these measures primarily register assessments of incumbent politicians rather than evaluations of the broader political system.[45] To Citrin, expressions of cynicism are

> ritualistic rather than genuine. The tendency to demean politics is a well-established cultural tradition in America ... precisely because the political culture sanctions expressions of political cynicism, their consequences may be purely symbolic. According to this point of view, to agree verbally that many people "running the government" are corrupt, incompetent, or untrustworthy is like shouting "Kill the umpire!" at a baseball game. Bloodthirsty rhetoric threatens neither the life expectancy of umpires nor the future of the national pastime.[46]

Despite the sustained low levels of public trust in government, there is little evidence that the serious consequences predicted by Miller and others have resulted. One detailed analysis of trust concluded in 1998 that "there is no indication that these attitudes are near a crisis stage."[47] Public levels of patriotism remain high, support for antidemocratic measures and activities has not noticeably increased, support for many government services has not decreased, and pleas for radical changes to the governmental system are uncommon. This, however, does not mean that cynical attitudes are largely ritualistic and without any effects, as Citrin would argue. Recent research conducted by Marc Hetherington demonstrates a variety of repercussions. Lower levels of trust lead to poorer evaluations of presidential performance and lessened support for the institutions of government, thus making it more challenging for political leaders to govern.[48] Trust also influences citizens' presidential vote choices. Those who are less trusting of government are more likely to vote for third-party or independent candidates, if such candidates are on the ballot. Absent this option, distrustful citizens are less likely to support the incumbent president (or the candidate from the president's party if the incumbent is not running) than are more trusting voters.[49]

Hetherington's most provocative argument, however, is that declining public trust has contributed to the increase in conservative public policies adopted by the national government.[50] Liberal solutions to public problems generally involve government, such as federal intervention to prevent racial discrimination or the provision of public money and subsidies to fight poverty. Conservatives, in contrast, tend to prefer minimal government involvement in the economic sector, so they generally favor policies that pursue this goal. Such policies have been more common in the United States since the 1960s, especially in contrast to President Lyndon Johnson's Great Society legislation that established a variety of government programs to fight racism and poverty. Public policy could have taken a conservative turn because citizens' attitudes became more conservative toward all issues over this time. Hetherington, however, demonstrates this is not the case. The public has not become less supportive of government funding for Social Security, Medicare, transportation, and education, for example.

Public opinion has fluctuated, however, toward certain social welfare policies, especially those that require most people to sacrifice so that others (the poor, racial minorities, etc.) will benefit. And these fluctuations have been largely driven by levels of public trust. When trust is higher, the public support liberal antipoverty and racial policies. As trust declines, public support for these policies is much lower, even though most citizens believe that poverty and racism should be eliminated. They simply do not believe the government is capable of solving these problems. Hetherington shows that four decades of increasing public distrust in government have "undermined public support for federal programs like welfare, food stamps, and foreign aid, not to mention the entire range of race-targeted programs designed to make equality between the races a reality."[51]

Finally, some have argued that public distrust is a good thing, so we should not worry about any negative implications. As liberal democrats posit, suspicion of those in power can be healthy for democracy, and thus declining trust might be a reasonable reaction to government actions.[52] Further, public distrust in the past has contributed to the inclusion of new groups into democratic decision making. As trust in government among certain groups declined, political movements such as the women's movement, the civil rights movement, and the environmental movement rose up to challenge existing power arrangements.[53] Increasing public distrust has also been mentioned as an indicator of the level of development of a nation. When a society's basic needs must be met by the government, trust in the government is expected to be high. Yet,

> [w]hen people no longer worry for their survival, they do not need to cling unquestionably to the authorities they hope will ensure their survival. Instead, as material well-being increases, trust in political institutions and elites is likely to decline as publics begin to evaluate their leaders and institutions by more demanding standards.[54]

SUPPORT FOR INSTITUTIONS

In addition to understanding citizens' trust in government in general, it is important to examine citizens' attitudes toward individual aspects of the political system, especially the institutions of government. We begin with a discussion of citizens' low levels of confidence in the Supreme Court, the executive branch, and Congress. As with trust in government, confidence in institutions is an important underpinning of a democratic nation. If citizens do not support governmental institutions, they are less likely to accept and comply with the outputs of those institutions. For example, citizens who lack confidence in institutions might be more willing to protest Supreme Court decisions or ignore legislation passed by Congress and signed into law by the president.[55] The questions used to measure confidence, however, tap into both attitudes toward the institutions and attitudes toward members of those institutions. Thus, it is difficult to know what to make of these low levels of confidence. Do they suggest a crisis for American democracy? Or do the low levels simply reflect citizens' dislike of the individuals within those institutions? We address these questions below.

Confidence in Institutions

How much confidence do citizens have in the Supreme Court, the executive branch, and Congress? Not much, according to national survey data collected by the General Social Survey (GSS).[56] Since the early 1970s, citizens have been asked the following:

> I am going to name some institutions in this country. As far as the people running these institutions are concerned, would you say you have a great deal

of confidence, only some confidence, or hardly any confidence at all in them? … Executive branch of the federal government … Congress … U.S. Supreme Court.

Of the three branches, citizens have the most **confidence in the Supreme Court** (see Figure 10-3). Between 1973 and 2004, 33 percent of citizens, on average, said they had a great deal of confidence in the Court. Support for the Supreme Court was at its all-time high in 1991 when 39 percent of citizens said they had a great deal of confidence in the institution. Its lowest point came in 1978 when only 29 percent felt that way.

Confidence in the executive branch has been quite a bit lower and not as stable as the Supreme Court. On average, 17 percent of Americans said they had a great deal of confidence in the executive branch between 1973 and 2004. The executive branch was held in highest esteem in 1973, when 30 percent of citizens said they had a great deal of confidence in the institution. The Watergate scandal was playing out at that point, yet confidence in the institution was high, relatively speaking. Unfortunately, the GSS did not ask the question prior to 1973, so we do not know whether the Watergate scandal had already taken a toll on confidence in the executive branch. By 1974, however, it is clear the scandal had tainted the presidency: confidence dropped to 14 percent. The low point for the executive branch came in 1996, when only 11 percent said they had a great deal of confidence.

Confidence in Congress is lower than both the Supreme Court and the executive branch. Similar to the executive branch, confidence in Congress is more

Figure 10-3   Confidence in the Supreme Court, Executive, and Congress

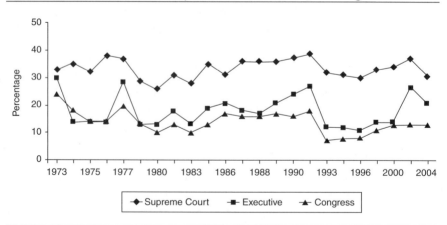

Source: Analysis of General Social Survey Cumulative Data File, 1972–2004.

Note: Data points are the percentage of respondents who have "a great deal" of confidence in each institution.

volatile than support for the Supreme Court. On average, only 14 percent of citizens said they had a great deal of confidence in Congress between 1973 and 2004. Congress's high point was in 1973 at 24 percent, and the low point was in 1993 when a mere 7 percent said they had a great deal of confidence in the legislative body. Not surprisingly, the "Republican Revolution" occurred in 1994, with the Republicans taking over the House of Representatives from the Democrats for the first time in forty years. Throughout much of the 1990s, public support for Congress was dismal. It has bounced back a bit in recent years, but disdain for Congress is still quite high.

As you have probably already noticed, the question wording used to measure confidence in these institutions conflates diffuse and specific support.[57] The survey question refers to "institutions" (thus implying diffuse support) and to "the people running these institutions" (thus implying specific support). Consequently, these data make it impossible to sort out whether American citizens have very limited faith in the fundamental institutions of our government or whether they simply hold political leaders in low esteem or both. This is problematic because if we are interested in combating low levels of confidence, we need to know what is driving the discontent. We would come up with very different solutions if the target of citizens' wrath was the institution versus the politicians themselves. We now turn to an important research project that tackles this issue.

Approval of Political Institutions and Their Members

John Hibbing and Elizabeth Theiss-Morse argue that political scientists must make a distinction between citizens' **attitudes toward the institutions of government** and their **attitudes toward the people in those institutions.**[58] To sort this out, Hibbing and Theiss-Morse designed and implemented their own national survey of 1,433 randomly selected respondents in 1992. In this survey, citizens were asked about their approval of each institution and their approval of members of each institution. See Table 10-3 for the wording of the questions used in this survey.

When attitudes toward the institutions are separated from attitudes toward the people running the institutions, you immediately see that citizens are actually quite supportive of the institutions: 88 percent or more of the respondents approved of each of the three institutions[59] (see Figure 10-4). Attitudes toward the people running these institutions, however, are a different story. Less than one-quarter of citizens approved of members of Congress, and less than one-half approved of the way the president was handling his job. Support for Supreme Court Justices was substantially higher with a 73 percent approval rating. Based on these data, Hibbing and Theiss-Morse conclude that the "confidence" questions overstate people's displeasure with the institutions of government.[60] Indeed, they argue citizens see the constitutional system of three branches of government as "goodness and light."[61] It is the people involved that citizens don't much care for, with one notable exception: citizens tend to like their own representative.

Table 10-3   Survey Questions Assessing Approval of Institutions and Members of Institutions

---

Approval of institutions:

"I have a few more questions about the institutions of the government in Washington—that is, the presidency, the Supreme Court, and Congress. In general, do you strongly approve, approve, disapprove, or strongly disapprove of the institution of the presidency, no matter who is in office?"

"What about the Supreme Court, no matter who the justices are?"

"What about the U.S. Congress, no matter who is in office?"

Approval of members of institutions:

"Again, thinking about people in government, please tell me if you strongly approve, approve, disapprove, or strongly disapprove of the way the people are handling their jobs. How do you feel about the way the nine justices on the Supreme Court have been handling their job?"

"What about President George Bush?"

"What about the 535 members of Congress?"

"What about your own representative in the U.S. House of Representatives?"

Source: John R. Hibbing and Elizabeth Theiss-Morse, *Congress as Public Enemy* (Cambridge: Cambridge University Press, 1995), 166.

Hibbing and Theiss-Morse also find that citizens perceive Congress as the most powerful institution of the three (despite the fact that most political scientists would point to the executive branch as the most powerful). Moreover, citizens do not just think it is powerful, they think it is *too powerful.*[62] Citizens have higher expectations for Congress and the presidency than for the Supreme Court when it comes to solving the nation's problems. They are not thrilled by the job that either Congress or the presidency is doing in addressing those problems, but they are particularly unimpressed by Congress. They are more likely to see Congress as blocking important things from happening than passing legislation to deal with problems.[63] As a result, citizens feel a great deal of disgust and anger toward Congress. Almost two-thirds of respondents said they felt anger and disgust at members of Congress, while one-third felt that way about the president, and only 7 percent felt that way about Supreme Court justices.[64]

To provide a more in-depth exploration of citizens' attitudes toward institutions, Hibbing and Theiss-Morse conducted eight focus groups in four areas of the country: southeast Nebraska, Minneapolis–St. Paul, Houston, and upstate New York. Each focus group was made up of six to twelve participants. Responding to a facilitator's broad questions about support for political institutions, the groups had open, free-flowing discussions that lasted about two hours each.[65] The participants in the focus groups echoed many of the survey research findings but also

Figure 10-4   Approval of Institutions and Members of Institutions, 1992

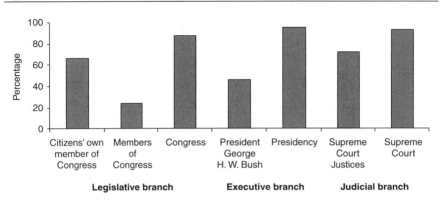

Source: John R. Hibbing and Elizabeth Theiss-Morse, *Congress as Public Enemy* (Cambridge: Cambridge University Press, 1995), 45.

Note: Bars represent the percentage of respondents who either "strongly approve" or "approve" of each attitude object.

added richness to our understanding of why citizens find members of Congress particularly distasteful.

So, why doesn't the public like members of Congress? "Congress is an enemy of the public *because* it is public."[66] Congress is an open institution; debates and decision making are on full display for the public to see. The gridlock, the partisan bickering, the compromises, and conflict—it's all there for citizens to evaluate. Furthermore, citizens are turned off by what they perceive as the inappropriate influence of lobbyists and interest groups on members of Congress. People are angered by members acting on behalf of interest groups in exchange for perks and ignoring the interests of common citizens. Table 10-4 contains quotations from focus group participants that illustrate these points.

But if citizens are so turned off by members of Congress, why do they like their *own* representative? Because members of Congress are an undifferentiated mass of people who do things the public does not like, whereas citizens have individuating information about their own representative that makes them like him or her. A citizen might know, for example, that her representative tracked down Grandpa Dale's lost farm subsidy check, or another citizen might know that his representative secured funding to build a new bridge in the community. Of course, when citizens see *other* members of Congress bringing home money to their districts, they often refer to it derisively as "pork," but projects brought to their *own* districts are considered sensible uses of taxpayer money.

While Congress is the most open institution, the Supreme Court is at the other end of the continuum.[67] It is the least public institution, heavily shielded from the

Table 10-4   Focus Group Discussion of Members of Congress

Participant from New York: "In Congress, they got cobwebs on their arms from sitting in chairs for three years. They got no new ideas. They just keep going back to the old stuff that keeps putting money in their pockets."

Participant from Minnesota: "When I think about it, [Congress] seems very removed from the people, and yet they're elected officials of the people, of course, but ... they don't seem accessible to me."

Participant from Texas: "These guys are up there, pardon my language, like fat cats as they've been called, doing this, that, and the other, and they're hob-nobbing with who? The people who have the influence, and who has the influence? The people with the money."

Participant from Nebraska: "I think Congress ... has gotten too big for their britches. They got used to all the freebies, the perks, the nice things that come to them, the power, and it's just become taken for granted. It's become abused."

Source: John R. Hibbing and Elizabeth Theiss-Morse, *Congress as Public Enemy* (Cambridge: Cambridge University Press, 1995), 97–99.

media and citizens. Debate occurs and votes are taken behind closed doors; the justice's own clerks are not even present during conferences. To be sure, interest groups try to influence judicial decision making by submitting amicus curiae briefs, but they do not take justices on golfing junkets or give money to reelection campaigns because justices serve for life. Consequently, the Supreme Court and its membership are seen as above the hurly burly of politics. The Court is perceived as a defender of the Constitution neutrally applying legal guidelines rather than a political actor.[68] As a result, citizens are substantially more favorable toward the Supreme Court and justices than toward Congress and its membership.

The president falls between these two extremes.[69] Internal debates and disagreement within the executive branch are not as visible as those in Congress. The hierarchical structure of the presidency allows it to put out a unified position. Interest groups certainly try to influence executive agencies, but this occurs largely out of the public eye; interest groups contribute to presidential campaigns, but lobbying of the White House happens behind closed doors rather than in public hearings as it does on Capitol Hill. In addition, many people view the president as a symbolic leader or a figurehead, comparing the president to the British monarchy, for example. Therefore, the less public, more ceremonial nature of the presidency makes it more palatable than the open divisiveness of Congress.

Overall, Hibbing and Theiss-Morse conclude that citizens do not like democratic processes, which leads them to view members of Congress with particular disdain. These scholars do not excuse the bad behavior on the part of some members of Congress, but they do argue that citizens should be better educated about how democracy actually works.[70] Democratic processes are "inevitably unruly."[71] If citizens had a better understanding of that, they would not be so turned off by the bickering and deal making occurring in the legislative branch. Ironically, citizens blame the members of Congress rather than the institution of Congress for the messy way in which democracy works. They do not seem to understand that Congress, not to mention the entire U.S. system of government, was designed to ensure conflict and compromise. If they did realize that, would citizens be as supportive of the constitutional system as they currently are? Would education lead people to appreciate members of Congress or would it lead citizens to lose respect for the institutions of democracy? These are hypothetical questions we cannot answer, but they are certainly important to consider.

Hibbing and Theiss-Morse's results are particularly troubling to pluralists and participatory democratic theorists. Pluralists, of course, think that citizens can be well represented by interest groups, but citizens don't agree. During Hibbing and Theiss-Morse's focus groups, one of the strongest complaints was about how interest groups do not represent the views of ordinary Americans. As a result of interest group influence, members of Congress pass legislation to please powerful groups but not to serve the interests of the people, according to many citizens. Participatory democratic theorists are challenged by the extreme dislike of politics that citizens revealed in the focus group discussions.[72] Participatory democratic theorists believe that citizens would be more engaged and participate at higher levels if they just had the opportunity to do so. Hibbing and Theiss-Morse's participants, however, were not interested in debate, conflict, uncertainty, and compromise— democracy, in other words. Citizens dislike democracy in practice and want no part of it. Instead, the public wants "government to do its job quietly and efficiently, sans conflict and sans fuss."[73] Thus, these findings undermine the arguments of participatory democratic theorists.

Elite democratic theorists would be most pleased with the findings discussed in this section. They believe citizens should have a healthy skepticism toward political leaders, yet maintain support for the institutions of government. That seems to best characterize citizens' attitudes toward institutions and the members of those institutions.

SOCIAL CAPITAL

For most people, their interactions with other individuals (at dinner, over the water cooler at work, or while volunteering to clean up a park) are more frequent and more significant than are their interactions with government. Social connectedness not only is important for people but also can be beneficial to a community, as observed nearly 100 years ago by the rural schools supervisor in West Virginia:

> The individual is helpless socially, if left to himself.... If he comes into contact with his neighbor, and they with other neighbors, there will be an

accumulation of social capital, which may immediately satisfy his social needs and which may bear a social potentiality sufficient to the substantial improvement of living conditions in the whole community.[74]

Lyda Hanifan further described social capital as "good will, fellowship, sympathy, and social intercourse." Contemporary definitions of social capital share much in common with this first usage of the term. For political scientist Robert Putnam, the most visible writer on this topic today, "social capital refers to connections among individuals—social networks and the norms of reciprocity and trustworthiness that arise from them."[75]

Social capital has two broad components: **civic engagement** ("individual and collective actions designed to identify and address issues of public concern"[76]) and **interpersonal trust** (the degree to which people think others can be trusted, are fair, and are helpful). Communities with high social capital consist of many citizens engaged in group activities and a public that has high levels of trust in other people. While most consider social capital to be a feature of a collective unit (town, state, country, etc.), some argue that we can consider social capital at the individual level. "It is not, after all, a 'community' that participates or builds trust, but the people who comprise that community who belong to civic organizations and acquire positive feelings towards others."[77] Despite this insight, following the lead of most social capital researchers, we focus our attention on **social capital** at the communal level.

Researchers have identified a number of specific consequences of social capital, including two that pertain to earlier portions of this chapter. Recent declines in social capital, which we will outline in the next section, have contributed to the lower levels of trust in government witnessed over the past few decades.[78] Why? "When citizens disengage from civic life and its lessons of social reciprocity, they are unable to trust the institutions that govern political life."[79] Additionally, confidence in national institutions, particularly the legislature, is higher in nations with greater social capital.[80] Beyond this influence of social capital on public attitudes, many benefits are presumed to accrue to communities with high levels of social capital, largely because such capital allows members to work together to address community problems. As Putnam writes, "life is easier in a community blessed with a substantial stock of social capital" because "networks of civic engagement … facilitate coordination and communication, amplify reputations, and thus allow dilemmas of collective action to be resolved."[81] Putnam backed up this assertion by demonstrating that compared with U.S. states with low social capital, those with high levels contained less violent crime, better environments for children (lower infant mortality rates, lower high school dropout rates, fewer children living in poverty, etc.), healthier citizens, and improved status for women (increased economic autonomy, better health and well-being, etc.).[82] Other researchers also have supported Putnam's point that members of a community are harmed when social capital in the community is low. For instance, the inability of blacks in the Mississippi Delta to coordinate with white civic organizations (due to white resistance) has contributed to the failure to reduce poverty among the black population even as more of the local elected officials in this region are black.[83]

Is social capital important for democratic governance? Democratic theorists disagree on this, largely because they differ on the proper level of citizen political engagement. Elite and pluralist democrats both propose that the public be minimally involved in governmental decision making, with the public's views represented via, respectively, elected officials or interest groups. Pluralists emphasize the importance of group activity in politics, as do social capital theorists, but these two disagree over the role of groups in democracy. Pluralists argue that competition among groups over governmental policy produces stable democracies by preventing one set of interests from being too powerful. The study of social capital, in contrast, emphasizes the benefits obtained by individuals who participate in civic groups as well as the benefits to community of having people engaged in politics.[84]

These latter views, of course, more closely resemble theories of classical and participatory democracy than pluralism. Both classical and participatory democrats stress the importance of a politically active public and thus would view social capital as valuable for democratic health. Participatory democrats, in particular, extol the virtues of citizen engagement with one another. Working with others can teach people tolerance of opposing views, trust in other people, and cooperation—qualities that are important for democratic governance. Communicating with others can also contribute to learning about politics and fine-tuning one's political attitudes. In addition to these individual benefits, participatory democrats believe that a citizenry more engaged in political activities and debate is good for democracy in that this is more likely to result in citizen views influencing government decisions. These normative theories of democracy, then, differ in whether they consider citizen connectedness important for democracy. What of the reality of social capital in the United States today? We answer that question next, by summarizing an influential study that tracked levels of social capital over the past few decades.

Putnam's Bowling Alone

Did you know that bowling is one of the most popular competitive sports in the United States? In fact, it became somewhat more popular near the end of the twentieth century. Between 1980 and the mid-1990s, the number of people who bowled increased by 10 percent. At the same time, however, participation in bowling leagues decreased by 40 percent. So, more Americans were bowling, but they were increasingly bowling on their own rather than as members of established leagues.[85] This fact led to the title of Robert Putnam's book examining social capital, *Bowling Alone.* At this point, you might be wondering what the connection between bowling and social capital is. For Putnam, the decline in league bowling was one of many indications that informal social connections among Americans were waning. Compared with nonleague bowlers, people who bowl in leagues not only bowl at the alley but also are much more likely to hang out together over food and drink. Connections are made and conversations—about bowling and many other topics—ensue. So, the imagery of bowling is particularly useful for illuminating one of the main themes of Putnam's book: rather than joining with others in a variety of political, social, and leisure activities, the public is increasingly acting alone.

To demonstrate that social capital is on the decline, Putnam and his research assistants marshaled an impressive amount of data covering many manifestations of social capital. The centerpiece of his analysis examines membership in **chapter-based civic associations,** such as parent-teacher associations, the American Legion, and the Jaycees, where members meet regularly in their local communities. For many of these groups, membership increased fairly steadily from 1900 to 1945, then grew tremendously until the mid-1960s. After a period of stability lasting through the 1970s or later, most groups have seen their membership numbers decrease substantially. Membership declines for a variety of civic associations are illustrated in Figure 10-5. These percentages represent the decline in membership rates for each association from the year of their highest membership until 1997. The number of people belonging to each group declined, quite significantly for some, during this time period. The American Association of University Women's membership rate is 84 percent lower than it was, and membership in the National Association for the Advancement of Colored People (NAACP) and the Elks each dropped 46 percent. The smallest decline presented here, at 25 percent, occurred for the Rotary.

In contrast, during these same decades some **national mass membership organizations** witnessed tremendous growth. Major environmental organizations, including the Sierra Club and National Wildlife Federation, saw their membership increase from 2 million in 1980 to 6.5 million in 1990, before leveling off.[86] One of the largest organizations in the nation, the American Association of Retired Persons (AARP), counted 33 million members in the mid-1990s, up from 400,000 in 1960. This expansion was remarkable and has contributed to the lobbying clout exercised by the AARP in Washington.[87] Yet, from a social capital perspective, membership in these types of organizations does not resemble belonging to an association with local chapters. For many who belong to mass membership organizations, participation entails sending in annual dues and perhaps reading newsletters, e-mail messages, and other communication sent by national headquarters. The connection between members of the AARP or the National Audubon Society is "like the bond between any two Red Sox fans ... they root for the same team and they share some of the same interests, but they are unaware of each other's existence. Their ties, in short, are to common symbols, common leaders, and perhaps common ideals, but not to one another."[88] Belonging to such groups, in other words, does not develop social capital.

Figure 10-5 Membership Declines for Civic Associations between Peak Year of Membership and 1997

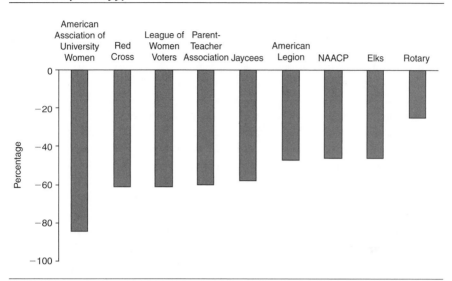

Source: Adapted from Appendix III of Robert D. Putnam, *Bowling Alone: The Collapse and Revival of American Community* (New York: Simon and Schuster, 2000), 438–439.

Note: Bars represent the percentage decline in membership rate (based on size of population eligible for membership) from year of highest rate for each organization to 1997.

Putnam's analysis did not stop with civic and political associations; he also considered other indicators of social capital's decline. Participation in religious activities (such as attending religious services) and groups (e.g., B'nai B'rith and the Knights of Columbus) is lower now than in prior decades. Labor union membership is down, as is membership in many professional organizations, including the American Nurses Association and the American Bar Association. In addition to membership in formal organizations, **informal social interaction** has also declined. Compared with past years, Americans are less likely today to socialize with their neighbors, to entertain friends at their house or be entertained at a friend's house. As Putnam concluded, "We spend less time in conversation over meals, we exchange visits less often, we engage less often in leisure activities that encourage casual social interaction. ... We know our neighbors less well, and we see old friends less often."[89]

Think about your own community. Are civic associations, religious organizations, and social groups thriving or do they have dwindling membership? While Putnam's data certainly indicate these trends are nationwide, considering the reality of your own community can provide concrete examples to illustrate Putnam's statistics and demonstrate the local relevance of national trends. For example, in one of our own neighborhoods—in Schenectady, New York—two organizations were recently forced to sell buildings because their small memberships made it financially impossible to keep and maintain the property. A hall run by the Knights of Columbus was torn down to make way for a parking lot for a local business, while a building owned by a men's social group was converted into an inn and restaurant (albeit with space reserved each month for the men's group to meet). One of us, Zoe Oxley, has also been approached by the League of Women Voters' local chapter to brainstorm about ways to encourage college students to join and participate in league activities. This local chapter not only has witnessed its membership roll shrink but is also concerned that the membership is aging, as is the case with many organizations that Putnam analyzed.

Why Has Social Capital Declined?

Over the past few decades, why "did the fabric of American community life begin to unravel?"[90] To explain this widespread and significant decline in social capital, Putnam considered many possible factors, ultimately concluding that four played contributing roles. The two that account for the smallest portion of the downward trend in social capital are changes in work patterns and the movement of people to the suburbs. With more women in the paid labor force and more two-career families than in the past, adults, especially women, have less time to devote to civic engagement, entertaining at home, and communal leisure activities. Suburbanization has played a role in decreasing social capital in part because those who live in the suburbs spend more time commuting to work, which eats into their time available for other activities. Suburbs not only contain residential areas but increasingly jobs and shops. The result is often a separation of one's home, work, and consumer lives. We might live in one town, work in a second, and do most of our shopping in a third. Further, our neighbors (or spouses!) might work in a fourth town and prefer to shop in a fifth. This leaves people without a strong attachment to any particular community, weakening social bonds and discouraging participation in local civic activities.

While these are important contributors to the decline in social capital, Putnam identifies generational replacement as more significant. Those who were born in the 1920s were especially civic minded and active, much more so than any generation born since. Putnam suggests that entering adulthood, a particularly formative period in one's life, during World War II separates this generation from others. Many members of this generation served in the military during the war, and the war was also felt on the home front. Factories were turned over to wartime production, people were asked to donate scrap metal and rubber when national supplies ran low, the rationing of food and other goods occurred, and volunteers participated in activities from civil defense to mailing books to service members overseas. Levels of patriotism and feelings of shared adversity were very high. Putnam argues that these experiences translated into a lifetime of civic participation and social connectedness. In short, "being raised after World War II was a quite different experience from being raised before that watershed."[91]

There is another crucial difference between this generation and ones that were born later: the former did not grow up watching television. Television viewing increased over the same decades that social capital was declining. More important, people who watch television a lot or rely on TV as their main form of entertainment are less likely to engage in a variety of social and civic activities, including attending meetings, going to church, and volunteering. In contrast, newspaper readership is related to belonging to civic organizations.[92] The relationship between TV watching and social capital is complex, however, in that not all types of TV shows depress social capital. In particular, the effect is greatest among those who view entertainment shows. As watching daytime television (soap operas, talk shows, etc.) increases, civic engagement decreases. Just as with reading the newspaper, however, watching news and current affairs programs on TV leads to increased civic participation.[93] Increased TV viewing, then, particularly of certain types of programs, eats away at social capital. As Putnam concludes,

> Heavy users of [television] are certainly isolated, passive, and detached from their communities, but we cannot be entirely certain that they would be more sociable in the absence of television. At the very least, television and its electronic cousins are willing accomplices in the civic mystery we have been unraveling, and more likely than not, they are ringleaders.[94]

Critiques of Putnam

Bowling Alone made a huge splash when it was published. Unlike most scholarly books, it received considerable national attention in the press and was read by many nonacademics, including politicians, activists, and leaders of associations. Putnam's work has thus been very influential in our thinking about social capital, and many people do support his conclusions. Yet, his research was not well received by everyone. While many do agree that Putnam's evidence of a decline in social connectedness is convincing, some feel he overlooked examples of citizen engagement and thus overstated his case that social capital is declining. For example, even though Americans are less likely to join the traditional civic associations that Putnam profiles, participation in small, less formal groups has increased. These include support groups (such as Alcoholics Anonymous), book clubs, coffee house gatherings, and tenants associations.[95] Putnam acknowledges these groups are common but argues they do not contribute to social capital in the same way that civic associations do because members of these types of small groups do not translate their participation into forms of civic engagement. Instead, the groups primarily provide an important support and caring network for members.[96]

While Putnam is correct, these small groups do provide meaningful person-to-person interaction and would seem to build interpersonal trust, one key feature of social capital.

By focusing so much attention on formal civic organizations, Putnam also overlooked social capital among citizens who have been marginalized in society, such as African Americans. Marginalized citizens often create social networks and social capital from their own locations, rather than only, or even primarily, through the type of civic associations favored by those in the majority. Furthermore, historical exclusion from many political and civic activities led to blacks forming bonds with each other in locales that Putnam neglected to examine, including homes, neighborhoods, black churches, the streets (especially during social protests), and possibly even prison. Although prison might not seem an obvious venue for building social capital, one scholar argues that "the prison is increasingly a venue of black civic action."[97] Some black organizations are active inside and outside prison, fostering links between prisoners and those on the outside. This has increased attention throughout the black community to issues related to prison life (including racial bias in the criminal justice system that leads to higher incarceration rates of blacks versus whites). Political activism around criminal justice has been one result.

Some reviewers of this chapter were concerned about our discussion of social capital among blacks in prison because they were worried that it might unintentionally perpetuate racial stereotypes among whites about the relationship between blacks and crime. We recognize this as a legitimate concern because racial prejudice among whites does still exist, as we discussed in chapters 6 and 9. Nevertheless, we think this point is important to highlight because it clearly illustrates the limitations of Putnam's focus on formal civic organizations. Furthermore, we view the building of social capital in prisons as a potentially quite positive phenomenon, not a negative one.

More common than these concerns that Putnam missed some examples of social connectedness are critiques that his explanations for the decline in social capital are incomplete. His generational replacement explanation is wanting in that he does not fully explain why the generation born in the 1920s is more engaged civically, other than postulating that the context of World War II is relevant. Further, Putnam implies that all members of this generation reacted to the war in the same way, whereas others have found that individuals can interpret and respond to the same historical events in very different ways.[98] To his credit, Putnam did examine many reasons for social capital's decline, but he overlooked some. The increase in public disillusionment with government in the wake of political scandals and government corruption has likely contributed to the decrease in explicitly political forms of civic engagement.[99] Messages from the political environment also likely played a role, such as conservative attacks on the protest movements of the 1970s and criticisms of the welfare state in the 1980s. Both types of rhetoric could have contributed to lowering trust in government and civic engagement (particularly among conservative citizens) and increasing mistrust across social groups.[100]

Finally, Putnam underemphasized an important trend: globalization. As the world has become more connected economically and transnational entities (including corporations, media conglomerates, and trade bodies) have become more prominent internationally,

> societies become more and more dominated by unbridled market forces that damage people's social relations and discourage civic engagement. In a world organized around the notion of individual liberty understood primarily as unrestrained economic entrepreneurship, traditional communal values of cooperation, solidarity, and civic participation are trumped by competitive market norms.[101]

What connects these additional explanations for the erosion of social capital is that they highlight structural or environmental causes, whereas Putnam focused his attention on individual people, implying that it was Americans' fault for social capital's decline: "we watch television instead of joining groups, and we have the wrong attitude to make democracy flourish."[102]

CONCLUSION

Do citizens trust their government? Not all that much, it turns out. In 2004, for example, less than 50 percent of citizens said they trust the government to do the right thing just about always or most of the time. Moreover, citizens' trust in government has declined significantly since 1964. What factors led to that decline? Tumultuous events, including war and scandals, and unmet expectations led to decreases in trust over time. Occasionally, upsurges in trust have occurred, and these have been attributed to the popularity of President Reagan, a strong economy, and a focus on terrorism and national security. Public trust is also a function of whether citizens are pleased with the policies produced by government and messages from the political environment. In general, demographic characteristics do not influence trust, although blacks demonstrate lower levels of trust than whites.

If citizens do not have high levels of trust for the government in general, perhaps they have confidence in specific governmental institutions? Again, the answer is no. On average, since the early 1970s, only about one-third of citizens have indicated they have confidence in the Supreme Court, even fewer citizens have expressed confidence in the executive branch, and fewer still in Congress. Scholars have argued, however, that this lack of confidence is more a function of citizens' dislike of the members of the institution rather than dislike for the institutions themselves. Indeed, when attitudes toward the members and the institutions are measured separately, it becomes apparent that citizens actually have a great deal of support for the basic institutions of government but are not as fond of the people running those institutions, particularly members of Congress.

Has social capital declined in the United States? Yes, indeed it has, according to research by Robert Putnam. Putnam identifies several factors leading to the decline in social capital, including changes in work patterns, the movement of people to suburbs, generational replacement, and television. Others have critiqued his work, however, arguing that structural or environmental factors, rather than individual people, are to blame for the decline in social capital.

Trust, support for institutions and their members, and social capital are all interrelated. Declines in social capital lead to less trust and less confidence in institutions, and low levels of trust lead to less support for institutions and their members. But, do low trust and social capital matter? Should we be concerned with citizens' disapproval of the people running government institutions (especially members of Congress)? Or should we be consoled by the high levels of approval for the institutions of government? Elite democratic theorists would not be concerned with a lack of social capital because they do not envision an active role for citizens. They would be pleased that citizens have a healthy skepticism toward members of institutions, yet maintain a high regard for the three branches of government. This support for the basic institutions of government will lead people to obey the law, thus creating a stable democracy, even if people do not like the particular people running the government.

In contrast, participatory democratic theorists would be troubled by low levels of trust and social capital and little faith in politicians because these indicate citizens are not actively engaged in politics. If citizens were involved, they could ensure that government officials were not crooked or wasting money or working on behalf of a few big interests. Thus, they could trust government to do what is right. Further, if citizens trusted government and the people running it, then more citizens would be willing to run for political office, something that would please participatory democratic theorists.

Democratic theorists of all stripes would be concerned if trust in government and confidence in the people running institutions became so low that the government could not function. Government officials might avoid trying to solve intractable problems (especially if solving them meant short-term pain) if they thought citizens would not support their efforts over the long haul. Trust in government and faith in elected officials are especially important in times of war. During the summer of 2007, political commentator Andrew Sullivan wrote, "Successfully prosecuting a long war requires a bond of trust between rulers and ruled. One reason why the current debate about what to do next in Iraq has become so bitter so quickly is precisely because none of us can trust what the government says or its motives."[103] Based on the evidence presented in this chapter, what do you think of Sullivan's provocative statement?

KEY CONCEPTS

attitudes toward the institutions
  of government / 295
attitudes toward the people in
  those institutions / 295
changes in public expectations of
  government / 286
chapter-based civic
  associations / 302
civic engagement / 300
confidence in Congress / 294
confidence in the executive
  branch / 294

confidence in the
  Supreme Court / 294
cynicism / 281
diffuse support / 279
informal social interaction / 303
interpersonal trust / 300
national mass membership
  organizations / 302
political reality model / 289
social capital / 300
specific support / 280
trust in government / 280

SUGGESTED SOURCES FOR FURTHER READING

Brace, Paul, and Barbara Hinckley. *Follow the Leader: Opinion Polls and the Modern Presidents.*
    New York: Basic Books, 1992.
Mueller, John E. *War, Presidents, and Public Opinion.* New York: Wiley, 1973.

These books examine presidential popularity. Brace and Hinckley find that the economy, dramatic events, time, and the personality of individual presidents influence popularity. Mueller's classic book demonstrates that when international crises occur, presidents will get a short-term bump in their approval ratings (i.e., the rally-round-the-flag effect).

Caldeira, Gregory A., and James L. Gibson. "The Etiology of Public Support for the Supreme
    Court." *American Journal of Political Science* 36 (1992): 635–664.
Gibson, James L., and Gregory A. Caldeira. "Blacks and the United States Supreme Court:
    Models of Diffuse Support." *Journal of Politics* 54 (1992): 1120–1145.

These classic articles by Caldeira and Gibson develop a measure of diffuse support for the Supreme Court. They find that blacks and whites are both supportive of the Court as an institution, but whites are more so. They also examine the factors that influence diffuse support for the Court.

Durr, Robert H., John B. Gilmour, and Christina Wolbrecht. "Explaining Congressional
    Approval." *American Journal of Political Science* 41 (1997): 175–207.

These scholars examine approval for Congress between 1974 and 1993. They find that public support for the institution declines when it carries out its duties as a legislative and representative body.

Durr, Robert H., Andrew D. Martin, and Christina Wolbrecht. "Ideological Divergence and Public Support for the Supreme Court." *American Journal of Political Science* 44 (2000): 768–778.

These scholars examine confidence in the Supreme Court between 1973 and 1993. They find that confidence in the Court increases when its rulings are consistent with the ideological leanings of the public.

Hero, Rodney E. *Racial Diversity and Social Capital: Equality and Community in America.* New York: Cambridge University Press, 2007.

In this important new book, Hero demonstrates that greater social capital is not associated with more positive results for all Americans. In some instances, higher levels of social capital are linked to worse conditions for blacks. Racial diversity, on the other hand, can have a positive effect on social and political outcomes for racial minorities.

Hetherington, Marc J. *Why Trust Matters: Declining Political Trust and the Demise of American Liberalism.* Princeton: Princeton University Press, 2005.

In this book, Hetherington focuses on the implications of declining public trust in government. Specifically, he presents a convincing case that lower levels of trust are responsible for the conservative shift in national public policy that has occurred since the 1960s.

Citrin, Jack. "The Political Relevance of Trust in Government." *American Political Science Review* 68 (1974): 973–988.
Miller, Arthur H. "Political Issues and Trust in Government: 1964–1970." *American Political Science Review* 68 (1974): 951–972.
——— ."Rejoinder to 'Comment' by Jack Citrin: Political Discontent or Ritualism?" *American Political Science Review* 68 (1974): 989–1001.

This exchange between Miller and Citrin highlights a number of issues in the empirical study of trust. Miller and Citrin disagree over how to define trust, the proper way to measure public trust in surveys, and what to make of declining levels of trust.

McLean, Scott L., David A. Schultz, and Manfred B. Steger, eds. *Social Capital: Critical Perspectives on Community and "Bowling Alone."* New York: New York University Press, 2002.
Putnam, Robert D. *Bowling Alone: The Collapse and Revival of American Community.* New York: Simon and Schuster, 2000.

In *Bowling Alone,* Putnam provides a wealth of information documenting recent declines in social capital and civic engagement. He also presents explanations for and describes many implications of these declines. The book edited by McLean, Schultz, and Steger contains essays that present critical interpretations of Putnam's work.

Warren, Mark E., ed. *Democracy and Trust.* Cambridge: Cambridge University Press, 1999.

This volume contains essays from both empirical political scientists and political theorists discussing public trust in a democracy. Among others, the authors explore topics such as whether declining trust is problematic, whether the public should actually be quite distrustful of government officials, and whether democracies require a minimum amount of trust to function.

The Saguaro Seminar, Civic Engagement in America: www.ksg.harvard.edu/saguaro/

This Web site summarizes various social capital-related initiatives directed by Robert Putnam. Research findings, a social capital blog, and methods for increasing social capital are some of the many features on the site.

SDA: Survey Documentation & Analysis: http://sda.berkeley.edu:8080/quicktables/quickconfig. do?gss04

This Web site allows you to easily analyze the General Social Survey (GSS) Cumulative Data File, 1972–2004. Let's say you are interested in whether there are racial differences in confidence in the Supreme Court. First, click on "Politics and Voting by Background Variables." Second, select the variable you want to analyze: Confidence in Supreme Court. Third, select the breakdown by race. Finally, click on create the table. The program will show you that whites have higher levels of confidence in the Supreme Court than blacks. This example is just the tip of the iceberg. This Web site will allow you to do all kinds of fun and informative data analysis. Check it out.

CHAPTER 11

Impact of Public Opinion on Policy

ON THE EVE of the U.S. invasion of Iraq in March 2003, nearly 60 percent of the American public supported U.S. military intervention to force Saddam Hussein from power.[1] In fact, according to polls conducted by the Pew Research Center, a majority of the public had favored sending troops into Iraq since November 2001 (see Figure 11-1). Polls conducted by other organizations showed "exceptionally consistent" results, with *all* demonstrating majority support for using U.S. troops to unseat Hussein.[2] With public support on his side (as well as congressional approval), President George W. Bush ordered the military into Iraq on March 19, 2003. In a nationally televised speech that evening, Bush announced this action as follows: "My fellow citizens, at this hour, American and coalition forces are in the early stages of military operations to disarm Iraq, to free its people and to defend the world from grave danger."[3]

During the first 18 months of the war, most Americans continued to express support for Bush's decision. Beginning in October 2004, however, less than 50 percent of the public felt that using military force in Iraq was the "right decision."[4] As the months ticked by, more and more Americans concluded that military action in Iraq should not have happened. By January 2007, only 40 percent labeled the military intervention as the right decision, whereas 51 percent believed it was the wrong decision. Furthermore, over these years, gradually increasing percentages of the public supported bringing U.S. troops home from Iraq. While only 32 percent of people expressed this view in September of 2003, nearly 50 percent did by the beginning of 2007.[5]

It was in this climate of decreased public support for the Iraq war that Bush proposed sending more than 20,000 additional troops to Iraq to serve alongside the approximately 140,000 servicemen and women already there. He argued that these extra troops were necessary to combat sectarian violence between Shiite and Sunni Muslims in Iraq and therefore improve safety and security in the nation, particularly in Baghdad.[6] Given the public's dissatisfaction with the war and increasing preference to return troops back to the United States, it is not surprising that support for the proposed surge was not high. In fact, only 31 percent of the public favored this proposal in January 2007. And of those that opposed, fully

Figure 11-1 Public Opinion and the Iraq War

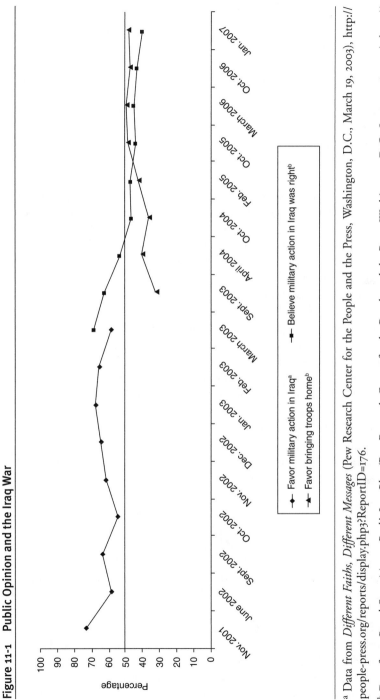

◆ Favor military action in Iraq[a]
■ Believe military action in Iraq was right[b]
◀ Favor bringing troops home[b]

[a] Data from *Different Faiths, Different Messages* (Pew Research Center for the People and the Press, Washington, D.C., March 19, 2003), http://people-press.org/reports/display.php3?ReportID=176.

[b] Data from *Broad Opposition to Bush's Iraq Plan* (Pew Research Center for the People and the Press, Washington, D.C., January 16, 2007), http://people-press.org/reports/display.php3?ReportID=301.

69 percent believed that Congress should actively try to prevent Bush from implementing his plan, even by withholding funding for the troops if necessary.[7] Despite this lack of public support, though, Bush did order more troops into Iraq in early 2007.

These two examples of policy decisions made by Bush present contrasting views of the relationship between public opinion and public policy. Bush's choice to engage in military action in Iraq coincided with the public's preferences, whereas his troop surge decision went against the wishes of a majority of Americans. Which is more common? Do policymakers generally enact policies that a majority of citizens support? Or is the discounting of public opinion more common? Under what circumstances will policy reflect the public's policy opinions? Does policy type matter? Are officials more or less likely to be responsive to public opinion when formulating foreign versus domestic policy? We address these questions in this chapter.

For a minute, though, let's think about the first example a bit more carefully. Before the Iraq war began, Bush attempted to persuade the public and other policymakers (notably members of Congress) that the United States should invade Iraq and topple Saddam Hussein. He presented two primary reasons why he felt this action was necessary.[8] First, he warned that Hussein was developing weapons of mass destruction and America's safety depended on stopping this effort. Second, he argued that Hussein must be removed from power because he was connected with al-Qaeda, the group responsible for the 9/11 attacks. Could his arguments have convinced the public to support his plan, which then became policy? If so, is this an example of Bush responding to public opinion or shaping opinion to support his own goals? These questions suggest that to truly understand the role of public opinion in policymaking, we must consider how officials monitor and use public opinion to further their own policy preferences, topics that we also take up in this chapter. First, however, we summarize democratic theorists' views on the role of the public in policymaking.

SHOULD PUBLIC OPINION INFLUENCE POLICY?

Regardless of whether public policy does respond to the wishes of the public, *should* it? As you have no doubt guessed by now, democratic theories provide quite different answers to this question. Before discussing these differences, recall that all democratic theorists support popular sovereignty. This is the belief that power in a democratic society ultimately rests with the citizenry. Differences across the theories emerge over how the people should exercise their power and how capable the public is for democratic governance.

Participatory democrats expect the influence of the public on policy to be quite substantial. Policymakers should, in their view, enact policy that coincides with the wishes of the majority. These theorists further believe that officials should debate policy openly, providing the public with meaningful and relevant information about policy options. Leaders should not attempt to manipulate or mislead the public. After listening to an information-rich policy debate, the public can form opinions about public policy, opinions which they communicate to the leaders. Because political equality is also important to participatory democrats, they expect that policymakers will respond to the wishes of the entire public, not only those citizens who are especially involved in politics or who have the financial means to express their opinions most loudly (such as by contributing to candidates for elective office).

Pluralists expect that public policy will reflect public opinion, but they prefer that citizens be somewhat removed from the policymaking process. For them, opinions are best expressed via *organized groups.*[9] Whereas citizens are not knowledgeable enough about policy issues to express clear preferences to officials, pluralists assume interest group representatives are. These groups lobby policymakers directly, trying to convince them to support policy that is in the interest of the group's members. Pluralists also argue that citizens are not attentive enough about politics to follow the goings-on of their elected officials, but interest group representatives do this and communicate details back to their members. Through the interest group link, though, only those people who are represented by groups are likely to have their preferences communicated to officials. This model thus privileges the opinions of those who are organized over those who do not have a group actively involved in lobbying government officials.

Of the democratic theories we have been profiling in this book, elite democrats posit the smallest role for the public in policymaking. These theorists believe that the public should be involved in electing officials, but should then leave the policy details up to the leaders. Elite democrats view the public as disinterested in following politics closely enough to make decisions over complex policy matters and incapable of seeing beyond their own interest to make choices that are in the best interest of the nation. Thus, they prefer to leave policymaking to those with expertise—the leaders. Policymakers can attempt to educate the public about the best policy option, but at the end of the day, the officials should do as they see fit. This view was clearly expressed in a July 2007 opinion column written by David Broder, a *Washington Post* journalist. After describing examples in which the "dangerously compliant congressional leadership" followed the wishes of the public by not enacting policies that Broder thought would be good for the country, he concluded with the following: "Politicians are wise to heed what people want. But they also have an obligation to weigh for themselves what the country needs. In today's Washington, the 'wants' of people count far more heavily than the nation's needs."[10]

Despite this view, elite democrats expect that policy might minimally correspond with public preferences. They see this outcome occurring via *elections.* Citizens elect leaders who they hope will follow their general policy preferences and then have the chance to remove these officials from office if they do not. Thus, elections can produce a connection between the opinions of voters and policy. The voters have control over who is elected, and officials have an incentive to keep the preferences of voters in mind or risk losing their office come Election Day. Finally, elite democrats do not hope for or expect that the preferences of all members of the public will be expressed through elections, but rather only the wishes of those who are most attentive to and involved in politics. For elite democrats, it is perfectly fine, even preferred, if the opinions of other members of the public do not influence policy decisions.

Judgments about politicians' responses to public opinion are not restricted to democratic theorists. Everyday conversations include negative descriptions of leaders who do not adopt the speaker's preferred behavior. Politicians who are perceived to follow the public's wishes too quickly and uncritically are said to *pander*, whereas those who make decisions contrary to public opinion are decried as *shirkers*. Indeed, you might have strong preferences about whether officials should or should not enact policy that corresponds with the wishes of the public. Whether you do or not, we encourage you to ponder over the normative democratic theories as we present findings from empirical research on public opinion and public policy.

Is Public Opinion Related to Policy?

As one scholar put it, "No one believes that public opinion always determines public policy; few believe it never does."[11] True enough, but sorting out how often public opinion is related to policy is not an easy task. Numerous decisions need to be made, including whether to examine public opinion for one or more issues and whether to focus on national or state policymaking. Thus, researchers have taken very different approaches to studying the relationship between opinion and policy. One method that has been used is a **case study**, which entails an in-depth analysis of one policy area (such as health care policy) or one policy decision (the passage of a specific bill). While many case studies of the opinion-policy relationship have been conducted,[12] we instead focus our attention in this section on research that examines many different policy areas and decades at once. After all, if a case study of tax policy in the 1990s finds that opinion influenced policymaking, we cannot be certain that this relationship exists for other issues or for other time periods. In contrast, **aggregate studies**, which examine many issue domains and years, provide more conclusive evidence about the overall relationship between public opinion and public policy.

Issue-Specific Opinion and Policy

When public support toward an issue changes, does policy then change? This question was addressed by Benjamin Page and Robert Shapiro.[13] They examined public opinion survey data between 1935 and 1979 and identified 357 cases in which policy preferences changed significantly over time. Page and Shapiro then studied national and state policies for each case at the time of the first public opinion measure and then again one year after the second measure to see if there had been any change in the policy. Their goal was to assess **opinion-policy congruence**. For example, imagine that the percentage of the public that wanted the government to spend more money to protect the environment increased from 48 percent in 1978 to 58 percent in 1983. To assess the relevant government policy, Page and Shapiro compared the level of actual spending on the environment in 1978 with that in 1984. Such an approach allowed them to determine whether public policy changed in the same direction as the opinion change (this is congruence), changed in the opposite direction, or did not change. Their underlying assumption is that if policy does respond to public opinion, this should be especially likely when public opinion changes.[14]

Across all of their cases, Page and Shapiro found that when both opinion and policy changed, 66 percent of these changes were congruent. They further demonstrated that congruence was more likely the larger the opinion change (see Figure 11-2). When public support for a policy changed only 6 or 7 percentage points and when the relevant public policy changed, it did so in the same direction as the opinion change 53 percent of the time. Opinion-policy congruence fairly steadily increased for larger opinion changes and reached 100 percent when the opinion change was 30 percentage points or higher.

A related approach to assessing the opinion-policy relationship is to examine public *preference for change* rather than actual opinion change. That is, instead of finding instances where public opinion did change over time as Page and Shapiro did, you could see whether the public desires that a specific government policy be

Figure 11-2   Congruence between Opinion Change and Policy Change, by Size of Opinion Change

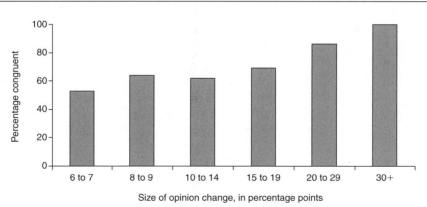

Source: Data from Table 3 of Benjamin I. Page and Robert Y. Shapiro, "Effects of Public Opinion on Policy," *American Political Science Review* 77 (1983): 180.

changed and then examine whether government policy does in fact change in response. This was the approach favored by Alan Monroe. Perusing the results from many public opinion polls, Monroe identified many examples of questions asking about policy change. He did this for two time periods: 1960–1976 and 1980–1993.[15] For each measure of public preferences, he then examined whether national policy changed or stayed the same

To assess consistency (Monroe's term for congruence), Monroe compared public preferences for change with actual policymaking for each policy issue in his analysis. When a majority of the public favored policy change and change did occur in the direction of the public's wishes, opinion-policy consistency was present. Similarly, consistency also occurred when the majority opinion favored the status quo (no change) and policy did not change. Overall, Monroe concluded that public preferences and policy were consistent 64 percent of the time for the first time period and 55 percent for the second. As you can see in Table 11-1, however, the preferences of the public were more in line with public policy when the public favored the status quo.[16] Between 1960 and 1976, for instance, when the public preferred that a specific policy not change, this policy stayed the same in 76 percent of the cases Monroe analyzed. When the public wanted change, they got it only 59 percent of the time. And during the sec-

Table 11-1   Consistency between Public Opinion and Public Policy

	Consistency for 1960–1976 Overall consistency: 64% (222 cases)	
Public policy	*Public preference*	
	Status quo	*Change*
Status quo	**76%**	41%
Change	24	**59**
	Consistency for 1980–1993 Overall consistency: 55% (566 cases)	
Public policy	*Public preference*	
	Status quo	*Change*
Status quo	**70%**	55%
Change	30	**45**

Sources: Data for top half from Table 1 of Alan D. Monroe, "Consistency between Public Preferences and National Policy Decisions," *American Politics Quarterly* 7 (1979): 9. Data for bottom half from Table 1 of Alan D. Monroe, "Public Opinion and Public Policy, 1980–1993," *Public Opinion Quarterly* 62 (1998): 13.

ond time period, when the public preferred that a policy be changed, this change occurred only 45 percent of the time, yet public preferences for the status quo were met for 70 percent of these cases. This **status quo bias** is perhaps not surprising. The U.S. political system with its three branches of government that share power and check each other's power was set up to make policy alterations occur slowly, if at all.

Opinion Trends and Policy

Other studies of the opinion-policy relationship have used broader measures of public opinion. This approach assumes that when formulating policies, policymakers focus on general **opinion trends** (such as liberal or conservative swings) in public opinion rather than opinion toward specific policy issues.[17] One broad measure of public opinion used in opinion-policy studies is labeled **policy mood** or **policy sentiment**.[18] The measure is obtained by aggregating across opinion toward dozens of specific issues. It captures whether the public feels that the government, in general, is doing too much or not doing enough. In other words, it measures "global preferences for a larger, more active federal government as opposed to a smaller, more passive one across the sphere of all domestic policy controversies."[19]

Examining over-time variation in the domestic policy mood is interesting in its own right. Americans' global preferences were quite liberal in the 1960s, then turned more conservative until 1980 (refer to the solid line in Figure 11-3). A more liberal policy mood returned and stayed until the early 1990s. The first half of the 1990s witnessed a trend toward conservatism.

For our purposes now, however, we want to know whether changes in the public's policy sentiment were accompanied by changes in public policy. This did happen for domestic policy issues, according to research conducted by Robert Erikson, Michael MacKuen, and James Stimson.[20] These authors assessed the direction of policymaking by determining the ideological direction of key laws passed by Congress (and not vetoed by the president) between 1954 and 1996. That is, for each two-year session of Congress, this measure shows whether laws enacted tended to be conservative or liberal. When comparing the ideology of policy with the ideology of the public, Erikson et al. found that when the public mood changed, public policy generally followed in the same direction (see the dotted line in Figure 11-3). In other words, a liberal shift in the public mood was followed by a liberal shift in policy. Likewise, conservative opinion shifts were accompanied by policy moving in a conservative direction. As Erikson et al. described this relationship, "Public sentiment shifts. Political actors sense the shift. And then they alter their policy behavior."[21]

The relationship between public opinion and policymaking in the U.S. states has also been examined. In one study, researchers used people's responses to poll questions asking them their ideological identification to determine the average ideology for each state.[22] For the years of their study (1976–1988), the

Figure 11-3   Correspondence between Public Mood and Policy

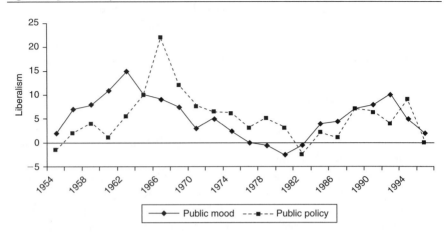

Source: Figure 2.2 of Robert S. Erikson, Michael B. MacKuen, and James A. Stimson, "Public Opinion and Policy: Causal Flow in a Macro System Model," in *Navigating Public Opinion: Polls, Policy, and the Future of American Democracy,* ed. Jeff Manza, Fay Lomax Cook, and Benjamin I. Page (Oxford: Oxford University Press, 2002), 43.

states with the most conservative citizens were Utah, Idaho, and Oklahoma. Massachusetts, Rhode Island, and New York were the most liberal. Each state's policy ideology was also assessed by examining the liberalness or conservativeness of state policies in specific areas (education, criminal justice, taxes, etc.). When the ideology of the public was compared with that of a state's policy, a clear pattern emerges: policy is more liberal in states where the citizens are more liberal. When more of a state's citizens identify as conservative, the state's policies are more conservative.[23] For example, the two states with the most liberal public policies were New York and Massachusetts. Among exceptions to this trend, the policies in Wisconsin and Delaware are more liberal than their citizenries, whereas people in Arkansas and Indiana are less conservative than their state's public policies.

Variation in Congruence

Despite the dissimilarities in research designs and goals, all of these scholars conclude that public opinion and public policy tend to be related.[24] They and others have also explored whether congruence is higher for certain policies or people. It is. First, issue salience matters. The more that the public is especially concerned about an issue or the more that an issue receives national attention, such as in the news media, the more likely that public opinions about the policy will closely match actual policy.[25] For his 1980–1993 analysis, for example, Monroe found that public preferences for change and policy outcomes were 69 percent consistent for issues that the public felt were the most important for the nation.[26] Consistency dropped to 60 percent for issues that were ranked the second to fifth most important, and to 56 percent for issues that were ranked lower than this. Among issues that were not considered important by the public, opinion and policy were consistent only 46 percent of the time.

Public attentiveness is also relevant. Congruence is higher for citizens who follow politics most attentively compared with citizens who pay lesser attention.[27] Members of the public who care deeply about a policy area as well as the attentive public are likely to know how their elected officials stand on issues and to take this into consideration when they vote.[28] Elected officials also know this, and if they wish to remain in office, they pay attention to the wishes of their aware and engaged constituents. Officials are also vigilant about especially salient issues. Such issues can provoke those citizens who are normally only marginally attentive to politics to tune in and become informed about the topics.[29] And if these citizens do not like their representatives' positions on salient issues, they can vote them out of office.

Finally, important recent work suggests that the more income that a person has, the more likely that public policy corresponds to his or her preferences.[30] This conclusion is particularly striking when we consider instances in which the preferences of those with high incomes differ from the opinions of either low- or middle-income Americans. In such situations, public policy is significantly likely to be related to the opinions of the high-income group but is unrelated to preferences of people with lower incomes. As Martin Gilens concludes, "influence over actual policy outcomes appears to be reserved almost exclusively for those at the top of the income distribution."[31] The primary instance when lower income citizens are likely to see their preferences reflected in public policy is when they have the same opinion as those of more means.

These findings concern proponents of participatory democracy greatly. Not only do the research conclusions suggest that not all Americans' preferences are equally likely to be related to the policy decisions of leaders, but they also suggest that economic inequalities are one source of such differing levels of responsiveness. This provides further evidence to these theorists that inequalities among the public need to be minimized, a view also favored by more modern variants of classical democratic theory, such as that proposed by Jean-Jacques Rousseau.[32] Elite democrats, in contrast, would likely applaud the findings. These theorists prefer that if the government's policies do match the preferences of the public, it is best if the opinions of the most involved and more aware citizens are followed. These citizens, after all, are most likely to have well-considered opinions on policy matters, according to elite democrats.

Public Opinion in Comparative Perspective
BOX 11-1   COMPARING OPINION-POLICY CONGRUENCE ACROSS DEMOCRACIES

Is the level of opinion-policy congruence in the United States typical among democratic nations? Unfortunately, examinations of this topic for other countries have been quite rare.[1] Some scholars have compared public opinion with the opinions of elected officials or candidates across nations. One such approach demonstrates that in the late 1970s the views of the public were generally more similar to the opinions of officials in Britain, West Germany, and especially France than in the United States.[2] While this research is informative, it does not directly examine enacted public policy, and thus is difficult to compare with the opinion-policy congruence studies presented in this chapter. The one scholar who has done cross-national research comparing opinion and policy is Joel Brooks, so we profile his work here.

Brooks compared public opinion and public policy in five nations: the United States, Canada, Great Britain, France, and West Germany.[3] His method for doing so was similar to that used by Page and Shapiro. Utilizing opinion poll results, Brooks categorized the majority of the citizens as either favoring or opposing a range of specific policy issues. He examined different time periods for each nation, analyzing at least ten years of opinion data for each country (refer to the figure below for specific years). He then categorized the nation's official policy for each of these issues, primarily by analyzing legislative and executive decisions. He assessed existing policy at the time that the survey data were collected and, to allow for the possibility that policy changed in response to public preferences, up until one year after. Finally, from these measures of opinion and policy, he was able to categorize each case as demonstrating opinion-policy consistency or inconsistency. For instance, if a majority of the citizens in West Germany opposed the conscription of women into the military and the German military did not draft women, opinion and policy would be consistent. When the West German public supported the death penalty for people convicted of murder and governmental policy did not allow capital punishment for murderers, as was the case in the late 1970s, there was inconsistency between opinion and policy.

As the figure below demonstrates, Brooks uncovered little variation across these nations in the consistency of opinion and policy. Consistency was lowest in Canada at 39 percent of cases analyzed and highest in Great Britain at 44 percent, with the other three nations falling in between these percentages. You will no doubt notice that the level of opinion-policy congruence found by Brooks is lower than what was found by Page and Shapiro and by Monroe. This is largely because of differences in how

(continued)

congruence or consistency was measured. Page and Shapiro calculated opinion-policy congruence only for those cases when both opinion and policy changed over time. When instead considering all of their cases (including instances of nonchange as well as change), they find that opinion and policy are congruent 43 percent of the time, a result very similar to Brooks'.[4]

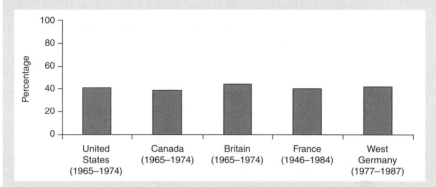

While all are democracies, these five nations differ in the structure of their governments. For instance, in the United States, Canada, and West Germany, power is shared between the federal and state or provincial governments. Great Britain and France have unitary governments, which means that most power resides in the federal government. Furthermore, three of these nations (Canada, Great Britain, and West Germany) have parliamentary governments. In contrast, the United States has a presidential system with power separated between the executive and the legislature. France has both a president and a parliament.

Do these institutional differences matter when it comes to opinion-policy congruence? Brooks' analyses suggest no. Despite the different governmental structures that exist across these five democracies, the likelihood that public opinion will be consistent with governmental policy is essentially the same in all five.

1. Russell J. Dalton, *Citizen Politics: Public Opinion and Political Parties in Advanced Western Democracies,* 2nd ed. (Chatham, N.J.: Chatham House Publishers, 1996), chap. 11.
2. Ibid. See also Russell J. Dalton, "Political Parties and Political Representation: Party Supporters and Party Elites in Nine Nations," *Comparative Political Studies* 18 (1985): 267–299.
3. Joel E. Brooks, "Democratic Frustration in the Anglo-American Polities: A Quantification of Inconsistency between Mass Public Opinion and Public Policy," *Western Political Quarterly* 38 (1985): 250–261; Joel E. Brooks, "The Opinion-Policy Nexus in France: Do Institutions and Ideology Make a Difference?" *Journal of Politics* 49 (1987): 465–480; Joel E. Brooks, "The Opinion-Policy Nexus in Germany," *Public Opinion Quarterly* 54 (1990): 508–529.
4. Brooks, "The Opinion-Policy Nexus in Germany," 514.

Do Politicians Follow or Lead the Public?

You just learned that there is considerable evidence that public opinion is related to policy outputs for both the national and state governments in the United States. Does this mean that the views of the public *influence* the decisions of policymakers? We need to know more before we can answer this question. Just because we see a *correlation* between opinion and policy, we cannot be sure that opinion caused the policy outcome. It is possible, after all, that the policy change caused the public's opinions to change. We can rule out this possibility for most of the studies we just discussed, however, because of the methods used by the researchers. For example, both Page and Shapiro and Erikson et al. measured public opinion at one point in time and policy at a later date. Thus, their results cannot be due to policy influencing opinion because public opinion was assessed before the policy changed.[33]

There is another possibility, however. Before public policy is changed, politicians unveil proposals and publicly debate their preferred policies. The news media often cover these developments. While politicians are debating the merits of various policy proposals, the public thus has the opportunity to learn about the pros and cons of each. And, because it can take many weeks, months, or even years before policy is changed, the opinions of the public can be influenced by the policymaking process. For example, as we suggested at the beginning of this chapter, Bush's appeals to the public to support his plan to invade Iraq likely influenced public opinion on this matter.

Why do we care about this? It is important to sort out the precise nature of the opinion-policy connection for many reasons, not least of which are democratic theory implications. **Democratic responsiveness** refers to leaders enacting policy that the public wants. Such responsiveness assumes that governmental policy reflects the *genuine opinions* of the public. This is what participatory democrats hope for. However, what if the public opinion that the officials seem to be responding to was actually largely created by these officials? If policymakers persuade the public to support the officials' preferred policy and then policymakers enact this policy, can we conclude that democratic responsiveness has occurred? It depends. If public support for the proposal is genuine, then politicians' influence on public opinion would not worry participatory democrats so much. What if, however, the public has been *manipulated*? Manipulation occurs when leaders use "false or misleading arguments or information to turn the public against its true interests (the preferences it would hold if information were accurate and complete)."[34] Such a circumstance would undermine participatory democrats' goal of responsiveness. So, before we can conclude that participatory democrats are happy with the evidence showing that public opinion and public policy are related, we need to know whether leaders are truly responding to the public as opposed to trying to shape, or even manipulate, citizens' opinions.

Unlike participatory theorists, elite democrats actually prefer that public preferences be shaped by leaders. The leaders, after all, are the ones who are most aware of what is in the best interest of the nation and who have the expertise to put forth specific policy proposals. Policymakers should share their proposals and reasons for supporting them to the public, thus providing **opinion leadership**. According to this view, educating the public is an important goal for leaders. If policy reflects the wishes of the public at all, according to elite democrats, it is best if the public's preferences have been influenced by the wisdom and expertise of the leaders.

To navigate among these competing theories, it is important to consider the context in which public policy opinions are formed. This entails moving beyond the aggregate studies of opinion and policy we just reviewed and into the "whole big, messy realm of public opinion and policymaking in the United States."[35] In particular, delving into the processes of policymaking and trying to determine the goals of politicians will help to address the debate between participatory and elite democrats. We do that in this section, first by examining how leaders learn about public opinion. Then, we discuss what politicians do with this public opinion information. Do they use it to inform their policy decisions? Or do they use it to try to direct public opinion?

How Do Politicians Learn about Public Opinion?

One way that politicians try to determine the opinions of the public is through opinion polls. This is especially the case with presidents. Before the 1930s, when modern opinion polling techniques were developed, presidents used other means to learn of public preferences. These included reading letters that were sent to the White House, talking to citizens, reading newspapers, interpreting past election outcomes, and counting the number of people attending rallies.[36] Franklin Roosevelt was the first president to hire a pollster to conduct private polls for him.[37] Presidents Harry S. Truman and Dwight Eisenhower chose not to follow Roosevelt's lead, but presidential opinion polling returned with the election of John F. Kennedy. With Kennedy's inauguration in 1961, "the White House became a veritable warehouse stocked with the latest public opinion data."[38]

Presidential Polling. All presidents since Kennedy have relied on **private polls** to gauge public opinion. These private polls are conducted specifically for the president and contain the questions designed by his personal pollster(s) and advisors. One reason why presidents use private polls is because they consider their own polls more trustworthy than other sources of public opinion. Opinion information collected by others (members of Congress, the news media, interest groups, etc.) likely reflects the goals of the collector. Thus, relying on his own polls gives the president an independent means to determine the public's wishes.[39]

Related to this point is John Geer's argument that private polling provides presidents with high-quality information about the public's preferences. Geer analyzed the various methods by which presidents have assessed public opinion over the decades.[40] He concludes that two features of polls allow them to more accurately gauge citizen opinion. First, polls measure citizens' views *directly* whereas other sources of public preferences (newspaper stories, interest group statements, etc.) indirectly portray the public's attitudes. Second, polls provide more *representative* assessments of the people's opinions. Letters sent to officials and conversations with people who attend rallies do represent the views of the letter writers and rally participants, of course. What about the views of less politically active segments of the public? Polling is more likely to capture these citizens' views and thus supplies a more thorough summary of the citizenry than do other methods of gathering public opinion.

The results from the president's private polls are distributed to many members of the administration, including top advisors (the Chief of Staff, Domestic Policy Advisor, Legal Counsel, Director of Communications, etc.) and even the president himself.[41] Richard Nixon was particularly keen on examining the polls. He "engaged his aides in 'long discussions' about poll results; at times, he became 'fascinated with the findings,' spending large blocks of time 'reviewing and reverting' to the results until he had accumulated extensive notes."[42]

Although private polling is now a permanent and institutionalized feature of presidential administrations, some presidents have commissioned more polls than others. Presidents tend to keep details of their private polling secret, but one way to track this activity is to consider how much money was spent on the president's polls. The White House is not permitted to spend public money on polling because this is considered an electoral or partisan activity. So, the national political party organizations (such as the Democratic and Republican National Committees) pay for the president's polls. Since 1975, the party committees have been required to report all of their spending, including that on White House polling, to the Federal Election Commission. Figure 11-4 presents the yearly amount paid to pollsters for Presidents Jimmy Carter through Bill Clinton during these presidents' first terms in office.[43] The figures were adjusted for inflation (they are reported in year 2000 dollars), so we can directly compare amounts across presidents. Finally, there are two bars for each president: the first presents the average for the first three years in office and the second is for money spent during the reelection year.

Two patterns are noteworthy. First, presidents spend much more on polling during their reelection years compared with the other years, presumably to track voter support for them and their opponents. Second, not all presidents devote the same amount of attention to polling in nonelection years. Ronald Reagan and Clinton were much more likely to commission polls in their first three years in office, spending respectively, on average, $2.1 and $2.3 million per year to do so. Carter's and George H. W. Bush's annual spending was much lower, each at about half a million dollars. The results of this analysis "suggest that Reagan and Clinton took survey research . . . much more seriously during the governing process than did Carter and Bush."[44]

Figure 11-4   Presidential Spending on Private Polls, First Term Only

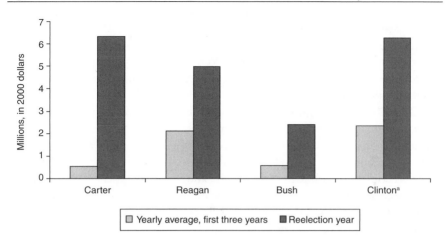

Source: Data from Table 1 of Shoon Kathleen Murray and Peter Howard, "Variation in White House Polling Operations: Carter to Clinton," *Public Opinion Quarterly* 66 (2002): 534.

[a] Figure for Clinton's reelection year spending includes $1.49 million for polling conducted that year but paid out two years later.

When reelection time rolled around, however, Carter and Bush did significantly increase spending on private polls, with Carter's spending during that year dwarfing the amount paid to pollsters during his first three years in office.[45]

What about polling in the George W. Bush administration? Since he is still in office, researchers have not yet had the opportunity to examine fully funding data for George W. Bush. One preliminary analysis of spending on private polls during 2001 and 2002, however, demonstrates that George W. Bush's monthly spending on polls was comparable with other recent presidents and that, as with his immediate predecessors, Bush's spending on polls did increase every month that he was in office.[46] The data complement anecdotal evidence from the news media and memoirs of administration officials that suggests Bush's private polling expenditures rival Reagan's and Clinton's.[47]

A variety of opinions are collected by presidents, including, not surprisingly, public support for specific policy issues. One analysis of the content of polls used by Presidents Richard Nixon through George H. W. Bush demonstrates that policy questions appeared more than other types of questions for Jimmy Carter, Ronald Reagan, and George H. W. Bush.[48] These items encompassed a wide range of domestic and foreign policies, although opinions on specific policies are most likely to be gathered for especially salient issues.[49] Richard Nixon and Gerald Ford were more interested in popularity data. Their polls contained more items assessing public approval of their own and Congress's job performance than items about policy matters. This discrepancy was especially clear for Nixon, whereas Ford was only slightly more likely to poll on popularity than issues.[50] Did this trend toward the collection of policy opinions and away from popularity continue for Presidents Clinton and George W. Bush? We do not know, since this study did not examine the two most recent presidents. Future analyses of these presidents' private polls will hopefully address this topic.

Other Sources of Public Opinion. Although commonly used by presidents, opinion polls are not the most frequent source of public opinion for all politicians. One reason is cost: polling is very expensive and not all officials have access to funds to pay for polls.[51] Some politicians, though, simply believe that there are better sources of public preferences. Reliance on polls appears to be less common in Congress than in the White House for this reason. Communicating in person as well as examining mail and phone calls received from constituents provides important information to representatives about the issue opinions, concerns, and intensity of feeling among members of the public. Polls are perceived by members of Congress to be especially poor at registering how strongly the public cares about an issue.[52]

In an analysis of the sources of public opinion information among staff members in the Illinois legislature, Susan Herbst finds that two stand out: the news media and interest groups.[53] These staffers assume that media presentations of policy issues (whether in news stories or editorials) reflect public sentiment on the issues. So, if newspapers positively portray a reform measure to make criminal sentences harsher, the legislative assistants infer that the public also perceives this policy favorably. More interesting, though, were Herbst's findings about interest groups as proxies for the public's attitudes. Consider the following two quotations from people she interviewed:[54]

> ... interest groups. That's how we gauge public opinion ... I would have to say that from a public opinion standpoint, we don't really care what the average Joe thinks. I don't say that as if we're not representing them, but we're representing the people who represent them. It's one step removed from the general public.

> Obviously I think that the lobbyists and organized groups are much more effective [than average citizens] because they have an organized message. They have money and they're here. Whereas a lot of people, I think there's a lot of people in the state that just really don't care what goes on in Springfield.

The sentiments expressed here are pluralism in action. The legislative staff members saw interest group positions as a better measure of public opinion than the *actual opinions* of the citizenry. The groups are organized, their messages are coherent, and their members are more knowledgeable and attentive to politics than is the general public. So, when a representative from an interest group, such as an agricultural or labor organization, communicates the group's position on an issue, legislative aides assume this is the same position held by farmers and union workers.

How Do Politicians Use Public Opinion Data?

After investing millions of dollars in private polls, what do politicians and their advisors do with the detailed public opinion information they receive? In their influential book, Lawrence Jacobs and Robert Shapiro argue that politicians use these details to try to influence public opinion.[55] In other words, responsiveness to wishes of the majority is not the main goal, but trying to convince the public to support specific policy proposals is. More precisely, polling results are used to create **crafted talk**—rhetoric and messages that officials communicate to the public. Opinion polls, Jacobs and Shapiro argue, demonstrate to officials which features of a proposal the public supports, which they oppose, and which they are uncertain about and thus open to persuasion on. Polling also helps politicians "identify the words, arguments and symbols about specific policies that the centrist public finds most appealing and that they believe to be most effective in changing public opinion to support their policy goals."[56] If politicians are successful at cultivating public support and their proposals become law, then during reelection campaigns they can claim to have enacted the public's wishes into policy. Rather than democratic responsiveness, Jacobs and Shapiro call this outcome **simulated responsiveness**.

Crafted Talk and Health Care Reform. To provide evidence in support of their crafted talk theory, Jacobs and Shapiro conducted a detailed case study of the formulation of and debate over President Clinton's proposal to reform health care in 1993–1994.[57] To determine how Clinton used public opinion, they interviewed key Clinton advisors, reviewed White House documents, examined public statements made by Clinton and others about health care reform, and considered poll results, including Clinton's private polls. They found that while Clinton polled extensively on health care, he did not do so to help him determine the details of his reform proposal. Instead, the policy details were driven by Clinton's own policy goals, his ideology, his vision of what would be the best health care system for the nation's citizens and economy, and the preferences of key interest groups. Once the specifics of the proposal had been decided on, Clinton's private pollster (Stanley Greenberg) was asked to gather public opinion data. Greenberg lamented that he was kept "out of the process … of designing the content of health care reform."[58] Rather than finding out the public's opinions about health care policy, he instead "polled the *presentation* of the policy."[59] In other words, polling data were used to make decisions about how to sell Clinton's proposal to the public. And getting the public behind his proposal was very important on the assumption that it would put pressure on Congress to pass Clinton's plan.

How exactly did public opinion shape Clinton's presentation of his proposal? It helped Clinton and his advisors identify which aspects of the complex plan were especially popular.[60] One of Clinton's policy goals was to provide universal health care coverage for all Americans, a goal that the public also supported. Thus, the overarching theme used to describe his proposal was "Security for All." Clinton also felt that health care reform was necessary to slow down the increase in health care costs. Since the public was less concerned about this problem, he deemphasized this aspect of his plan when discussing the proposal with the public.

Meanwhile, opponents of Clinton's reforms (primarily congressional Republicans and interest groups representing business and health insurers) were not silent. In fact, they were also relying on polling data to determine how to communicate their message to the public.[61] Their polls demonstrated that the public was concerned about too much government control over their own health care decisions. Clinton's plan was thus described as mandating a substantial increase in the government's health care bureaucracy. Key Republicans in Congress labeled the plan a "monstrosity" and "the most destructively big government approach ever proposed" and argued that the proposal would require "upwards of 50,000 additional bureaucrats to meddle with our health care."[62] Furthermore, knowing that citizens were generally happy about their own health coverage but also uneasy about how their coverage might change, Clinton's opponents also emphasized the possible negative effects they would witness under Clinton's policy.

Responsiveness, Opinion Leadership, and Manipulation. In the end, public support for Clinton's plan declined from nearly 60 percent in September 1993 to 40 percent of the citizens in favor the following July. The reform plan died in Congress before it reached the floor for a formal vote. This could be interpreted as evidence of opinion leadership and democratic responsiveness. Perhaps the public listened to the politicians' policy debate, were more persuaded by Clinton's opponents than by Clinton and his supporters, and changed their opinions accordingly. This interpretation further implies that policymakers responded to the well-informed and meaningful wishes of the public in deciding not to enact Clinton's reforms.

Jacobs and Shapiro draw quite a different conclusion from their case study. They argue that the public's preferences were manipulated by the policy debate. Citizens grew to oppose Clinton's plan not because of the plan's actual content but because of the rhetoric that opponents used to undermine the plan. While the opponents were successful at influencing public opinion, Clinton's crafted talk failed to resonate with the public. The results from one opinion poll demonstrate this point quite clearly. In March 1994, when respondents were asked whether they supported "the Clinton health plan," less than a majority did. Yet when asked what they thought about a plan that provided coverage for all people, promoted competition in the health care industry, required employers to provide insurance for their employees, and gave government some power to control health care costs, 76 percent felt that plan had "a great deal" or "some" appeal.[63] The details of this hypothetical plan were actually the exact provisions contained *in Clinton's plan*. In other words, the public wanted the features of Clinton's proposal, but not if it were described as "Clinton's plan." This could be seen as evidence that the public did not learn enough from the elites' health care policy debate to develop meaningful opinions toward Clinton's plan. In Jacobs and Shapiro's interpretation, opinion was manipulated.

If their interpretation is correct, participatory democrats would be concerned. Perhaps more disturbing for them, however, is Jacobs and Shapiro's evidence that politicians on both sides of this debate felt it more important to try to shape public opinion than to respond to it. In their own words, "Our interviews with officials in the Clinton administration as well as staff to Republican and Democratic members of Congress revealed a strong and consistent disdain for the public's competence to understand policy and offer reasoned input into policymaking."[64] These views would please elite democrats, though, as they coincide with these theorists' beliefs that the public's capabilities are minimal and that officials should thus discount public opinion when making policy decisions.

So, is it safe to conclude that democratic responsiveness is rare and that manipulation of public opinion is the norm? While Jacobs and Shapiro's arguments are compelling, we are not ready to make this conclusion. Research in this area is quite new so there is not a clear consensus. In fact, some scholars have concluded that presidents are responsive to public opinion, especially for salient policies, domestic policy issues, or when large majorities (more than 70 percent) of the public support an issue.[65] Other research demonstrates that while presidents do collect opinion data in order to market their preferred policies, the mere collection of the data allows them to monitor the public's attitudes. This monitoring can result in presidents responding to the public's wishes and it also helps presidents determine when the public is unlikely to be swayed by crafted talk.[66] Even Jacobs and Shapiro uncover some evidence of policymakers (particularly congressional Republicans) responding to public preferences during the health care debate.[67] Finally, and probably not surprisingly, the likelihood that elected officials will respond to rather than attempt to lead public opinion varies throughout their terms. Responsiveness to public wishes increases as Election Day nears.[68]

Thus the empirical research does not clearly identify whether politicians try to manipulate the public or provide guidance and arguments to lead the public to well-considered opinions. No doubt both motivations exist, but more work needs to be done to determine when one goal is likely to be pursued over another and also when these strategies are likely to be successful. Furthermore, and not surprisingly, when officials do try to shape public opinion, it is very difficult to determine whether they are educating or manipulating citizens.[69] Yet, these topics need to continue to be explored if we want to link the empirical study of public opinion to normative democratic theory. From a normative standpoint, it is not enough to know that opinion and policy are often related. We also need to know how the opinions of the public are influenced by policymakers, what the quality of public opinion is, and what the officials do once they know public preferences.

PUBLIC OPINION AND FOREIGN POLICY

There are many reasons to suspect that governmental policy might be more likely to follow public opinion for domestic policy than for foreign policy.[70] For one, foreign policies are often less salient to the public than are domestic policies. As we discussed earlier, opinion-policy congruence is higher for more salient issues. Some people, including policymakers, believe that since the public is not knowledgeable or sophisticated enough to hold coherent, well-reasoned foreign policy opinions, foreign policy officials should discount public preferences. Compared with other issue domains, policymakers might be more likely to rely on arguments and evidence from experts (intelligence analysts, military officials, etc.) when it comes to foreign policy.

Finally, elected officials might feel as if they have flexibility to ignore the public when it comes to foreign policy and not suffer electoral consequences. Given that foreign policies are removed from the day-to-day lives of most Americans, some leaders think they can be successful at educating the public on these issues. Consider, for example, the following comments of Congressman Brian Baird, a Democrat from Washington. When asked in the summer of 2007 how he would justify to his constituents his view that U.S. troops needed to stay in Iraq longer when he had initially been an opponent of military intervention in Iraq, Baird responded:

> I would just say to people who are upset, if you could take the time that I have taken over the last number of months to meet with, not only the Iraqi leaders on all sides but our military troops on the ground, their leaders, our ambassadors, leaders from throughout the region, I think you'd have a different impression—I certainly do. And my hope would be people would say someone who's been there on the ground several times now, met with people throughout the region, may have a different insight than just someone who's reading about it second or third hand in the media.[71]

Despite these assumptions that opinion-policy congruence might be lower for foreign compared with domestic policy, early aggregate analyses did not provide supporting evidence.[72] Monroe even concluded that foreign policy was *more* likely than domestic issues to reflect public preferences.[73] Further, case studies of specific policy topics tended to confirm that opinion does influence foreign policy. Public preferences for defense spending are related to the size of the defense budget.

When the public believes too little is being spent, the budget generally increases, and vice versa.[74] Public opinion has also been shown to have constrained policy-makers' decisions regarding U.S. military interventions, such as during the 1991 Persian Gulf War. As the author of this research concludes, "Public opinion is increasingly recognized as a central factor in the decisions about U.S. foreign relations."[75]

Reconsiderations of Public Influence

A number of recent studies paint a somewhat different picture of the relationship between the public and foreign policy. These conclusions appear in research utilizing different methods or new sources of data. One analysis of Reagan's policy behavior shows that his foreign policy decisions were consistent with public preferences (as measured by his pollster) only 35 percent of the time, compared with 58 percent for domestic policy. The author concludes that Reagan felt he had wiggle room when it came to his foreign policy decisions, in part because the public's foreign policy attitudes tend not to be as firm as they are toward domestic matters.[76] Archival research of Clinton's decisions to launch military interventions in Somalia and Bosnia also demonstrates a lack of responsiveness to public opinion. In both cases, Clinton made these decisions despite his own polling evidence showing that the public did not support either intervention.[77] Finally, a very interesting analysis of the mail received by President Lyndon Johnson uncovers a key relationship between the views expressed by certain letter writers and Johnson's decisions regarding the Vietnam War.[78] Even though a majority of the American public did not support Johnson escalating the war, his public statements and military policy became more "hawkish" when he received more letters encouraging him to step up military activity in Vietnam. In this way, Johnson did follow public opinion, but only the opinions of a subset of the public (those who were especially attentive and informed) rather than the wishes of the broader populace.

Benjamin Page, one of the coauthors of an aggregate analysis of opinion-policy congruence, has even reconsidered his earlier conclusion that congruence is similar for domestic and foreign policies.[79] Since "policymakers may have more success in the foreign than the domestic realm at influencing—educating or manipulating—public opinion to harmonize with intended or existing policies," we have to be careful how we interpret findings of congruence in foreign affairs.[80] A high correlation between public opinion and foreign policy thus might not be evidence of democratic responsiveness as much as simulated responsiveness. Furthermore, Page goes on to argue that opinion manipulation might be especially likely in foreign affairs: "Foreign policy issues are often obscure, distant from everyday life, and the executive often enjoys a high degree of information control as well as substantial bipartisan deference from other elites."[81]

Page's critique of the earlier research does not stop with these arguments, however. In two separate projects, he has provided compelling empirical evidence that public preferences shape foreign policy minimally, if at all. In the first, Lawrence Jacobs and Page examine the influence of the public, business interests, labor unions, and foreign policy experts (academics, think-tank researchers, and leaders of foreign policy organizations) on foreign policy officials' views.[82] Their approach is noteworthy because they consider the *comparative* influence of these groups, whereas most studies of the opinion-policy relationship have only examined whether public opinion influences policy. In reality, policymakers have many people and groups attempting to sway their policy decisions, so Jacobs and Page's research design more closely matches actual policymaking conditions. For data, they rely on surveys conducted by the Chicago Council on Foreign Relations (CCFR). Between 1974 and 2002, the CCFR measured the opinions of government officials engaged in foreign policymaking (from presidential administrations, the Senate, and the House of Representatives). Note that the data do not indicate which *policy decisions* government officials made but rather what their views are. While this limits Jacobs and Page's conclusions about what influences foreign policy somewhat, they are likely correct when they argue that "the survey-expressed policy preferences of government officials can be used as reasonable indicators of the policies that they enact or pursue."[83]

The CCFR also gathered the foreign policy opinions of the public, business and labor representatives, and foreign policy experts. Jacobs and Page compared the opinions for each of those groups with the opinions of the government officials. So, which has the strongest influence on the views of foreign policy officials? Business. As Jacobs and Page put it, "internationally oriented business leaders exercise strong, consistent, and perhaps lopsided influence on the makers of U.S. foreign policy."[84] The effect of business leaders on officials in presidential administrations was especially strong. Foreign policy experts were also influential, but less so than business. Further down the influence ladder came labor unions, and weakest of all was the public. Public preferences were more consequential in influencing the opinions of members of the House, for highly salient issues, and for economic matters. Yet, overall, these effects were dwarfed by the substantial impact of business leaders on foreign policy officials.

Results from Page's second project appeared in his book with Marshall Bouton.[85] This book provides a careful and thorough analysis of the content of the public's foreign policy attitudes. For their data, they rely on CCFR surveys conducted between 1974 and 2004, with a particularly strong emphasis on the 2002 survey results. They draw two key conclusions regarding the foreign policy opinions of the public. First, of the many possible goals Americans could want U.S. foreign policy to pursue, three broad goals are most important: security from attack, domestic well-being, and international justice and humanitarianism.[86] Table 11-2 presents the five specific goals most supported by the public in each of these three categories. Some of these, as you will see, fulfill more than one broad goal, so they are listed in two of the three categories. Very large majorities

(90 percent or more) of the public view the security goals of fighting terrorism and stopping the spread of nuclear weapons as very important. Close behind, however, is support for such domestic well-being goals as protecting jobs and preventing illegal drugs from entering the nation (85 percent and 81 percent, respectively). While the public believes that the foreign policy goal of international justice and humanitarianism is less important than security or domestic well-being, this goal is not unimportant. Indeed, 61 percent of Americans believe U.S. foreign policy should aim to fight world hunger, and 47 percent view the promotion of human rights in other nations as very important. Although these specific data are from the 2002 survey, Page and Bouton also demonstrate that citizens' foreign policy goals have been quite stable since 1974.[87]

In terms of which specific foreign policies the United States should pursue to meet these goals, the public has a preference for **multilateralism**.[88] This is Page and Bouton's second primary conclusion about foreign policy opinions.

Table 11-2 Americans' Foreign Policy Goals, 2002

Foreign policy goal	Percentage agreeing goal should be "very important foreign policy goal of the United States"
Security from attack	
Combat international terrorism	91
Prevent spread of nuclear weapons	90
Maintain superior military power worldwide	68
Strengthen UN (also justice goal)	57
Defend U.S. allies' security (also justice goal)	57
Domestic well-being	
Protect jobs of U.S. workers	85
Stop flow of illegal drugs into U.S.	81
Secure adequate energy supplies	75
Control and reduce illegal immigration	70
Improve global environment (also justice goal)	66
International justice and humanitarianism	
Combat world hunger	61
Promote and defend human rights in other nations	47
Strengthen international law and institutions (also security goal)	43
Protect weaker nations against aggression	41
Promote market economies abroad (also domestic goal)	36

Source: Data from Table 2.1 of Benjamin I. Page with Marshall M. Bouton, *The Foreign Policy Disconnect: What Americans Want from Our Leaders but Don't Get* (Chicago: University of Chicago Press, 2006), 41.

Multilateral foreign policies emphasize working with other nations and international bodies such as the United Nations (UN) rather than "going it alone." Support for a multilateral approach was evident in the build-up to the Iraq war. Although majorities of the public did support sending the U.S. military to Iraq (as we documented at the beginning of the chapter), when asked whether the U.S. military should be the sole force in Iraq or whether the United States "should only invade Iraq with UN approval and the support of its Allies," 65 percent preferred the latter while only 20 percent supported the former.[89] More broadly, the public has consistently supported (a) U.S. alliances, (b) participating in UN peacekeeping missions, (c) engaging in diplomacy (with allies and adversaries) rather than using force, (d) using international legal bodies for people who violate human rights, and (e) entering into international treaties to solve global problems (such as the Kyoto Protocol to reduce global warming).

Do the public's preferences coincide with U.S. foreign policy? Not so much, say Page and Bouton. Throughout their examination of the public's attitudes, they provide numerous examples of actual foreign policy decisions that have differed from the public's wishes. These include privileging the policy goal of security from attack over domestic well-being, stopping the payment of dues to the UN in the 1990s, the longstanding refusal to engage in diplomatic relations with Cuba, and President George W. Bush's decisions not to sign the Kyoto Protocol or the International Criminal Court treaty.

In a more systematic analysis, Page and Bouton compare citizens' and policymakers' responses to the CCFR surveys.[90] These are the same surveys that Jacobs and Page used. And, in line with these earlier findings, Page and Bouton conclude that the policy opinions of policymakers often diverge from those of the public (see Figure 11-5). For instance, the public is significantly more likely than foreign policy officials in Congress, the Defense Department, or the White House to believe protecting domestic jobs and strengthening the UN are very important U.S. foreign policy goals. Citizens also display more support for the Kyoto Protocol, the International Criminal Court, and decreasing legal immigration. Foreign policy officials are more likely than the public to believe the United States should pursue **unilateral foreign policies** (i.e., to "go it alone"), to think that the North American Free Trade Agreement is good, and to support the elimination of tariffs. As you can see in Figure 11-5, some of these differences in opinions between the public and policymakers are substantial. It is because of findings such as these that Page and Bouton subtitled their book "What Americans Want from Our Leaders but Don't Get."

CONCLUSION

Does public opinion influence public policy? As you learned at the beginning of this chapter, aggregate empirical studies do demonstrate that policy is related to opinion more often than not. This congruence between opinion and policy is not

**Figure 11-5   Foreign Policy Preferences of Public versus Policymakers,
1994 and 2002**

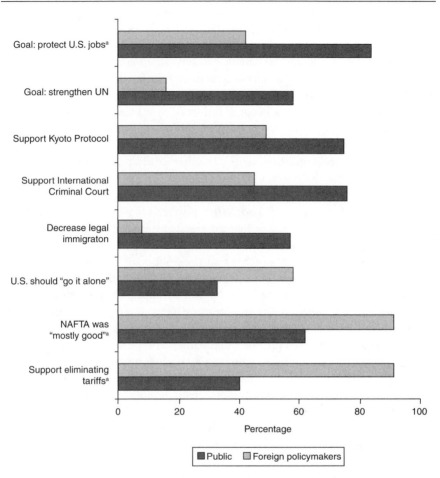

Source: Data from Benjamin I. Page with Marshall M. Bouton, *The Foreign Policy Disconnect:
What Americans Want from Our Leaders but Don't Get* (Chicago: University of Chicago Press,
2006), 213, 215.

[a]Results are from 1994; all others from 2002.

the same for all policy areas. Rather, it is highest for salient issues. Congruence also
varies across individuals: attentive and higher income people are most likely to have
their preferences realized in public policy. Yet, the general finding that opinion is
related to policy in the United States was well documented by these studies.

Later sections of the chapter, however, highlighted topics and new evidence
that raise questions about this conclusion. Considering whether policymakers try

to influence public opinion during policymaking encouraged us to examine how leaders use information about public opinion. Ample evidence suggests that officials, particularly the president, collect public opinion for the dual purposes of *responding to* and *shaping* public opinion. When policies reflect the preferences of the public after the public's opinions have been influenced, perhaps even manipulated, by leaders, we would hesitate to conclude that democratic responsiveness has occurred. Finally, recent scholarship on foreign policy demonstrates that public opinion influences foreign policies less than was once thought. Business interests and policy experts exert a stronger influence over foreign policy, which perhaps explains why policy decisions are often out of step with public preferences.

Overall, then, we agree with others that when it comes to control over public policy, citizens are "semi-sovereign."[91] In other words, public policy only sometimes coincides with the public's policy opinions.

What do democratic theorists make of these empirical findings? Elite democrats would likely be most satisfied. When public policy does coincide with the preferences of the public, it is best that the views of the most attentive citizens are heeded. The fact that politicians are increasingly using polls to try to shape public opinion to support policy options that the politicians have already designed (without following the wishes of the public to do so) would please elite democrats. They would also be heartened to learn that leaders appear to be exercising discretion in the realm of foreign policy and are more likely to rely on the views of business leaders and policy experts than the uninformed public.

The empirical research also provides some, albeit limited, support for the views of pluralists. Those officials who do not conduct private polls appear to rely on interest groups to assess the public's wishes. The nation's foreign policies also are more likely to match the preferences of interest groups (business and labor) than the public.

Finally, there is much in this chapter that worries participatory democrats. The greater influence of attentive and wealthy citizens on policy undermines these theorists' goal of political equality. More concerning, though, is the evidence that politicians believe there are times when they should not follow the wishes of the public. Whether ignoring the public, as seems to be the case in foreign policymaking, or trying to alter citizens' views with crafted rhetoric and perhaps misleading information, the end result is a lack of democratic responsiveness.

Key Concepts

aggregate studies / 316	opinion leadership / 325
case study / 316	opinion-policy congruence / 317
crafted talk / 329	opinion trends / 319
democratic responsiveness / 324	policy mood / 319
multilateralism / 335	policy sentiment / 319

SUGGESTED SOURCES FOR FURTHER READING

Erikson, Robert S., Michael B. MacKuen, and James A. Stimson. *The Macro Polity.* Cambridge:
    Cambridge University Press, 2002.
Page, Benjamin I., and Robert Y. Shapiro. "Effects of Public Opinion on Policy." *American Politi-
    cal Science Review* 77 (1983): 175–190.

These influential studies demonstrate that national policies do correspond with the
wishes of the public.

Geer, John G. *From Tea Leaves to Opinion Polls: A Theory of Democratic Leadership.* New York: Co-
    lumbia University Press, 1996.
Heith, Diane. *Polling to Govern: Public Opinion and Presidential Leadership.* Palo Alto, Calif.: Stan-
    ford University Press, 2003.

These two works examine the use of polling by presidents. Geer pays particular
attention to how polling has changed politicians' behavior. Along the way, he has
much to say about democratic leadership and how we should expect politicians to
lead. Heith has compiled interesting data on what type of opinion information
presidents collect and for what purposes.

Jacobs, Lawrence R., and Robert Y. Shapiro. *Politicians Don't Pander: Political Manipulation and
    the Loss of Democratic Responsiveness.* Chicago: University of Chicago Press, 2000.
Page, Benjamin I., with Marshall M. Bouton. *The Foreign Policy Disconnect: What Americans Want
    from Our Leaders but Don't Get.* Chicago: University of Chicago Press, 2006.

These scholars argue that policy does not necessarily respond to the wishes of the
public. Jacobs and Shapiro demonstrate that politicians can be motivated to manipulate public opinion rather than enact policies the public truly wants. In their
new work, Page and Bouton show that for decades the foreign policies pursued by
leaders have differed from public preferences.

Mettler, Suzanne, and Joe Soss. "The Consequences of Public Policy for Democratic Citizenship:
    Bridging Policy Studies and Mass Politics." *Perspectives on Politics* 2 (2004): 55–73.
Soss, Joe, and Sanford F. Schram. "A Public Transformed? Welfare Reform as Policy Feedback."
    American Political Science Review 101 (2007): 111–127.

While public opinion scholars have long been interested in whether opinion influences policy, the authors of these articles argue that there is much we need to
know about whether policy influences opinion. They suggest that the long-term
influences of specific policies on the mass public could be substantial, possibly
affecting issue salience and opinions, evaluation of political parties, and group

identities. Soss and Schram further argue that these effects are likely to differ across policy areas. In fact, they find that attitudes toward welfare policy were not changed after welfare reforms were enacted during the 1990s.

Pew Research Center for the People and the Press: http://people-press.org/

Pew has conducted many surveys of foreign policy attitudes since 1990. The results from these polls, including many regarding public views of the Iraq war, are available on their Web site.

Council on Foreign Relations: www.cfr.org

This Web site contains a wealth of information about contemporary foreign policy issues. The CFR has been analyzing global affairs and U.S. foreign policy since 1921.

PART VI

What Do We Make of Public Opinion in a Democracy?

CHAPTER 12

Conclusion

CITIZENS MATTER in a democratic society. Democracy comes from the Greek words *demos* and *kratein*. *Demos* means the people, and *kratein* means to rule. Thus, by definition, democracy is rule by the people. Now, *to what extent* citizens should rule in a democratic nation depends largely on your normative perspective, as we have discussed at some length.

In this concluding chapter, we grapple with what to make of public opinion in a democracy. Specifically, we address the five questions that have organized our discussion throughout this book: What should the role of citizens be in a democratic society? Are citizens pliable? Do citizens organize their political thinking? Do citizens endorse and demonstrate democratic basics? And what is the relationship between citizens and their government? We base our answers to these overarching questions on the empirical research and in light of normative democratic theories. But, ultimately, we ask you to judge the evidence, weigh the theories, and draw your own conclusions regarding the capacity of citizens to function effectively in a democracy.

WHAT SHOULD THE ROLE OF CITIZENS BE IN A DEMOCRACY?

This question cuts to the heart of the matter. Should citizens be at the center of decision making or should they be at the periphery of power? The answer, of course, depends on your normative perspective. Classical democratic theorists envisioned a fundamental role for citizens. Citizens should be informed, interested, and intimately involved in political decision making. By engaging in political activities, people would become good citizens with concerns beyond their own narrow self-interest. Yet, empirical evidence suggests that many—if not most—people are not the ideal citizens specified by the classical democratic theorists. Most citizens are not intensely interested in politics, nor are they particularly well informed about the issues of the day. Further, many citizens dislike politics and do not want to be involved with decision making on a regular basis; rather, they prefer representatives to act on their behalf.

In response to the empirical evidence on the limitations of citizens, elite democratic theories sprung up. Elite democratic theorists stressed that democracy is still possible even though citizens do not meet the high expectations of classical democratic theory. Instead of citizens directly influencing governmental decision making, elite democratic theorists argued that citizens should exert indirect control by voting in competitive elections. Citizens are only expected to participate in elections, not to fully engage in the ins and outs of policymaking. From this perspective, the goal of democracy is system stability rather than the development of good citizens. Pluralists also envisioned a more limited role for citizens, but they emphasized interest groups as fundamental intermediaries linking the public to elites. According to pluralists, citizens can still have their views articulated to elites through the actions of interest groups without becoming knowledgeable about issues themselves.

Participatory democratic theories were developed to challenge the narrow role of citizens asserted by elite democratic theorists. While acknowledging that direct democracy is not feasible in a nation as geographically large and highly populous as the United States, participatory democratic theorists emphasized a much more central place for citizens. Indeed, these theorists argued that citizens *could* live up to the ideals of classical democratic theorists *if* systemic barriers keeping people from reaching their potential were removed. Participatory democratic theorists emphasized the benefits that would accrue to individuals as they participated in politics: citizens would learn more about politics and become more knowledgeable about the interests of others and therefore become more open and tolerant. These theorists also stressed that all citizens, not just the advantaged in society, should have a voice. If participation were widespread, inequities in society would be redressed.

By now you are an expert on these varying theoretical approaches. You probably even have a favorite theoretical lens through which to assess the empirical evidence. In the next section, we rely on these theories as we review the research that addresses the question: are citizens pliable?

ARE CITIZENS PLIABLE?

Yes, to some extent citizens are pliable. That is not to say they are completely malleable. Citizens do not enter the political arena as blank slates simply waiting to be written on by interested political elites. Nevertheless, they are influenced by the environment around them, including sometimes being swayed by elite behavior.

Children are shaped by agents of socialization, including schools, peers, and current political events. Parents in particular have an effect on their children's political development. In their early 20s, young adults go through a period of attitude instability, yet remnants of their childhood socialization tend to stick with people throughout their lives. We can think of the predispositions developed early on—especially party identification—as anchors that keep citizens from being buffeted too much by elite storms of influence.

This understanding is consistent with the research regarding the power of the mass media. The media are not able to simply inject citizens with their messages, yet citizens are not fully constrained by their existing attitudes either. The subtle effects model best characterizes the influence of the media on citizens. That is, citizens are affected by the media through agenda setting, priming, and framing, but this influence often works in ways that make sense, for example, through credible sources or a thoughtful process of weighing what values are most important.

Now, it is important to recognize that the extent to which citizens are pliable differs across individuals. Research on attitude stability and change, for example, shows that politically unaware citizens tend to hold unstable attitudes. Citizens' predispositions also matter. Citizens who are aware rely more on their predispositions (such as party identification) to decide whether to accept messages from elites compared with those who are less aware. Attitude stability is also influenced by the different ways in which citizens process persuasive messages. That is, citizens who process political messages quickly and without much detailed thought (i.e., using a peripheral route) tend to end up with unstable attitudes. In contrast, citizens who process messages using a central route, which involves more careful consideration of persuasive messages, are more apt to have durable attitudes.

Elite democratic theorists would assess the empirical evidence and focus on the movement of citizens' attitudes. They would conclude that citizens do not have well-considered, meaningful opinions and thus should rightly take cues from more rational political elites. Participatory democratic theorists, on the other hand, would emphasize the structural factors that lead citizens to have unstable attitudes. For example, they might point to the media's preference for soft news as a barrier to citizens having informed, stable opinions. Moreover, participatory democratic theorists would argue that not all attitude change is bad. Citizens should learn from political events and experiences, perhaps changing their attitudes as a result. Citizens who never modify their opinions in response to new information are close-minded and short-sighted, not thoughtful and reasonable. Thus, participatory democratic theorists would argue that both "excessive instability and excessive stability of public opinion can be liabilities in a democracy."[1] What do you think? Does the pliability of the American public constitute excessive instability? Or do the levels of pliability indicate citizens are open to information from the environment, yet anchored by meaningful predispositions?

DO CITIZENS ORGANIZE THEIR POLITICAL THINKING?

According to Philip Converse, the answer is a resounding no. His research demonstrates quite persuasively that citizens do not organize their political thinking along a liberal-conservative dimension. Other scholars, however, counter that view by relying on a broader understanding of ideology. Further, if we move beyond ideology and look to other factors that might structure citizens' issue positions, we see there are a variety of forces that influence citizens, including attitudes toward social and political groups, values, personality, historical events, and occasionally self-interest. Thus, it seems that citizens organize their thinking a lot more than Converse's original research would lead us to believe.

Nevertheless, Converse's work raises serious questions about how well citizens and elites can communicate since they are not speaking the same ideological language. Moreover, how can citizens hold elites accountable if they are not on the same ideological page? Both participatory and elite democratic theorists worry about accountability, so neither is comforted by Converse's findings. Pluralists, however, point out it is not surprising that groups play such an important role in organizing citizens' political thinking. From the pluralist perspective, of course, groups are central to politics. Thus, Converse's early findings that citizens conceptualize politics in terms of groups and more recent scholars' findings that group attitudes have a strong influence on citizen thinking allow pluralists to resurrect a more optimistic view of citizen capabilities. But is the heavy reliance of citizens on group-based thinking good enough for participatory democratic theorists? Probably not, especially given that stereotypes and prejudice against groups play such a large role in shaping the attitudes of white Americans.

Do Citizens Endorse and Demonstrate Democratic Basics?

To answer this question, we really need to separate it into two separate propositions. First, do citizens *endorse* democratic basics? Yes, citizens endorse many fundamental democratic principles. In the abstract, citizens show high levels of support for civil liberties. People believe, for example, in freedom of speech and legal rights for citizens regardless of their political views. Similarly, many people approve of civil rights in principle. For instance, citizens are highly supportive of blacks and whites attending the same school.

But, do citizens *demonstrate* democratic basics? The answer to this question is often no. Citizens do not show much support for civil liberties in practice, especially during times of war and for groups they despise. Likewise, citizens are significantly less supportive of civil rights in practice than in principle. For example, when it comes to school busing to ensure school integration, the majority of white citizens are not on board. And although a majority of blacks support busing, it is a much smaller proportion than the number of blacks who favor school integration in theory. Overall then, most citizens endorse civil liberties and civil rights in the abstract, but many do not demonstrate support for the implementation of these principles.

A similar type of phenomenon occurs with regard to political interest and knowledge. Citizens express at least modest interest in politics and are quite attentive to political campaigns and the war in Iraq. Thus, citizens seem to realize the importance of politics in theory. Yet, many citizens lack the practical political knowledge needed to participate effectively in a democratic society.

Elite democratic theorists look at the limited levels of political knowledge and low levels of support for civil rights and liberties in practice and conclude that citizens are not capable of a central role in democratic governance. In the minds of these theorists, the lack of support for democratic basics justifies elites dominating decision-making processes. In contrast, participatory democratic theorists lament the democratic deficiencies of the American people, yet see hope in the high levels of support for democratic principles. Participatory democratic theorists argue that if barriers were removed and citizens got the chance to participate more actively, then they would learn how to put their support of democratic principles into practice.

WHAT IS THE RELATIONSHIP BETWEEN CITIZENS AND THEIR GOVERNMENT?

If we were to think about the relationship between citizens and their government in the same way we think about a marital relationship, we would characterize it as on the rocks and possibly heading for divorce court. Many citizens do not trust the government, and they do not have much respect for the people running the government, especially members of Congress as a whole. The one saving grace is that citizens support the basic institutions of government. This may be what keeps the relationship from completely falling apart.

Participatory democratic theorists argue that low levels of trust in government and citizens' disapproval of the people running government institutions stem from people not participating in the political process. If more people were involved, government would be more responsive and citizens would feel more trusting. This would lead to a virtuous circle of influence because more trust would lead to more participation, which would lead to more trust, and so forth. Unfortunately, the empirical evidence suggests more of a vicious circle, with less trust leading to lower approval of political leaders, which leads to less participation, which feeds back into less trust, and the pattern repeats. Elite democratic theorists are not overly concerned by this vicious circle. They expect citizens to be skeptical of their government. But, if trust were to become so low as to undermine the stability of the political system, elite democratic theorists would be concerned. To return to our marriage analogy, if citizens actually decided to divorce the government, it would most definitely get the attention of elite democratic theorists.

Are elected officials responsive to the public? The evidence on this point is most consistent with the views of elite democratic theorists. The research shows that citizens have a fairly minimal effect, especially in the realm of foreign policy in which experts and interest groups carry the day. When the public does have an impact, it is typically the voices of the most attentive and wealthiest individuals who are most influential. There is an exception to this general pattern of elite unresponsiveness to citizens: when issues—either foreign or domestic—are highly salient, policy is more likely to follow the wishes of the public.

Overall, elite democratic theorists are pleased by the limited role citizens play in shaping policy outcomes, and pluralists appreciate the prominence of interest groups in formulating foreign policy. Participatory democratic theorists, on the other hand, are troubled that the general public has so little influence on the policymaking process. Moreover, the evidence that elites try to manipulate public opinion is particularly disconcerting to participatory democratic theorists.

What Do We Make of Public Opinion in a Democracy?

At the end of the day, what do we make of public opinion? There is empirical evidence that provides support for elite democratic theorists, pluralists, and participatory democratic theorists. In our view, the evidence is most consistent with elite and pluralist views of politics. Additional public opinion research is needed to determine why citizens don't meet the ideals of participatory democratic theorists. A better understanding of the obstacles to citizen competence and engagement would be helpful. Participatory democratic theorists look to greater political participation as a route through which people can become better citizens—more knowledgeable, tolerant, and respectful of civil rights, for example. But does greater participation actually have that effect on citizens? More research on this would certainly help us evaluate whether participation is the panacea suggested by these theorists.

In closing, you are now an expert on normative democratic theories and the empirical research on public opinion. Which normative democratic theory is most appealing to you? How do you assess the empirical evidence? In short, what do *you* make of public opinion in a democracy?

Appendix
Studying Public Opinion Empirically

In this appendix, we describe a variety of methods for empirically studying public opinion. For each, we also point to specific studies using the method that we have profiled in chapters of this text. Turning to these examples will further illuminate the particular research methods as well as their strengths and weaknesses.

PUBLIC OPINION SURVEYS

Today, the most common method for assessing public opinion is via a **survey** or **public opinion poll**. Most of us are familiar with polls or, at the very least, the results of polls. The survey results that we frequently encounter (in the news media, on the Internet, etc.) are based on the responses provided by a **sample** of people to the same list of questions. Survey respondents are typically randomly selected to represent a specific **population** (students at the University of Kansas, residents of New Mexico, citizens of the United States, etc.). Survey respondents answer a series of questions, often by selecting one response from a list of options provided by the survey interviewer. For example, to gauge public sentiment on the issue of capital punishment, a survey might include the following question: "Are you in favor of the death penalty for a person convicted of murder?" Those being surveyed would respond by selecting "favor" or "oppose" or, in some cases, "no opinion" or "I don't know." These types of questions, with a limited set of response options, are called **closed-ended questions**.

Questions can be worded in a variety of ways, and the choice of which words to include can have important effects. People are more likely to favor the death penalty, for instance, when the question is worded as above compared with other wording options (see Box A-1). Conclusions as to whether the American public has become more tolerant toward politically unpopular groups, such as communists, have also depended on which survey questions were used to measure attitudes. We show how in chapter 8 when we contrast the measurement approach used by Samuel Stouffer versus that adopted by John Sullivan, James Piereson, and George Marcus. Chapter 5 describes how conclusions about the level of ideological thinking among the public were influenced by the wording of survey questions. Debates over the best ways to measure the public's levels of knowledge and political trust have also hinged, at least in part, on survey question wording (see, respectively, chapters 7 and 10).

BOX A-1 Question Wording Matters

In May 2004, the Gallup Organization polled 1,000 American adults about their opinions toward the death penalty. About one-half of the respondents were asked whether they support the death penalty for convicted murderers, whereas the other half were asked to indicate which they favor more, the death penalty or life in prison. Here is a summary of the responses to these two questions:

Option A: "Are you in favor of the death penalty for a person convicted of murder?"

Favor	71%
Oppose	26
No opinion	3

Option B: "If you could choose between the following two approaches, which do you think is the better penalty for murder: the death penalty or life imprisonment with absolutely no possibility of parole?"

Death penalty	50%
Life in prison	46
No opinion	4

We see that nearly three-fourths of the public support the death penalty when they are asked about it alone, but only one-half do when they have a choice of punishments for convicted murderers. This is a substantial difference, and very different conclusions would be drawn about public support for the death penalty depending on which result is referenced. So, when you come across poll results, it is important to know the question that was asked of the respondents rather than only the results. Similarly, if you ever report the results of an opinion poll, you also need to provide the question wording. Otherwise, it is very easy to mislead, whether intentionally or not, those who are reading your summary of the results.

Source: Data available at www.pollingreport.com/crime.htm.

Public opinion polls have a number of advantages. Randomly sampling people from a specified population allows us to draw conclusions about the opinions of the entire population. Why is that the case? Because a **random sample** is one in which chance alone determines which elements of the population make it into the sample. For example, let's say you want to draw a sample of 25 students from a class of 100 students, and you want the opinions of the 25 students to reflect the opinions of all 100 students. How would you draw that sample? You could have each student write his or her name on a slip of paper, collect the 100 names in a hat, give it a good shake to make sure the names are all mixed up, and then draw out 25 names. Consequently, it is chance alone that determines which 25 students end up in your sample. When respondents are selected in this manner, and *not* on the basis of their specific characteristics (such as race, political views, etc.), we can generalize results from the sample to the larger population from which the sample was drawn. The ability to draw such conclusions is known as **external validity**. For polls that include only respondents who *opt* to participate (such as the online polls that have become ubiquitous), the results are applicable *only* to those people who answered the survey questions. In other words, such polls cannot provide information about a larger population.

Another advantage of surveys is that answering a closed-ended question is not very time consuming, so each respondent can answer many questions without being overly burdened. Also, many individuals can be asked the same questions, again because the time commitment per person is not great. Providing survey respondents the same questions with the same response options facilitates the tallying of results (such as, 71 percent of Americans support the death penalty) and also allows for over-time comparison of public opinion, provided, of course, that the same questions are asked over time. For instance, as shown in Figure A-1, public support for the death penalty has fluctuated since 1991. In the early 1990s, three-quarters (or more) of the public favored the death penalty, but by 2000 only two-thirds did. After 2001, perhaps because of the 9/11 terrorist attacks, support for the death penalty increased somewhat (to 70–72 percent), before then decreasing.

We present many results from public opinion surveys throughout this text. A few examples are the trends in party identification that appear in chapter 1, levels of public knowledge of political figures and events in chapter 7, post-9/11 attitudes toward civil liberties in chapter 8, and Americans' foreign policy opinions and views toward the Iraq war in chapter 11. Further, examples of the public's views toward civil rights are presented throughout chapter 9. These include support for female, black, Mormon, and atheist presidential candidates; changes over time in support for gay rights; and opinions toward school busing and affirmative action.

Surveys also have many uses. News media organizations use polls to measure the public's political and social opinions, whereas candidates conduct polls to determine which voters support them and why. Public opinion scholars find surveys

Figure A-1   Public Opinion toward the Death Penalty, 1991–2004

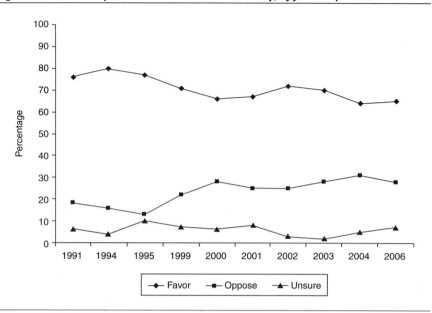

Source: Data available at www.pollingreport.com/crime.htm.

Note: These polling data are from the Gallup Organization and are based on national representative samples. The survey question was worded as follows: "Are you in favor of the death penalty for a person convicted of murder?"

useful for assessing the content of the public's opinions as well as describing how people's opinions differ. A survey containing the previously discussed capital punishment question might also ask respondents for their racial classification. Comparing responses to these two questions will allow a researcher to conclude whether support for the death penalty varies by the race of the respondent. It does. In a survey conducted in 2000, 76 percent of whites and 75 percent of Hispanics favored the death penalty, whereas only 52 percent of African Americans indicated that they support capital punishment for convicted murderers.[1]

A specific type of survey, called a **panel** or **longitudinal survey**, allows scholars to determine whether people's opinions have stayed the same over time. In a panel study, the *same* people are asked their opinions on the same issues more than once. As we profile in chapter 2, important conclusions about the stability of attitudes socialized during adolescence were drawn from a panel study conducted by Kent Jennings and Richard Niemi. Also, Philip Converse analyzed data from a panel study conducted between 1956 and 1960 to examine whether Americans' political attitudes changed during these years. We present Converse's findings in chapters 4 and 5.

EXPERIMENTS

Another common method used by public opinion researchers is experimentation. While many types of public opinion **experiments** have been conducted, in the most common form, the researcher manipulates a feature of the study and then assesses individual or group responses. Imagine you wanted to know whether a politician's gender influences public opinion toward the politician, for example. To assess this experimentally, you would provide information about a politician to some people. Everyone would read the same details, with one exception: half would be told the politician is male and the other half would be told the politician is female. After reading the descriptions, these individuals would be asked whether they approve of the politician. Many news media studies use experimental designs whereby some people read/watch/hear one type of news story while others are exposed to a different type. Both groups are then assessed along the same criteria to see whether the varying content of the news stories influenced their opinions or behaviors. Or, to examine experimentally the influence of popular culture on death penalty opinions, some people could be assigned to watch the movie *Dead Man Walking* while others would not watch it. Opinions about the death penalty would be gathered from both groups, with opinions measured after watching the movie for those who had been assigned to watch *Dead Man Walking*. This movie, originally released in 1995 and based on the actual experiences of Sister Helen Prejean, explores the relationship between a nun and a man who has been sentenced to death in the months before his execution.

Two features of experiments that distinguish them from other methods and that allow for powerful causal conclusions to be drawn from experimental studies are manipulation and random assignment.[2] **Manipulation** involves the researcher varying access to information, events, or whatever is the focus of the research among experimental participants. **Random assignment** refers to the process by which people are assigned to experimental groups, such as watching a movie or not watching it. Individuals are randomly assigned to these groups, perhaps by flipping a coin to establish one's assignment, in the expectation that individual characteristics that might be related to the study's goals are equally likely to appear in all groups. Since whites are more supportive of capital punishment than are African Americans, for instance, it is important that not all African Americans be assigned to the same group in an experiment designed to assess the impact of a movie on capital punishment opinions. With random assignment, chance alone, rather than one's personal characteristics, determines experimental group assignment.

With successful random assignment, a researcher can be very certain that any differences in opinions or behaviors found across experimental groups are due to their exposure to the original stimulus (i.e., due to the experimenter's manipulated feature). Experiments thus allow researchers to conclude that one factor causes another—a feature of research designs called **internal validity**. The ability to draw such causal conclusions is the primary advantage of experiments over other research methods. For example, one could conduct a survey and ask people if they have seen *Dead Man Walking* and whether they support the death penalty. If those who have seen the movie are less likely to favor capital punishment, it would be tempting to conclude that watching this movie influenced individuals' opinions. But you could not rule out the possibility that those who opposed capital punishment *before* the movie was released were more likely to attend the movie. So, one's political opinions might have influenced one's movie watching habits rather than the other way around. If, however, you expose some people to the movie and others do not see it (and have never seen it), and you still find that those watching the movie are less supportive of the death penalty, you can be much more certain that the movie influenced their opinions.

Experimental research is featured in many chapters of this text. We demonstrate, for example, how experiments were used to examine the mass media effects of agenda setting, priming, and framing in chapter 3. Many models of attitude change have used experiments to test their hypotheses, as we detail in chapter 4. Further, in chapter 8, we summarize a series of studies conducted by George Marcus, John Sullivan, Elizabeth Theiss-Morse, and Sandra Wood that examine the influence of contextual factors on political tolerance judgments.

While experiments possess internal validity, they have less external validity. That is, by using convenience samples (such as college students enrolled in introductory psychology courses) rather than random samples, experimenters cannot claim that their sample represents the broader population in terms of demographic characteristics or political opinions. One way to address this weakness is to include an experimental design within a nationally representative survey. This method, called a **survey-based experiment** or **split-half survey**, entails randomly assigning survey respondents to experimental conditions. Thus, this approach "combine[s] the causal power of the randomized experiment with the representativeness of the general population survey."[3] Examples of survey experiments appear in chapter 6 (Karen Stenner's work on the authoritarian personality and Dennis Chong and colleague's research on self-interest) and chapter 7 (Jeffery Mondak and Belinda Creel Davis's study of how encouraging "don't know" responses influences people's answers to political knowledge questions). The death penalty example presented in Box A-1 also used a split-half survey design.

INTERVIEWS

Asking people about their political views is also accomplished by **in-depth interviewing**. Unlike surveys in which hundreds (or thousands) of people are asked a series of closed-ended questions, interviewers ask their respondents much broader questions that are often **open-ended**. That is, interviewers typically do not provide their respondents with a list of response options and ask them to select one but rather allow the interviewee to answer a question however she wants. An interviewer interested in public opinion toward the death penalty might ask questions such as the following: "Do you support the death penalty?" or "What do you think about the death penalty?" The former obviously directs the respondent to consider her opinion on this issue, whereas the latter might prompt her to reveal her opinion or instead to assess the issue more broadly. Topics such as racial disparities in the application of the death penalty, the deterrent effect of the death penalty, or popular culture references to the death penalty might emerge in response to the second question. Note that neither question provides response options, allowing the respondent to answer the questions in multiple ways. Further, in answering either question, a respondent could explain why she holds the opinion that she does, or an interviewer might ask her directly to explain her opinion if she does not volunteer this information. Such "Why?" questions, since they are open-ended, do not appear frequently on opinion surveys, yet they can provide very useful information about an individual's opinion.

Because open-ended questions typically take longer to answer, the number of individuals participating in an interview is usually much smaller than the number who responds to a survey. When a researcher spends many hours with his interview subjects, as Robert Lane did when he interviewed fifteen men about their political ideology (see chapter 5), the volume of respondent comments can be enormous. The transcripts of Lane's questions and his interviewees' responses totaled 3,750 pages! With a smaller number of participants in a study, who have not been randomly selected to participate, it is inappropriate to draw conclusions that can apply to a larger population. Thus, studies using interview respondents are often criticized for not being representative of a larger population, a weakness that does not apply to surveys of randomly selected individuals.

In-depth interviewing can sometimes more accurately represent the opinions of those who are actually interviewed, however. By allowing respondents to decide what is most appropriate when answering questions, the responses are more likely to reflect their actual thinking (no matter how organized or how messy) on the topic. By forcing respondents to select a preconceived option, surveys might not measure real opinions on an issue. To take an obvious example, survey respondents confronted with the "favor" or "oppose" option to a death penalty question will typically select one of these options even if their real attitude is "I support the death penalty when I am certain that the person convicted of murder did, without a doubt, commit the murder, but often one cannot be certain, beyond a doubt, that the person actually did commit the murder and there are now many examples coming to light when incorrect decisions were made by juries." An in-depth interview is very likely to capture the nuances of this person's view, whereas a public opinion survey with closed-ended questions simply cannot. Such benefits of interviewing are detailed in chapter 5, in which we discuss how in-depth interviewing has been used to examine citizens' ideology. Chapter 11 also presents results from a study that used interviews. In this case, Susan Herbst interviewed staff members in the Illinois legislature to determine how they assess public opinion regarding policy issues that the legislators are debating.

Focus Groups

Focus groups resemble interviews in a number of ways, including that they both are used by researchers to examine how people think about political issues and that they use open-ended questions. The primary differences are that focus group research is conducted on multiple people at once and consists of a group discussion that is moderated and guided by a trained individual. Focus group researchers are often interested in learning how individuals construct political issues in their mind, how people communicate about a particular issue, and how an individual's discussion of a topic responds to communication from others in a group. In this way, focus groups are "a way to observe interaction among people that is important in understanding political behavior that is not possible to observe using more traditional empirical methodology."[4] To examine public opinion on capital punishment, for example, a focus group could be used to assess how people discuss this issue, including which features of it are especially compelling or relevant. A focus group could also be assembled to view news media stories or movies about capital punishment and then discuss their reactions, in order to determine how a group constructs meaning from such stories.

In this text, we examine Doris Graber's use of focus groups to better understand how people use the political knowledge they have accumulated (see chapter 7). Chapter 10 presents a description of how focus group participants assembled by John Hibbing and Elizabeth Theiss-Morse evaluated Congress.

Content Analysis

The final method that we profile here is content analysis. As its name indicates, **content analysis** is a technique used to analyze the content of communication. More specifically, it has been defined as "a research technique for the objective, systematic and quantitative description of the manifest content of communication."[5] Content analysis can be applied to any type of communication, such as a news media story, a speech by a politician, a popular television show, an Internet site, or a novel. The primary object of content analysis is to systematically summarize the content of the selected source or item. This is done by selecting specific criteria of the communication to analyze, then carefully coding a selection (stories, speeches, etc.) along these criteria. For example, a speech could be analyzed for the number of times a specific word is used, the number of times a topic is mentioned, and whether the speaker uses any examples from his or her personal life.

In terms of public opinion research, many topics can be examined using content analysis. If one wishes to know how the news media present public opinion on an issue, such as capital punishment, the content of news stories can be analyzed. Is public opinion represented as opinion survey results or as quotations from individual people? Or are elected officials asked what they think the public thinks about this issue? In studies that seek to determine whether news media coverage is related to public opinion, content analysis is also used to examine this coverage. As we discuss in chapter 3, this was the approach used by Maxwell McCombs and Donald Shaw to examine agenda setting by the news media and by Paul Kellstedt to study the effects of the news on racial policy opinions.

We also examine a different use of content analysis earlier in this text. Martin Gilens and Craig Hertzman examined newspaper coverage of the 1996 Telecommunications Act. Their goal was to determine if the coverage differed according to whether the owners of the newspapers also owned television stations. Since the Telecom Act proposed to loosen the federal rules regarding television ownership, Gilens and Hertzman expected that media ownership might be related to coverage of this act. As we describe in chapter 3, they were correct.

CONCLUSION

These five methods—surveys, experiments, interviews, focus groups, and content analysis—are the most common approaches used to assess public opinion. Surveys are the most frequently used approach, whereas focus groups and content analysis are the least common. As was mentioned in the prior paragraphs, each method has advantages and disadvantages, and, as has been better illustrated in the chapters in the book, each is well suited to addressing particular types of public opinion questions.

Lastly, most of these research methods require human participation. Conducting research on people involves a host of ethical considerations. Chief among these concerns, participants should voluntarily agree to participate, they should offer their informed consent before the study begins, and they should not suffer undue physical or psychological harm while participating in the study or after. For a detailed discussion of these and other ethical matters involved when using people as research subjects, refer to The Belmont Report (listed as a suggested reading below).

KEY CONCEPTS

closed-ended questions / 349
content analysis / 356
experiments / 353
external validity / 351
focus groups / 356
in-depth interviewing / 354
internal validity / 353
longitudinal survey / 352
manipulation / 353
open-ended questions / 354

panel / 352
population / 349
public opinion poll / 349
random assignment / 353
random sample / 351
sample / 349
survey / 349
survey-based experiment / 354
split-half survey / 354

SUGGESTED SOURCES FOR FURTHER READING

Aronson, Elliot, Phoebe C. Ellsworth, James Merrill Carlsmith, and Marti Hope Gonzales. *Methods of Research in Social Psychology*, 2nd ed. Boston: McGraw-Hill, 1989.
Krueger, Richard A., and Mary Anne Casey. *Focus Groups: A Practical Guide for Applied Research*, 3rd ed. Thousand Oaks, Calif.: Sage, 2004.
Rubin, Herbert J., and Irene S. Rubin. *Qualitative Interviewing: The Art of Hearing Data,* 2nd ed. Thousand Oaks, Calif.: Sage, 2004.
Weber, Robert Philip. *Basic Content Analysis*, 2nd ed. Thousand Oaks, Calif.: Sage, 1990.

Each of these books focuses on a specific research method: experiments, focus groups, interviewing, and content analysis, respectively. These authors provide a more detailed overview of each method than do the general research methods texts listed below.

Asher, Herbert. *Polling and the Public: What Every Citizen Should Know*, 7th ed. Washington, D.C.: CQ Press, 2007.
Traugott, Michael W., and Paul J. Lavrakas. *The Voter's Guide to Election Polls*, 3rd ed. Lanham, Md.: Rowman & Littlefield, 2004.

The most common method for measuring public opinion is the opinion poll or survey. Asher's book is an informative and readable introduction to all aspects of survey research, while Traugott and Lavrakas focus on interpreting poll results properly.

Carlson, James M., and Mark S. Hyde. *Doing Empirical Political Research*. Boston: Houghton Mifflin, 2003.
Johnson, Janet Buttolph, H. T. Reynolds, and Jason D. Mycoff. *Political Science Research Methods*, 6th ed. Washington, D.C.: CQ Press, 2007.

These two books provide useful overviews of the dominant research methods used in the study of politics, including the study of public opinion.

"Ethical Principles and Guidelines for the Protection of Human Subjects of Research" (also known as The Belmont Report): www.hhs.gov/ohrp/humansubjects/guidance/belmont.htm.

The Belmont Report was produced by the National Commission for the Protection of Human Subjects of Biomedical and Behavioral Research in 1979. This influential report established basic ethical principles that should be followed by scholars conducting research on human subjects. This report is a must-read for anyone who collects data from human subjects.

Gilens, Martin. "An Anatomy of Survey-Based Experiments." In *Navigating Public Opinion: Polls, Policy, and the Future of American Democracy*, ed. Jeff Manza, Fay Lomax Cook, and Benjamin I. Page. Oxford: Oxford University Press, 2002.

In this short essay, Gilens discusses the benefits of survey experiments. He also provides many examples of survey-based experiments that have been conducted to study public opinion.

Notes

CHAPTER 1

1. "President Bush Disappointed by Congress's Failure to Act on Comprehensive Immigration Reform," June 28, 2007, www.whitehouse.gov/news/releases/2007/06/20070628-7.html.
2. "Enforcing Our Borders and Our Laws," August 10, 2007, http://mcconnell.senate.gov/record.cfm?id=281072&start=1.
3. "This Week: The Iowa Debates; Democratic Candidates," *ABC News,* August 19, 2007.
4. William E. Hudson, *American Democracy in Peril: Seven Challenges to America's Future,* 2nd ed. (Chatham, N.J.: Chatham House, 1998), 2.
5. David Held, *Models of Democracy,* 2nd ed. (Stanford: Stanford University Press, 1996).
6. These and other features of classical democracy are outlined by Aristotle in *The Politics,* especially the beginning of Book VI, pages 359–367. Aristotle was not a proponent of this form of democracy, however, in part because he preferred that those with wealth have more control over decision making. Aristotle, *The Politics,* trans. T. A. Sinclair (Middlesex, England: Penguin Books, 1986).
7. Thucydides, *History of the Peloponnesian War, Books I and II,* trans. Charles Forster Smith (Cambridge, Mass.: Harvard University Press, 1991), 2.37.2, 2.40.3–5.
8. Jean-Jacques Rousseau, *The Social Contract,* trans. Maurice Cranston (London: Penguin Books, 1988), 69, 136.
9. Ibid., 72.
10. Held, *Models of Democracy,* 44.
11. Philip Green, "'Democracy' as a Contested Idea," in *Democracy: Key Concepts in Critical Theory,* ed. Philip Green (Atlantic Highlands, N.J.: Humanities Press, 1993); Held, *Models of Democracy.*
12. Held, *Models of Democracy*; C. B. Macpherson, *The Life and Times of Liberal Democracy* (Oxford: Oxford University Press, 1977).
13. Held, *Models of Democracy.*
14. Hudson, *American Democracy in Peril,* 5; see also Held, *Models of Democracy.*
15. Joseph A. Schumpeter, *Capitalism, Socialism and Democracy,* 5th ed. (London: Allen and Unwin, 1976), 269.
16. Robert A. Dahl, *Who Governs? Democracy and Power in an American City* (New Haven: Yale University Press, 1961); David B. Truman, *The Governmental Process* (New York: Knopf, 1951).
17. Bernard R. Berelson, Paul F. Lazarsfeld, and William N. McPhee, *Voting: A Study of Opinion Formation in a Presidential Campaign* (Chicago: University of Chicago Press, 1954), 307.
18. Berelson, Lazarsfeld, and McPhee, *Voting*; Macpherson, *Life and Times*; Jack L. Walker, "A Critique of the Elitist Theory of Democracy," *American Political Science Review* 60 (1966): 285–295.

19. Henry S. Kariel, "The Democratic Revisionists," in *Frontiers of Democratic Theory*, ed. Henry S. Kariel (New York: Random House, 1970); Macpherson, *Life and Times*.

20. Robert A. Dahl, *A Preface to Democratic Theory* (Chicago: University of Chicago Press, 1956), 63.

21. Held, *Models of Democracy*.

22. Alexander Hamilton, James Madison, and John Jay, *The Federalist Papers*, ed. Clinton Rossiter (New York: Penguin, 1961), 78.

23. Ibid., 79.

24. Ibid., 82.

25. Schumpeter, *Capitalism, Socialism and Democracy*, 283.

26. Dahl, *Who Governs*.

27. Peter Slevin and Robin Wright, "Pentagon Was Warned of Abuse Months Ago; U.S. Officials, Rights Groups Sought Changes," *Washington Post*, May 8, 2004, p. A12.

28. E. E. Schattschneider, *The Semi-Sovereign People: A Realist's View of Democracy in America* (New York: Holt, Rinehart and Winston, 1960), 35.

29. Dahl, *Who Governs*, 228. See also Dahl, *A Preface to Democratic Theory*.

30. Held, *Models of Democracy*.

31. Hudson, *American Democracy in Peril*.

32. Walker, "Critique of the Elitist Theory," 289. For a similar argument, see Peter Bachrach, *The Theory of Democratic Elitism: A Critique* (Washington, D.C.: University Press of America, 1980).

33. Walker, "Critique of the Elitist Theory," 288–289.

34. Macpherson, *Life and Times*; Carole Pateman, *Participation and Democratic Theory* (Cambridge: Cambridge University Press, 1970).

35. Macpherson, *Life and Times*, 94.

36. Held, *Models of Democracy*.

37. Benjamin Barber, *Strong Democracy: Participatory Politics for a New Age* (Berkeley: University of California Press, 1984), 272.

38. Walker, "Critique of the Elitist Theory."

39. Held, *Models of Democracy*; Macpherson, *Life and Times*.

40. Barber, *Strong Democracy*; Pateman, *Participation and Democratic Theory*.

41. Bachrach, *Theory of Democratic Elitism*, 101.

42. Bachrach, *Theory of Democratic Elitism*.

43. Macpherson, *Life and Times*; Pateman, *Participation and Democratic Theory*.

44. Hudson, *American Democracy in Peril*, 21.

45. Raymond E. Wolfinger and Jonathan Hoffman, "Registering and Voting with Motor Voter," *PS: Political Science and Politics* 34 (2001): 85–92.

46. John R. Hibbing and Elizabeth Theiss-Morse, *Stealth Democracy: Americans' Beliefs about How Government Should Work* (Cambridge: Cambridge University Press, 2002); Diana C. Mutz, *Hearing the Other Side: Deliberative versus Participatory Democracy* (Cambridge: Cambridge University Press), 2006.

47. V. O. Key Jr., *Public Opinion and American Democracy* (New York: Alfred A. Knopf, 1961), 14.

48. Alan D. Monroe, *Public Opinion in America* (New York: Dodd, Mead, 1975), 6.

49. Herbert Blumer, "Public Opinion and Public Opinion Polling," *American Sociological Review* 13 (1948): 544.

50. Ibid., 547.

51. Ibid., 546.

52. Philip E. Converse, "Changing Conceptions of Public Opinion in the Political Process," *Public Opinion Quarterly* 51 (1987): S12–S24. For a critique of the dominance of polls in the study of public opinion, see Taeku Lee, "The Sovereign Status of Survey Data," in *Navigating Public Opinion: Polls, Policy, and the Future of American Democracy*, ed. Jeff Manza, Fay Lomax Cook, and Benjamin I. Page (Oxford: Oxford University Press, 2002).

53. Robert Weissberg, *Polling, Policy, and Public Opinion: The Case against Heeding the "Voice of the People"* (New York: Palgrave Macmillan, 2002).

54. Ibid., 139.

55. Daniel Yankelovich, *Coming to Public Judgment: Making Democracy Work in a Complex World* (Syracuse, N.Y.: Syracuse University Press, 1991), 6.

56. Gordon W. Allport, "Attitudes," in *A Handbook of Social Psychology*, ed. Carl Murchison (Worcester, Mass.: Clark University Press, 1935), 804.

57. Alice H. Eagly and Shelly Chaiken, *The Psychology of Attitudes* (Fort Worth: Harcourt Brace Jovanovich College, 1993), 1.

58. Richard E. Petty and John T. Cacioppo, *Attitudes and Persuasion: Classic and Contemporary Approaches* (Dubuque, Iowa: William C. Brown, 1981), 7.

59. Jon A. Krosnick, "Government Policy and Citizen Passion: A Study of Issue Publics in Contemporary America," *Political Behavior* 12 (1990): 59–92.

60. James H. Liu and Bibb Latané, "The Catastrophic Link between the Importance and Extremity of Political Attitudes," *Political Behavior* 20 (1998): 105–126

61. Martin Gilens, *Why Americans Hate Welfare* (Chicago: University of Chicago Press, 1999).

62. Milton Rokeach, *The Nature of Human Values* (New York: Free Press, 1973), 5.

63. Donald R. Kinder and David O. Sears, "Public Opinion and Political Action," in *Handbook of Social Psychology*, vol. II, 3rd ed., ed. Gardner Lindzey and Elliot Aronson (New York: Random House, 1985), 674.

64. Kinder and Sears, "Public Opinion and Political Action."

65. Rokeach, *The Nature of Human Values*; Stanley Feldman, "Structure and Consistency in Public Opinion: The Role of Core Beliefs and Values," *American Journal of Political Science* 32 (1988): 416–440.

66. Donald R. Kinder, "Pale Democracy: Opinion and Action in Postwar America," in *The Evolution of Political Knowledge: Theory and Inquiry in American Politics*, ed. Edward D. Mansfield and Richard Sisson (Columbus: Ohio State University Press, 2004).

67. Along with behavior, cognitions and affect are considered to be the three components of an attitude. Behavior "encompasses people's actions with respect to the attitude object" (Eagly and Chaiken, *Psychology of Attitudes*, 10). Examples include discriminating against a member of a group for which one holds negative stereotypes or signing a petition in support of a policy that one views favorably. For a helpful overview of this tripartite view of attitudes and limitations to viewing attitudes as consisting of three separate components, refer to chapter 1 of Eagly and Chaiken, *Psychology of Attitudes*.

68. Angus Campbell et al., *The American Voter* (New York: Wiley, 1960), 121.

69. American National Election Studies, conducted at the Center for Political Studies, University of Michigan.

70. General Election Exit Polls, conducted by Voter News Service.

71. Philip E. Converse, "The Nature of Belief Systems in Mass Publics," in *Ideology and Discontent*, ed. David E. Apter (New York: Free Press, 1964); Philip E. Converse and Gregory B. Markus "Plus ça change . . . : The New CPS Election Study Panel," *American Political Science Review* 73 (1979): 32–49; Donald P. Green, Bradley Palmquist, and Eric Schickler, *Partisan Hearts and Minds: Political Parties and the Social Identities of Voters* (New Haven: Yale University Press, 2002).

72. Macpherson, *Life and Times*, 4.

CHAPTER 2

1. Richard M. Merelman, "Revitalizing Political Socialization," in *Political Psychology*, ed. Margaret G. Hermann (San Francisco: Jossey-Bass, 1986), 279.

2. Donald R. Kinder, "Politics and the Life Cycle," *Science* 312 (2006): 1907.

3. Herbert H. Hyman, *Political Socialization* (Glencoe, Ill.: Free Press, 1959), 69.

4. Virginia Sapiro, "Not Your Parents' Political Socialization: Introduction for a New Generation," *Annual Review of Political Science* 7 (2004): 2.

5. David Easton and Jack Dennis, *Children in the Political System: Origins of Political Legitimacy* (New York: McGraw-Hill, 1969).

6. Merelman, "Revitalizing Political Socialization," 296.

7. Fred I. Greenstein, *Children and Politics*, rev. ed. (New Haven: Yale University Press, 1969), 1.

8. Robert D. Hess and Judith V. Torney, *The Development of Political Attitudes in Children* (New York: Anchor Books, 1968).

9. Fred I. Greenstein, "The Benevolent Leader: Children's Images of Political Authority," *American Political Science Review* 54 (1960): 934–943.

10. Robert D. Hess and David Easton, "The Child's Changing Image of the President," *Public Opinion Quarterly* 24 (1960): 632–644.

11. Greenstein, "Benevolent Leader."

12. Roberta S. Sigel, "Image of a President: Some Insights into the Political Views of School Children," *American Political Science Review* 62 (1968): 216–226.

13. Ibid., 218.

14. Ibid., 220, 219.

15. Greenstein, "Benevolent Leader"; Hess and Easton, "Child's Changing Image"; Dean Jaros and Kenneth L. Kolson, "The Multifarious Leader: Political Socialization of Amish, 'Yanks,' Blacks," in *The Politics of Future Citizens,* ed. Richard G. Niemi (San Francisco: Jossey-Bass, 1974); Sarah F. Liebschutz and Richard G. Niemi, "Political Attitudes among Black Children," in *The Politics of Future Citizens,* ed. Richard G. Niemi (San Francisco: Jossey-Bass, 1974).

16. Hess and Easton, "Child's Changing Image," 640.

17. Dean Jaros, Herbert Hirsch, and Frederic J. Fleron Jr., "The Malevolent Leader: Political Socialization in an American Sub-Culture," *American Political Science Review* 62 (1968): 564–575.

18. Hess and Easton, "Child's Changing Image."

19. Fred I. Greenstein, "The Benevolent Leader Revisited: Children's Images of Political Leaders in Three Democracies," *American Political Science Review* 69 (1975): 1371–1398.

20. Jaros and Kolson, "The Multifarious Leader"; Liebschutz and Niemi, "Political Attitudes."

21. Paul R. Abramson, "Political Efficacy and Political Trust Among Black Schoolchildren: Two Explanations," *Journal of Politics* 34 (1972): 1243–1275.

22. Kim L. Fridkin, Patrick J. Kenney, and Jack Crittenden, "On the Margins of Democratic Life: The Impact of Race and Ethnicity on the Political Engagement of Young People," *American Politics Research* 34 (2006): 605–626.

23. Hess and Easton, "Child's Changing Image"; Hess and Torney, *Development of Political Attitudes.*

24. Greenstein, "Benevolent Leader," 941.

25. Jaros, Hirsch, and Fleron, "The Malevolent Leader," 565.

26. Abramson, "Political Efficacy and Political Trust"; Fridkin, Kenney, and Crittenden, "On the Margins."

27. Hess and Torney, *Development of Political Attitudes,* 126.

28. Dean Jaros and Bradley C. Canon, "Transmitting Basic Political Values: The Role of the Educational System," *The School Review* 77 (1969): 94–107.

29. Richard G. Niemi and Jane Junn, *Civic Education: What Makes Students Learn* (New Haven: Yale University Press, 1998).

30. Roberta Sigel and Marilyn Brookes, "Becoming Critical about Politics," in *The Politics of Future Citizens,* ed. Richard G. Niemi (San Francisco: Jossey-Bass, 1974).

31. Ibid., 108.

32. Sigel and Brookes, "Becoming Critical about Politics."

33. Greenstein, "Benevolent Leader Revisited."

34. Amy Carter and Ryan L. Teten, "Assessing Changing Views of the President: Revisiting Greenstein's *Children and Politics,*" *Presidential Studies Quarterly* 32 (2002): 453–462.

35. Greenstein, "Benevolent Leader."

36. M. Kent Jennings and Richard G. Niemi, "The Transmission of Political Values from Parent to Child," *American Political Science Review* 62 (1968): 169.

37. Jennings and Niemi, "Transmission of Political Values."

38. Ibid., 173.

39. Ibid., 183.

40. John R. Alford, Carolyn L. Funk, and John R. Hibbing, "Are Political Orientations Genetically Transmitted?" *American Political Science Review* 99 (2005): 153–167.

41. Ibid., 153.
42. Paul R. Abramson, "Generational Change and the Decline of Party Identification in America: 1952–1974," *American Political Science Review* 70 (1976): 469–478.
43. David O. Sears and Nicholas A. Valentino, "Politics Matters: Political Events as Catalysts for Preadult Socialization," *American Political Science Review* 91 (1997): 45–65.
44. Ibid., 50.
45. Nicholas A. Valentino and David O. Sears, "Event-Driven Political Communication and the Preadult Socialization of Partisanship," *Political Behavior* 20 (1998): 127–154.
46. Ibid., 145.
47. Sears and Valentino, "Politics Matters," 58.
48. M. Kent Jennings and Gregory B. Markus, "Partisan Orientations over the Long Haul: Results from the Three-Wave Political Socialization Panel Study," *American Political Science Review* 78 (1984): 1000–1018.
49. Ibid., 1016.
50. M. Kent Jennings and Laura Stoker, *The Persistence of the Past: The Class of 1965 Turns Fifty* (Berkeley: University of California, Institute of Governmental Studies, 2001), http://repositories.cdlib.org/igs/WP2001-16.
51. Jennings and Markus, "Partisan Orientations."
52. M. Kent Jennings, Laura Stoker, and Jake Bowers, *Politics across Generations: Family Transmission Reexamined* (Berkeley: University of California, Institute of Governmental Studies, 2001), http://repositories.cdlib.org/igs/WP2001-15.
53. Jennings and Niemi, "Transmission of Political Values."
54. Ibid.
55. Jennings, Stoker, and Bowers, *Politics across Generations*; Richard G. Niemi and M. Kent Jennings, "Issues and Inheritance in the Formation of Party Identification," *American Journal of Political Science* 35 (1991): 970–988.
56. Niemi and Jennings, "Issues and Inheritance."
57. Paul Allen Beck and M. Kent Jennings, "Family Traditions, Political Periods, and the Development of Partisan Orientations," *Journal of Politics* 53 (1991): 742–763; Jennings and Markus, "Partisan Orientations."
58. Jennings and Markus, "Partisan Orientations," 1000.
59. Abramson, "Generational Change."
60. David O. Sears, "Whither Political Socialization Research? The Question of Persistence," in *Political Socialization, Citizenship Education, and Democracy*, ed. Orit Ichilov (New York: Teachers College Press, 1990), 75.
61. Diana Owen, "Service Learning and Political Socialization," *PS: Political Science and Politics* 33 (2000): 639.
62. Sapiro, "Not Your Parents' Political Socialization."
63. Paul Allen Beck, "Opinion and Action in Postwar America: Additional Perspectives," in *The Evolution of Political Knowledge: Theory and Inquiry in American Politics*, ed. Edward D. Mansfield and Richard Sisson (Columbus: Ohio State University Press, 2004), 151.

CHAPTER 3

1. *Gratz et al. v. Bollinger et al.*, 539 U.S. 244 (2003); *Grutter v. Bollinger et al.*, 539 U.S. 306 (2003).
2. *Regents of the University of California v. Bakke* 438 U.S. 265 (1978); in *Bakke*, the Court ruled that race could be used as a factor in admissions decisions but that a set number of seats could not be reserved for underrepresented minorities.
3. *Bush v. Gore*, 531 U.S. 98 (2000).
4. Terri L. Towner, Rosalee A. Clawson, and Eric N. Waltenburg, "Media Coverage of the University of Michigan Affirmative Action Decisions," *Judicature* 90 (2006): 120–128.
5. Roland E. Wolseley, *The Black Press, U.S.A.,* 2nd ed. (Ames: Iowa State University Press, 1990).
6. Towner, Clawson, and Waltenburg, "Media Coverage."
7. John D. Richardson and Karen M. Lancendorfer, "Framing Affirmative Action: The Influence of Race on Newspaper Editorial Responses to the University of Michigan Cases,"

Harvard International Journal of Press/Politics 9 (2004): 74–94; William A. Gamson, *Talking Politics* (Cambridge: Cambridge University Press, 1992).

8. This section draws heavily from Denis McQuail, *Media Accountability and Freedom of Publication* (Oxford: Oxford University Press, 2003), and David Croteau and William Hoynes, *By Invitation Only: How the Media Limit Political Debate* (Monroe, Maine: Common Courage, 1994); also see James Curran, "What Democracy Requires of the Media," in *The Press,* ed. Geneva Overholser and Kathleen Hall Jamieson (Oxford: Oxford University Press, 2005), chap. 7.

9. W. Lance Bennett and William Serrin, "The Watchdog Role," in *The Press,* ed. Geneva Overholser and Kathleen Hall Jamieson (Oxford: Oxford University Press, 2005), chap. 10.

10. For a discussion of the term "fourth estate," see McQuail, *Media Accountability,* 52.

11. Robert G. Picard, "Money, Media, and the Public Interest," in *The Press,* ed. Geneva Overholser and Kathleen Hall Jamieson (Oxford: Oxford University Press, 2005), chap. 20; Michael Schudson and Susan E. Tifft, "American Journalism in Historical Perspective," in *The Press,* ed. Geneva Overholser and Kathleen Hall Jamieson (Oxford: Oxford University Press, 2005), chap. 2.

12. James T. Hamilton, *All the News That's Fit to Sell: How the Market Transforms Information Into News* (Princeton: Princeton University Press, 2004), chap. 4.

13. For a fascinating history of these events, see Ken Auletta, *Three Blind Mice: How the TV Networks Lost Their Way* (New York: Random House, 1991).

14. Thomas E. Patterson, *Doing Well and Doing Good: How Soft News and Critical Journalism Are Shrinking the News Audience and Weakening Democracy—And What News Outlets Can Do about It* (Cambridge, Mass.: Harvard University, Joan Shorenstein Center on the Press, Politics and Public Policy, John F. Kennedy School of Government, 2000), www.ksg.harvard.edu/presspol/research_publications/reports/softnews.pdf.

15. Ibid., 3.

16. Ibid., 3.

17. Ibid., 4.

18. Ibid., 3.

19. Ibid., 7.

20. Bill Carter, "Is It the Woman Thing, or Is It Katie Couric?" *New York Times,* May 14, 2007, C1.

21. *Paris Hilton Becomes a National News Story* (Pew Research Center for the People and the Press, Washington, D.C., June 14, 2007), http://people-press.org/reports/display.php3?ReportID=338.

22. Phil Rosenthal, "Scrubbed, by the Ivory People," *Chicago Sun-Times,* August 20, 2001, 34.

23. For other examples of Proctor and Gamble influence, see Ben H. Bagdikian, *The New Media Monopoly* (Boston: Beacon Press, 2004), 236–240.

24. Bagdikian, *The New Media Monopoly.*

25. Ibid., 3.

26. "Who Owns What," *Columbia Journalism Review* (July 10, 2006), www.cjr.org/resources/?c=cbs.

27. See News Corporation's Web site for information on their media holdings: www.newscorp.com/.

28. Croteau and Hoynes, *By Invitation Only,* 23.

29. Martin Gilens and Craig Hertzman, "Corporate Ownership and News Bias: Newspaper Coverage of the 1996 Telecommunications Act," *Journal of Politics* 62 (2000): 369–386.

30. Also see Hamilton, *All the News,* chap. 5. Hamilton finds that television stations held by companies owning multiple stations provide significantly less hard news coverage on their local broadcasts than those stations that are not part of concentrated media companies.

31. Gilens and Hertzman, "Corporate Ownership," 383.

32. See GE's Web site for information on their products: www.ge.com/products_services/index.html.

33. "Random House: Number One in the World of Book Publishing," www.bertelsmann.com/bertelsmann_corp/wms41/bm/index.php?ci=24&language=2.

34. See Bertelsmann's Web site for information on their corporate divisions: www.bertelsmann. com/bertelsmann_corp/wms41/bm/index.php?ci=99&language=2.

35. McQuail, *Media Accountability,* 80.

36. See Hamilton, *All the News,* 148. Hamilton examines whether television stations promote the stars and programs of the networks with which they are affiliated; he finds, for example, that ABC affiliates devoted significantly more attention to *Who Wants to Be a Millionaire?* and Regis Philbin (the game show's original host) on their local newscasts than did the CBS, NBC, or Fox affiliates. *Who Wants to Be a Millionaire?,* of course, is a popular ABC program.

37. See the CBS News Web site: http://cbsnews.com.

38. The information in this paragraph is drawn from "Who Owns What," *Columbia Journalism Review* (June 27, 2006), www.cjr.org/resources/?c=disney.

39. "Company Overview," http://corporate.disney.go.com/corporate/overview.html.

40. See the PBS and NPR Web sites for more detailed information: www.npr.org and www.pbs. org.

41. *Public Knowledge of Current Affairs Little Changed by News and Information Revolutions* (Pew Research Center for the People and the Press, Washington, D.C., April 15, 2007), http://people-press.org/reports/display.php3?ReportID=319.

42. Steven Kull, Clay Ramsay, and Evan Lewis, "Misperceptions, the Media, and the Iraq War," *Political Science Quarterly* 118 (2003–2004): 569–598.

43. The full text of this question was not provided in the Kull, Ramsay, and Lewis "Misperceptions" article but was available at http://65.109.167.118/pipa/pdf/oct03/IraqMedia_Oct03_quaire.pdf.

44. See Croteau and Hoynes, *By Invitation Only,* chap. 5, and Ralph Engelman, *Public Radio and Television in America: A Political History* (Thousand Oaks, Calif.: Sage Publications, 1996), chap. 10.

45. Wolseley, *The Black Press, U.S.A.,* chap. 5.

46. Christopher P. Campbell, *Race, Myth and the News* (Thousand Oaks, Calif.: Sage Publications, 1995); Ronald N. Jacobs, *Race, Media, and the Crisis of Civil Society: From Watts to Rodney King* (Cambridge: Cambridge University Press, 2000); Pamela Newkirk, "The Minority Press: Pleading Our Own Cause," in *The Press,* ed. Geneva Overholser and Kathleen Hall Jamieson (Oxford: Oxford University Press, 2005), chap. 5; Towner, Clawson, and Waltenburg, "Media Coverage."

47. Rosalee A. Clawson, Harry C. "Neil" Strine IV, and Eric N. Waltenburg, "Framing Supreme Court Decisions: The Mainstream versus the Black Press," *Journal of Black Studies* 33 (2003): 784–800; Michael Huspek, "Black Press, White Press, and Their Opposition: The Case of the Police Killing of Tyisha Miller," *Social Justice* 31 (2004): 217–241.

48. Jacobs, *Race, Media,* 52.

49. For an analysis of Latino media, see América Rodriguez, *Making Latino News: Race, Language, Class* (Thousand Oaks, Calif.: Sage Publications, 1999).

50. McQuail, *Media Accountability,* 58.

51. John Carey and Nancy Hicks Maynard, "The Future of News: The Future of Journalism," in *The Press,* ed. Geneva Overholser and Kathleen Hall Jamieson (Oxford: Oxford University Press, 2005), 424; Curran, "What Democracy Requires," 127.

52. Hamilton, *All the News,* chap. 7.

53. Schudson and Tifft, "American Journalism," 40–41.

54. Robert M. Entman, "The Nature and Sources of News," in *The Press,* ed. Geneva Overholser and Kathleen Hall Jamieson (Oxford: Oxford University Press, 2005), chap. 3; Herbert J. Gans, *Deciding What's News,* 25th anniversary ed. (Evanston, Ill.: Northwestern University Press, 2004), 175–176.

55. Gans, *Deciding What's News*; Leon Sigal, *Reporters and Officials* (New York: D.C. Heath, 1973); Entman, "The Nature and Sources."

56. W. Lance Bennett, "Toward a Theory of Press-State Relations in the United States," *Political Communication* 40 (1990): 103–125.

57. Timothy E. Cook, *Governing with the News,* 2nd ed. (Chicago: University of Chicago Press, 2005), 93.

58. Ibid., 20.
59. See Hamilton, *All the News,* chap. 2.
60. Timothy E. Cook, "Domesticating a Crisis: Washington Newsbeats and Network News after the Iraqi Invasion of Kuwait," in *Taken by Storm,* ed. W. Lance Bennett and David L. Paletz (Chicago: University of Chicago Press, 1994), 105–130.
61. Gaye Tuchman, *Making News* (New York: Free Press, 1978).
62. Jonathan S. Morris and Rosalee A. Clawson, "Media Coverage of Congress in the 1990s: Scandals, Personalities, and the Prevalence of Policy and Process," *Political Communication* 22 (2005): 297–313.
63. Michael Robinson and Margaret Sheehan, *Over the Wire and on TV: CBS and UPI in Campaign '80* (New York: Russell Sage Foundation, 1980).
64. Thomas E. Patterson, *Out of Order* (New York: Alfred A. Knopf, 1993).
65. Ibid., 69.
66. Joseph N. Cappella and Kathleen Hall Jamieson, *Spiral of Cynicism* (New York: Oxford University Press, 1997).
67. Ibid., 33–34.
68. Based on 2004 data from the American National Election Studies (www.electionstudies.org), *The ANES Guide to Public Opinion and Electoral Behavior* (Ann Arbor: University of Michigan, Center for Political Studies, producer and distributor).
69. Gans, *Deciding What's News,* 285.
70. Daniel Hallin, *The Uncensored War* (Cambridge: Cambridge University Press, 1986); John R. Zaller, *The Nature and Origins of Mass Opinion* (Cambridge: Cambridge University Press, 1992).
71. Howard Kurtz, "The Post on WMDs: An Inside Story," *Washington Post,* August 12, 2004, A1; "The Times and Iraq," *New York Times,* May 26, 2004, A10.
72. Patrick O'Heffernan, "A Mutual Exploitation Model of Media Influence in U.S. Foreign Policy," in *Taken by Storm,* ed. W. Lance Bennett and David L. Paletz (Chicago: University of Chicago Press, 1994), 231–249.
73. Bennett and Serrin, "The Watchdog Role."
74. Dana Priest and Anne Hull, "Soldiers Face Neglect, Frustration at Army's Top Medical Facility," *Washington Post,* February 18, 2007, A1.
75. Entman, "The Nature and Sources."
76. Clawson, Strine, and Waltenburg, "Framing Supreme Court Decisions"; Huspek, "Black Press, White Press."
77. Entman, "The Nature and Sources," 62.
78. Denis McQuail, *Mass Communication Theory: An Introduction* (Beverly Hills: Sage Publications, 1984), chap. 7.
79. Paul F. Lazarsfeld, Bernard R. Berelson, and Hazel Gaudet, *The People's Choice: How the Voter Makes Up His Mind in a Presidential Campaign,* 2nd ed. (New York: Columbia University Press, 1948); also see Bernard R. Berelson, Paul F. Lazarsfeld, and William N. McPhee, *Voting: A Study of Opinion Formation in a Presidential Campaign* (Chicago: University of Chicago Press, 1954).
80. For a discussion of selective exposure, selective perception, and selective retention, see Joseph T. Klapper, *The Effects of Mass Communication* (New York: Free Press, 1960), chap. 2.
81. Lazarsfeld, Berelson, and Gaudet, *The People's Choice,* 151.
82. Ibid., 151.
83. Maxwell E. McCombs and Donald L. Shaw, "The Agenda-Setting Function of Mass Media," *Public Opinion Quarterly* 36 (1972): 176–187.
84. Ibid., 177; emphasis in original.
85. Bernard C. Cohen, *The Press and Foreign Policy* (Princeton: Princeton University Press, 1963), 13; emphasis in original.
86. For a discussion of agenda-setting research conducted in other countries, see David Weaver, Maxwell McCombs, and Donald L. Shaw, "Agenda-Setting Research: Issues, Attributes, and Influences," in *Handbook of Political Communication Research,* ed. Lynda Lee Kaid (Mahwah, N.J.: Erlbaum, 2004), 257–282.

87. Shanto Iyengar, Mark D. Peters, and Donald R. Kinder, "Experimental Demonstrations of the 'Not-So-Minimal' Consequences of Television News Programs," *American Political Science Review* 76 (1982): 848–858.

88. Ibid., 851.

89. Iyengar, Peters, and Kinder, "Experimental Demonstrations."

90. Thomas E. Nelson, Rosalee A. Clawson, and Zoe M. Oxley, "Media Framing of a Civil Liberties Conflict and Its Effect on Tolerance," *American Political Science Review* 91 (1997): 567.

91. Adam J. Berinsky and Donald R. Kinder, "Making Sense of Issues through Media Frames: Understanding the Kosovo Crisis," *Journal of Politics* 68 (2006): 640–656.

92. Shanto Iyengar, "Framing Responsibility for Political Issues: The Case of Poverty," *Political Behavior* 12 (1990): 19–40.

93. Ibid., 25.

94. Ibid., 25.

95. Nelson, Clawson, and Oxley, "Media Framing."

96. Ibid., 571.

97. Ibid., 571.

98. Ibid., 571.

99. Russell H. Fazio, "A Practical Guide to the Use of Response Latency in Social Psychological Research," in *Review of Personality and Social Psychology, vol.* 11: *Research Methods in Personality and Social Psychology,* ed. Clyde Hendrick and Margaret S. Clark (Newbury Park, Calif.: Sage Publications, 1990).

100. Nelson, Clawson, and Oxley, "Media Framing," 579.

101. For additional evidence on this point, see Thomas E. Nelson and Zoe M. Oxley, "Issue Framing Effects on Belief Importance and Opinion," *Journal of Politics* 61 (1999): 1040–1067, and James N. Druckman, "On the Limits of Framing Effects: Who Can Frame?" *Journal of Politics* 63 (2001): 1041–1066.

102. Others scholars have also provided a more redeeming view of the citizen by showing that accessibility does not lead to priming. Instead, citizens who are politically knowledgeable and who trust the media infer that issues covered by the media are important and thus rely on those issues when evaluating politicians. See Joanne M. Miller and Jon A. Krosnick, "News Media Impact on the Ingredients of Presidential Evaluations: Politically Knowledgeable Citizens Are Guided by a Trusted Source," *American Journal of Political Science* 44 (2000): 301–315.

103. Paul M. Kellstedt, *The Mass Media and the Dynamics of American Racial Attitudes* (Cambridge: Cambridge University Press, 2003).

104. Druckman, "On the Limits."

CHAPTER 4

1. Robin Toner, "The 2000 Campaign: The Abortion Issue; Shifting Views over Abortion Fog Gore Race," *New York Times,* February 25, 2000, sec. A, late edition.

2. Ibid.; Walter V. Robinson and Ann Scales, "Campaign 2000; Gore Record Scrutinized for Veracity," *Boston Globe,* January 28, 2000, sec. A, third edition.

3. Al Gore, The First Gore-Bush Presidential Debate, Boston, October 3, 2000, www.debates. org/pages/trans2000a.html (accessed October 5, 2006).

4. Richard Norton Smith, "George Bush: The Life of a Lone State Yankee—Book Reviews," *Washington Monthly,* March 1998, http://findarticles.com/p/articles/mi_m1316/is_n3_v30/ai_20388962/pg_1 (accessed October 5, 2006).

5. Richard Brookhiser, "A Visit with George Bush," *The Atlantic Monthly,* August 1992, www.theatlantic.com/issues/92aug/brookhiser.htm (accessed October 5, 2006).

6. George Bush, Acceptance Speech, Republican National Convention, New Orleans, August 18, 1988, www.presidency.ucsb.edu/shownomination.php?convid=4 (accessed October 5, 2006).

7. Toner, "The 2000 Campaign."

8. Brookhiser, "Visit with George Bush."

9. For more details regarding the ANES series, visit www.electionstudies.org.

10. Philip E. Converse, "The Nature of Belief Systems in Mass Publics," in *Ideology and Discontent,* ed. David E. Apter (New York: Free Press, 1964).

11. Ibid., 240.

12. Ibid., 241.

13. Philip E. Converse, "Attitudes and Non-Attitudes: Continuation of a Dialogue," in *The Quantitative Analysis of Social Problems,* ed. Edward R. Tufte (Reading, Mass.: Addison-Wesley, 1970).

14. Converse, "Nature of Belief Systems," 245.

15. Converse, "Nature of Belief Systems."

16. Benjamin I. Page and Robert Y. Shapiro, *The Rational Public: Fifty Years of Trends in Americans' Policy Preferences* (Chicago: University of Chicago Press, 1992), 1. For a similar conclusion, see James A. Stimson, *Tides of Consent: How Public Opinion Shapes American Politics* (Cambridge: Cambridge University Press, 2004).

17. Ibid., 56.

18. Ibid., 16.

19. Philip E. Converse, "Popular Representation and the Distribution of Information," in *Information and Democratic Processes,* ed. John A. Ferejohn and James H. Kuklinski (Urbana, Ill.: University of Illinois Press, 1990), 382.

20. A wonderful resource for understanding the vast psychology literature on attitudes is Alice H. Eagly and Shelly Chaiken's *The Psychology of Attitudes* (Fort Worth: Harcourt Brace Jovanovich, 1993).

21. Gregory M. Herek, "The Instrumentality of Attitudes: Toward a Neofunctional Theory," *Journal of Social Issues* 42 (1986): 99.

22. Daniel Katz, "The Functional Approach to the Study of Attitudes," *Public Opinion Quarterly* 24 (1960): 163–204.

23. Ibid., 172.

24. M. Brewster Smith, Jerome S. Bruner, and Robert W. White, *Opinions and Personality* (New York: Wiley, 1956).

25. Mark Snyder and Kenneth G. DeBono, "A Functional Approach to Attitudes and Persuasion," in *Social Influence: The Ontario Symposium,* vol. 5, ed. Mark P. Zanna, James M. Olson, and C. Peter Herman (Hillsdale, N.J.: Erlbaum, 1987), 109.

26. Katz, "Functional Approach," 188.

27. Snyder and DeBono, "Functional Approach to Attitudes." For a similar argument, see Herek, "Instrumentality of Attitudes."

28. Carl I. Hovland, Irving L. Janis, and Harold Kelley, *Communication and Persuasion: Psychological Studies of Opinion Change* (New Haven: Yale University Press, 1953).

29. Jon A. Krosnick, Andrew L. Betz, Lee J. Jussim, and Ann R. Lynn, "Subliminal Conditioning of Attitudes," *Personality and Social Psychology Bulletin* 18 (1992): 152–162.

30. Richard E. Petty and John T. Cacioppo, *Attitudes and Persuasion: Classic and Contemporary Approaches* (Dubuque, Iowa: William C. Brown, 1981); Richard E. Petty and John T. Cacioppo, *Communication and Persuasion* (New York: Springer-Verlag, 1986).

31. Richard E. Petty, John T. Cacioppo, and Rachel Goldman, "Personal Involvement as a Determinant of Argument-Based Persuasion," *Journal of Personality and Social Psychology* 41 (1981): 847–855.

32. Petty and Cacioppo, *Attitudes and Persuasion,* 225.

33. Eagly and Chaiken, *Psychology of Attitudes.*

34. Petty and Cacioppo, *Attitudes and Persuasion,* 256.

35. John R. Zaller, *The Nature and Origins of Mass Opinion* (Cambridge: Cambridge University Press, 1992).

36. See, for example, William J. McGuire, "The Nature of Attitudes and Attitude Change," in *The Handbook of Social Psychology,* 2nd ed., vol. 3, ed. Gardner Lindzey and Elliot Aronson (Reading, Mass.: Addison-Wesley, 1969).

37. Zaller, *Nature and Origins,* 1.

38. Ibid., 19.
39. Ibid., 44–45.
40. Dennis Chong, "Free Speech and Multiculturalism In and Out of the Academy," *Political Psychology* 27 (2006): 29–54.
41. Ibid., 34.
42. Zaller, *Nature and Origins,* 40.
43. Pablo Briñol et al., "Individual Differences in Resistance to Persuasion: The Role of Beliefs and Meta-Beliefs," in *Resistance and Persuasion,* ed. Eric S. Knowles and Jay A. Linn (Mahwah, N.J.: Erlbaum, 2004); Julia Zuwerink Jacks and Maureen E. O'Brien, "Decreasing Resistance by Affirming the Self," in *Resistance and Persuasion,* ed. Eric S. Knowles and Jay A. Linn (Mahwah, N.J.: Erlbaum, 2004).
44. Respectively, Briñol et al., "Individual Differences"; Kathleen Fuegen and Jack W. Brehm, "The Intensity of Affect and Resistance to Social Influence," in *Resistance and Persuasion,* ed. Eric S. Knowles and Jay A. Linn (Mahwah, N.J.: Erlbaum, 2004); and Jeffrey M. Quinn and Wendy Wood, "Forewarnings of Influence Appeals: Inducing Resistance and Acceptance," in *Resistance and Persuasion,* ed. Eric S. Knowles and Jay A. Linn (Mahwah, N.J.: Erlbaum, 2004).
45. Jacks and O'Brien, "Decreasing Resistance."
46. George Y. Bizer and Richard E. Petty, "How We Conceptualize Our Attitudes Matters: The Effects of Valence Framing on the Resistance of Political Attitudes," *Political Psychology* 26 (2005): 553–568.
47. Ibid.
48. Richard R. Lau, "Two Explanations for Negativity Effects in Political Behavior," *American Journal of Political Science* 29 (1985): 119–138.
49. Leon Festinger, *A Theory of Cognitive Dissonance* (Stanford: Stanford University Press, 1957).
50. Leon Festinger and James Merrill Carlsmith, "Cognitive Consequences of Forced Compliance," *Journal of Abnormal and Social Psychology* 58 (1959): 203–210.
51. Daryl J. Bem, "Self-Perception Theory," in *Advances in Experimental Social Psychology,* vol. 6, ed. Leonard Berkowitz (New York: Academic Press, 1972), 5. See also Daryl J. Bem, "Self-Perception: An Alternative Interpretation of Cognitive Dissonance Phenomena," *Psychological Review* 74 (1967): 183–200.
52. Eagly and Chaiken, *Psychology of Attitudes.*
53. Ibid., 546.
54. Ibid.

CHAPTER 5

1. Bob Minzesheimer, "Insults Thrown, Left and Right," *USA Today,* June 1, 2003, www.usatoday.com/life/books/news/2003-06-01-book-expo_x.htm (accessed July 23, 2007), emphasis added.
2. "Bipartisan Immigration Bill Faces Bipartisan Fight," CNN.com, May 18, 2007, www.cnn.com/2007/POLITICS/05/18/immigration.bill/index.html?iref=newssearch (accessed July 23, 2007).
3. Nina Totenberg, "The Roberts Court and the Role of Precedent," *Morning Edition,* National Public Radio, July 3, 2007.
4. Kent Tedin, "Political Ideology and the Vote," *Research in Micropolitics* 2 (1987): 65.
5. Kathleen Knight, "Transformations of the Concept of Ideology in the Twentieth Century," *American Political Science Review* 100 (2006): 619–635.
6. Philip E. Converse, "The Nature of Belief Systems in Mass Publics," in *Ideology and Discontent,* ed. David E. Apter (New York: Free Press, 1964), 214.
7. Ibid., 207.
8. Ibid.
9. See also Angus Campbell, Philip E. Converse, Warren E. Miller, and Donald E. Stokes, *The American Voter* (New York: Wiley, 1960), chap. 10.

10. Converse used "Ideologue" to refer to those people who demonstrated the most abstract ideological thinking, even though this term is often reserved for people who display a dogmatic attachment to their beliefs. In other words, while Converse's ideologues displayed high levels of political reasoning, we more commonly think of ideologues as those who are not open-minded to new information or who do not think carefully about political matters. This distinction was not lost on Converse. Despite the potential confusion over his use of ideologue, he selected this term because he could not locate another term or short phrase that conveyed the meaning he intended. "[U]sers of ideological reference points as an heuristic for better understanding of political objects and events," or similar phrases were simply too long (Philip E. Converse, "Democratic Theory and Electoral Reality," *Critical Review* 18 [2006]: 310).

11. Campbell, Converse, Miller, and Stokes, *The American Voter,* 231.

12. Ibid., 236.

13. Ibid., 224.

14. Converse, "Nature of Belief Systems," 223.

15. Ibid., 243.

16. Donald R. Kinder, "Belief Systems after Converse," in *Electoral Democracy,* ed. Michael B. MacKuen and George Rabinowitz (Ann Arbor: University of Michigan Press, 2003), 13.

17. Samuel L. Popkin, "The Factual Basis of 'Belief Systems': A Reassessment," *Critical Review* 18 (2006): 233–234.

18. Norman H. Nie, Sidney Verba, and John R. Petrocik, *The Changing American Voter,* enlarged ed. (Cambridge, Mass.: Harvard University Press, 1979), chap. 8. See also Norman H. Nie with Kristi Andersen, "Mass Belief Systems Revisited: Political Change and Attitude Structure," *Journal of Politics* 36 (1974): 541–591.

19. Nie, Verba, and Petrocik, *Changing American Voter,* 137.

20. James A. Stimson, "Belief Systems: Constraint, Complexity and the 1972 Election," *American Journal of Political Science* 19 (1975): 393–417; Tedin, "Political Ideology."

21. Converse, "Democratic Theory and Electoral Reality," 305. See also Stephen Earl Bennett, "Democratic Competence, Before Converse and After," *Critical Review* 18 (2006): 105–141.

22. Philip E. Converse and Gregory B. Markus, "Plus ça change ... : The New CPS Election Study Panel," *American Political Science Review* 73 (1979): 32–49; M. Kent Jennings, "Ideological Thinking among Mass Publics and Political Elites," *Public Opinion Quarterly* 56 (1992): 419–441; Converse, "Democratic Theory and Electoral Reality."

23. John L. Sullivan, James E. Pierson, and George E. Marcus, "Ideological Constraint in the Mass Public: A Methodological Critique and Some New Findings," *American Journal of Political Science* 22 (1978): 233–249.

24. Kinder, "Belief Systems after Converse."

25. Christopher H. Achen, "Mass Political Attitudes and the Survey Response," *American Political Science Review* 69 (1975): 1220. See also Jon A. Krosnick and Matthew K. Berent, "Comparisons of Party Identification and Policy Preferences: The Impact of Survey Question Format," *American Journal of Political Science* 37 (1993): 941–964.

26. Sullivan, Pierson, and Marcus, "Ideological Constraint"; Donald R. Kinder and David O. Sears, "Public Opinion and Political Action," in *Handbook of Social Psychology,* vol. II, 3rd ed., ed. Gardner Lindzey and Elliot Aronson (New York: Random House, 1985).

27. The seven issues for 1980 were defense spending, school busing, environmental regulations, relations with the Soviet Union, abortion, the Equal Rights Amendment, and inflation. Eight issues were analyzed for 2004: government provision of services, defense spending, government versus private medical insurance, government job guarantee, aid to blacks, environmental protection, death penalty, and women's role.

28. The 1980 results are from Jennings, "Ideological Thinking."

29. Jennings, "Ideological Thinking."

30. We excluded three issues from our analysis because we worried that public responses to these items would have been affected by the events of September 11, 2001. The excluded items were spending on crime, foreign aid, and border security. When these items are included, the correlation decreases slightly from .44 to .40.

31. Jennings, "Ideological Thinking."
32. Robert E. Lane, *Political Ideology: Why the American Common Man Believes What He Does* (New York: Free Press, 1962), 9–10.
33. Ibid., 485–487.
34. Ibid., 441.
35. Ibid., chap. 22.
36. Converse, "Democratic Theory and Electoral Reality"; Kinder and Sears, "Public Opinion and Political Action."
37. Michael C. Dawson, *Black Visions: The Roots of Contemporary African-American Political Ideologies* (Chicago: University of Chicago Press, 2001), 65.
38. Dawson, *Black Visions;* Melissa Harris-Lacewell, *Barbershops, Bibles, and BET: Everyday Talk and Black Political Thought* (Princeton: Princeton University Press, 2004).
39. Dawson does discuss a sixth ideology—black Marxism—but argues that it played a more prominent role in black political thought in the past than in contemporary times.
40. Harris-Lacewell, *Barbershops, Bibles, and BET,* 1.
41. Ibid., chap. 5.
42. For similar conclusions, see Donald R. Kinder, "Belief Systems Today," *Critical Review* 18 (2006): 197–216, and Bennett, "Democratic Competence."
43. Kathleen Knight, "Ideology in the 1980 Election: Ideological Sophistication Does Matter," *Journal of Politics* 47 (1985): 828–853. See also Tedin, "Political Ideology."
44. Knight, "Transformations."
45. David C. Barker and James D. Tinnick III, "Competing Visions of Parental Roles and Ideological Constraint," *American Political Science Review* 100 (2006): 249–263.
46. B. Dan Wood and Arnold Vedlitz, "Issue Definition, Information Processing, and the Politics of Global Warming," *American Journal of Political Science* 51 (2007): 552–568.
47. Paul M. Sniderman, Richard A. Brody, and Philip E. Tetlock, *Reasoning and Choice: Explorations in Political Psychology* (Cambridge: Cambridge University Press, 1991); Popkin, "The Factual Basis."
48. Pamela Johnston Conover and Stanley Feldman, "The Origins and Meaning of Liberal/Conservative Self-Identification," *American Journal of Political Science* 25 (1981): 617–645; Kinder, "Belief Systems Today."
49. John T. Jost, "The End of the End of Ideology," *American Psychologist* 61 (2006): 651–670.
50. Ibid.
51. Michael Schudson and Susan E. Tifft, "American Journalism in Historical Perspective," in *The Press,* ed. Geneva Overholser and Kathleen Hall Jamieson (Oxford: Oxford University Press, 2005).
52. *News Audiences Increasingly Politicized* (Pew Research Center for the People and the Press, Washington, D.C., June 8, 2004), http://people-press.org/reports/display.php3? PageID=833.
53. *Online Papers Modestly Boost Newspaper Readership* (Pew Research Center for the People and the Press, Washington, D.C., July 30, 2006), http://people-press.org/reports/display.php3? PageID=1064.
54. Bennett, "Democratic Competence," 119.
55. Ibid., 105.
56. Jennings, "Ideological Thinking," 421.

CHAPTER 6

1. Donald R. Kinder, "Diversity and Complexity in American Public Opinion," in *Political Science: The State of the Discipline*, ed. Ada Finifter (Washington, D.C.: American Political Science Association, 1983).
2. Ibid., 401.
3. T. W. Adorno, Else Frenkel-Brunswik, Daniel J. Levinson, and R. Nevitt Sanford, *The Authoritarian Personality* (New York: Harper & Brothers, 1950).
4. Ibid., 228.
5. Ibid., 385.

6. See, for example, Richard Christie and Marie Jahoda, eds., *Studies in the Scope and Method of "The Authoritarian Personality": Continuities in Social Research* (Glencoe, Ill.: Free Press, 1954); and Bob Altemeyer, *Right-Wing Authoritarianism* (Winnipeg, Manitoba, Canada: University of Manitoba Press, 1981).
7. Karen Stenner, *The Authoritarian Dynamic* (New York: Cambridge University Press, 2005).
8. Ibid., 14.
9. Ibid., chap. 6.
10. Ibid., 177.
11. Ibid., 24; emphasis in original.
12. Unfortunately, these questions about child-rearing values were not available for all years of the General Social Survey. When these questions were not available, Stenner used a sophisticated statistical technique to impute authoritarianism scores for respondents. See Stenner, *The Authoritarian Dynamic*, Appendix D, www.karenstenner.com/AD3_appendix%20D.pdf.
13. Stenner, *The Authoritarian Dynamic*, 190.
14. Ibid., 86.
15. Ibid., chap. 7.
16. Ibid., chap. 8.
17. Ibid., 17.
18. Ibid., 26.
19. Ibid., 291.
20. Stenner includes several additional conditions in her experiment, but these three are most revealing for our purposes here.
21. Stenner, *The Authoritarian Dynamic*, 292.
22. Alexander Hamilton, James Madison, and John Jay, *The Federalist Papers*, ed. Clinton Rossiter (New York: Penguin, 1961), 82.
23. For a review of this literature, see Jack Citrin and Donald P. Green, "The Self-Interest Motive in American Public Opinion," *Research in Micropolitics* 3 (1990): 1–28; David O. Sears and Carolyn L. Funk, "The Role of Self-Interest in Social and Political Attitudes," *Advances in Experimental Social Psychology* 24 (1991): 1–91.
24. See, for example, David O. Sears, Carl P. Hensler, and Leslie K. Speer, "Whites' Opposition to 'Busing': Self-Interest or Symbolic Politics?" *American Political Science Review* 73 (1979): 369–384. Kinder and Sanders show the limited effect of self-interest on white and black opinion toward several racial issues; see Donald R. Kinder and Lynn M. Sanders, *Divided by Color* (Chicago: University of Chicago Press, 1996).
25. Donald R. Kinder and D. Roderick Kiewiet, "Sociotropic Politics: The American Case," *British Journal of Political Science* 11 (1981): 129–161.
26. David O. Sears and Jack Citrin, *Tax Revolt: Something for Nothing in California*, enlarged ed. (Cambridge, Mass.: Harvard University Press, 1985).
27. Donald Philip Green and Ann Elizabeth Gerken, "Self-Interest and Public Opinion toward Smoking Restrictions and Cigarette Taxes," *Public Opinion Quarterly* 53 (1989): 1–16; Richard D. Dixon, Roger C. Lowery, Diane E. Levy, and Kenneth F. Ferraro, "Self-Interest and Public Opinion toward Smoking Policies: A Replication and Extension," *Public Opinion Quarterly* 55 (1991): 241–254.
28. Robin M. Wolpert and James G. Gimpel, "Self-Interest, Symbolic Politics, and Public Attitudes toward Gun Control," *Political Behavior* 20 (1998): 241–262.
29. Citrin and Green, "The Self-Interest Motive," 18.
30. Dennis Chong, Jack Citrin, and Patricia Conley, "When Self-Interest Matters," *Political Psychology* 22 (2001): 541–570.
31. Ibid., 542.
32. Kinder, "Diversity and Complexity," 406.
33. For a review of the values literature, see Stanley Feldman, "Values, Ideology, and the Structure of Political Attitudes," in *Oxford Handbook of Political Psychology*, ed. David O. Sears, Leonie Huddy, and Robert Jervis (New York: Oxford University Press, 2003).
34. Stanley Feldman, "Structure and Consistency in Public Opinion: The Role of Core Beliefs and Values," *American Journal of Political Science* 32 (1988): 416–440; Kinder and Sanders, *Divided by Color*.

35. Feldman and Steenbergen make an interesting distinction between egalitarianism and humanitarianism; see Stanley Feldman and Marco R. Steenbergen, "The Humanitarian Foundation of Public Support for Social Welfare," *American Journal of Political Science* 45 (2001): 658–677.
36. Feldman, "Structure and Consistency."
37. Kinder and Sanders, *Divided by Color*; Donald R. Kinder and Nicholas Winter, "Exploring the Racial Divide: Blacks, Whites, and Opinion on National Policy," *American Journal of Political Science* 45 (2001): 439–453.
38. Kinder and Sanders, *Divided by Color*, 134.
39. Kinder and Winter, "Exploring the Racial Divide," 441.
40. Kinder and Winter demonstrate that black-white differences in egalitarianism and support for limited government explain nearly one-half of the racial gap in opinions on social welfare policies; see Kinder and Winter, "Exploring the Racial Divide," 439–453, for further details on the principle of limited government.
41. Herbert F. Weisberg, "The Structure and Effects of Moral Predispositions in Contemporary American Politics," *Journal of Politics* 67 (2005): 648; Paul R. Brewer, "The Shifting Foundations of Public Opinion about Gay Rights," *Journal of Politics* 65 (2003): 1208–1220.
42. Weisberg makes a distinction between moral traditionalism and moral judgment. He argues that moral judgment (i.e., an evaluation of people's lifestyles) is a better predictor of attitudes on some cultural issues than moral traditionalism; see Weisberg, "The Structure and Effects."
43. Thomas E. Nelson and Donald R. Kinder, "Issue Frames and Group-Centrism in American Public Opinion," *Journal of Politics* 58 (1996): 1055–1078.
44. See, for example, Pamela Johnston Conover, "The Role of Social Groups in Political Thinking," *British Journal of Politics* 18 (1988): 51–76; Fay Lomax Cook and Edith Barrett, *Support for the American Welfare State* (New York: Columbia University Press, 1992); and James R. Kluegel and Eliot R. Smith, *Beliefs about Inequality* (New York: Aldine de Gruyter, 1986).
45. Howard Schuman, Charlotte Steeh, Lawrence Bobo, and Maria Krysan, *Racial Attitudes in America*, revised ed. (Cambridge, Mass.: Harvard University Press, 1997).
46. Scott B. Blinder, "Dissonance Persists: Reproduction of Racial Attitudes among Post-Civil Rights Cohorts of White Americans," *American Politics Research* 35 (2007): 299–335.
47. For a brief overview of the literature on new forms of racism, see Appendix A in Kinder and Sanders, *Divided by Color*, 291–294.
48. Ibid., 105–106.
49. Kinder and Sanders, *Divided by Color*.
50. Ibid., 106.
51. Ibid., 107.
52. Ibid., 117.
53. Much of the research on public opinion toward race-targeted policies has focused on white attitudes toward policies targeted to blacks. It is clear that more research is needed on white attitudes toward policies targeted to other minority groups. Furthermore, more research is needed on minority attitudes toward race-targeted policies.
54. Martin Gilens, *Why Americans Hate Welfare* (Chicago: University of Chicago Press, 1999).
55. The death penalty is another race-coded issue. See the fascinating study by Mark Peffley and Jon Hurwitz, "Persuasion and Resistance: Race and the Death Penalty in America," *American Journal of Political Science* 51 (2007): 996–1012.
56. Gilens, *Why Americans Hate Welfare*, 67.
57. Ibid., 81.
58. Ibid., 90.
59. For an experimental demonstration of the effect of racialized welfare images on public opinion, see James M. Avery and Mark Peffley, "Race Matters: The Impact of News Coverage of Welfare Reform on Public Opinion," in *Race and the Politics of Welfare Reform*, ed. Sanford F. Schram, Joe Soss, and Richard C. Fording (Ann Arbor: University of Michigan Press, 2003).
60. Gilens, *Why Americans Hate Welfare*, 128.
61. Rosalee A. Clawson and Rakuya Trice, "Poverty as We Know It: Media Portrayals of the Poor," *Public Opinion Quarterly* 64 (2000): 53–64.
62. Ibid., 58.

63. See, for example, Patricia Gurin, Shirley Hatchett, and James S. Jackson, *Hope and Independence* (New York: Russell Sage Foundation, 1989).

64. Patricia Gurin, "Women's Gender Consciousness," *Public Opinion Quarterly* 49 (1985): 144.

65. Note that while scholars tend to agree that there are several components of group consciousness, they often disagree about what to label those components.

66. Michael C. Dawson, *Behind the Mule* (Princeton: Princeton University Press, 1994); Katherine Tate, *From Protest to Politics*, enlarged ed. (Cambridge, Mass.: Harvard University Press, 1994). For a discussion of black feminist consciousness, see Evelyn M. Simien, *Black Feminist Voices in Politics* (Albany: State University of New York Press, 2006).

67. Katherine Tate, "Black Opinion on the Legitimacy of Racial Redistricting and Minority-Majority Districts," *American Political Science Review* 97 (2003): 45–56.

68. Gabriel R. Sanchez, "The Role of Group Consciousness in Latino Public Opinion," *Political Research Quarterly* 59 (2006): 435–446.

69. Many scholars have noted the powerful influence of party identification on other political attitudes. For the earliest account of the influence of party identification, see Angus Campbell, Philip E. Converse, Warren E. Miller, and Donald E. Stokes, *The American Voter* (New York: Wiley, 1960).

70. Wendy M. Rahn, "The Role of Partisan Stereotypes in Information-Processing about Political Candidates," *American Journal of Political Science* 37 (1993): 472–496.

71. Brian J. Gaines, James H. Kuklinski, Paul J. Quirk, Buddy Peyton, and Jay Verkuilen, "Same Facts, Different Interpretations: Partisan Motivation and Opinion on Iraq," *Journal of Politics* 69 (2007): 957–974.

72. Ibid., 972.

73. Ibid., 967.

74. John E. Mueller, *War, Presidents, and Public Opinion* (New York: Wiley, 1973); Paul Brace and Barbara Hinckley, *Follow the Leader: Opinion Polls and the Modern Presidents* (New York: Basic Books, 1992).

75. Brian J. Gaines, "Where's the Rally? Approval and Trust of the President, Cabinet, Congress, and Government Since September 11," *PS: Political Science & Politics* 35 (2002): 531–536.

76. Paul Allen Beck, "Partisan Dealignment in the Postwar South," *American Political Science Review* 71 (1977): 477–498; Earl Black and Merle Black, *The Rise of Southern Republicans* (Cambridge, Mass.: Harvard University Press, 2002).

77. For an analysis of this Southern realignment, see Nicholas A. Valentino and David O. Sears, "Old Times There Are Not Forgotten: Race and Partisan Realignment in the Contemporary South," *American Journal of Political Science* 49 (2005): 672–688.

78. Samantha Luks and Laurel Elms, "African-American Partisanship and the Legacy of the Civil Rights Movement: Generational, Regional, and Economic Influences on Democratic Identification, 1973–1994," *Political Psychology* 26 (2005): 735–754.

79. Taeku Lee, *Mobilizing Public Opinion: Black Insurgency and Racial Attitudes in the Civil Rights Era* (Chicago: University of Chicago Press, 2002).

80. Ibid., 31; emphasis in original.

81. The Montgomery bus boycott was instigated by Rosa Parks's refusal to give up her bus seat to a white man on December 1, 1955. Some observers have characterized Parks's actions as the beginning of the modern civil rights movement; see Paula Giddings, *When and Where I Enter: The Impact of Black Women on Race and Sex in America* (New York: William Morrow, 1984). Freedom Summer refers to the events of summer 1964. During that summer, civil rights organizations registered and organized African Americans in Mississippi in the face of extreme brutality carried out by the white power structure. Bloody Sunday in Selma refers to the events of March 7, 1965. Civil rights activists were beaten mercilessly by white law enforcement officers as they attempted to march from Selma to Montgomery, Alabama.

82. Lee, *Mobilizing Public Opinion*, 127.

83. Ibid., 132.

84. Ibid., 123.

85. Ibid., 208; emphasis in original.

Chapter 7

1. *Public Knowledge of Current Affairs Little Changed by News and Information Revolutions* (Pew Research Center for the People and the Press, Washington, D.C., April 15, 2007), http://people-press.org/reports/display.php3?ReportID=319.
2. Michael X. Delli Carpini and Scott Keeter, *What Americans Know about Politics and Why It Matters* (New Haven: Yale University Press, 1996), 8.
3. Samuel L. Popkin, *The Reasoning Voter* (Chicago: University of Chicago Press, 1994).
4. Paul M. Sniderman, Richard A. Brody, and Philip E. Tetlock, *Reasoning and Choice: Explorations in Political Psychology* (New York: Cambridge University Press, 1991), 19.
5. John A. Ferejohn, "Information and the Electoral Process," in *Information and Democratic Processes,* ed. John A. Ferejohn and James H. Kuklinski (Urbana: University of Illinois Press, 1990), chap. 1.
6. Delli Carpini and Keeter, *What Americans Know,* 42.
7. This section draws heavily from Delli Carpini and Keeter, *What Americans Know.* Delli Carpini and Keeter provide an excellent review of the various strands of thought regarding levels of citizen knowledge.
8. Anthony Downs, *An Economic Theory of Democracy* (New York: Harper & Row, 1957).
9. Ibid., 259.
10. John A. Ferejohn and James Kuklinski, *Information and Democratic Processes* (Urbana: University of Illinois Press, 1990); Arthur Lupia and Mathew D. McCubbins, *The Democratic Dilemma* (Cambridge: Cambridge University Press, 1998); Popkin, *The Reasoning Voter.*
11. Susan T. Fiske and Shelley E. Taylor, *Social Cognition,* 2nd ed. (New York: McGraw-Hill, Inc., 1991); Doris A. Graber, *Processing Politics* (Chicago: University of Chicago Press, 2001).
12. See John R. Hibbing and Elizabeth Theiss-Morse, *Stealth Democracy* (Cambridge: Cambridge University Press, 2002).
13. Ferejohn, "Information and the Electoral Process," 3.
14. Delli Carpini and Keeter, *What Americans Know,* 10.
15. Dell Carpini and Carter, *What Americans Know.*
16. Ibid., chap. 2.
17. Ibid., 101.
18. Richard L. Fox and Robert W. Van Sickel, *Tabloid Justice* (Boulder, Colo.: Lynne Rienner, 2001), 130.
19. James H. Kuklinski et al., "Misinformation and the Currency of Democratic Citizenship," *Journal of Politics* 62 (2000): 790–816.
20. Ibid., 792–793; emphasis in original.
21. Also see Jennifer Jerit and Jason Barabas, "Bankrupt Rhetoric: How Misleading Information Affects Knowledge about Social Security," *Public Opinion Quarterly* 70 (2006): 278–303.
22. Delli Carpini and Keeter, *What Americans Know,* 106–116.
23. Ibid., 107.
24. Ibid., 106–116.
25. Neil Postman, *Amusing Ourselves to Death* (New York: Viking Penguin, 1985).
26. Ibid., 3–4.
27. Delli Carpini and Keeter, *What Americans Know,* 291–293.
28. Ibid., 116; but also see Bennett, who argues that citizens were slightly less informed in 1987 than they were in 1967: Stephen Earl Bennett, "Trends in Americans' Political Information, 1967–1987," *American Politics Quarterly* 17 (1989): 422–435.
29. Delli Carpini and Keeter, *What Americans Know,* chap. 4.
30. Also see *Public Knowledge,* 7–8.
31. Delli Carpini and Keeter, *What Americans Know,* appendix 2.
32. Ibid., 147–151.
33. Ibid., 146; also see Vincent L. Hutchings, *Public Opinion and Democratic Accountability: How Citizens Learn about Politics* (Princeton: Princeton University Press, 2003).

34. Markus Prior, "Political Knowledge after September 11," *PS: Political Science & Politics* 35 (2002): 523–529.

35. Jeffery J. Mondak and Belinda Creel Davis, "Asked and Answered: Knowledge Levels When We Will Not Take 'Don't Know' for an Answer," *Political Behavior* 23 (2001): 199–224; Jeffery J. Mondak, "Developing Valid Knowledge Scales," *American Journal of Political Science* 45 (2001): 224–238.

36. Jeffery J. Mondak and Mary R. Anderson, "The Knowledge Gap: A Reexamination of Gender-Based Differences in Political Knowledge," *Journal of Politics* 66 (2004): 492–512.

37. Mondak and Davis, "Asked and Answered"; Mondak, "Developing Valid Knowledge Scales"; Mondak and Anderson, "The Knowledge Gap."

38. *Public Knowledge.*

39. The American National Election Studies (www.electionstudies.org). *The 2004 National Election Study* [dataset]. Ann Arbor: University of Michigan, Center for Political Studies (producer and distributor).

40. Graber, *Processing Politics*; Doris A. Graber, "Why Voters Fail Information Tests: Can the Hurdles Be Overcome?" *Political Communication* 11 (1994): 331–346.

41. Graber, *Processing Politics,* 7.

42. Ibid., chap. 2.

43. Ibid., 30.

44. Ibid., chap. 3; also see William A. Gamson, *Talking Politics* (Cambridge: Cambridge University Press, 1992).

45. Graber, *Processing Politics,* 57.

46. Ibid., 56.

47. Ibid., 64.

48. Delli Carpini and Keeter, *What Americans Know*; Staci L. Rhine, Stephen Earl Bennett, and Richard S. Flickinger, "Gaps in Americans' Knowledge about the Bosnian Civil War," *American Politics Research* 29 (2001): 592–607; Bennett, "Trends in Americans' Political Information"; Jennifer Jerit, Jason Barabas, and Toby Bolsen, "Citizens, Knowledge, and the Information Environment," *American Journal of Political Science* 50 (2006): 266–282.

49. Delli Carpini and Keeter, *What Americans Know,* 147–151.

51. *Public Knowledge,* 7.

52. Kim L. Fridkin, Patrick J. Kenney, and Jack Crittendon, "On the Margins of Democratic Life: The Impact of Race and Ethnicity on the Political Engagement of Young People," *American Politics Research* 34 (2006): 605–626.

53. Richard G. Niemi and Jane Junn, *Civic Education: What Makes Students Learn* (New Haven: Yale University Press, 1998).

54. Ibid., 13.

55. *Public Knowledge,* 19.

56. Delli Carpini and Keeter, *What Americans Know,* 182–184; Jerit, Barabas, and Bolsen, "Citizens, Knowledge."

57. Stephen E. Bennett, Richard S. Flickinger, and Staci L. Rhine, "Political Talk Over Here, Over There, Over Time," *British Journal of Political Science* 30 (2000): 99–119.

58. Jonathan S. Morris and Richard Forgette, "News Grazers, Television News, Political Knowledge, and Engagement," *Harvard International Journal of Press/Politics* 12 (2007): 91–107.

59. Ibid., 92.

60. Markus Prior, "News vs. Entertainment: How Increasing Media Choice Widens Gaps in Political Knowledge and Turnout," *American Journal of Political Science* 49 (2005): 577–592.

61. Delli Carpini and Keeter, *What Americans Know.*

62. Niemi and Junn, *Civic Education.*

63. Mark A. Smith, "Ballot Initiatives and the Democratic Citizen," *Journal of Politics* 64 (2002): 892–903.

64. Stacy B. Gordon and Gary M. Segura, "Cross-National Variation in the Political Sophistication of Individuals: Capability or Choice?" *Journal of Politics* 59 (1997): 126–147.

65. Nancy Burns, Key Lehman Schlozman, and Sidney Verba, *The Private Roots of Public Action* (Cambridge, Mass.: Harvard University Press, 2001).

66. Ibid., 343.
67. Jerit, Barabas, and Bolsen, "Citizens, Knowledge."
68. Also see Rhine, Bennett, and Flickinger, "Gaps in Americans' Knowledge." These authors argue that the knowledge gap about the Bosnian civil war declined over time because television news provided significant coverage of the conflict.
69. Delli Carpini and Keeter, *What Americans Know,* chap. 6.
70. Ibid., 265.
71. Kuklinski et al., "Misinformation."
72. Martin Gilens, "Political Ignorance and Collective Policy Preferences," *American Political Science Review* 95 (2001): 379–396.
73. Larry M. Bartels, "Uninformed Votes: Information Effects in Presidential Elections," *American Journal of Political Science* 40 (1996): 194–230.
74. Stephen Earl Bennett and Linda L.M. Bennett, "Out of Sight, Out of Mind: Americans' Knowledge of Party Control of the House of Representatives, 1960–1984," *Political Research Quarterly* 46 (1993): 67–80; Stephen Earl Bennett, Staci L. Rhine, and Richard S. Flickinger, "The Things They Cared About: Change and Continuity in Americans' Attention to Different News Stories, 1989–2002," *Harvard International Journal of Press/Politics* 9 (2004): 75–99; Delli Carpini and Keeter, *What Americans Know.*
75. The American National Election Studies (www.electionstudies.org). *The ANES Guide to Public Opinion and Electoral Behavior.* Ann Arbor: University of Michigan, Center for Political Studies (producer and distributor).
76. Ibid.
77. Ibid.
78. Burns, Schlozman, and Verba, *The Private Roots.*
79. Lonna Rae Atkeson, "Not All Cues Are Created Equal: The Conditional Impact of Female Candidates on Political Engagement," *Journal of Politics* 65 (2003): 1040–1061.
80. David E. Campbell and Christina Wolbrecht, "See Jane Run: Women Politicians as Role Models for Adolescents," *Journal of Politics* 68 (2006): 233–247.
81. Data from Iraq Coalition Casualty Count, http://icasualties.org/oif/.
82. *Iraq Dominates News Landscape in First Six Months of 2007* (Pew Research Center for the People and the Press, Washington, D.C., June 28, 2007), http://people-press.org/reports/display.php3?ReportID=340.
83. Ibid., 1.
84. Ibid., 3–4.

CHAPTER 8

1. David G. Barnum, "Decision Making in a Constitutional Democracy: Policy Formation in the Skokie Free Speech Controversy," *Journal of Politics* 44 (1982): 493.
2. James L. Gibson and Richard D. Bingham, "Skokie, Nazis, and the Elitist Theory of Democracy," *Western Political Quarterly* 37 (1984): 34.
3. Barnum, "Decision Making," 506.
4. John L. Sullivan, James Piereson, and George E. Marcus, "An Alternative Conceptualization of Political Tolerance: Illusory Increases 1950s–1970s," *American Political Science Review* 73 (1979): 784.
5. Samuel A. Stouffer, *Communism, Conformity, and Civil Liberties: A Cross-Section of the Nation Speaks Its Mind* (Garden City, N.Y.: Doubleday, 1955), 54.
6. See, in particular, *Federalist* nos. 10 and 51. Alexander Hamilton, James Madison, and John Jay, *The Federalist Papers,* ed. Clinton Rossiter (New York: Penguin, [1787] 1961).
7. Hazel Erskine, "The Polls: Freedom of Speech," *Public Opinion Quarterly* 34 (1970): 485, 486.
8. Respectively, James W. Prothro and Charles M. Grigg, "Fundamental Principles of Democracy: Bases of Agreement and Disagreement," *Journal of Politics* 22 (1960): 282, and John L. Sullivan, James Piereson, and George E. Marcus, *Political Tolerance and American Democracy* (Chicago: University of Chicago Press, 1982), 203.

9. Prothro and Grigg, "Fundamental Principles"; Herbert McClosky, "Consensus and Ideology in American Politics," *American Political Science Review* 58 (1964): 361–382.

10. Erskine, "The Polls," 482.

11. David G. Lawrence, "Procedural Norms and Tolerance: A Reassessment," *American Political Science Review* 70 (1976): 80–100; James L. Gibson and Richard D. Bingham, "On the Conceptualization and Measurement of Political Tolerance," *American Political Science Review* 76 (1982): 603–620.

12. Stouffer, *Communism, Conformity, and Civil Liberties.*

13. For a more detailed description of the General Social Survey, visit www.norc.uchicago.edu/projects/gensoc.asp.

14. Others finding increases in tolerance since the 1950s include James A. Davis, "Communism, Conformity, Cohorts, and Categories: American Tolerance in 1954 and 1972–73," *American Journal of Sociology* 81 (1975): 491–513; Lawrence, "Procedural Norms"; J. Allen Williams Jr., Clyde Z. Nunn, and Louis St. Peter, "Origins of Tolerance: Findings from a Replication of Stouffer's Communism, Conformity, and Civil Liberties," *Social Forces* 55 (1976): 394–408; and John Mueller, "Trends in Political Tolerance," *Public Opinion Quarterly* 52 (1988): 1–25.

15. For a similar conclusion, see Thomas C. Wilson, "Trends in Tolerance Toward Rightist and Leftist Groups, 1976–1988: Effects of Attitude Change and Cohort Succession," *Public Opinion Quarterly* 58 (1994): 539–556.

16. Sullivan, Piereson, and Marcus, "Alternative Conceptualization"; Sullivan, Piereson, and Marcus, *Political Tolerance.* See also John L. Sullivan and George E. Marcus, "A Note on 'Trends in Tolerance,'" *Public Opinion Quarterly* 52 (1988): 26–32, and Michal Shamir and John Sullivan, "The Political Context of Tolerance: The United States and Israel," *American Political Science Review* 77 (1983): 911–928.

17. Sullivan, Piereson, and Marcus, "Alternative Conceptualization," 793.

18. George E. Marcus et al., *With Malice Toward Some: How People Make Civil Liberties Judgments* (Cambridge: Cambridge University Press, 1995).

19. Sullivan, Piereson, and Marcus, *Political Tolerance,* 257.

20. Stouffer, *Communism, Conformity, and Civil Liberties,* chap. 4; Prothro and Grigg, "Fundamental Principles"; Davis, "Communism, Conformity, Cohorts"; Clyde Z. Nunn, Harry J. Crockett Jr., and J. Allen Williams Jr., *Tolerance for Nonconformity* (San Francisco: Jossey-Bass, 1978); James L. Gibson, "Alternative Measures of Political Tolerance: Must Tolerance Be 'Least-Liked'?" *American Journal of Political Science* 36 (1992): 560–577; Wilson, "Trends in Tolerance"; Ewa A. Golebiowska, "Individual Value Priorities, Education, and Political Tolerance," *Political Behavior* 17 (1995): 23–48.

21. Prothro and Grigg, "Fundamental Principles"; Lawrence Bobo and Frederick C. Licari, "Education and Political Tolerance: Testing the Effects of Cognitive Sophistication and Target Group Affect," *Public Opinion Quarterly* 53 (1989): 285–308.

22. John L. Sullivan et al., "The Sources of Political Tolerance: A Multivariate Analysis," *American Political Science Review* 75 (1981): 92–106.

23. Stouffer, *Communism, Conformity, and Civil Liberties*; Golebiowska, "Individual Value Priorities."

24. Prothro and Grigg, "Fundamental Principles," 291. For a similar argument, see Lawrence, "Procedural Norms."

25. Nunn, Crockett, and Williams, *Tolerance for Nonconformity,* 170.

26. Bobo and Licari, "Education and Political Tolerance."

27. For examples of some, or all, of these conclusions, see Stouffer, *Communism, Conformity, and Civil Liberties*; Nunn, Crockett, and Williams, *Tolerance for Nonconformity*; Gibson, "Alternative Measures"; Bobo and Licari, "Education and Political Tolerance"; Wilson, "Trends in Tolerance"; Golebiowska, "Individual Value Priorities"; Ewa A. Golebiowska, "Gender Gap in Political Tolerance," *Political Behavior* 21 (1999): 43–66; Dennis Chong, "Free Speech and Multiculturalism In and Out of the Academy," *Political Psychology* 27 (2006): 29–54.

28. Stouffer, *Communism, Conformity, and Civil Liberties,* 130.

29. Ibid., 221.

30. Williams, Nunn, and St. Peter, "Origins of Tolerance."
31. Ibid.
32. Sullivan et al., "Sources of Political Tolerance," 103. See also Bobo and Licari, "Education and Political Tolerance," and Gibson, "Alternative Measures."
33. Gibson, "Alternative Measures"; Sullivan et al., "Sources of Political Tolerance"; James L. Gibson, "Homosexuals and the Ku Klux Klan: A Contextual Analysis of Political Tolerance," *Western Political Quarterly* 40 (1987): 427–448; Marcus et al., *With Malice*; Marcus et al., "The Emotional Foundation of Political Cognition: The Impact of Extrinsic Anxiety on the Formation of Political Tolerance Judgments," *Political Psychology* 26 (2005): 949–963.
34. Gibson, "Homosexuals and the Ku Klux Klan"; Marcus et al., *With Malice*.
35. Stouffer, *Communism, Conformity, and Civil Liberties*; Sullivan et al., "Sources of Political Tolerance"; Gibson, "Homosexuals and the Ku Klux Klan"; Gibson, "Alternative Measures"; Marcus et al., *With Malice*.
36. Golebiowska, "Gender Gap."
37. Mueller, "Trends in Political Tolerance."
38. Marcus et al., *With Malice*.
39. Ibid., 69–70.
40. Ibid., 81.
41. Gibson, "Homosexuals and the Ku Klux Klan."
42. Patricia G. Avery et al., "Exploring Political Tolerance with Adolescents," *Theory and Research in Social Education* 20 (1992): 386–420.
43. Marcus et al., *With Malice,* 123–124.
44. Ibid., 127.
45. For a complete list of types of leaders analyzed, refer to page 17 of Stouffer, *Communism, Conformity, and Civil Liberties.*
46. Ibid., chap. 2.
47. Nunn, Crockett and Williams, *Tolerance for Nonconformity.*
48. McClosky, "Consensus and Ideology," 367.
49. David G. Barnum and John L. Sullivan, "The Elusive Foundations of Political Freedom in Britain and the United States," *Journal of Politics* 52 (1990): 719–739.
50. Robert W. Jackman, "Political Elites, Mass Publics, and Support for Democratic Principles," *Journal of Politics* 34 (1972): 753–773. For a similar conclusion, see Nunn, Crockett, and Williams, *Tolerance for Nonconformity.*
51. V.O. Key Jr., *Public Opinion and American Democracy* (New York: Alfred A. Knopf, 1961); Robert A. Dahl, *Who Governs? Democracy and Power in an American City* (New Haven: Yale University Press, 1961); McClosky, "Consensus and Ideology."
52. John L. Sullivan et al., "Why Politicians Are More Tolerant: Selective Recruitment and Socialization among Political Elites in Britain, Israel, New Zealand and the United States," *British Journal of Political Science* 23 (1993): 53.
53. Viet Dinh, "Freedom and Security after September 11," in *Civil Liberties vs. National Security in a Post-9/11 World,* ed. M. Katherine B. Darmer, Robert M. Baird, and Stuart E. Rosenbaum (Amherst, N.Y.: Prometheus Books, 2004), 107; emphasis in original.
54. Jay Stanley and Barry Steinhardt, "Bigger Monster, Weaker Chains: The Growth of an American Surveillance Society," in *Civil Liberties vs. National Security in a Post-9/11 World,* ed. M. Katherine B. Darmer, Robert M. Baird, and Stuart E. Rosenbaum (Amherst, N.Y.: Prometheus Books, 2004), 65.
55. Lynn M. Kuzma, "The Polls—Trends: Terrorism in the United States," *Public Opinion Quarterly* 64 (2000): 90–105.
56. Darren W. Davis and Brian D. Silver, "Civil Liberties vs. Security: Public Opinion in the Context of the Terrorist Attacks on America," *American Journal of Political Science* 48 (2004): 30.
57. Ibid., 31.
58. For an overview of public attitudes toward terrorism policies since 9/11, see Yaeli Bloch-Elkon, "The Polls—Trends: Preventing Terrorism after the 9/11 Attacks," *Public Opinion Quarterly* 71 (2007): 142–163.

59. CNN poll, conducted May 16–17, 2006, www.pollingreport.com/terror2.htm.
60. ABC News/*Washington Post* polls, www.pollingreport.com/terror2.htm.
61. *Dimming the Beacon of Freedom: U.S Violations of the International Covenant on Civil and Political Rights* (American Civil Liberties Union, New York, N.Y., June 2006), www.aclu.org/pdfs/iccprreport20060620.pdf.
62. *Americans Taking Abramoff, Alito and Domestic Spying in Stride* (Pew Research Center for the People and the Press, Washington, D.C., January 11, 2006), http://people-press.org/reports/display.php3?ReportID=267.
63. Costas Panagopoulos, "The Polls—Trends: Arab and Muslim Americans and Islam in the Aftermath of 9/11," *Public Opinion Quarterly* 70 (2006): 608–624.
64. Linda Greenhouse, "Justices, 5–3, Broadly Reject Bush Plan to Try Detainees," *New York Times,* June 29, 2006, sec. A, late edition.
65. Kate Zernike, "Senate Approves Broad New Rules to Try Detainees," *New York Times,* September 29, 2006, sec. A, late edition.
66. McClosky, "Consensus and Ideology," 376; emphasis in original.
67. Avery et al., "Exploring Political Tolerance with Adolescents," 411.
68. Sullivan, Piereson, and Marcus, *Political Tolerance,* 9.
69. Barnum, "Decision Making," 497.

CHAPTER 9

1. *Women in National Parliaments* (Inter-Parliamentary Union, Geneva, Switzerland, 2007), www.ipu.org/wmn-e/classif.htm (accessed August 29, 2007).
2. Carole Kennedy, "Is the United States Ready for a Woman President? Is the Pope Protestant?" in *Anticipating Madam President,* ed. Robert P. Watson and Ann Gordon (Boulder, Colo.: Lynne Rienner Publishers, 2003), 133; "2004 Presidential Election," www.archives.gov/federal-register/electoral-college/2004/popular_vote.html (accessed August 3, 2007).
3. Edward S. Greenberg and Benjamin I. Page, *America's Democratic Republic,* 2nd ed. (New York: Pearson Education, 2007), 101.
4. For a noteworthy exception, see Lawrence D. Bobo and Devon Johnson, "Racial Attitudes in a Prismatic Metropolis: Mapping Identity, Stereotypes, Competition, and Views on Affirmative Action," in *Prismatic Metropolis: Inequality in Los Angeles,* ed. Lawrence D. Bobo, Melvin L. Oliver, James H. Johnson Jr., and Abel Valenzuela Jr. (New York: Russell Sage Foundation, 2000), 81–163.
5. Jeffrey M. Jones, "Some Americans Reluctant to Vote for Mormon, 72-Year-Old Presidential Candidates," *The Gallup Poll,* February 20, 2007, www.galluppoll.com/content/default.aspx?ci=26611&pg=2 (accessed July 14, 2007).
6. Mariana Servín-González and Oscar Torres-Reyna, "Trends: Religion and Politics," *Public Opinion Quarterly* 63 (1999): 592–621.
7. Survey by Gallup Organization, September 21–September 24, 2006. The iPOLL Databank, The Roper Center for Public Opinion Research, University of Connecticut, www2.lib.purdue.edu:4076/ipoll.html (accessed September 23, 2007).
8. Ibid.
9. Ibid.
10. Ibid.
11. Jennifer L. Lawless, "Women, War, and Winning Elections: Gender Stereotyping in the Post–September 11th Era," *Political Research Quarterly* 57 (2004): 479–490.
12. Ibid., 483–487.
13. Survey by Gallup Organization.
14. Ibid.
15. On this distinction between principles of equality and implementation, see Howard Schuman, Charlotte Steeh, Lawrence Bobo, and Maria Krysan, *Racial Attitudes in America,* rev. ed. (Cambridge, Mass.: Harvard University Press, 1997).

16. Ibid., 108.
17. See the research by Bobo and Kluegel, which makes a distinction between opportunity-enhancing policies and equal outcome policies: Lawrence Bobo and James R. Kluegel, "Opposition to Race-Targeting: Self-Interest, Stratification Ideology, or Racial Attitudes?" *American Sociological Review* 58 (1993): 443–464.
18. *Trends in Political Values and Core Attitudes: 1987–2007* (Pew Research Center for the People and the Press, Washington, D.C., March 22, 2007): 40, 70, http://people-press.org/reports/display.php3?ReportID=312. The question wording and context have varied over time. In 2007, the wording was: "As I read some programs and proposals that are being discussed in the country today, please tell me whether you strongly favor, favor, oppose, or strongly oppose each … Affirmative action programs designed to help blacks, women and other minorities get better jobs and education." In 1995, the question opened with "In order to overcome past discrimination …" and was not part of a list of items.
19. Rosalee A. Clawson, Katherine Tate, and Eric N. Waltenburg, *Blacks and the U.S. Supreme Court Survey*, 2003.
20. These findings are also consistent with survey data collected in 2000. See Michael C. Dawson and Rovana Popoff, "Reparations: Justice and Greed in Black and White," *Du Bois Review: Social Science Research on Race* 1 (2004): 47–91.
21. Philip J. Mazzocco, Timothy C. Brock, Gregory J. Brock, Kristina R. Olson, and Mahzarin R. Banaji, "The Cost of Being Black: White Americans' Perceptions and the Question of Reparations," *Du Bois Review: Social Science Research on Race* 3 (2006): 261–297.
22. Ibid., 286.
23. For additional data on support for gay rights, see Gary R. Hicks and Tien-tsung Lee, "Public Attitudes toward Gays and Lesbians: Trends and Predictors," *Journal of Homosexuality* 51 (2006): 57–77; for an analysis of gender differences in support for gay rights, see Gregory M. Herek, "Gender Gaps in Public Opinion about Lesbians and Gay Men," *Public Opinion Quarterly* 66 (2002): 40–66.
24. Robin Toner, "For 'Don't Ask, Don't Tell,' Split on Party Lines," *New York Times,* June 8, 2007, A1.
25. *Bowers v. Hardwick*, 478 U.S. 186 (1986).
26. *Lawrence and Garner v. Texas*, 539 U.S. 558 (2003).
27. For additional data, see Paul R. Brewer and Clyde Wilcox, "Trends: Same-Sex Marriage and Civil Unions," *Public Opinion Quarterly* 69 (2005): 599–616.
28. *Relationship Recognition in the U.S.* (Human Rights Campaign, Washington, D.C., 2007), www.hrc.org/Template.cfm?Section=Your_Community&Template=/ContentManagement/ContentDisplay.cfm&ContentID=16305; *State Prohibitions on Marriage for Same-Sex Couple* (Human Rights Campaign, Washington, D.C., 2007), www.hrc.org/Template.cfm?Section=Your_Community&Template=/ContentManagement/ContentDisplay.cfm&ContentID=19449.
29. Thomas R. Marshall, *Public Opinion and the Supreme Court* (London: Unwin Hyman, 1988).
30. *Trends in Political Values*, 37.

CHAPTER 10

1. Arthur H. Miller, "Political Issues and Trust in Government: 1964–1970," *American Political Science Review* 68 (1974): 951.
2. The Declaration of Independence, July 4, 1776, www.ushistory.org/declaration/document/index.htm.
3. David Easton, *A Systems Analysis of Political Life,* with a New Preface (Chicago: University of Chicago Press, 1979); Joseph S. Nye Jr., "Introduction: The Decline of Confidence in Government," in *Why People Don't Trust Government,* ed. Joseph S. Nye Jr., Philip D. Zelikow, and David C. King (Cambridge, Mass.: Harvard University Press, 1997); Arthur H. Miller, "Rejoinder to 'Comment' by Jack Citrin: Political Discontent or Ritualism?" *American Political Science Review* 68 (1974): 989–1001.
4. Easton, *Systems Analysis of Political Life.*

5. Ibid., 273–274.
6. Ibid., 274.
7. Arthur H. Miller, Edie N. Goldenberg, and Lutz Erbring, "Type-Set Politics: Impact of Newspapers on Public Confidence," *American Political Science Review* 73 (1979): 67.
8. Miller, "Rejoinder to 'Comment,'" 989.
9. Marc J. Hetherington, *Why Trust Matters: Declining Political Trust and the Demise of American Liberalism* (Princeton: Princeton University Press, 2005).
10. Jack Citrin, "The Political Relevance of Trust in Government," *American Political Science Review* 68 (1974): 973–988; Marc J. Hetherington, "The Political Relevance of Political Trust," *American Political Science Review* 92 (1998): 791–808.
11. Miller, Goldenberg, and Erbring, "Type-Set Politics," 67.
12. Mark E. Warren, "Democratic Theory and Trust," in *Democracy and Trust,* ed. Mark E. Warren (Cambridge: Cambridge University Press, 1999).
13. Hetherington, *Why Trust Matters.*
14. Warren, "Democratic Theory and Trust," 341.
15. Russell Hardin, "Do We Want Trust in Government?" in *Democracy and Trust,* ed. Mark E. Warren (Cambridge: Cambridge University Press, 1999).
16. Hetherington, *Why Trust Matters.*
17. Originally, five questions were created; the fifth asked whether respondents believed that politicians are smart. This item is generally not analyzed by scholars examining public trust as it does not correlate that well with the other four trust items. Perhaps for this reason, the question has not appeared on an ANES survey since 1980.
18. Donald E. Stokes, "Popular Evaluations of Government: An Empirical Assessment," in *Ethics and Bigness: Scientific, Academic, Religious, Political, and Military,* ed. Harlan Cleveland and Harold D. Lasswell (New York: Harper, 1962), 64.
19. Citrin, "Political Relevance," 974.
20. Ibid., 975.
21. M. Stephen Weatherford, "Economic 'Stagflation' and Public Support for the Political System," *British Journal of Political Science* 14 (1984): 187–205; Paul R. Abramson and Ada W. Finifter, "On the Meaning of Political Trust: New Evidence from Items Introduced in 1978," *American Journal of Political Science* 25 (1981): 297–307.
22. Miller, "Rejoinder to 'Comment,'" 989.
23. Hetherington, *Why Trust Matters*; Luke Keele, "Social Capital and the Dynamics of Trust in Government," *American Journal of Political Science* 51 (2007): 241–254.
24. John R. Zaller, "Monica Lewinsky's Contribution to Political Science," *PS: Political Science & Politics* 31 (1998): 182–189.
25. Jane Mansbridge, "Social and Cultural Causes of Dissatisfaction with U.S. Government," in *Why People Don't Trust Government,* ed. Joseph S. Nye Jr., Philip D. Zelikow, and David C. King (Cambridge, Mass.: Harvard University Press, 1997).
26. Jack Citrin and Donald Philip Green, "Presidential Leadership and the Resurgence of Trust in Government," *British Journal of Political Science* 16 (1986): 450.
27. Citrin and Green, "Presidential Leadership."
28. Weatherford, "Economic 'Stagflation'"; M. Stephen Weatherford, "How Does Government Performance Influence Political Support?" *Political Behavior* 9 (1987): 5–28; Hetherington, *Why Trust Matters.* For a counterargument, see the essays in *Why People Don't Trust Government,* ed. Joseph S. Nye Jr., Philip D. Zelikow, and David C. King.
29. Hetherington, *Why Trust Matters.*
30. Ibid., 34–35.
31. Miller, "Political Issues."
32. David C. King, "The Polarization of American Parties and Mistrust of Government," in *Why People Don't Trust Government,* ed. Joseph S. Nye Jr., Philip D. Zelikow, and David C. King (Cambridge, Mass.: Harvard University Press, 1997).
33. Thomas E. Patterson, *Out of Order* (New York: Knopf, 1993); Joseph N. Cappella and Kathleen Hall Jamieson, *Spiral of Cynicism: The Press and the Public Good* (Oxford: Oxford University Press, 1997).
34. Miller, Goldenberg, and Erbring, "Type-Set Politics."

35. Gary Orren, "Fall from Grace: The Public's Loss of Faith in Government," in *Why People Don't Trust Government,* ed. Joseph S. Nye Jr., Philip D. Zelikow, and David C. King (Cambridge, Mass.: Harvard University Press, 1997), 95.

36. John Woolley and Gerhard Peters, *The American Presidency Project* [online]. Santa Barbara: University of California (hosted), Gerhard Peters (database), www.presidency.ucsb.edu/ws/?pid=53091.

37. Shmuel T. Lock, Robert Y. Shapiro, and Lawrence R. Jacobs, "The Impact of Political Debate on Government Trust: Reminding the Public What the Federal Government Does," *Political Behavior* 21 (1999): 244.

38. Stokes, "Popular Evaluations of Government"; Orren, "Fall from Grace"; Hetherington, *Why Trust Matters.*

39. Miller, "Political Issues"; Susan E. Howell and Deborah Fagan, "Race and Trust in Government: Testing the Political Reality Model," *Public Opinion Quarterly* 52 (1988): 343–350; James M. Avery, "Race, Partisanship, and Political Trust Following *Bush versus Gore* (2000)," *Political Behavior* 29 (2007): 327–342.

40. Paul R. Abramson, *Political Attitudes in America* (New York: Freeman, 1983).

41. Howell and Fagan, "Race and Trust," 345.

42. Melissa Marschall and Paru R. Shah, "The Attitudinal Effects of Minority Incorporation: Examining the Racial Dimensions of Trust in Urban America," *Urban Affairs Review* 42 (2007): 629–658.

43. Miller, "Rejoinder to 'Comment,'" 989.

44. Miller, "Political Issues"; Miller, "Rejoinder to 'Comment.'" For similar arguments, see Stokes, "Popular Evaluations of Government"; William A. Gamson, *Power and Discontent* (Homewood, Ill.: Dorsey Press, 1968); and Orren, "Fall from Grace."

45. Also see Timothy E. Cook and Paul Gronke, "The Skeptical American: Revisiting the Meanings of Trust in Government and Confidence in Institutions," *Journal of Politics* 67 (2005): 784–803.

46. Citrin, "Political Relevance," 978.

47. Introduction and Summary, *How Americans View Government: Deconstructing Distrust* (Pew Research Center for the People and the Press, Washington, D.C., March 10, 1998), http://people-press.org/reports/display.php3?ReportID=95.

48. Hetherington, "Political Relevance of Political Trust." See Weatherford, "How Does Government Performance," and Orren, "Fall from Grace" for similar conclusions.

49. Marc J. Hetherington, "The Effect of Political Trust on the Presidential Vote, 1968–96," *American Political Science Review* 93 (1999): 311–326.

50. Hetherington, *Why Trust Matters.*

51. Ibid., 139.

52. Hardin, "Do We Want Trust?"

53. Russell J. Dalton, *Democratic Challenges, Democratic Choices: The Erosion of Political Support in Advanced Industrial Democracies* (Oxford: Oxford University Press, 2004).

54. Mark E. Warren, "Introduction," in *Democracy and Trust,* ed. Mark E. Warren (Cambridge: Cambridge University Press, 1999), 8.

55. Rosalee A. Clawson, Elizabeth R. Kegler, and Eric N. Waltenburg, "The Legitimacy-Conferring Authority of the U.S. Supreme Court: An Experimental Design," *American Politics Research* 29 (2001): 566–591.

56. James A. Davis, Tom W. Smith, and Peter V. Marsden, General Social Surveys, 1972–2004: Cumulative file [Computer file], 2nd ICPSR version. Chicago: National Opinion Research Center [producer], 2005. Storrs: University of Connecticut, Roper Center for Public Opinion Research; Ann Arbor, Mich.: Interuniversity Consortium for Political and Social Research; Berkeley: University of California, Computer-Assisted Survey Methods Program (http://sda.berkeley.edu) [distributors], 2005.

57. James L. Gibson, Gregory A. Caldeira, and Lester Kenyatta Spence, "Measuring Attitudes toward the United States Supreme Court," *American Journal of Political Science* 47 (2003): 354–367.

58. John R. Hibbing and Elizabeth Theiss-Morse, *Congress as Public Enemy* (Cambridge: Cambridge University Press, 1995).

59. Ibid., 45.
60. Also see Gibson, Caldeira, and Spence, "Measuring Attitudes."
61. Hibbing and Theiss-Morse, *Congress as Public Enemy,* 104.
62. Ibid., 51–53.
63. Ibid., 52–54.
64. Ibid., 58.
65. Ibid., 171–173.
66. Ibid., 149.
67. Ibid., chap. 5.
68. Jeffery J. Mondak and Shannon Ishiyama Smithey, "The Dynamics of Public Support for the Supreme Court," *Journal of Politics* 59 (1997): 1114–1142; Vanessa A. Baird and Amy Gangl, "Shattering the Myth of Legality: The Impact of the Media's Framing of Supreme Court Procedures on Perceptions of Fairness," *Political Psychology* 27 (2006): 597–614.
69. Hibbing and Theiss-Morse, *Congress as Public Enemy,* chap. 5.
70. Ibid., 156–158.
71. Ibid., 162.
72. On this point, also see John R. Hibbing and Elizabeth Theiss-Morse, *Stealth Democracy* (Cambridge: Cambridge University Press, 2002).
73. Hibbing and Theiss-Morse, *Congress as Public Enemy,* 147.
74. Lyda Hanifan, "The Rural School Community Center," *Annals of the American Academy of Political and Social Science,* 67 (1916): 130, quoted in Robert D. Putnam, *Bowling Alone: The Collapse and Revival of American Community* (New York: Simon and Schuster, 2000), 19.
75. Putnam, *Bowling Alone,* 19.
76. "Civic Engagement and Service Learning," American Psychological Association, www.apa.org/ed/slce/civicengagement.html (accessed June 29, 2007).
77. John Brehm and Wendy Rahn, "Individual-Level Evidence for the Causes and Consequences of Social Capital," *American Journal of Political Science* 41 (1997): 1002–1003.
78. Keele, "Social Capital and the Dynamics."
79. Ibid., 241.
80. Kenneth Newton, "Trust, Social Capital, Civil Society, and Democracy," *International Political Science Review* 22 (2001): 201–214.
81. Robert D. Putnam, "Bowling Alone: America's Declining Social Capital," *Journal of Democracy* 6 (1995): 67.
82. Putnam, *Bowling Alone,* chaps. 16–20; Amy Caiazza and Robert D. Putnam, "Women's Status and Social Capital in the United States," *Journal of Women, Politics & Policy* 27 (2005): 69–84.
83. Sharon D. Wright Austin, *The Transformation of Plantation Politics: Black Politics, Concentrated Poverty, and Social Capital in the Mississippi Delta* (Albany: State University of New York Press, 2006).
84. David A. Schultz, "The Phenomenology of Democracy: Putnam, Pluralism, and Voluntary Associations," in *Social Capital: Critical Perspectives on Community and "Bowling Alone,"* ed. Scott L. McLean, David A. Schultz, and Manfred B. Steger (New York: New York University Press, 2002).
85. Putnam, *Bowling Alone,* 111–113.
86. Ibid., chap. 9.
87. Ibid., 50–52; Putnam, "Bowling Alone."
88. Putnam, *Bowling Alone,* 71.
89. Ibid., 115.
90. Ibid., 184.
91. Robert D. Putnam, "Tuning In, Tuning Out: The Strange Disappearance of Social Capital in America," *PS: Political Science and Politics* 28 (1995): 676.
92. Putnam, *Bowling Alone,* chap. 13; Putnam, "Tuning In, Tuning Out." See also Pippa Norris, "Does Television Erode Social Capital? A Reply to Putnam," *PS: Political Science and Politics* 29 (1996): 474–480; Brehm and Rahn, "Individual-Level Evidence."
93. Putnam, *Bowling Alone,* chap. 13; Norris, "Does Television Erode Social Capital?"

94. Putnam, *Bowling Alone,* 246.
95. Robert Wuthnow, *Sharing the Journey: Support Groups and America's New Quest for Community* (New York: Free Press, 1994); Kenneth Newton, "Social Capital and Democracy," *American Behavioral Scientist* 40 (1997): 575–586; Carl Boggs, "Social Capital as Political Fantasy," in *Social Capital: Critical Perspectives on Community and "Bowling Alone,"* ed. Scott L. McLean, David A. Schultz, and Manfred B. Steger (New York: New York University Press, 2002).
96. Putnam, *Bowling Alone,* 148–152.
97. Michael J. Shapiro, "Post-Liberal Civil Society and the Worlds of Neo-Tocquevillean Social Theory," in *Social Capital: Critical Perspectives on Community and "Bowling Alone,"* ed. Scott L. McLean, David A. Schultz, and Manfred B. Steger (New York: New York University Press, 2002), 115.
98. Scott L. McLean, "Patriotism, Generational Change, and the Politics of Sacrifice," in *Social Capital: Critical Perspectives on Community and "Bowling Alone,"* ed. Scott L. McLean, David A. Schultz, and Manfred B. Steger (New York: New York University Press, 2002).
99. Boggs, "Social Capital as Political Fantasy."
100. R. Claire Snyder, "Social Capital: The Politics of Race and Gender," in *Social Capital: Critical Perspectives on Community and "Bowling Alone,"* ed. Scott L. McLean, David A. Schultz, and Manfred B. Steger (New York: New York University Press, 2002).
101. Manfred B. Steger, "Robert Putnam, Social Capital and a Suspect Named Globalization," in *Social Capital: Critical Perspectives on Community and "Bowling Alone,"* ed. Scott L. McLean, David A. Schultz, and Manfred B. Steger (New York: New York University Press, 2002).
102. Schultz, "The Phenomenology of Democracy."
103. Andrew Sullivan, "Clinton, Trust, and The War," *The Atlantic Online,* July 20, 2007, http://andrewsullivan.theatlantic.com/the_daily_dish/2007/07/clinton-trust-a.html (accessed July 25, 2007).

CHAPTER 11

1. *Different Faiths, Different Messages* (Pew Research Center for the People and the Press, Washington, D.C., March 19, 2003), http://people-press.org/reports/display.php3?Report ID=176.
2. Ole R. Holsti, *Public Opinion and American Foreign Policy,* rev. ed. (Ann Arbor: University of Michigan Press, 2004), 278.
3. "President Bush Addresses the Nation," March 19, 2003, www.whitehouse.gov/news/releases/2003/03/20030319-17.html.
4. *Broad Opposition to Bush's Iraq Plan* (Pew Research Center for the People and the Press, Washington, D.C., January 16, 2007), http://people-press.org/reports/display.php3?ReportID=301.
5. Ibid.
6. "President's Address to the Nation," January 10, 2007, www.whitehouse.gov/news/releases/2007/01/20070110-7.html.
7. *Broad Opposition.*
8. Benjamin I. Page with Marshall M. Bouton, *The Foreign Policy Disconnect: What Americans Want from Our Leaders but Don't Get* (Chicago: University of Chicago Press, 2006), chap. 4.
9. For a description of this and other mechanisms linking opinion and policy, see Alan D. Monroe and Paul J. Gardner Jr., "Public Policy Linkages," in *Research in Micropolitics,* vol. 2, ed. Samuel Long (Greenwich, Conn.: JAI Press, 1987).
10. David S. Broder, "A Mob-Rule Moment," *Washington Post,* July 5, 2007.
11. Paul Burstein, "The Impact of Public Opinion on Public Policy: A Review and an Agenda," *Political Research Quarterly* 56 (2003): 29.
12. See, for example, Lawrence R. Jacobs, *The Health of Nations: Public Opinion and the Making of American and British Health Policy* (Ithaca, N.Y.: Cornell University Press, 1993); Bruce Russett, *Controlling the Sword: The Democratic Governance of National Security* (Cambridge, Mass.: Harvard University Press, 1990); and Elaine B. Sharp, *The Sometime Connection: Public Opinion and Social Policy* (Albany: State University of New York Press, 1999).

13. Benjamin I. Page and Robert Y. Shapiro, "Effects of Public Opinion on Policy," *American Political Science Review* 77 (1983): 175–190.
14. For a compelling argument that shifts in public opinion produce strong effects in national politics, see James A. Stimson, *Tides of Consent: How Public Opinion Shapes American Politics* (Cambridge: Cambridge University Press, 2004).
15. Alan D. Monroe, "Consistency between Public Preferences and National Policy Decisions," *American Politics Quarterly* 7 (1979): 3–18; Alan D. Monroe, "Public Opinion and Public Policy, 1980–1993," *Public Opinion Quarterly* 62 (1998): 6–28.
16. See also Martin Gilens, "Inequality and Democratic Responsiveness," *Public Opinion Quarterly* 69 (2005): 778–796.
17. James A. Stimson, Michael B. MacKuen, and Robert S. Erikson, "Opinion and Policy: A Global View," *PS: Political Science and Politics* 27 (1994): 29–35.
18. Respectively, James A. Stimson, *Public Opinion in America: Moods, Cycles, and Swings* (Boulder, Colo.: Westview Press, 1991), and Robert H. Durr, "What Moves Policy Sentiment?" *American Political Science Review* 87 (1993): 158–170.
19. James A. Stimson, Michael B. MacKuen, and Robert S. Erikson, "Dynamic Representation," *American Political Science Review* 89 (1995): 548.
20. Robert S. Erikson, Michael B. MacKuen, and James A. Stimson, *The Macro Polity* (Cambridge: Cambridge University Press, 2002), chap. 9; Stimson, MacKuen, and Erikson, "Dynamic Representation."
21. Stimson, MacKuen, and Erikson, "Dynamic Representation," 543.
22. Robert S. Erikson, Gerald C. Wright, and John P. McIver, *Statehouse Democracy: Public Opinion and Policy in the American States* (Cambridge: Cambridge University Press, 1993), chap. 2.
23. Ibid., chap. 4.
24. See also Burstein, "Impact of Public Opinion."
25. Page and Shapiro, "Effects of Public Opinion"; Monroe, "Consistency Between"; Burstein, "Impact of Public Opinion"; Sharp, *Sometime Connection*; Shoon Kathleen Murray, "Private Polls and Presidential Policymaking: Reagan as a Facilitator of Change," *Public Opinion Quarterly* 70 (2006): 477–498.
26. Monroe, "Public Opinion."
27. Donald J. Devine, *The Attentive Public: Polyarchical Democracy* (Chicago: Rand McNally, 1970).
28. Vincent L. Hutchings, *Public Opinion and Democratic Accountability* (Princeton: Princeton University Press, 2003).
29. V. O. Key Jr., *Public Opinion and American Democracy* (New York: Alfred A. Knopf, 1961), chap. 21; Stimson, *Tides of Consent*, chap. 6; R. Douglas Arnold, *The Logic of Congressional Action* (New Haven: Yale University Press, 1990); John R. Zaller, "Coming to Grips with V. O. Key's Concept of Latent Opinion," in *Electoral Democracy*, ed. Michael B. MacKuen and George Rabinowitz (Ann Arbor: University of Michigan Press, 2003).
30. Gilens, "Inequality."
31. Ibid., 794.
32. Jean-Jacques Rousseau, *The Social Contract*, trans. Maurice Cranston (London: Penguin Books, 1988).
33. For further discussion of causality and aggregate studies of opinion and policy, see Robert S. Erikson, Michael B. MacKuen, and James A. Stimson, "Public Opinion and Policy: Causal Flow in a Macro System Model," and Benjamin I. Page, "The Semi-Sovereign Public," both in *Navigating Public Opinion: Polls, Policy, and the Future of American Democracy*, ed. Jeff Manza, Fay Lomax Cook, and Benjamin I. Page (Oxford: Oxford University Press, 2002).
34. Page with Bouton, *Foreign Policy Disconnect*, 223.
35. Page, "Semi-Sovereign Public," 329.
36. John G. Geer, *From Tea Leaves to Opinion Polls: A Theory of Democratic Leadership* (New York: Columbia University Press, 1996), chap. 2; Robert M. Eisinger, *The Evolution of Presidential Polling* (New York: Cambridge University Press, 2003).

37. Eisinger, *Evolution of Presidential Polling*; Lawrence R. Jacobs, "The Recoil Effect: Public Opinion and Policymaking in the U.S. and Britain," *Comparative Politics* 24 (1992): 199–217.

38. Jacobs, "The Recoil Effect," 210.

39. Eisinger, *Evolution of Presidential Polling*; Lawrence R. Jacobs and Robert Y. Shapiro, "The Rise of Presidential Polling: The Nixon White House in Historical Perspective," *Public Opinion Quarterly* 59 (1995): 163–195.

40. Geer, *Tea Leaves*, chap. 2.

41. Diane Heith, *Polling to Govern: Public Opinion and Presidential Leadership* (Palo Alto, Calif.: Stanford University Press, 2003), chap. 2. See also Shoon Kathleen Murray and Peter Howard, "Variation in White House Polling Operations: Carter to Clinton," *Public Opinion Quarterly* 66 (2002): 527–558.

42. Jacobs and Shapiro, "Rise of Presidential Polling," 166.

43. Murray and Howard, "Variation in White House Polling."

44. Ibid., 533.

45. See also Kathryn Dunn Tenpas and James A. McCann, "Testing the Permanence of the Permanent Campaign: An Analysis of Presidential Polling Expenditures, 1977–2002," *Public Opinion Quarterly* 71 (2007): 349–366.

46. Ibid.

47. Heith, *Polling to Govern*, chap. 8.

48. Ibid., chap. 3.

49. James N. Druckman and Lawrence R. Jacobs, "Lumpers and Splitters: The Public Opinion Information that Politicians Collect and Use," *Public Opinion Quarterly* 70 (2006): 453–476.

50. Heith, *Polling to Govern*, 44–45.

51. Susan Herbst, *Reading Public Opinion: How Political Actors View the Democratic Process* (Chicago: University of Chicago Press, 1998), chap. 2.

52. Eisinger, *Evolution of Presidential Polling*, 188–190; Lawrence R. Jacobs and Robert Y. Shapiro, *Politicians Don't Pander: Political Manipulation and the Loss of Democratic Responsiveness* (Chicago: University of Chicago Press, 2000), chap. 4.

53. Herbst, *Reading Public Opinion*, chap. 2.

54. Ibid., 53, 54.

55. Jacobs and Shapiro, *Politicians Don't Pander*.

56. Ibid., 48.

57. Ibid., chap. 3.

58. Quoted in ibid., 96.

59. Ibid., 108; emphasis in original.

60. Ibid., 106–112.

61. Ibid., chap. 4.

62. Ibid., 137.

63. Hilary Stout, "Many Don't Realize It's Clinton's Plan They Like," *Wall Street Journal*, March 10, 1994.

64. Jacobs and Shapiro, *Politicians Don't Pander*, 301.

65. Murray, "Private Polls"; Druckman and Jacobs, "Lumpers and Splitters."

66. Jacobs, "The Recoil Effect"; Geer, *Tea Leaves*; Heith, *Polling to Govern*.

67. Jacobs and Shapiro, *Politicians Don't Pander*, 147–148.

68. Brandice Canes-Wrone, *Who Leads Whom? Presidents, Policy, and the Public* (Chicago: University of Chicago Press, 2006); Jacobs and Shapiro, *Politicians Don't Pander*, chap. 9.

69. For one attempt to do just this, see Benjamin I. Page and Robert Y. Shapiro, "Educating and Manipulating the Public," in *Manipulating Public Opinion: Essays on Public Opinion as a Dependent Variable*, ed. Michael Margolis and Gary A. Mauser (Pacific Grove, Calif.: Brooks-Cole, 1989).

70. For overviews of this topic, see Holsti, *Public Opinion*, chap. 1, and Page with Bouton, *Foreign Policy Disconnect*, 219–223.

71. "Iraq Trip Sways Congressman against Pullout," *All Things Considered*, National Public Radio, August 21, 2007.

72. Page and Shapiro, "Effects of Public Opinion"; Burstein, "Impact of Public Opinion."
73. Monroe, "Consistency Between"; Monroe, "Public Opinion."
74. Larry M. Bartels, "Constituency Opinion and Congressional Policy Making: The Reagan Defense Buildup," *American Political Science Review* 85 (1991): 457–474; Thomas Hartley and Bruce Russett, "Public Opinion and the Common Defense: Who Governs Military Spending in the United States?" *American Political Science Review* 86 (1992): 905–915.
75. Richard Sobel, *The Impact of Public Opinion on U.S. Foreign Policy Since Vietnam: Constraining the Colossus* (New York: Oxford University Press, 2001), 240. For a similar conclusion, see Holsti, *Public Opinion.*
76. Murray, "Private Polls."
77. Robert Y. Shapiro and Lawrence R. Jacobs, "Public Opinion, Foreign Policy, and Democracy: How Presidents Use Public Opinion," in *Navigating Public Opinion: Polls, Policy, and the Future of American Democracy*, ed. Jeff Manza, Fay Lomax Cook, and Benjamin I. Page (Oxford: Oxford University Press, 2002).
78. Brandon Rottinghaus, "Following the 'Mail Hawks': Alternative Measures of Public Opinion on Vietnam in the Johnson White House," *Public Opinion Quarterly* 71 (2007): 367–391.
79. The original finding was presented in Page and Shapiro, "Effects of Public Opinion."
80. Page, "Semi-Sovereign Public," 336.
81. Ibid., 337.
82. Lawrence R. Jacobs and Benjamin I. Page, "Who Influences U.S. Foreign Policy?" *American Political Science Review* 99 (2005): 107–123.
83. Ibid., 110.
84. Ibid., 120. For a similar conclusion, see G. William Domhoff, "The Power Elite, Public Policy, and Public Opinion," in *Navigating Public Opinion: Polls, Policy, and the Future of American Democracy*, ed. Jeff Manza, Fay Lomax Cook, and Benjamin I. Page (Oxford: Oxford University Press, 2002).
85. Page with Bouton, *Foreign Policy Disconnect.*
86. Ibid., chap. 2.
87. Ibid., 46–52.
88. Ibid., chaps. 4 and 5.
89. Ibid., 109.
90. Ibid., chap. 7.
91. E. E. Schattschneider, *The Semi-Sovereign People: A Realist's View of Democracy in America* (New York: Holt, Rinehart and Winston, 1960); Page, "Semi-Sovereign Public."

CHAPTER 12

1. Dennis Chong and James N. Druckman, "Framing Theory," *Annual Review of Political Science* 10 (2007): 120.

APPENDIX

1. These results are from the 2000 American National Election Study, a survey of the American adult population. The death penalty question was worded as follows: "Do you favor or oppose the death penalty for persons convicted of murder?"
2. Donald R. Kinder and Thomas R. Palfrey "On Behalf of an Experimental Political Science," in *Experimental Foundations of Political Science*, ed. Donald R. Kinder and Thomas R. Palfrey (Ann Arbor: University of Michigan Press, 1993).
3. Martin Gilens, "An Anatomy of Survey-Based Experiments," in *Navigating Public Opinion: Polls, Policy, and the Future of American Democracy*, ed. Jeff Manza, Fay Lomax Cook, and Benjamin I. Page (Oxford: Oxford University Press, 2002), 232.
4. James M. Carlson and Mark S. Hyde, *Doing Empirical Political Research* (Boston: Houghton Mifflin, 2003), 297.
5. Bernard R. Berelson, *Content Analysis in Communications Research* (New York: Free Press, 1952), 18. See also Klaus Krippendorff, *Content Analysis: An Introduction to Its Methodology* (Newbury Park, Calif.: Sage, 1980).

Glossary

Acceptance. Stage in the political persuasion process during which people decide they agree with the content of a persuasive argument. (Chapter 4)

Accessibility model. A model of opinion formation that says that easily accessible concepts (e.g., due to media coverage) influence people's political judgments. (Chapter 3)

Accuracy. A news norm that calls for journalists to provide correct information, often achieved by relying on official sources. (Chapter 3)

Activated mass opinion. Beliefs that are salient to citizens and lead them to be politically active. (Chapter 6)

Activation effect. Occurs when political communication encourages citizens to support presidential candidates who share their preexisting values and predispositions. (Chapter 3)

Advocacy journalism. A form of journalism that is committed to only some of the news norms because it is also concerned with providing news from a particular perspective. (Chapter 3)

Affirmative action. An umbrella term for a variety of policies that ensure equal treatment of minorities and whites in education and employment. (Chapter 9)

Agenda-setting phenomenon. Occurs when the media influence which issues citizens view as important. (Chapter 3)

Aggregate studies. Examinations of more than one political event or topic, such as analyzing policymaking in many issue domains across multiple years. (Chapter 11)

Atheists. People who oppose churches or formal religion. (Chapter 8)

Attitude. Positive or negative evaluation of an object (person, issue, etc.). (Chapter 1)

Attitude change. Degree to which political opinions fluctuate over time. (Chapter 4)

Attitude constraint. Situation that exists when political opinions are related to one another; degree to which one can predict a person's opinion toward a political object when knowing his or her opinions toward other objects. (Chapter 5)

Attitude crystallization. Development of more concrete and stable political opinions. (Chapter 2)

Attitude importance. Degree to which a specific attitude is personally meaningful or relevant. (Chapter 1)

Attitude stability. Degree to which political opinions remain the same over time. (Chapters 4, 5)

Attitudes toward the institutions of government. Attitudes toward the Congress, presidency, and Supreme Court. (Chapter 10)

Attitudes toward the people in those institutions. Attitudes toward members of Congress, the president, and Supreme Court justices. (Chapter 10)

Authoritarians. People who have a predisposition to value sameness and conformity to group norms. (Chapter 6)

Belief system. Set of related, coherent political attitudes; attitudes are related because they derive from overarching worldview (such as political ideology). (Chapter 5)

Beliefs. Thoughts or information regarding an attitude object, often concerning what one thinks to be true about the object. (Chapter 1)

Benevolent leader imagery. Viewing political leaders in very positive terms, believing that leaders do good deeds. (Chapter 2)

Bill of Rights. The first ten amendments to the Constitution. (Chapter 8)

Black political ideology. Political belief system present among African Americans; specific views often include group-based perspectives, such as beliefs regarding the status of blacks in society. (Chapter 5)

Case study. An in-depth analysis of a specific political event or arena, such as the passage of a piece of legislation or policymaking surrounding one issue. (Chapter 11)

Causal responsibility. Identifying causes for a political problem, such as poverty. (Chapter 3)

Central route to persuasion. Process by which attitudes change when a person is motivated and able to carefully consider persuasive communication; resulting attitude change is likely to endure. (Chapter 4)

Changes in public expectations of government. Changes in what people think the government should do when new problems that the government is ill equipped to handle are forced onto the government's agenda. (Chapter 10)

Chapter-based civic associations. Community-based organizations whose members meet regularly, such as parent-teacher associations, the American Legion, and the Jaycees. (Chapter 10)

Citizen apathy. Lack of interest or involvement in political matters. (Chapter 1)

Civic education. Education about government and politics in schools. (Chapter 7)

Civic engagement. Actions by individuals and collectives to identify and address public issues. (Chapter 10)

Civil liberties. Rights granted to citizens that are protected from government suppression, such as freedom of speech or freedom of religion. (Chapter 8)

Civil rights. Government guarantees of political equality for people. (Chapter 9)

Classical models of democracy. Theories based on ancient Athenian democracy; key characteristics include active citizen participation in political debates and decisions. (Chapter 1)

Closed-ended questions. Survey questions with a limited set of response options. (Appendix)

Cognitive dissonance theory. Approach to understanding attitudes that posits people prefer to maintain consistency across their beliefs, attitudes, and attitude-relevant behaviors; when inconsistencies arise, people will work to regain consistency. (Chapter 4)

Collective public opinion. Political attitudes of an aggregation of people, such as all citizens of a nation. (Chapter 4)

Communists. People who favor communism as a system of government, particularly wanting a society without the evils of capitalism so that people can fully benefit from their own labor. (Chapter 8)

Concentrated. A few large companies own the majority of the media in the United States. (Chapter 3)

Confidence in Congress. Faith in the people running Congress. (Chapter 10)

Confidence in the executive branch. Faith in the people running the executive branch of the federal government. (Chapter 10)

Confidence in the Supreme Court. Faith in the people running the Supreme Court. (Chapter 10)

Conglomerate. Large corporations that own several media companies as well as nonmedia companies. (Chapter 3)

Consensual politics. Context during which disagreements between the major political parties are relatively minor and the political environment is not dominated by discussion of conflictual issues. (Chapter 5)

Conservatives. People whose political ideology emphasizes order, tradition, individual responsibility, and minimal government intervention in economic matters. (Chapter 5)

Considerations. Pieces of information or reasons held by individuals that cause them to support or oppose a political issue. (Chapter 4)

Constitutional framework. Formal system of government, as enshrined in the Constitution. (Chapter 8)

Content analysis. Research technique used to examine the content of communication. (Chapter 3, Appendix)

Context. Broader environment, potentially including the features of one's community or nation, or events occurring in other nations. (Chapter 8)

Conversion effect. Occurs when political communication leads citizens to change from one candidate to another. (Chapter 3)

Corporations. Organizations with the primary goal of making money; describes most media outlets. (Chapter 3)

Counterterrorism policies. Government actions that are intended to combat terrorism. (Chapter 8)

Crafted talk. Rhetoric and messages that officials communicate to the citizenry in an attempt to influence public opinion. (Chapter 11)

Cross-sectional study. Method for assessing political opinions by examining a sample of individuals at one point in time. (Chapter 4)

Cynicism. A lack of trust in government that stems from the belief that government is not functioning well. (Chapter 10)

Democratic elitists. Democratic theorists who view competitive elections as the primary mechanism by which citizen preferences are expressed; also believe that governmental decisions are better made by political elites than the public. (Chapter 1)

Democratic responsiveness. Occurs when political leaders enact public policy that coincides with the genuine opinions of the public. (Chapter 11)

Democratic theory. Field of study that focuses on defining the proper characteristics, often normative, of a democracy. (Chapter 1)

Diffuse support. Public opinions about the political system, such as contentment with the form of government and attachment to the norms and structure of the regime. (Chapters 2, 10)

Direct democracy. Governmental system whereby citizens meet, discuss, and decide on the content of the laws. (Chapter 1)

Efficacy. Belief that one can influence the decisions of government officials and that officials are responsive to the public. (Chapter 2)

Egalitarianism. Belief that people are equal and should be treated the same regardless of their personal characteristics. (Chapters 3, 6)

Ego defense. Theory that people have specific attitudes because the attitudes protect their egos or images of themselves from outside threats. (Chapter 4)

Elaboration likelihood model. Approach for understanding persuasion that focuses on the degree to which people generate cognitive responses to persuasive communication. (Chapter 4)

Elite discourse. Discussion of political topics (issues, candidates, etc.) by leaders that is communicated to the public. (Chapter 4)

Emotions. Feelings about or affect regarding an attitude object. (Chapter 1)

Empirical analyses. Examinations that focus on accurately describing and/or explaining real-life phenomena. (Chapter 1)

Enemy combatants. Government designation used to classify those people suspected of threatening national security or waging war against the nation. (Chapter 8)

Entertainment. Shows that may have political content, but their primary purpose is to entertain, not inform. (Chapter 3)

Episodic frames. A media frame that focuses on individual people. (Chapter 3)

Ethnographic research. Method for assessing political attitudes and behaviors by which researchers immerse themselves into a setting or community, observing individuals, asking them questions, and more generally interacting with them. (Chapter 5)

Experiment. A type of research design that has two key characteristics: (a) the experimenter manipulates a feature of the study, and (b) subjects are randomly assigned to experimental conditions. (Appendix)

Experimenter control. The experimenter determines the experimental treatment and when and how it will be introduced to subjects. (Chapter 3)

Exposure to diversity. Degree to which one is in contact with people who are different, particularly people who hold different political views from one's own. (Chapter 8)

External validity. A characteristic of a study in which the findings can be generalized beyond the sample and context used in that study. (Chapter 3, Appendix)

Extremity. Degree to which support or opposition toward an attitude object is strong or slight. (Chapter 1)

Factions. Groups of citizens who pursue their self-interest rather than advocating for the common good of the community or nation. (Chapter 1)

Focus groups. A type of research method for assessing political attitudes in which citizens are brought together in a group and asked what they think about political topics using open-ended questions. (Chapter 7, Appendix)

Forum for diverse views. Place where a range of political opinions is provided. (Chapter 3)

Framing effects. When media frames influence public opinion on the issue being framed. (Chapter 3)

Free speech frame. A media frame that emphasizes the rights of individuals to speak. (Chapter 3)

Functional theories. Approach for understanding the development of attitudes by focusing on the motivations people have for holding specific attitudes; examples of motivations include knowledge and ego defense. (Chapter 4)

Game schema. How journalists organize their coverage of political candidates by focusing on the ins and outs of the campaign. (Chapter 3)

Gay marriage. Same-sex marriage, probably the most controversial gay rights issue of our times. (Chapter 9)

Gender gap in political knowledge. Studies of political knowledge commonly show that men are significantly more knowledgeable about politics than women; the gap decreases when the propensity to guess is taken into account. (Chapter 7)

Gender stereotypes. Beliefs about males as a group and females as a group that citizens apply to individual men or individual women. (Chapter 9)

Generalist. Someone who is knowledgeable across all political topics. (Chapter 7)

Generational effect. Changes in political attitudes to an entire age cohort, caused by events or features of the political context. (Chapter 2)

Genetic inheritance. Transmission of traits, opinions, and so forth from parents to offspring via genes. (Chapter 2)

Geneva Conventions. An international treaty that governs, among other matters, the treatment of prisoners of war and the rights of foreign nationals who are accused of committing criminal acts. (Chapter 8)

Governing schema. How citizens organize their thinking about politics by focusing on political issues. (Chapter 3)

Government expenditures frame. A frame that focuses on government spending. (Chapter 3)

Group attitudes. Attitudes toward important social and political groups that shape public opinion. (Chapter 6)

Group consciousness. An awareness of how membership in a particular group shapes the life chances of individuals. (Chapter 6)

Hard news. News regarding political leaders, important issues, and significant events. (Chapter 3)

Heuristics. Mental shortcuts used for processing and understanding information; one example is relying on the ideology of the sponsor of a new policy to determine one's own opinion toward the policy. (Chapter 5)

Historical events. Important political events that shape public opinion. (Chapter 6)

Homosexuals. Individuals who have intimate relationships with people of their same sex. (Chapter 8)

Humanitarian frame. A frame that focuses on the needs of poor people. (Chapter 3)

Hypodermic model. Perspective that views the media as quite persuasive and citizens as unable to resist media messages. (Chapter 3)

Ideologically contentious. Context during which salient political actors (such as members of political parties) disagree over the key issues of the day, particularly when the disagreements fall along ideological lines. (Chapter 5)

Ideology. Overarching set of beliefs regarding the proper role of government in society, in regulating the economy and in individuals' lives. (Chapter 5)

Implementation. Translating abstract policies into practice. (Chapter 9)

Importance model. A model of opinion formation that says that important concepts are weighted more heavily in citizens' minds (e.g., due to media coverage), which then influence people's political judgments. (Chapter 3)

Impressionable years model. Pattern by which political attitudes change during late adolescence and early adulthood, then remain more stable throughout the rest of the life span. (Chapter 2)

In-depth interviewing. A type of research method for assessing political attitudes by asking respondents very broad questions and allowing respondents to answer how they wish and in as much detail as they want to provide. (Chapter 5, Appendix)

Individualism. Belief that people should get ahead on the basis of their own efforts. (Chapters 3, 6)

Informal social interaction. Casual interaction among neighbors or friends. (Chapter 10)

Information environment. Refers to how much information about politics is present in the media. (Chapter 7)

Informed. Citizens who hold accurate factual beliefs about politics. (Chapter 7)

Interest groups. Organizations or collections of individuals who attempt to influence governmental decision makers regarding specific issues. (Chapter 1)

Intermediary. Link between citizens and political elites. (Chapter 3)

Internal validity. A characteristics of a study that allows a researcher to conclude that one factor causes another. (Appendix)

Internet. Provides an outlet for information, contains both entertainment and political news. (Chapter 3)

Interpersonal communication. Discussion of political matters among individuals. (Chapter 2)

Interpersonal trust. The degree to which people think others can be trusted, are fair, and are helpful. (Chapter 10)

Knowledge function. Theory that people have specific attitudes because the attitudes help them to understand the world around them. (Chapter 4)

Leaners. Individuals who describe themselves as partisan independents but who do feel closer to one political party than others. (Chapter 1)

Learning theory. Approach for understanding the development of attitudes; basic premise is that attitudes are obtained much like habits are, people grow to like or dislike attitude objects after repeated exposure to the object. (Chapter 4)

"Least liked" group. Group whose political views or behaviors a person loathes the most; survey research method for assessing public tolerance of those holding unpopular political views. (Chapter 8)

Liberals. People whose political ideology favors government intervention in the economy when necessary to combat features of the free market (such as discrimination and low wages); also individuals who value equality and openness to dissenting views. (Chapter 5)

Libertarians. People who have a predisposition to value diversity and individual freedom. (Chapter 6)

Life cycle. Pattern by which political attitudes are strongly influenced by one's age rather than, for example, developing only when one is young. (Chapter 2)

Likert question. Type of item appearing on an opinion poll whereby a statement is presented to respondents who are asked whether they agree or disagree with the statement. (Chapter 5)

Limited information processors. People do not have the cognitive abilities to systematically process complex political information, which is why they use heuristics. (Chapter 7)

Low-information rationality. Occurs when citizens use heuristics, such as party identification or cues from trusted groups, to figure out their political stances. (Chapter 7)

Mainstream effect. When political elites agree on an issue, the more politically aware a person is, the more likely he or she will hold the same opinion as the elites. (Chapter 4)

Malevolent leader imagery. Viewing political leaders quite negatively, believing that leaders are not good people. (Chapter 2)

Manipulation. Involves the researcher varying access to information, events, or whatever is the focus of the research among experimental participants. (Appendix)

Marketplace of ideas. Availability of many different political views in the public arena. (Chapter 8)

Measurement error. Difference between the assessment of political attitudes and what the real content of those attitudes actually is. (Chapter 5)

Media communication. Coverage of political topics or events in the news or via other mass market formats. (Chapter 2)

Militarists. People who believe that military leaders rather than elected officials should rule a nation. (Chapter 8)

Minimal effects model. Perspective that views citizens as resistant to media messages because they filter media content through their preexisting attitudes. (Chapter 3)

Minority press. Newspapers that serve minority communities. (Chapter 3)

Misinformed. Citizens who hold inaccurate factual beliefs about politics. (Chapter 7)

Moral traditionalism. Citizens' beliefs regarding the organization of family and society. (Chapter 6)

Multilateralism. Foreign policy goals that emphasize working with other nations and international bodies such as the United Nations. (Chapter 11)

Multiple choice questions. Questions that provide several possible answers from which a respondent can select. (Chapter 7)

National mass membership organizations. Organizations that are not community based; individuals participate by paying dues, but rarely by working with other citizens to solve problems. (Chapter 10)

National probability sample. Selection of people who have been chosen randomly to accurately represent a larger population; generally used for selecting individuals for opinion polls. (Chapter 2)

Neutrality. A news norm that calls for journalists to not inject their personal opinions into news coverage. (Chapter 3)

News grazers. People who follow the news on television, but quickly flip to another channel when they lose interest. (Chapter 7)

News norms. Standards and customs that shape the behavior of journalists. (Chapter 3)

Newsbeats. A news norm that calls for journalists to be assigned to cover specific institutions or topic areas, called beats. (Chapter 3)

Newsworthiness. A news norm that calls for journalists to cover conflict. (Chapter 3)

Nonattitudes. Political opinions that are fleeting, not well considered, or lacking meaning for people who hold them. (Chapter 4)

Nonprofit media corporations. Media organizations whose goal is to serve the public interest rather than make money. (Chapter 3)

Normative. Conclusions or statements that focus on how the world should operate; in the realm of democratic theory, views regarding how government and society ought to be structured, including what ought to be the role of the citizenry. (Chapter 1)

Normative threats. A situation in which core values are called into question. (Chapter 6)

Objectivity. A news norm that calls for journalists to provide both sides of an issue. (Chapter 3)

Official sources. News sources that primarily include government officials but also other powerful people in society. (Chapter 3)

Old-fashioned racism. A set of beliefs about the innate inferiority of black Americans. (Chapters 6, 9)

Open-ended questions. Survey items that allow respondents to answer however they see fit; these items do not present respondents with predetermined response options. (Chapter 5, Appendix)

Opinion. Expression of a preference toward an object; verbal or written expression of an attitude. (Chapter 1)

Opinion leadership. Act of political elites educating or shaping the attitudes of the citizenry, such as by describing policy proposals and reasons for supporting them. (Chapter 11)

Opinion trends. General direction of aggregate public preferences, such as liberal or conservative swings. (Chapter 11)

Opinion-policy congruence. Degree to which citizen preferences and governmental decisions are the same. (Chapter 11)

Pack journalism. Occurs when journalists assigned to the same newsbeats all cover the same stories (and don't cover other stories). (Chapter 3)

Panel or longitudinal study/survey. Assessing the political opinions of the same people at two or more points in time. (Chapter 2, Appendix)

Participatory democracy. Theory of democracy that emphasizes the importance of political participation by the public and believes the public to be capable of meaningful participation. (Chapter 1)

Partisan independence. Viewing oneself as not identifying with a political party. (Chapter 1)

Partisans. People who identify with a political party. (Chapter 1)

Party identification. Allegiance with or attachment to a political party (typically the Democratic Party or the Republican Party); a self-classification rather than a description of one's behavior. (Chapter 1)

People and players. A type of political knowledge about key people and groups. (Chapter 7)

Perceived discrimination. Belief that discrimination is an important problem limiting life chances. (Chapter 6)

Period effects. Results when features of the political period influence the political attitudes of many people, regardless of one's age. (Chapter 2)

Peripheral route to persuasion. Process by which attitudes change under conditions when a person is not motivated or able to carefully consider persuasive communication; resulting attitude change is likely to be only temporary. (Chapter 4)

Pluralistic roots. Perspective that public opinion is shaped by several factors, not just ideology. (Chapter 6)

Pluralists. Democratic theorists who believe that groups perform an essential role as intermediaries between the public and political elites. (Chapter 1)

Pocketbook issues. Issues that deal with people's personal economic circumstances. (Chapter 6)

Polarization effect. When political elites disagree on an issue, the attitudes of more politically aware citizens will coincide with their existing predispositions, especially when the elite disagreement falls along party or ideological lines. (Chapter 4)

Policy mood. Broad measure of aggregate public opinion; generally captures whether the public feels that the government is too active or not active enough. (Chapter 11)

Policy sentiment. Broad measure of aggregate public opinion; synonym of policy mood. (Chapter 11)

Political awareness. Degree to which people follow political matters closely. (Chapter 4)

Political expertise. Degree to which people are knowledgeable about and interested in political matters. (Chapter 8)

Political knowledge. Facts about politics stored in citizens' long-term memories. (Chapter 7)

Political opinionation. Degree to which people have attitudes on political matters. (Chapter 2)

Political predispositions. People's existing political orientations, including core values and enduring beliefs. (Chapter 4)

Political reality explanation/model. Political attitudes are based on real political phenomena; for example, lower levels of trust among blacks due to the fact that they have less political power than whites. (Chapters 2, 10)

Political socialization. Process by which people learn about politics and develop political opinions. (Chapter 2)

Political structure. Institutional features of a political system. (Chapter 7)

Political times. Features of the broader environment during a particular era that can shape public opinion toward specific issues or people. (Chapter 8)

Political tolerance. Public support for civil liberties, particularly when supporting the rights of individuals or groups whose views one opposes. (Chapter 8)

Popular sovereignty. Principle that the power in a democratic society ultimately rests with the citizenry. (Chapter 1)

Population. All the elements of interest. (Appendix)

Prejudice. Negative affect that is felt toward a specific societal group. (Chapter 1)

Priming effects. Occur when the media cover particular issues and then citizens rely on those issues as they evaluate political leaders. (Chapter 3)

Principles of equality. Abstract beliefs that blacks and whites should be treated equally. (Chapter 9)

Private polls. Opinion surveys that are conducted for political leaders (most notably the president) to assess public opinion. (Chapter 11)

Propensity to guess. The likelihood that someone will guess when answering survey questions. (Chapter 7)

Public judgment. Opinions that result once people have thoroughly considered a political issue and the consequences of their views. (Chapter 1)

Public opinion. The preferences of people toward governmental and policy matters, generally considered as the aggregation of individuals' views. (Chapter 1)

Public opinion poll. A type of research method for assessing political attitudes in which a large sample of citizens (typically randomly selected from the population) are each asked the same list of questions. (Chapter 1, Appendix)

Public order frame. A media frame that emphasizes that violence might occur at a public event. (Chapter 3)

Question wording. Content of items on an opinion poll as well as the content of response options that are provided to respondents. (Chapter 5)

Race-coded policies. Policies that are race-neutral, yet have become linked with racial minorities in the minds of white citizens. (Chapter 6)

Race-neutral policies. Policies that affect citizens regardless of race. (Chapter 6)

Race-targeted policies. Policies designed to specifically aid racial minorities, such as affirmative action and the government taking steps to ensure fair treatment in employment. (Chapter 6)

Racial gap in political knowledge. In general, whites are more knowledgeable about politics than racial minorities; the gap disappears when it comes to knowledge of issues particularly important to minorities. (Chapter 7)

Racial identity. Belief that one's fate is tied to the fate of his or her racial group. (Chapter 6)

Racial profiling. Selecting someone for questioning or extra scrutiny on the basis of race or ethnicity. (Chapter 8)

Racial resentment. A form of prejudice that focuses on the moral character of blacks and contends that blacks do not work hard enough and that they take what they have not earned (similar to symbolic racism). (Chapter 6)

Racists. People who believe members of their own race are superior to members of other racial groups. (Chapter 8)

Random assignment. Process of assigning subjects to experimental conditions such that chance alone determines which subject gets in which condition. (Chapter 3, Appendix)

Random sample. A sample in which chance alone determines which elements of the population make it into the sample. (Appendix)

Receive-accept-sample model. Framework for understanding political persuasion; whether attitude change results will depend on exposure to and agreement with persuasive communication as well as what considerations are at the top of one's head at a given point in time. (Chapter 4)

Reception. Stage in the political persuasion process during which people are exposed to, attend to, and understand persuasive communication. (Chapter 4)

Reinforcement effect. Occurs when political communication reinforces people's existing political preferences. (Chapter 3)

Reparations. Remedial policies that would address the harmful effects of slavery on Americans living today. (Chapter 9)

Representative democracy. Governmental system whereby citizens elect officials to represent their views and make decisions. (Chapter 1)

Resistance. Processes by which people ensure that persuasive communication does not change their attitudes; also, motivations people hold to withstand attitude change. (Chapter 4)

Rules of the game. A type of political knowledge about the institutions and processes of politics. (Chapter 7)

Sample. A subset of the elements of interest (i.e., a subset of the population). (Appendix)

Self-interest. A person's narrow, economic interests. (Chapter 6)

Self-perception theory. Approach to understanding attitude formation and change; key premise is that people infer their attitudes from their own behaviors. (Chapter 4)

Shared environment. Experiences and upbringing that are the same between individuals; particularly relevant when examining twins. (Chapter 2)

Short answer questions. Open-ended questions that require respondents to answer without providing any answer options. (Chapter 7)

Simulated responsiveness. When public policy corresponds with the opinions of the public but only after citizen views have been cultivated by leaders to reflect the policy goals of the leaders; in other words, public policy does not necessarily reflect the genuine wishes of the public. (Chapter 11)

Social adjustment function. Theory that people have specific attitudes because the attitudes conform to those of peers in their social network. (Chapter 4)

Social capital. Degree to which people connect with and trust other citizens and engage in civic activities in their communities. (Chapter 10)

Social isolation. Degree to which one does not interact with other people. (Chapter 8)

Social movements. Citizens organizing and working together to influence politics. (Chapter 6)

Social network. The collection of individuals with whom a person discusses politics regularly. (Chapter 4)

Socialists. People who favor socialism or, more specifically, government ownership of private property. (Chapter 8)

Socialization agents. Sources of political learning or political opinions; individuals or institutions that foster learning or development of opinions. (Chapter 2)

Socialization gains. Acquisition or further development of political opinions. (Chapter 2)

Socially undesirable. True attitudes that are politically incorrect that people do not want to reveal when asked survey questions on sensitive topics, such as race or religion. (Chapter 9)

Sociotropic concerns. General concerns about society. (Chapter 6)

Soft news. News that has nothing to do with public policy. (Chapter 3)

Specialist. Someone who has knowledge on some topics but not others. (Chapter 7)

Specific support. Attitudes toward the performance of political leaders and governmental outputs, such as public policies. (Chapters 2, 10)

Split-half survey. An experiment embedded in a survey whereby one-half of the respondents are randomly assigned to one condition and the other one-half are randomly assigned to another condition. (Chapter 7, Appendix)

Status quo bias. The likelihood that public policy will remain the same when the public does not desire a policy change is higher than the likelihood that policy will change when the public desires change. (Chapter 11)

Stereotypes. Beliefs about the characteristics of members of social groups; can be positive or negative. (Chapter 1)

Substance of politics. A type of political knowledge about political issues. (Chapter 7)

Subtle effects model. Perspective that views the media as having influence over citizens via agenda setting, priming, and framing. (Chapter 3)

Survey. A type of research method for assessing political attitudes in which a large sample of citizens (typically randomly selected from the population) are each asked the same list of questions. (Appendix)

Survey-based experiment. An experiment embedded in a survey whereby subjects are randomly assigned to experimental conditions. (Appendix)

Symbolic racism. The belief that blacks do not work hard enough and that black disadvantage cannot be explained by discrimination (similar to racial resentment). (Chapter 9)

Tabloid journalism. A form of journalism that is much less committed, if at all, to news norms. (Chapter 3)

Thematic frame. A media frame that focuses on society. (Chapter 3)

Threat perceptions. Beliefs that a person or a group endangers one's personal security, way of life, or the security of the nation. (Chapter 8)

Timebound. A study has this characteristic when it only applies to a limited time period. (Chapter 7)

Tolerance curriculum. Educational lessons and activities designed to increase public support for civil liberties, particularly for groups holding unpopular political views. (Chapter 8)

Traditional journalism. A form of journalism that exhibits a strong commitment to news norms. (Chapter 3)

Transfer of affect. Emotions held toward one attitude object are passed on to a related object and thus influence attitudes toward the second object. (Chapter 4)

Treatment responsibility. Identifying solutions for a political problem, such as poverty. (Chapter 3)

Trust. Degree to which people agree that political leaders are honest and act in the public's interests. (Chapter 2)

Trust in government. A positive evaluation of the government in Washington; particularly having faith in the performance of government and in political leaders. (Chapter 10)

Two-step flow of communication. When political information first flows from the media to attentive citizens, called opinion leaders, and then these attentive citizens pass on the information to their friends and family who are not as engaged in politics. (Chapter 3)

Unilateral foreign policies. Governmental actions that feature one nation "going it alone" rather than working together with other nations or international organizations. (Chapter 11)

Uninformed. Citizens who do not hold factual beliefs about politics. (Chapter 7)

Unshared environment. Experiences and upbringing that differ between individuals; particularly relevant when examining twins. (Chapter 2)

USA Patriot Act. National legislation granting certain powers to government officials with the goal of fighting terrorism. (Chapter 8)

Utilitarian function. Theory that people have specific attitudes toward an object because of the benefits provided by or the punishment inflicted by the attitude object. (Chapter 4)

Valid measure. One that measures what it is supposed to measure. (Chapter 7)

Value of free expression. Importance of people discussing and debating a wide range of political views in public. (Chapter 8)

Value-expressive function. Theory that people have specific attitudes because these attitudes allow them to express their core beliefs and values. (Chapter 4)

Values. Abstract, enduring beliefs regarding how the world should work. (Chapters 1, 6)

Watchdog. When the media scrutinize and investigate the actions of public officials. (Chapter 3)

Index

Note: Tables, figures, boxes, and notes are indicted by *t, f, b,* and *n,* respectively.